NATIONALIZING CRISES

The Political Economy of Public Policy in Contemporary India

NATIONALIZING CRISES

The Political Economy of Public Policy in Contemporary India

Edited by

Bhabani Shankar Nayak

ATLANTIC

PUBLISHERS & DISTRIBUTORS (P) LTD

Published by

ATLANTIC

PUBLISHERS & DISTRIBUTORS (P) LTD

B-2, Vishal Enclave, Opp. Rajouri Garden,
New Delhi-110027
Phones : 25413460, 25429987, 25466842

Sales Office
7/22, Ansari Road, Darya Ganj,
New Delhi-110002
Phones : 23273880, 23275880, 23280451
Fax : 91-11-23285873
web : www.atlanticbooks.com
e-mail : info@atlanticbooks.com

ISBN 81-269-0481-X

Printed in India
at Nice Printing Press, Delhi

DEDICATED TO

My grandmother

Tiranabala Nayak has been living

in crises throughout her life.

Acknowledgements

Many people have contributed enormously and took trouble for the making of this volume. I am thankful to all the academicians, teachers and research scholars whose academic generosity and contributions enabled me to complete this volume.

I owe a lot to all my comrades for their inspiration to fight with all the spirit against the crisis conditions imposed by this system. I have spent my innocent childhood, enjoying colorful youth and crisis-ridden student life which helped me in learning about the wider horizons of society.

I am thankful to all my teacher friends especially Mr. Suresh Mishra and Mr. Anup Kumar Mallick (S.N. College, Rajkanika), Prof. Sudhanshu Pattnaik and Prof. Sarada Rath (Utkal University, Orissa), Prof. Shantha Sinha and Prof. G. Haragopal (University of Hyderabad), Dr. Ian Duncan, Dr. Vinita Damodaran (University of Sussex, UK) who have taken all the pain to contour my ideas and thoughts in an academic direction with a concern and commitment for the society.

All my friends have been standing by me to share my pain and pleasure in all the times. Lipsa's friendly-funny talks and positive criticism, Elamathi, Daniel, Clare Rogers, Narayan, Laura and Prasanta's supportive company helped me in many ways. Bijaya, Baga, Dilu, Bidu, Badu and Tribhuban are true pals since childhood and moulded my thoughts. Sanju's unfailing smile is a consistent source of inspiration and a secure company.

Tuku, Sansia, Pachha are not only brothers but also true pals who have contributed immensely for the development of my academic life. My grandmother, parents and relatives are taking all the troubles by granting me absolute freedom and standing by me during my mental and material crises.

I am thankful to Dr. K.R. Gupta of the Atlantic Publishers & Distributors (P) Ltd., New Delhi who is always inspiring and took all the trouble to publish this volume in time.

All shortcomings in this volume are mine and mine alone. I hope if any shortcomings remain in this volume, they may help to continue further research. I thank all the contributors and many others who have directly or indirectly helped in bringing out this volume.

BHABANI SHANKAR NAYAK

Contents

Introduction

It is quite unlikely to edit a volume without reviewing the papers incorporated in the volume. But deliberately thought of not to review the papers incorporated in this volume as the papers speak according to their own languages with their own identity. The contributors and their papers to this volume speak in different languages in response to different issues, theoretical and disciplinary agendas in the shadow of different ideological and normative commitments. Therefore, the notions and ethos of political economy implicitly or explicitly animating different papers vary. For me, political economy is more an approach than a concept whose definition can unite all the papers in this volume under a single theme. Both classical and marxian academics tend to assume a political economy in which power is reflexive of economic relations. Engel's assertion speaks for both the classical and marxian traditions. In his words, "political economy in the widest sense is the science of laws governing the production and exchange of the material means of subsistence in human society".[1] Thus, 'crises' in the society indicates 'crises' in the laws or conditions governing the production and exchange relations or the power that controls the economic relations. Any attempt to study 'crises' in a society must cover the laws governing production and exchange relations or the power that controls it.

The volume aims to make innovative contributions to key debates in the burgeoning field of society, economy and politics in contemporary India. The arguments in this volume moves beyond the traditional analysis of 'cause and effect' relationship while addressing 'crises' in its different forms. The 'condition' is more important than the 'cause-effect' relationship to study 'crisis' because the study of 'conditions' covers the 'cause-effect' relationship but the study of 'cause-effect' relationship most of the time overlooks 'conditions'. The study of 'conditions' of crisis helps to understand the process of transition and national restructuring of India and its society, economy and politics. This understanding of the structural processes in India is the recognition of the dialectic of the contradictory forces and process at work, will enable us to identify the 'crises' which is reinforced by the state through its ruling and governing elites, multinational and transnational corporations through its production and distribution mechanisms and markets. The public policy making institutions in India helps this process of creating conditions of crisis. At the samc time, both international and domestic forces, agencies and processes influence and help in strengthening the conditions of crisis. In the process of regime change of elites or ruling class, the density of crises also changes. The crisis condition reinforces scarcity and inequality. Any attempt towards the removal of scarcity depends on the progress towards egalitarian order which can generate potential for productive capacity to overcome crises. This indicates a process of transformation in all levels of the society; from the material production to production of reason based consciousness in the individual and in the society together. The state and government which have the authority must strive to achieve these goals through making public policy towards social and economic transformation. However, the public policy making institutions of the state and government work in reverse which help to reinforce crises. A good knowledge about crises and its reinforcing agencies will be essential for all future struggles for alternatives.

This study intends to map out the crises which are reinforced by the ruling class in India since decades in the process of identity formations based on race, religion, caste and culture in politics and dismantling the role of state in economy through the process of market led reforms. The idea is that the markets will resolve everything. In fact, both economic theory and the practice of market principles for decades absolutely don't show that. Consciously or not, users of the neoliberal theory can all too simply presume that if an economy is working well, it must be those market mechanisms which are causing it to do well. When market has failed to provide their 'economic miracle', then they call it as 'negative wealth effect'. Thus, neoliberal theorist has no other causal explanation other than this. We need serious investigation to understand the way; the present economic system is working and working badly. Then the neoliberal analysts must give us casual analysis whether market failure or government interference is preventing the economy from positive development as modeled. If the economy modeled by the neoclassicals fails to deliver positive development then they define it as market failure caused by negative wealth effect. So, the entire concept of 'free market' is less informative and blind towards openness. In this way the neoclassical theory and its propagating individuals and institutions actively discourages people from observing or understanding the necessary role of government and state in the market mechanisms themselves if they are to work efficiently, or in many cases if they are to work at all. Of course, the reality compels neo-classics to acknowledge some market failures and some need for public intervention, for example to deter monopoly. But the very word 'intervention' implies an absurd belief in the possibility of an ungoverned market economy. However, the dichotomy between the preachings, practices and realities have led to the augmentation of discontent between mainstream neoclassical economics instruction and reality. It is interesting; if you watch the advocates of neoliberalism regularly, you will definitely find that they tell us one thing today and tomorrow exactly the opposite, both with same commitment and sincerity. The neoclassical economist see crises as the result of recession and depressions caused by some sort of external forces to economy such as, war, business failure, stock market panic, and bad weather etc. They have never tried to locate the important role of state and its institutions of public policy making. Former World Bank economist Lant Pritchett's study has found that the inequality among and between the rich and poor nations has increased between the period of 1870 and 1960. He makes satire of neoliberal economists hope for a convergence between rich and poor countries in terms of per capita GDP in near future. His study and example of India's economic growth is again interesting where he says, "...a few developing countries were actually 'converging', that is, they are growing faster than the United States. When are these lucky 'convergers' going to overtake United States? India, for example, registered an annual average growth rate of 3 per cent between 1980 and 1993. If India could sustain this pace for another 100 years, its income would reach the level of high income countries today. And if India can sustain this growth differential for 377 years, my great-great-great-great-great-great-great-great-great-great-great grand children will be alive to see India's income level 'converge'"[2]. Another study was conducted by the economists of the Centre for Economic and Policy Research (CEPR) in which they have tried to put neoliberal hypothesis to test by looking at the difference between poor and rich countries from 1980 to 2000. They have found that the poor countries fell far behind the rich countries and there is a diminishing progress of poor countries. The period between 1980 and 2000 is the 'period of triumph for neoliberalism', the political program of neoliberalism and its advocates[3]. Continuous fall of their arguments and ground reality compels them to change their language and talk about 'long run'. The capitalist media disseminates the language of 'long run' in such a way that one can understand by the following small example. When I talk to my father (who is a small farmer with little knowledge about journalistic economics) on the neoliberal politics-policies and its negative effects then he talks about 'long run'. He says, "we have to sacrifice something now to achieve many things in the long run; these policies will help the economy to boom and help to eradicate poverty and inequality in the long run". When I give him empirical examples of the practice and fall of neoliberal economy then he either becomes angry or makes fun of marxian economy and uses his prejudiced patriarchy position to control me like World Bank and IMF controls the third world countries through its conditional lending programmes in the name of development. This neoliberal economist's language of 'long run' is like the theological promise of salvation or better life in the heaven. Thus, there is no time limit to achieve prosperity, patiently one can wait till death and may achieve it after death! This is the way the neoliberals keep the masses out of the reality. This is the tactic by which the neoliberals are generating a liberal class in the society with its own hegemony of ideas. Many people are the victims of these neoliberal ideas and my father is a glaring example. Thus, these neoliberal ideas which help people to remain far from reality, I call it as "growth of negative consciousness". The growth of negative consciousness facilitates crisis condition in a society.

The crisis in the economy and society is being produced out of the difference between instruction and reality. It leads to unbelievable alienation, reductionist thinking, social ruthlessness and the arrogant ignorance of many conventional 'academicians' concerning the nature of India we live in. But the neoclassical economists refuse to admit that their approach is 'sycophantic to capitalism' and generates 'crises'. Those academicians have their own set of ideas. So, we can't ignore the academic foundations for what's going on in political and economic fields. The academic research, teaching and history are the worst victims of this process of neoclassical developments in political economy and patronization of religion, culture and other identities in the society. There is a continuous attack on history for its formalization, which is an effort to facilitate complete indoctrination of the Indian society to carry out such an agenda where there is no place for critical and reflective thought. Thus, it is necessary to have a strong plural academic foundation to create a critical mass in which you have all the perspectives along with a progressive thought to guide. While advocating for a plural academic research, I am not promoting liberal pluralism[4] on the grounds that such knowledge is necessary for effective governance and for improving the conditions of life via economic and political modernization. However, scientific and academic basis of ideas for criticism, and other approaches are legitimate in a society.

The crisis is again reinforced by the given political economy of the Indian society where masses have to sacrifice their development for the pleasure of others. Instead of solving these acute problems, the Indian ruling class tries to overcome it by diverting people from the real life issues through the process of spreading the venom of communalism and other emotive issues. The society and culture are being shaped by the economy, and economics doesn't lead politics, it follows politics. Thus, it is necessary precondition to shape politics for the better economy that works for the masses. Apart from the market based advocacy, the ruling class in India also advocates for the technology and information. Of course, we need technology but till now it is in the hands of the few and far away from the masses. Thus, the technological revolution which was launched in India in the form of technology transfer during Rajiv Gandhi era, has failed to overcome the crisis rather reinforced it. Again the appearance of a minority Congress government under the leadership of Prime Minister Narasimha Rao, then the fall of Congress regime and growth of third force at the centre of Indian politics to the growth of the BJP led National Democratic Alliance (NDA) and emergence of the present United Progressive Alliance (UPA) mark the dynamics of Indian politics and it also reflects the crisis inherent in the system and its potential for alternative transformation too. The potential of the crisis ridden system produces new forces, forms, structures and sites of resistance nationwide. In spite of universalizing inequality tendencies of these global, national and local actors, new forms of particularism and alternatives are cropping up. Thus, it is necessary to be united behind critical concepts, striving for comprehensiveness, continuous fighting against the ruling and non ruling elite's class needs to be stressed to underline the fragile nature of the process. At all levels of the fight to transform the public policy, state, government and its institutions committed and accountable to the masses, need organized and unexpected intellectual encounters, strategic planning for alternatives along with sufficient information that will pave the way to overcome crisis in the contemporary Indian society, economy and politics.

The crisis in one field enforces crisis in the other. So, it is very difficult to study crisis in a society separately without looking at the political and economic set up along with its cultural settings. It is necessary to have an interdisciplinary outlook while looking at crisis. In a way, the book is trying to break away from the narrow silo that departmentalization of academic research is becoming. It's becoming somewhat sterile, almost a subset of methodological individualism[5] and moving towards a model-driven rigid disciplinary boundary, which gives certain insights, but doesn't provide full insights into the way knowledge actually operates in a society. The knowledge that operates in a society may be scientific but may not be derived through methodological research. Many researchers and academicians especially in social science fail to understand this concept that, "we have now moved into an epoch...where truth is entirely a product of consensus values, and where 'science' itself is just the name we attach to certain modes of explanation"[6]. Therefore, the book will be a product of interdisciplinary research by covering different aspects of the crisis ridden Indian Society to start a debate over the present paradigm of development and public policy setting in India. With the onslaught of liberalization, privatization and globalization, the demand for an integrated, broad-based, culturally accepted social and economic policies as well as people at the centre of development and economy have come to the centre stage of the debate. Hence, the book argues for the integrated development policy along with the cultural requirements and economy at the service of the humane needs of the masses. It requires a constant and continual flow of decisions by the authorities in charge of public policy. These decisions can be made at different heights in the politico-bureaucratic hierarchy of authorities in India in the national, state, district, municipality, block and gram panchayat level, etc.

Notes

1. Engel, Friedrich (1954), Anti-Dühring: Herr Eugen Dühring's Revolution in Science, Foreign Language Publishing House, Moscow, p. 203.

2. Pritchett's article on "Forget Convergence: Divergent Past, Present, and Future", can be found in the World Bank's website at http://www.worldbank.org/fandd/english/0696/articles/090696.htm.
3. Mark Weisbrot, Dean Baker, Egor Kraev, and Judy Chen, " The Scorecard on Globalization 1980-2000: Twenty Years of Diminished Progress" can be found in the webpage of CEPR at http://www.cepr.net/globalization/scorcard_on_globalization.htm.
4. Here the term 'liberal pluralism' used in the context of a political ideology, associated most often with modern capitalist democracies that incorporates a recognition of global and local difference based on cultural, ethnic, regional, religious, socio-economic, linguistic, etc. and promotes, through state, market, and civil institutions, knowledge of those differences. By creating such an artificial demarcation of the differences, the bourgeoning ruling class could able to dismantle the commonness among the people and their problem which has the potential to unite them.
5. By 'methodological individualism' I mean the knowledge based on and derived from methodological research that is 'only scientific knowledge'. The basic argument is that the knowledge cannot be scientific without a method of study. Thus, methodological individualism means scientific knowledge that is only methodological knowledge. While attacking methodological individualism, I do not believe in the method of postmodernism which attack against theory and methodology. They are claiming to relinquish all attempts to create new knowledge in a systematic fashion, but instead an "anti-rules" fashion. However, my argument is neither against theory nor against methodology. It is for an interdisciplinary approach towards science-knowledge and truth. There is no single approach or methodology to acquire scientific knowledge. Any attempt to acquire knowledge through monolithic model driven methodological research makes research incomplete that produces inadequate knowledge. In the same way, without theoretical and methodological background the research and knowledge derived from it, is fragile, limited and bias.
6. Norris, Christopher (1990), *What's Wrong with Postmodernism*, England: Harvester Wheatsheaf, p. 169. One can refer Norris, Christopher (1979), *Deconstruction: Theory and Practice*, New York: Routledge, for a greater understanding.

PART I

POLITICAL ECONOMY OF PUBLIC POLICY

The Color of Crisis: The 21st Century Culture of Science*

Brij Mohan

1

"Vijnanadipena Samsarabhayam Nivartate"
Chanakyanitisutra 565[1]

1. Knowledge and Social Welfare

Science and social development ought to enhance human development. The social science imperative of advancement is liberation. The incompleteness of the human animal therefore remains a daunting challenge for all scientists and thinkers. The idea of social science, after Peter Winch thought in terms of philosophy and methodology (1960), has come of age. Despite a sea change in our growing conceptual repertoire, ideology and polemics continue to impact the quality and content of intended inquiry and research. Strides in medicine, physics, engineering and other fields, including humanities and social sciences, also include human ingenuity's awesome power of mass murders and self-annihilation. The Enlightenment paradox continues to be a challenge (Becker, 1968). Archeology of knowledge, however, calls for scientificity and also calls for unity of discourse and discursive formulations (Foucault, 1972; Mohan, 1999).

Fallacies of social development abound (Mohan, 2005). Human-social-national development is a process of social transformation. This involves societal renewal which heavily depends on progressive social changes inclusive of peoples' old

---

*Partly based on papers delivered to the Social Science Faculty, Department of Social Work, M.K. Gandhi Kashi Vidyapith University, Varanasi, June 21, 2004 (following acceptance of an honorary D.Lit., Kashi University, India, June 19, 2004) and the 14th Symposium, IUCISD, Recife, Brazil, July 24-28, 2005.

habits of thoughts and institutional regulatory dominance. Unabashed militarism and ubiquitous terrorism globally dehumanize people. Such a state of development hardly qualifies to be universally progressive in the face of staggering social misery: More than 13 million children in America are struggling to survive. It's a catastrophe that is rarely reported (Relin, 2004: 6-8).[2] More than a billion children do not get drinking water and about 2 billion people live under disgraceful human conditions on this planet. The ILO report cites 10 million child slaves in many Afro-Asian countries. June Kane, author of report says: "Sadly, many countries don't see domestic child labor as a problem" (Fowler, 2004: 17A). Add the elements of fear and terror to this compound and the life poisoning cauldron of reality is ready.

The advent of the twenty-first century is a crucial juncture. We had hardly overcome the millennium angst, de-developmental signs unraveled by the post-ideological society manifested a new array of syndromes defying rationality: rising inequality in the wake of global economy, daunting fundamentalism in the age of reason, nearly pervasive terror—not to mention the new and age-old social maladies—and, above all, the invincibility of an essentially anti-state force representing the melt down of an established order.[3] Still worrisome is the state of the world's model democracy.[4]

2. Designing Social Contract II: The Developmental Crisis

Enlightenment unleashed a specter of hope. Again, paradoxically, expanding horizons of human quest for knowledge triggered cannons of alienation and despair, the twin gifts of modernity. The age of reason made humans think about themselves beyond the ossified structures of dogmas. The chimeras of hope, if you will, demolished certain barriers but nourished the seeds of a new religion named science. Human ingenuity, one could argue, is not essentially a liberating force. Under the strontium of nuclear clouds, there is an inevitable cold winter which will annihilate life on this planet. Also, evident is the fact that humans can be good and evil at the same time.

Any discourse on human nature and social evolution evokes a perennial debate about the innate character of the *naked ape*.[5] Evilness of our biological ancestors in the evolutionary stages may have undergone several phases. If the ape was a natural killer, humanity's destiny remains sealed as a self-destructive instinctual impulse. Notwithstanding interpretations of Hobbes, Darwin and Freud, it is hard to reject Rousseauean notions of primitive innocence which became corrupt (and evil) after the advent of a civil society premised on private property.

About five million years ago, chimpanzees and humans shared a common ape ancestor. In his brilliant analysis, Franz de Waal explodes the myth of a "killer ape." "Morality is not a superficial thing that we added on very late in our evolution. It relates to very old affectionate and affiliative tendencies that we have as a species and that we share with all roots of animals (quoted by Conniff, 2003: 62). Human behaviours are indeed embedded in the animal nature. When the idea of chimpanzee politics intrigued public, reporters asked,

> "Who do you consider the biggest chimpanzee in our present government?" De Waal declined to make such a comparison. "People do it to mock the politicians," he remarked, "but I feel they insult my chimps." On the other hand, politicians themselves have sometimes seen a resemblance (Conniff, 2003: 66).

There is enough scientific evidence to support the claim that instinctual behaviour is prone to socialization. It is, therefore, instructive to assume knowledge as a vehicle of social transformation. The communist utopia might fall under the deadly weight of its own bureaucracy, secrecy and lies. Knowledge itself does not lie; it is however vulnerable to its users who can prostitute it for their own nefarious end. Scientism, not science, is a fearsome instrument of oppression. However, knowledge and science are meaningless unless they are employable for lifting the human condition. I would argue that this is positivism at its best.

Social science is an oxymoron. However, organizations and research institutions in private and public sectors use and abuse it for their own objectives regardless of its impact on humanity. In other words, science and human development are not necessarily positively correlated. This uncertainty has turned the basic premises of the social contract upside down. Organizational goal-displacement is not a local or regional calamity. It is post-modernity's uncontrolled outcome which raises its ugly head in the guise of rapacious corporatization, unilateral neo-globalism, and mindless quantitativism.

Society is a *social* construct. Human animal is *social* in the sense that s/he subscribes to certain norms, values and goals. The well-being of a civil society depends on how we become social. A civil society, as we have seen, is not necessarily a free and responsible society. Two important tasks entail all social scientists and citizens: (1) Rethink what it means to be *social* and (2) Why is it necessary to remain *social* in an increasing violent and *asocial* climate?

A 'unified social construct' implies collective reaffirmation of basic human dignities on a par with inalienable universal rights. These *rights* should mean more than a shibboleth; their existence is crucial to what I call "social." An insane society can neither insure nor promote such dignities. An irresponsible culture that perpetuates oppression cannot by definition nourish good citizens. Human dysfunctionalities mirror societal contradictions, anomalies and perversities. A new culture warrants social transformation based on *Social Contract II*, hypothetical vision of a decent society.

A unified *social* construct, however, is a prerequisite. This involves diversity without inhumanity. It is not a prescription for any standardized notion of civility. It is a universal mandate for creative co-existence. The social contract that helped evolve society as a governmentally embedded state has become obsolete. The classic social contract theorists may have differed relative to the nature of human societies, but they all agreed about certain norms and regulations that would save the members of a society from each other. In other words, society was constructed on the premise of a commonly agreed contract that would help develop a system of governance in the interest of the future well-being of its entire membership. Since reality betrays this contract, it is about time for a renewed relationship between individual and society (Mohan, 2004).

Contemporary ideologies of self-governance from hedonism, capitalism, and *laissez faire* to fascism, statism, and terrorism have broken the fundamental premises of this social contract. While human beings—members of a society in general—remain short-changed by the illusionary power of democratic rule, a massive epidemic of alienation empowers the ruling class regardless of the ideological background. Put simply, a new state of jungle pervades all aspects of life leaving individuals, families and groups at the mercy of nearly despotic ruling elites, warlords and corporations. The consequences of this de-development have given rise to Brazilianization on one hand and unilateral aggression on the other—a delusional culture with imperial fantasies in the name of freedom.

The main premise of this presentation is: Enlightenment II precedes a new social contract which world societies need to survive each other. *Social Contract II* should partake of basic human needs, governance included, beyond the ideological clichés and propound a framework for a new civil society that is based on mutual acceptance without cutting each other's throat. The existing system not only promotes an atavistic will to power, it emboldens the rapaciousness of the mighty which, in a post-industrial society, leads to industrial-corporate despotism.

Reconceptualization of social transformation, therefore, posits social theory and practice in a new societal context (Mohan, 1999). Someone's martyr or freedom fighter is another's terrorist. Vocabularies of conflict posit the post-industrial society as a post-Leviathan phenomenon.

When does ethnic cleansing become genocide? Ten years ago[6] the world, especially the champions of democracy, chose to remain bystanders when the most horrific crimes against humanity were committed in Rwanda. Today's Africa, a continent cursed by the ravages of war, poverty and genocide, still remains an isolated world in the grip of its own First World War.[7] Liberia, Sudan, Congo and Afghanistan represent a new area of darkness where devolution of the State and Government is in the process. Iraq's case is uniquely different. Even after the transfer of power, one remains uncertain about its future security and integrity as a free nation. Is it not safe to conclude that greed, territoriality and neo-colonialism still remain de-socializing motivational forces?

Science and social transformation are not necessarily antagonistic constructs. The ideal situation will be to establish a symbiosis of the two toward achieving a free society. So far this has not happened because the politics of science and reform have always eclipsed the twin purposes of these important forces: social justice and diversity. If we could synergize discourse, decision-making, and developmental policy with this mission in mind, we can perhaps achieve a new meaning of *social* existence. Social scientists of the world have to commit themselves to reconstruction of social reality that may instill hope against despair.

Contemporary social sciences, it seems, have lost confidence in their mission, method and power. The corporatized academia which favours funded research and quantifiable versions of scholarship has demoralized social theorists, philosophers and thinkers. Being a "philosopher" euphemistically implies inanity and uselessness. Consumers of knowledge in a global economy aspire to achieve success in materially quantifiable term. The icon of success is a CEO, not a Socrates. The problem here is not inherent in philosophy; it is the lure and perversion of science which promotes spurious scholarship and rewards mendacious mediocrity that alienates otherwise genuine seekers of knowledge.[8]

Qualitative research as we in America study, teach and conduct is the same as anywhere else. However, the growing neo-empiricist fad at the expense of qualitative inquiry is a matter of serious concern for the future of social science education and research here and abroad. *It may be argued that much of social research is essentially qualitative as we deal with human-social situations*. The phenomena we study are all social constructs. Our models borrowed from natural sciences fall short of explanations let alone interpreting the complexity of variegated human reality. "Nature abhors vacuum" and science itself is an uncertainty. Let us review some laws of hard sciences:

> Clifford Pickover's Law of Mutating Conjectures posits that every law ever made "has been broken or will crumble after a time." Princeton astrophysicist Paul Steinhard's law is "Good science creates two challenging puzzles for each puzzle it solves." Anton Zeilinger's Fundamental Law is, "There is no fundamental Law." Finally, Maddox's Second Law based on his long experience as Editor of the famed *Nature* is: "Reviewers who are best placed to understand an author's work are the least likely to draw attention to its achievements, but are prolific sources of minor criticism, especially the identification of typos" (Cited by Rothstein, 2004: a15).

Like politics, "All laws are local" (Alan Alda cited *ibid.*). Our tools of evaluating quality are apolitical. All interpretations, however, reflect bias. The mythology of objective review process has evolved into a perfect vehicle of inclusion and exclusion. But for a few exceptions, it is not uncommon to come across mutual glorification by guest editors and writers recycling their self-plagiarized pieces at the expense of space and resources which others might utilize more creatively. Legitimization of the inauthentic leads to counter productivity. The point is: spurious science corrupts both rationality and humanity. Contemporary academic culture promotes a false consciousness of scientificity unrelated to the reality of life. This hiatus is a major impediment in the development of knowledge that beholds life, human spirit and progress in togetherness.

Human evolution has been a fascinating odyssey in search for survival. Societies and cultures have developed their systems of self-perpetuation premised on their myths and artifacts. Development of science and civilization is an outcome of this diverse cultural manifestation which has resulted into hierarchized structures of privilege, control and domination (Mohan, 1996). The outcome of this journey has not been functional. Civilizational crises have come and gone. The contemporary juncture, however, is unique in its direction as well as nature. Afghanistanization, Iraqification on the one hand and *Brazilianization* (Lind, 1995) on the other, represent the new global reality of an increasingly Balkanizing world. The former represents a melt down of the apparatus of the state and the latter—Brazilianization[9]—heralds the advent of a new overclass which is reclusive and rapacious, powerful and insensitive, and insecure and guilty at the same time. The cocktail of Afghanistanization and Brazilianization creates a dangerous toxin for the future well-being of civil society. A preemptive strategy against this "anti-social development" stage mandates new definitions of social class, contract and society. This involves radical changes in the international linkages of economic and political systems.

The post-Cold War realities have compounded the post-ideological world. 9/11 has further unleashed a specter of chimera and nightmares. Adam Curtis, in a BBC documentary *The Power of Nightmares* asserts that Al Qaeda is a phantom of US anxieties and it "seeks nothing less than to reframe the past several decades of American foreign policy...to argue that neo-conservatives...have vastly exaggerated those threats in their quests to remake the world in the image of the United States" (Bergen, 2005: 25). It is difficult to envision a world without the impact of globalization which euphemistically brings in the new wave of western conceptions of democracy, freedom and capitalism. China has triumphantly exploded the myth of ideological piety; its new capitalism without human rights insults Mao and Marx, rebukes Adam Smith, and challenges the Wilsonian world order. China's communist government and India's dysfunctional-populist democracy raise concerns that seem to define the colors, contours and complexities of the crisis that the world economy faces today. A developing nation, like India, must however eschew complacence; equally, perhaps even more, important is to harness the "imperial hubris" (Scheuer, 2004) of the world's only superpower.

Wisdom suggests that Asia's rise is no reason to panic (Hogland, 2005: 7B). "China sells what it can produce...India produces what it can sell," concludes Kamal Nath, India's commerce secretary (quoted by Hogland, 2005: 7B). The well deserved demise of communism should be no cause for comfort to functional free-market—a system which will not devour its own children. "Rigid ideology is a threat, not an asset" (Garson,

2005: B7). The failures of such policies have played havoc with the lives of poor all over the world:

> Cholera is an extreme result of development scheme. But then, privatizing water in Africa is an extreme application of the World Bank's private investment theory.... Even in the First World, it is often more profitable to siphon off than to 'develop.' ...A quarter of a century day-in and day-out asset stripping sponsored by the IMF and the World Bank left millions of poor people poorer. Meanwhile, unregulated capital flows—an other tenet of Washington Consensus—lead to speculative booms and currency crashes that pushed hundreds of millions of people down into dollar-a-day poverty (Garson, 2005: B17).

It is imperative that social development and science remain in harmony with each other. The world needs a reasonable climate of cooperation and interdependence which does not cause humane-made catastrophes like we have witnessed in Bosnia, New York (9/11), Rwanda, Darfur and Guntánamo Bay. A three-fold strategy to achieve this goal involves scientific, cultural and political synergy toward an international world order. These dimensions are directions for new global development which posits both *individual* and *social* in a universal context. This formulation is validated by world's general moral and ethical standards of civility. Utopian it may sound, but the present state of chaos and decadence demands nothing less if democracy, equality and justice mean more than feckless shibboleths. The point is human-social development cannot be separated. Scientists in general and social scientists in particular have bureaucratized their disciplines without knowing the color of crisis. While social developmentalism offers simplistic, often questionable, scenarios of limited social and economic growth (Midgley, 1995), human behaviorists are still snooping in the Plato's Cave. To see that humanity survives its own trappings, we must embrace the synthesis of *benign* facts and *finer* values (Mohan, 2005b).

The Crisis of India (Segal, 1965) is deeply rooted in "the deposits of time," to paraphrase Nirad Chaudhuri (1966: 38). India's recent economic recovery—thanks to globalization—has not addressed the basic issues: A sort of cultural atavism that thwarts India against herself. Casteism, communalism and regionalism are ugly heads of a hydra that threaten India's future. If India has to rise as a whole, she must resolve its cultural contradictions that torment her soul. A great civilization has to rise above its own trappings. Criminalizations of politics, pervasive public corruption and outrageous class-and-caste factions have harnessed a democratic populism that is hardly progressive (Mohan, 1996b). The impressive indices of economic growth and educational advancements are encouraging but they become meaningless in the vast ocean of inequalities and social injustices that the poor and oppressed peoples undergo in an otherwise promising nation.

3. Will the Butterflies Fail? Contextualizing the Challenge

The social chaos that paralyzes the progress of nations may be contextualized in light of the problems that perpetually plague the humankind: poverty, violence and war.

A tripartite implication of this formulation involves: Declaration of poverty and war as a crime against humanity; acceptance of global responsibility for regional tragedies; and universalization of social justice as a mandatory criteria for international co-existence. Translation of this mega-project involves courage and imagination on the part of all peoples and their allies. Social scientists in general have a collective obligation to raise consciousness for achieving a free society.

Social work education, practice and research calls for a self-renewal in light of new realities (2005a). Once we fine-tune our mission, we can initiate pedagogical innovations to impart knowledge, skills and values that can be effectively applied in the real world. Borrowed constructs and indigenous fads do not really make an enduring model. As I have contended, social work's main goal ought to be its own end: once a world without undue oppression becomes a reality, a practice of hope will instill and inculcate a new consciousness which is a prerequisite to all progressive social change. The future of social justice will determine the fate of social work's legitimacy crisis (Mohan, 1993; 2002; 2003).

José Ortega y Gasset's masterful metaphors may help summarize the contemporary predicament.

> Nature is always with us. It is self-supporting. In the forests of Nature we can be savages with impunity.... Civilization is not "just there," it is not self-supporting. It is artificial and requires the artist or the artisan. If you want to make use of the advantages of civilization, but are not prepared to concern yourself with the upholding of civilization—you are done. In a trice you find yourself left without civilization.... The jungle is always primitive and vice versa, everything primitive is jungle (Ortega y Gasset, 1930 [1957]: 88).

We developed this civilization and took it for granted. Ideologies of power masquerading as positivist scenarios of revolutionary changes left us in a trice. The surrealism of our crisis is: we do not know what to make of this civilization. As a result of our inability to recognize this barrier, our new developments present advancements without progress. Modern artificiality lacks both substance and humanity as a universal reality. No wonder why terror and nuclear horrors remind us of a jungle without any self-supportive quality. What we have is a self-destructive civilization in which *social* has lost its meaning and *asocial* has become "modern," or "objective," if you will.

It has been argued that science and government have become each other's pawns since World War II (Greenberg, 1999: 51). With historical empathy, as Giambattista Vico taught all scientists, social scientists must decode the general laws of social and cultural evolution if we need to signify the prescient power of ordinary people who have been lost ever since the dawn of Rousseauean civil society (Vico, 1744 [1999]). Modern society, it seems, is a civilizational jungle where individual liberties and social cohesion have become victims of the external forces of oppression. To regain a semblance of humanity under the uncertain horizons, one must continue to achieve freedom and dignity:

> It is the problem of survival, not revolution that has obsessed us: in recent years, survival for the victims of oppression and

> for [humankind] itself, as the state risks total destruction to ensure its prestige and dominance. It is proper and necessary that this should be so (Chomsky, 1971: 110).

A new culture of science warrants a symbiosis of success and progress,[10] the two fundamental elements of constructive evolution. We as a "community of communities"[11] have failed to achieve either. Will the butterflies of varied hues come out of the Plato's Cave and help us out of the chaos that engulfs much of the world? I still don't know.

Notes

1. "The lamp of Vijnana (knowledge or science) removes the fear of Samsara, the circle of births and deaths," *trans.* Ashok Kalia, University of Lucknow, India.
2. "Last year, according to the Department of Agriculture, 34.9 million Americans like the Compeans were "food insecure"—the government's term for those who must survive on a diet not nutritious enough to keep a child health. More than 13 million of those people were children. The U.S. Conference of Mayors expects that requests for emergency food from families with children will increase in 91 per cent of the nation's cities this year. They also document that emergency food outlets in 56 per cent of the nation's cities turned away hungry families last year because they run out of resources" (Relin, 2004: 6).
3. The implicit reference alludes to Al Qaeda and terrorist Bin Ladin's force.
4. Walter Cronkite laments on the state of current American democracy: "This is a dangerous condition for any representative democracy. The tight control of information, as well as the dissemination of misleading information and outright falsehoods, conjures up a disturbing image of a very different kind of society. Democracies are not well-run nor long-preserved with secrecy and lies" (Cronkite, 2004: 6B).
5. From Desmond Morris' *The Naked Ape* and Konrad Lorenz's *On Aggression* to Antony Jay's *Corporate Man* and Franz de Waal's *Chimpanzee Politics* scientists have linked human behaviour to primate instincts with varied degrees of emphasis on learning and instincts.
6. It was April 6, 1996, about 10 years ago.
7. *The New York Times* reporter S. Sen Gupta calls it Africa's First World War propelled by greedy nations surrounding resourceful Congo (*NPR*, Talk of the Nation, April 6, 2004).

8. "Discussion groups based on the teachings of Socrates are reviving the art of conversation" (*See* Hamilton, 2004: 65-66).
9. "The real threat is not Balkanization but Brazilianization of America, not fragmentation along racial lines but fissioning along class lines. Brazialianization is symbolized by the increasing withdrawal of the white American overclass into its own barricaded nation-within-a-nation, a world of private neighbourhoods, private schools, private police, private health care, and even private roads, walled off from the spreading squalor beyond. Like a Latin American oligarchy, the rich and well-connected members of the overclass can flourish in a decadent America with Third World levels of inequality and crime" (Lind, 1995: 14).
10. Jean Paul Sartre once famously said, "Success is not progress."
11. The expression is owed to my grand teacher, Dr. Radha Kamal Mukerjee, the father of Indian Sociology, Lucknow University, India.

References

Becker, Ernest (1968), *The Structure of Evil.* New York: The Free Press.

Bergen, Peter (2005), Beware the Holy War. *The Nation,* June 20: 25-34.

Chaudhuri, Nirad C. (1966), *The Continent of Circe: An Essay on the Peoples of India.* Bombay: Jaico Pub.

Chomsky, Noam (1971), *Problems of Knowledge and Freedom: The Russell Lectures.*

Conniff, Richard (2003), Rethinking Primate Aggression. *Smithsonian,* August, 34, 1: 60-67.

Cronkite, Walter (2004), Government Secrecy and Lies. *The Advocate,* April 3: 6B (distributed by King Features Syndicate).

De Waal, Frans (1982) (2000), *Chimpanzee Politics: Power and Sex Among Apes.* Baltimore, MD: Johns Hopkins Paperbacks.

Foucault, Michel (1972), *The Archeology of Knowledge & the Discourse on Language.* Trans. A.M. Sheridan. New York: Barnes & Nobles.

Fowler, Jonathan (2004), Report Cites 10 Million Child Slaves. *The Advocate,* June 11, 2004, 17A.

Garson, Barbara (2005), True Believers at the World Bank. *The Advocate,* May 30: B17.

Greenberg, Daniel S. (1999), *The Politics of Pure Science.* Chicago: University of Chicago Press.

Hamilton, Anita (2004), All the Right Questions. *Time,* April 5: 65-66.

Hogland, Jim (2005), Asia's Rise No Reason to Panic. *The Advocate,* June 6: 7B.

Lind, Michael (1995), *The American Nation: The New Nationalism and the Fourth American Revolution.* New York: The Free Press.

Midgley, James (1995), *Social Development: The Developmental Perspective in Social Welfare.* Thousand Oak, CA: Sage.

Mohan, Brij (2005), *Fallacies of Development.*

Mohan, Brij (2005a), *Reinventing Social Work: Reflections on the Metaphysics of Social Practice.* Lewiston, NY: The Edwin Mellen Press.

Mohan, Brij (2005b), Social Exclusions: Toward New Social Development. Paper delivered to the 14th Symposium, Inter-University Consortium of International Social Development, Recife, Brazil, July 24-28.

Mohan, Brij (2004), Redefining *Social*: Evolution of a Construct: From Oxymoron to Interdisciplinarity. Paper [to be] delivered to the Hawaiian International Conference of Social Sciences, Honolulu, Hawaii, June 15-19: 10.

Mohan, Brij (2003), *The Practice of Hope.* Philadelphia, PA: Xlibris.

Mohan, Brij (2002), *Social Work Revisited.* Philadelphia, PA: Xlibris.

Mohan, Brij (1999), *Unification of Social Work: Rethinking Social Transformation.* Westport, CT: Praeger.

Mohan, Brij (1996), Self, Society and Science: On Transforming Social Reality. *International Journal of Contemporary Sociology,* 33, 1: 59-78.

Mohan, Brij (1996a), *Democracies of Unfreedom: India and the United States.* Westport, CT: Praeger.

Mohan, Brij (1993), *Eclipse of Freedom.* Westport, CT: Praeger.

Ortega y Gasset, José (1930) (1957), *The Revolt of the Masses.* Trans. Anonymous. New York: W.W. Norton.

Relin, David O. (2004), Won't You Help Feed Them? *Parade,* April 4.

Rothstein, Edward (2004), Finding the Universal Laws that are There, Waiting.... *The New York Times,* January 10, 2004: a15.

Scheuer, Michael (2004), *Imperial Hubris: Why the West is Losing the War on Terror?* Dulles, VA: Brassey's Inc.

Segal, Ronald (1965), *The Crisis of India.* Harmondsworth, England: Penguin Books.

Vico, Giambattista (1744) (1999), *New Science.* London: Penguin Classics.

Winch, Peter (1960), *The Idea of a Social Science and Its Relation to Philosophy.* London: Routledge & Kegan Paul.

2

Political Economy of Centralisation in India: Some Critical Notes from a Decentralist Perspective

Pritam Singh

Introduction

The project and process of centralisation of economic and political power in India has been ongoing almost unquestioned and unchecked for the last approximately 60 years. The initial outline of the centralisation project can be observed right back in the 1930s and 1940s except that it had countervailing forces then in the shape of some economic aspects of Gandhian thinking, some regionally based political voices in the Congress Party and the Muslim opposition to the Hindu majoritarian consequences of political centralisation. The 1947 partition swung the pendulum strongly in favour of centralisation. The path of state-directed capitalist development that the Indian policy-makers followed until 1991 strengthened the process and forces of centralisation. The Balance of Payment (BoP) crisis of 1991 which resulted in the new regime of liberal economic reforms has opened some avenues for decentralisation especially in the economic domain but at the same time has given more power to the Centre in the process of closer integration of the national economy into the global capitalist economy than what existed before 1991.

This chapter is divided into five parts. **Part 1** attempts to construct a historical overview of the emergence of Centre-State relations in post-colonial India with particular emphasis on the debates in the Constituent Assembly which led to the formulation of the Indian Constitution in 1950. **Part 2** examines the importance of the historically-shaped triangular relationship between Indian capitalism, Indian State and Indian nationalism in explaining the structure of Centre-State relations. In **Part 3** the New Economic Policy of 1991 and its implications for the centralisation process are considered. **Part 4** evaluates very briefly the political, economic and cultural consequences of centralisation and **Part** 5 offers concluding remarks.

1. Historical Background to the Centralisation Debate

Prior to India's independence on 15 August 1947, the pattern of India's Centre-State relations were shaped by the British rule over India for about two centuries from mid-18th century onwards and the Moghul rule from about mid-15th century onwards.

Centre-Province Relations in Ancient and Medieval India

In the ancient period prior to the Moghul rule, a reasonably high degree of decentralisation seemed to exist. In these ancient empires "each province led its own life, continued its old familiar system of Government (though under the agents of the Central power) and used its own language" (Jadunath Sarkar, quoted in Govt. of India, 1988: 5). Another historical account of the ancient period states that "...the conquered states generally continued to retain their identity, and were ready to emerge into independence at a suitable opportunity" (Sastri, 1987: 116).

During the Moghul rule, the states continued to enjoy regional autonomy until the last Moghul ruler "made a strong bid for complete centralisation and abolition of traditional diversities and autonomy of the regions" (Govt. of India, 1988: 5). Shortly after his death, the regional forces re-asserted their independence.

Centre-Province Relations during the British Rule

The British colonisation of India was completed by 1858 following the annexation of the last sovereign State of Punjab in 1849 and the defeat of the 'Sepoy Mutiny' in 1857.[1] During the 1857 conflict, the British discovered that 500 and odd Princely States in India could be allies of the British rule in India. As a result, the earlier British colonial policy of expansion through 'direct rule' in the subcontinent was substituted partially by one of 'indirect rule' for these Princely States. A dual system of direct rule in British Indian Provinces and indirect rule in the Princely States emerged. The remote and inaccessible areas with strong local tribal customs and beliefs and long history of isolation, retained varying degrees of autonomy (Govt. of India, 1988: 6). The British rulers also found a highly centralised administration to be incompatible with the size and diversity of the country. The result was administrative inefficiency and local discontent, making some degree of decentralisation inevitable. The first small but significant step in the direction of decentralisation was taken by the Indian Councils Act, 1861. The Act reversed the centralising trend that had been set by the Charter Act of 1833.[2] It provided for participation by non-officials in the Legislative Council of the Governor-General. Similar provisions were made for the Legislative Councils of the Provinces. The principle of indirect election to these Legislative Councils was established in 1892 and the functions were enlarged to include the right of discussion of the budget and interpellation in matters of public interest.

The process of decentralisation of finances which was started with the Mayo Scheme in 1871 was continued until its formalisation by the Government of India Act, 1919 which contributed further to the evolution of a 'dispersed' political system in India.

The association of Indians with local self-government through elected municipalities and district boards, although with strictly limited authority, was initiated in 1882 by Lord Rippon.

The emergence of the Indian National Congress in 1885 and the consequent growth of Indian nationalism encouraged the British rulers to devolve more powers to the states with the purpose of giving the Indians some feeling of participation in power. The Indian Council Act, 1909 (Morley-Minto Reforms) which further extended the association of Indians with State power, though with separate electorates, narrow franchise and indirect election, was a continuation of the British policy of co-opting some Indians into State power.

The most significant step undertaken by the British to introduce devolution of power to the states was the Government of India Act, 1919.[3] By the Devolution Rules framed under the Act, the 'dyarchical' system of Centre and Provinces provided for delegation of powers to the Provinces not only in the administrative but also in the legislative and financial spheres. For this purpose, separate Central and Provincial Lists of subjects were drawn up. The subjects in the Provincial List were further subdivided into 'reserved' and 'transferred' subjects. The Departments dealing with the 'transferred' subjects were placed in the charge of elected Ministers responsible to the Provincial legislature, while the Departments in respect of 'reserved' subjects were administered by the Governor assisted by an Executive Council nominated by him. Although with respect to 'transferred' subjects, the Provinces derived substantial authority by devolution from the Central Government, yet the Governor-General in Council remained in control at the apex of this centralised system ultimately responsible to the Secretary of State for India in the UK. Finance was a 'reserved subject' in charge of a member of the nominated Executive Council. The main instruments of administration, namely, the Indian Civil Service and the Indian Police were under the control of the Secretary of State and were responsible to him and not to the Minister. The Governor had the discretionary power of not acting on the advice of the Ministers. No bill could be moved in the Provincial Legislature without the permission of the Governor-General. No bill could become law without his assent. Although the 1919 Act formally devolved some powers to the provinces, in reality, the structure of Centre-Province relations remained unitary with the Governor-General in Council in effective ultimate control.

The failure of the extremely limited devolution set in motion by the 1919 Act in meeting the Indian nationalist demands for power-sharing forced the British Government to appoint a Statutory Commission under Sir John Simon in November 1927 to consider the extension of some more power to the Indians. However, the composition of the Commission—all the seven members were British—provoked boycott of the Commission by almost all Indian political tendencies. The Congress Party pressed the British Government to accede to the national demand for convening a Round Table Conference or Constituent Assembly to determine the future constitution of India.

The British Government published a White Paper in 1933, embodying the principles of Constitutional reforms in India. This eventually led to the 1935 Government of India Act which provided a new framework for Centre-State Relations by dividing the governmental subjects into three lists—Federal, Provincial and Concurrent. As a follow up of the Act, elected governments responsible to legislature assumed offices in 1937. However, as a protest against the Centre's continuous intrusion into Provincial autonomy, the governments in the Provinces led by the Congress Party resigned in 1939.

Congress in the pre-independence period in its party organisational structure made a formal response to regional aspirations of the States but in reality remained a highly centralised party. According to Santhanam (1960: 61), the pre-independence Congress party structure "...had become very highly centralised.... The Provincial Congress Committees had become accustomed to look for guidance and take directions from the All-India Congress Committee and the All-India Congress Committee used to take its guidance from the Working Committee, and generally the Working Committee from the leader or the leaders." In March 1942, Sir Stafford Cripps presented proposals of the British Government to elect a Constituent Assembly through proportional representation by the Provincial Legislatures to frame a new Constitution of India after the end of World War II. It was also suggested that the British Government would accept the new Constitution subject, *inter alia*, to the condition that any Province could opt out of it and retain its constitutional position as laid down in the 1935 Act. The rejection of Cripps' proposals by the dominant tendencies in the Indian nationalist movement led to a new initiative by the British Government, *viz.* the announcement of the British Cabinet Mission Plan by Mr. Atlee, the British Prime Minister, on May 16, 1946. The plan envisaged a federalist political structure for India that allowed considerable devolution of power to the provinces. This pro-States federal framework with a weak Centre and residual power vested in the States had been advocated to accommodate the Muslim League's fear of Hindu domination resulting from an excessively powerful Centre. By adopting a seemingly accommodationist strategy, ensuring sufficient autonomy to those States with a Muslim majority, the Congress leadership was hoping to avert the creation of a separate Muslim-majority Pakistan. Nevertheless, on 3 July 1947 the British government announced its decision to partition the country.

There are two ways of interpreting the reason for the breakdown of this plan, which led to the partition of India into two separate countries on 15 August 1947. One interpretation could be that the failure of the Congress leadership's attempt at seeking accommodation with Muslim League could have been the result of the Muslim League's intransigence, leaving Congress opposed to any devolutionary approach in the future. Conversely, it could be argued that the Congress devolutionary-cum-accommodation offer was flawed from the beginning since Congress leadership was already centralist in its political orientation. This forced Jinnah to be more resolute in his determination to seek a separate Pakistan in order to protect what he saw as the Muslim interests. Once Pakistan was created, Congress leadership was more convinced than before that only an uncompromising centralist approach could prevent any further partition of the country. K. Santhanam, a strong votary of decentralisation, cites Maulana Abul Kalam Azad to point out that "one of the reasons which induced Sardar Patel to agree to partition was that it would give an opportunity to establish a strong Central Government as against the weak Central Government which was all that was possible if the Cabinet Mission had been accepted and the Constitution had been drawn up in accordance with the Cripps Plan" (Santhanam, 1960: 60). According to Ayesha Jalal it was the Congress's unwillingness to take account of Muslim League's concerns by agreeing to a federal set-up that pushed Jinnah to the path of partition (Jalal, 1985).

Whatever interpretation of the reasons behind the creation of Pakistan the historians may find to be more acceptable, the partition of India into Hindu-majority "Bharat" (the alternative official name given to India in its Constitution) and the Muslim-majority Pakistan at the time of independence from British rule had a decisive influence on the character of Centre-State relations in post-independence India. The partition led to a sharp reversal in the approach of the Constituent Assembly regarding Centre-State relations. The absence of Muslim League after partition removed the counter-balancing force to the Congress, which became practically the sole political party in India (Santhanam, 1960: 60). Consequently, the political leadership of independent India, the Indian National Congress, did not face any serious political resistance to their preferred perspective of constructing a constitutional arrangement with strong centralist bias as opposed to the pro-States federalist political structure envisaged prior to 1947. This change is expressed in the Second Report of the Union Powers Committee, dated July 5, 1947: "Now that the partition is a settled fact, we are unanimously of the view that it would be injurious to the interests of the country to provide for a weak Central authority which will be incapable of ensuring peace, of co-ordinating vital matters of common concern...and that the soundest framework of our Constitution is a federation with a 'strong Centre'" (Govt. of India, 1988: 7). Once the partition plan was accepted, the Indian political leadership (at least the majority) was relieved to be able to implement their plan of a strong Centre.

The Indian Constitution and the Debate in the Constituent Assembly

This strong pro-Centre bias in the structure of Centre-State relations was enshrined in the Constitution of India framed by the Constituent Assembly of independent India, which came into force on January 26, 1950 (Bhattacharya, 1992; Govt. of India, 1988; Austin 2004/1966).

During the transition period from August 15, 1947 to January 26, 1950, two sets of considerations can be identified as having influenced the framers of the new Constitution in opting for a 'strong-Centre'-oriented Constitutional framework: dealing with immediate contingent problems and, more importantly, realising some long-term political objectives. The immediate problems were: the large-scale sectarian violence against the Muslims in India, and against the Hindus and Sikhs in Pakistan; rehabilitation of these mainly forced refugees, armed intervention in Kashmir to secure its accession to India, the use of military and diplomatic means to secure the accession of some of the Princely States aspiring to set up their own sovereign states and the military suppression of the armed Communist uprising in

Telengana in the south of India. The immediate and short-term contingental developments contributed to strengthening pro-Centre institutional structures like the military and the centralised bureaucracy and also to generating a general political climate in the country and general opinion among the Constitutional framers which were strongly favourable to introducing a pro-Centre bias in the Constitutional framework. The immediate problems seemed to make a strong Centre a historic necessity enabling the newly independent nation to face the potential threat of "Balkanisation" and disintegration of the country. This nationalist sentiment was also shared by the overwhelming Hindu population of India especially in the Hindi speaking 'cow belt' of North India. The long-term politico-economic vision of the dominant and majority group among the members of the Constituent Assembly can be described as consisting of the following elements: (a) A strong Centre was necessary to build one unified Indian national identity out of the multiple national and ethnic identities in India;[4] (b) a strong Centre was more effective than the provincial government in shaping a State-Capitalist path of development[5] (Bettelheim, 1968; Chattopadhyay, 70; Desai, 1984); (c) a strong Centre was necessary to reduce regional inequalities to foster a spirit of balanced national development;[6] and (d) a strong Centre is more likely than the provincial governments to be able to reduce class inequalities to make the socio-economic system stable and endurable.[7] The long-term politico-economic vision shared by the majority among the Constitution-makers reinforced the tendency towards centralisation set in by the necessity of strong Central intervention in the context of immediate contingental problems. The immediate contingental developments could not have by themselves led to framing a pro-Centre Constitution without the long-term politico-economic vision mentioned above. It is, perhaps, plausible to argue in a contra-factual manner that had the dominant majority of the Constitution makers had a political vision strongly favourable to the autonomy of the States, then after the resolution of the contingental post-partition problems, they would have put their weight behind a pro-State autonomy constitutional framework.

It seems, therefore, that the long-term politico-economic and historical goals set by the Constitution makers played a more decisive role than the compulsions of dealing with immediate contingental problems in shaping the Centre oriented structure of the Indian Constitution.

In May 1947 K.M. Panikkar, one of the leading figures in the Constituent Assembly, wrote: "Federation with limited powers for the Centre, was an unavoidable evil in India, so long as the Muslim majority provinces had to be provided for in an all-India centre.... It is no longer necessary to provide for the very large measure of power for the units, which a full union with the Muslim majority provinces would have rendered unavoidable" (quoted by Bhattacharya, 1992: 99). This statement seemed to reflect a sense of relief that the Muslim bargaining power had vanished and the centralising agenda could now be implemented without any opposition. Nehru articulated similar views. He argued that "the severe limitations on the scope of central authority in the Cabinet Mission's plan was a compromise accepted by the Assembly much, we think against its judgment of the administrative needs of the country in order to accommodate the Muslim League. Now that partition is a settled fact we are unanimously of the view that it would be injurious to the interests of the country to provide for a weak central authority...." (quoted by Bhattacharya, 1992: 96).

Other members of the Constituent Assembly, namely Jaspat Roy Kapoor and Ram Chandra Gupta (both from UP) as well as Jagat Narain Lal (Bihar) expressed a Hindutva view of history as a justification for a strong Centre. Quoting Kapoor, "history undoubtedly proves that whenever there has been no centralisation in this country it has been overrun by foreigners" (*Constituent Assembly Debates* [henceforth *CAD*], November 21, 1949, Vol. XI, 760). Anyone questioning centralisation was almost dubbed as a spy of a foreign government by Kapoor. "The two fundamental things about this Constitution are the unity of the country and a strong Central Government...nobody should be sorry for it excepting one who would like to bring about confusion and chaos in this country because his sympathies may be lying somewhere else outside the borders of this country"[8]

(*CAD*, November 21, 1949, Vol. XI, 762). In his speech Kapoor expressed his disenchantment with "the special provisions for Kashmir" (*CAD*, November 21, 1949, Vol. XI, 762) and concluded with a strong Hindu nationalist fervour: "Our motto and slogan hereafter should be: *Bharat samvidhan ki Jaya ho, Bharat Mata ki Jaya ho*"[9] (*CAD*, November 21, 1949, Vol. XI, 763). In the opinion of Ram Chandra Gupta, centralisation resulted from the partition process and the consequent emergence of Pakistan. He also expressed a Hindutva-oriented view arguing: "Prior to the partition of the country, it was thought that all the provinces should be practically independent of the Centre except in certain matters—defence, communication, etc.—the residuary powers to vest in the units; but the partition did demand, and rightly demanded that Centre should be made as strong as possible. The Constitution has effected this change.... *A strong Central Government is the need of the hour* (italics original).... All along the ages, and our history bears ample testimony to this fact, the overmastering problem before India has been one of integration, and consolidation and unification" (*CAD*, November 24, 1949, Vol. XI, 920).[10] To Jagat Narain Lal[11] more Central power implied greater national solidarity. He said, "Time after time in history, we have found this solidarity being broken and India falling at the feet of the foreign conquerors" (*CAD*, November 25, 1949, Vol. XI, 946). Although in a weaker Hindutva tone, K.M. Munshi[12] followed Kapoor, Gupta and Lal by praising the virtues of "strong central authority" in the Indian historical experience (CAD, Vol. VIII, 927-28).

There were others who also spoke in favour of centralisation giving different justifications, the most prominent being Ambedkar. There seemed to be a convergence of positions: Hindu nationalists, secular Indian nationalists (Nehru) and Ambedkar all seemed to agree on the need for a strong Centre for different reasons. Though a centraliser, Ambedkar also played the most influential role in critiquing Nehru's over-centralising approach on many issues. Ambedkar opposed and defeated Nehru's position that a simple majority of parliament should have the power to amend some features of the Constitution. He also showed critical awareness of the fact that many of the centralising features of the proposed Constitution in the framing of which he had played a key role, "invaded provincial autonomy" (Austin, 2004: 262-64).

Strong resistance to a highly centralised political structure came mainly from Southern States: N.G. Ranga, K. Santhanam, Mahboob Ali Baig and Ramalingam Chettiar all opposed the move to centralisation. According to Professor Ranga, "...centralisation, I wish to warn this house, would only lead to Sovietisation and totalitarianism and not democracy" (*CAD*, November 9, 1948, Vol. VII, 350). Mahboob Ali Baig supported institutional mechanisms like the electoral system of proportional representation to ensure that the interests of religious minorities are safeguarded and disapproved of the move towards a unitarist political system: "...in the hands of a Central Government which wants to override and convert this federal system into a unitary system, it can be easily done. Now there is a danger of this sort of Government becoming totalitarian. This is the danger in the form of the Constitution that is embodied in the Draft Constitution" (*CAD*, November 8, 1948, Vol. VII, 296). T.T. Krishnamachari was sympathetic to giving some powers to the Centre for introducing uniform labour standards (as proposed by Jagjivan Ram) and for maintaining public health standards, but feared that creating a strong Centre "would also mean the enslavement of people who do not speak the language of the legislature, the language of the Centre" (*CAD*, November 5, 1948, Vol. VII, 234-35). Krishnamachari feared "Hindi imperialism" and "totalitarianism" as a result of centralisation...." (*CAD*, November 5, 1948, Vol. VII, 234-35). Socialists H.V. Kamath and Professor Shibban Lal Saksena were extremely critical of the many pro-centralisation proposals especially the ones relating to the President's Rule. Kamath considered these measures to be a threat to democracy and characterised them as a Hitler-like takeover by the Union Government (*CAD*, August 3, 1949, Vol. XI, 135-42 for Kamath and 142-45 for Saksena).

The jurist H.N. Kunjru and the United Provinces premier G.B. Pant, who "seems to have been the unofficial spokesman of the provincial premiers in the Assembly" (Austin, 2004 : 315), were other well-known critics of the centralisation process. Kamplapati Tiwari opposed a strong Centre from a Gandhian standpoint: "The first fundamental defect of the Constitution appears to be that it is terribly centre-ridden.... Everyone knows that effective power in the hands of the centre can only be based on military strength and the concentration of military power is the sure road leading to the complete destruction of popular rights. This is a historic truth. Our Constitution obviously presents this danger" (*CAD*, 1949: 863-64).

Another group opposed to the centralisation proposals was the Sikhs. Justice Ajit Singh Bains has highlighted the well-known historical fact that, "the Sikh representative in the Constituent Assembly did not sign the Constitution of India as it had not given any autonomy to the states" (Bains, 1996: 179). Hukam Singh, a Sikh representative, stated: "...the Sikhs feel utterly disappointed and frustrated. They feel that they have been discriminated against. Let it not be misunderstood that the Sikh community has agreed to this Constitution. I wish to record an emphatic protest here. My community cannot subscribe its assent to this historic document. ...In our Constitution, each article tends to sap the local autonomy and make the provinces irresponsible. ...The minorities and particularly the Sikhs have been ignored and completely neglected. The Provincial units have been reduced to Municipal Boards...there is enough provision in our Constitution...to facilitate the development of administration into a fascist State" (*CAD*, November 21, 1949, Vol. XI, 753). Another Sikh representative Bhupinder Singh Mann (spelt wrongly in the *CAD Official Report* as Man) expressed the Sikhs' sentiment by stating: "I will be failing in my duty if I do not give the reactions of my own community, the Sikhs of East Punjab, so far as this Constitution goes. Their feeling is that they cannot give unstinted support or full approval to this Constitution" (*CAD*, November 21, 1949: 722). Bains argues that the Sikh unrest in Punjab since Independence in 1947 and especially during the 1980s and 1990s can be attributed to this unitarist Constitution which empowers the Centre *vis-à-vis* the States.

Bajpai captures the dominant Hindu majoritarian and nationalist mood in the Constituent Assembly debates and points out that, "minorities were referred to as 'disfigurement,' 'cancerous,' 'poisonous' for the body politic" (Bajpai, 2000: 1839). Khilnani (1997: 29) observes that "Hindu voices" had become "emboldened" in the Congress Party after the 1947 Partition.[13]

Although there were other supporters of centralisation, the most dedicated proponents of strong centralisation and Union power prior to and after independence were Hindu nationalists. Strong Central power in the Indian Constitutional framework and the Indian political structure is associated, in the Hindutva vision, with strong Indian Hindu nationhood. Decentralisation and minority rights are viewed, in this vision, with suspicion as potential threats to that nationhood. When secular Indian nationalists equated Central power with unity and territorial integrity of the country, they moved, almost imperceptibly, into the territory of Hindu nationalist discourse. The convergence between Hindu Indian nationalism and secular Indian nationalism on the question of support for strong centralisation both before as well as after independence is a striking feature of the Indian political culture.

2. Troika of Capital, State and Nation: The Phase of Planned Capitalist Development

There is a growing consensus in the literature that the Indian Constitution contained a strong bias in favour of the Centre. Furthermore, since the framing of the Constitution, the changes which have taken place have further strengthened the powers of the Centre (Mitra, 1987; Sathyamurthy, 1996; Gulati, 1987; Govt. of India, 1987). The historically-shaped triangular relationship between Indian capitalism, Indian State and Indian nationalism is of prime importance in explaining the structure of Centre-State relations in India and thus the process of centralisation of economic and political power as well as the dynamics of macro-political economy of India in general. In the shaping of the Indian Constitution, the ideology of Indian nationalism found a legal-constitutional framework to give expression to its centralist perspective (Austin, 2004; Jennings, 1953). The strategy of State capital accumulation, followed in independent India with a critical role assigned to central planning, further reinforced the trend towards strengthening the forces of centralisation (Chattopadhyay, 1970 and 1992; Bettelheim, 1968; Chakravarty, 1987/89; Bardhan, 1984/89). The Indian capitalist class fully endorsed this strategy of State-directed industrialisation, participated in it and benefited hugely from it (Desai, 1975; Desai, 1984; Patnaik, 1975; Sen, 1982; Byres, 1993b; Harriss 1989).

The troika of Capital, State and Nation thus entered into a mutually reinforcing relationship. A Nation needed a State and Capital, the Capital needed a Nation and a State and the State needed Capital and a Nation.[14]

Indian State and Indian Nationalism

Given the structure of the Indian Constitution, the power of the Indian state is articulated through the Central government and the various state (provincial) governments. With the balance of power between the Central government and the provincial governments being decisively in favour of the Centre, the Indian State can be characterised as a Centralist State. Historically, the role of this Centralist Indian State has been as the architect and articulator of one unified Indian nationalism (Banerjee, 1992; Ramasubramaniam, 1992; Nandy, 1992). In other words, Indian nationalism is the ideology of the Centralist Indian State though at times, Indian nationalism may transform itself in an almost unnoticeable manner into Hindu nationalism. Whilst secular and Hindu nationalism are opposed to each other in their premises and perspectives in several ways, their insistence on the rejection of multiple nationalisms in India unites these two versions of Indian nationalism.

Indian Capitalism and Indian State

A state is situated in the context of a mode of production, which can be feudal, capitalist or socialist. During the 1990s, the mode of production in Indian industry and agriculture was, indisputably, capitalist[15] (Sen, 1992; Chattopadhyay, 1992; Sathyamurthy, 1995). The Indian State is, therefore, situated, both globally and nationally, in the context of a capitalist mode of production. The specific character of the capitalist State shapes and is shaped by a specific capital accumulation strategy, which is historically determined in a complex way and varies in its form within the capitalist mode of production. The capital accumulation strategy pursued in India is influenced significantly by the centralist character of the Indian State and the Indian nationalism. Hence, the specific accumulation strategy pursued in India is legitimised by the ideology of Indian nationalism and subsequently contributes towards shaping the character of the Indian State as a centralist State. On the other hand, Indian nationalism and its centralism dictate the specific accumulation strategy followed by the Indian State.

Indian Capitalism and Indian Nationalism

Due to the existence of provincial States, the process of capital accumulation, despite being global in scope, is fundamentally shaped by the national context. The specific way in which the State is influenced by nationalism, affects the capital accumulation strategy in a nation-state (Jessop, 1990). The capital accumulation strategy pursued by the Indian State can be described as a relatively independent state capitalist development strategy (Patnaik, 1975; Desai, 1975; Desai, 1984; Sen, 1982). The roots of this strategy lie in the national movement for independence from British imperialism and the strategy is a reflection of the convergence of two perspectives in the national movement for independence: the perspective of the political leadership of the Indian National Congress, which was the major political force behind the independence movement and the perspective of the Indian bourgeoisie. The political leadership of the Indian National Congress, especially Nehru, considered the role of State through the planning mechanism in a mixed economy as fundamental to industrialisation (Chandra, 1969; Chakravarty, 1987/1989). The Indian bourgeoisie, which having experienced the role of the colonial State in obstructing the growth of indigenous Indian Capitalism, regarded the independent national State as a source of strength and help for further capitalist expansion (Chandra, 1992; Mukherjee, 1976). Common to both perspectives was the ideology of Indian nationalism, which can therefore be regarded as the legitimising ideology behind the specific capital accumulation strategy followed in independent India after 1947. The emphasis on maintaining relative independence from imperialism was also imparted by the national ideology of gaining and maintaining national sovereignty.

It follows that the driving force behind the capital accumulation strategy of relatively independent state capitalist development was the legitimising ideology of Indian nationalism. This capital accumulation strategy, in turn, by placing crucial reliance upon planning and, hence, on the central government, legitimised centralisation of power and the creation of a centralist State (Bardhan, 1984/1989).

This accumulation strategy and the emergence of a centralist Indian State which it legitimised, in turn, legitimised Indian nationalism. The crucial point, which is often obfuscated in the discourse of Indian nationalism and which hence needs to be emphasised is that India contains within its geographical territory many nations and potential nations. The accumulation strategy of planned development by its emphasis on the crucial role of Central Government in central planning, justified the need for political unification of the country and such a political unification required subjugation of other national identities to one Indian identity.

The general theoretical point which emerges from the analysis of the triangular relationship between Capital, State and Nation is that in a multinational society, a capital accumulation strategy and an ideology of one unifying nationalism that relies upon the central role of the State for economic management and political unification, leads to the creation of a Centralist State. The emergence of such a Centralist State has crucial implications for the conduct of State intervention in situations of conflict between its long-term goal of one unitarist nationalism and the historical aspirations of other nations and potential nations that exist within the geographical boundaries of the nation state.

It may be fruitful to elaborate further on the relationship between Indian nationalism and the Centralist State, which is a mediated relationship rather than a direct one. The mediation is provided by the political economy of the accumulation strategy in a multinational country. The ideology of nationalism by its value-emphasis on sovereignty/independence/autonomy assigns a crucial role to the State in implementing the accumulation strategy. Empowerment of the Central Government is the only way in which the State in a multinational country can continue with this accumulation strategy, since the successful implementation of any economic development strategy (in any mode of production) requires political stability. It must be mentioned in passing here that political stability within a given mode of production is discussed as one of the main prerequisites of economic development. It is entirely reasonable to argue for the desirability or necessity of political instability which may eventually lead to the transition to a new mode of production where this transition may be required in order to initiate economic development. The reference situation in our case is economic development and political stability within the parameters of a capitalist mode of production in a multinational country. Political stability in this situation can be shattered either by class conflicts or nationalist conflicts. It follows that capitalist development in a multinational situation, requires the submerging of diverse national identities to one unifying national identity. In a multinational country such as India where the capitalist development strategy calls for an active interventionist State, the successful implementation of this strategy requires the State to articulate the ideology of one unifying nationalism. Furthermore, in a constitutional structure like India with State power divided between the Centre and the provinces, the ideology of one unifying nationalism demands a powerful Centre which, in turn, imparts a Centralist character to the State.

Indian Nationalism: The Ideology of the Indian State

The thesis that Indian nationalism is the ideology of the Indian State is fairly well-established with sufficient scholarly literature to support it (Desai, 1959; Archarya, 1993; Mukarji and Arora, 1992; Nandy, 1992; Joshi and Josh, 1994). What is new is the claim on my part to bring this relationship into the analysis of Indian macro-political economy in its multinational dimension. The significance of this claim is the fact that the ideology of Indian nationalism of the Indian State puts it in conflict with nationalism of the nations based in the provinces. However, it must be qualified that since in the Hindi speaking provinces Indian nationalism is itself the dominant ideological current, this conflict between Indian nationalism as the ideology of the Indian State and the nationalisms of the nations based in the provinces is confined only to the non-Hindi speaking states.

In the Hindi-speaking states, either there is no regional party (Madhya Pradesh and Rajasthan and, to some extent, Himachal Pradesh) or regional parties articulate regional concerns through caste based parties as opposed to the upper caste dominated Indian nationalist parties; UP and Bihar fall into this category.

In the non-Hindi speaking states, the State power at the province level articulates itself in an ambiguous and contradictory way. On the one hand, with the State power being highly centralised at the Centre, the institutions of State power in the constituent provinces find themselves increasingly forced to articulate the ideology of Indian nationalism. On the other hand, these institutions have to manage the nationalist pressure of a nation based in a particular province to articulate the ideology of nationalism of that nation. The exact nature of the contradictory pressures to which the State power in a constituent province is subjected, is determined by the degree of development of nationalism (movements, organizations, ideology) in that particular province.

There is unevenness in the growth of province based nationalisms. In those constituent provinces with well-developed nationalism (Southern provinces but especially Tamil Nadu and Andhra Pradesh, Kashmir, Punjab, Assam, Nagaland, Mizoram), the State power, if it is being articulated through a democratically elected government, comes under greater pressure from the nationalism of the nations located in these provinces than in provinces with a weaker degree of development of nationalism (*e.g.* Orissa, Maharashtra and Gujarat). Consequently, the Centre as the articulator of one unified Indian nationalism is always apprehensive of democratically elected governments in those provinces where the nationalism of the nation is relatively well-developed. The increasing phenomena of the imposition of the

President's rule in such provinces are not incidental but are rooted in the structural conflict between one unified Indian nationalism articulated by the Centre and the nationalisms of the nations based in such provinces.

The Centre-State relations in India will be the arena where the conflicts between Indian nationalism and the nationalisms of the nations based in the provinces will be fought out. As it has happened in the past sometimes, the short-term ephemeral political changes like the same party rule at the Centre and in the states or the same kind of coalition rule at the Centre and in the states, personal rapport between political leadership at the Centre and in the states may disguise this conflict. However, in the long-term these ephemeral changes will be overtaken by the more enduring historical basis of structural conflict between the Centre and the states. The Indian capitalist class aiming to preserve a unified national marked for capital accumulation and expansion, will be an ally of the Centre in its conflict with the states. The ideology of "one Indian nation" will be used as much by the big capitalist class to conceal its naked economic interests as by the Central State to generate sentiments of national unity and territorial integrity.

3. The New Economic Policy of 1991

The stance of India's economic policy underwent a fundamental change on 24 July 1991 when the Indian minority Government of Prime Minister P.V. Narsimha Rao with Dr. Manmohan Singh as Finance Minister embarked on a process of economic liberalization, aimed at moving the country away from its previous inward-oriented and state-directed policy regime towards greater market orientation.

The Macroeconomic Crisis of 1991

India's economic reform process had modestly started in 1985 but was significantly accelerated in the wake of the severe and acute 1991 Balance of Payments (BoP) crisis (Cassen and Joshi, 1995). This crisis saw India close to defaulting on its external debt obligations as the country's international credit-worthiness collapsed, foreign private lending was cut off and foreign exchange reserves fell to $1 billion in June 1991—a level hardly sufficient to meet India's import needs for two weeks.[16] The underlying causes of India's macroeconomic crisis lay primarily in accelerating inflation rates, high and persistent fiscal and current account deficits as well as a heavy and growing burden of domestic and foreign debt (Joshi and Little, 1996). In August 1991, India's inflation rate stood at 16.7 per cent and India's fiscal deficit had reached a peak level of 8.4 per cent of GDP in 1990-91 (Prasad, 1995). The BoP crisis was thus primarily the consequence of unsound economic policies whilst external shocks such as the Gulf crisis only played a minor role (Joshi and Little, 1996). Major external driving forces behind the reforms were the collapse of the Soviet Union, the spectacular growth of China after its opening up in 1978, as well as external creditor and donor pressure (Srinivasan, 2000; Cassen and Joshi, 1995). "In the light of the situation, economic stabilisation and seeking help from the IMF followed as a matter of course" (Nayar, 2001: 133). Financial support from the IMF, however, was provisional on the fulfilment of conditionalities[17] requesting the liberalization and deregulation of the Indian economy. In the face of the crisis, the new Indian government's immediate objective was to restore domestic and external macroeconomic stability but it went beyond IMF conditionalities and initiated wide-ranging long-term structural reforms aimed at achieving its goal of extension of the internal market through poverty reduction and acquisition of a major role in international economic affairs.

The Gradualist Path of India's Economic Reforms

In contrast to the "big bang" or "shock therapy" reforms underway in other countries, India took a gradual approach to economic liberalization which has provoked criticism from reform radicals (Cassen and Joshi, 1995). "The reforms that have been initiated are many, and they have continued to arrive in many little moves almost continually" (Ahluwalia and Little, 1998: 36). Gradualism or incrementalism resulted partly from the fact that the economic reforms were introduced in response to a sudden rather than a prolonged economic crisis. Furthermore, political compulsions of the Rao government placed limitations on the speed and scope of the reforms. According to Manmohan Singh, "... the dilemma of a reformer is compounded in as much as he has to balance economic logic with political and social acceptability and carry out the tasks laid out" (Nayar, 2001: 151). Rao's government as a minority government was dependent on the support of other political parties to enact policy, making radical structural reforms difficult (Cassen and Joshi, 1995).

The New Economic Policy and its Impact on Centralisation

Although the economic reforms have transferred some powers from the Centre to the provinces to enable negotiations with foreign capital, the major levers of economic policy (industrial policy, agricultural policy and in the new global context still more important monetary and fiscal policy) are still controlled by the Centre (Guhan, 1995; Singh, 1993). Some weakening of the planning mechanism has transformed the mode of operation of the Centre's intervention in the economy, it has not weakened its powers to initiate policy changes and regulate and control the economy.

Economic reforms have not brought about any change to the ideology of the Central State as the builder of unified Indian nationalism. The big capitalist class sees the Central State as a key instrument to facilitate the building of a unified national market which is integrated well with the global capitalist economy. The troika of Capital, State and Nation that mutually reinforced each other and created conducive conditions for the growth of centralisation in the State led path of capitalist development till 1991, still persists with minor modifications. There has not been any serious challenge to the project and process of centralisation so far. We cannot, however, preclude the possibility in future of the strong emergence of regional nationalisms and regional parties. If a coalition of Left and regional parties comes to power which weakens the two pro-Centre parties (Congress and the BJP), a new era of decentralisation might get initiated in India.

4. Political, Economic and Cultural Implications of the Centralisation Process

The major political and cultural implications of centralisation are that it weakens the range of regional diversities located in the various states of India. The centralisation process facilitates hegemonisation of the so-called national culture over regional nationalist identities and cultures. This hegemonisation contains within it the further risk of strengthening homogenisation. The growing tendency towards hegemonisation and homogenisation is bound to lead to conflicts with state-based regional identities. The biggest negative economic consequence of centralisation is the concentration of economic power in the hands of a small elite located in the key metropolitan centres and especially in Delhi, the seat of political power. The concentration of political power follows from the concentration of economic power. Such concentration of economic and political power gives birth to anti-democratic authoritarian political tendencies.

5. Conclusion

India has a long tradition of continuing conflict between the centralist and the decentralist tendencies. The British Rule in India contributed to consolidating the power of centralist tendencies. The national movement for independence from British Rule was riddled with a contradiction. Its conflict with British Rule pushed it towards supporting decentralisation but the ideological vision of the leaders of the Indian National Congress, the dominant party in the national movement, was one of building a strong central government once India became independent. This vision got incorporated in the Indian Constitution.

The strategy of State capitalist development followed in India after independence provided the material and ideological basis for constructing a powerful centralist State. The economic reforms of 1991 have merely changed the mode of regulation of the economy by the Centre, they have not abolished the key role of the Centre. The project and process of centralisation in India after 1947, therefore, has remained largely unchallenged so far. However, the development of capitalism in the different regions of India is bound to give a fillip to the growth of regional nationalisms whose urge for decentralisation may bring about a coalition of forces that could bring into power a government whose vision and programme could include dismantling the structures of economic and political power that have been created by the project and process of centralisation. The Left in India is faced with a historical choice.[18] Either the Left remains a minor ally of the pro-Centre Congress Party as it is now to thwart the possibility of coming back to power of the Hindu nationalist BJP—another pro-Centre party—or it takes an initiative to lead a coalition of regional parties to form a Third Alternative to the two main parties of Indian centralisation (the Congress and the BJP). The Third Alternative will have to construct a coherent project of decentralisation in India in order to make it sustainable on a long-term basis. The struggle and conflict between the centralist and decentralist tendencies is going to be a key determinant in the shaping of Indian political economy in the coming decades.

(I am thankful to Kathrin Weisspfennig for the assistance she provided in writing this paper).

Notes

1. On the annexation of Punjab, see Singh, K. (1966/1984). For the books with several editions like this one, the method of citing the dates in this article has followed the procedure of citing the later date for the edition consulted and the earlier date for the first edition of the book. See also Grewal (1990). On the 'Sepoy Mutiny', see Omissi (1994). Though there were a few other states that were annexed after Punjab, they were not strategically that important for the British Empire in India as Punjab was.
2. The discussion which follows on various developments regarding the Centre-State relations during the British Rule in India is based upon the evidence provided by the Commission on Centre-State Relations Report (CCSRR) Part I, Govt. of India, 1988. The Commission is more popularly known as Sarkaria Commission because it was headed by Justice Ranjit Singh Sarkaria, a retired judge of India's Supreme Court. Any additional supporting evidence is mentioned specifically at the relevant points.
3. The Montagu-Chelmsford Report led to the enactment of 1919 Act (Govt. of India, 1988:6).
4. M.C. Setalvad, who later became an Attorney-General of India, observes: "the founding fathers were painfully conscious that the feeling of Indian/nationhood was still in the making and required to be carefully nurtured. They therefore built a constitutional structure with a powerful Central Government envisaging the emergence of an indivisible and integrated India" (Setalvad, M.C. Union and State

Relations under the Indian Constitution [Tagore Law Lectures], cited in: Government of India [1988], *Commission on Centre-State Relations: Report Part I.* Government of India, 7).

5. "Not much had been done for economic development of the country in the pre-independence era. To catch up with the industrially developed nations, the progress that took them centuries, had to be compressed in decades" (Govt. of India, 1988: 8).
6. "The Constitution framers were aware that several Provinces, regions or areas of India were economically and industrially far behind relatively to others. There were great economic disparities. The problem of economic integration had many facets" (Govt. of India, 1988: 8). "Two questions, however, stood out: one question was how to achieve a federal, economic and fiscal integration, so that the economic policies affecting the interests of India as a whole could be carried out without putting an ever-increasing strain on the unity of India, particularly in the context of a developing economy. The second question was how to foster the development of areas which were underdeveloped without creating too many preferential or discriminative barriers." *Automobile Transport Ltd* vs. *State of Rajasthan*. AIR 1962 SC 1406, quoted in Govt. of India, 1988: 8.
7. "The nation was committed to a socio-economic revolution designed not only to secure the basic needs of the common man and economic unity of the country, but further to bring about a fundamental change in the structure of the Indian society in accordance with egalitarian principles. It was felt by the Constitution framers that such a transformation could be brought about only by a strong Central Government" (Govt. of India, 1988: 8).
8. From the context of the debate, it is clear that the reference here is to Pakistan.
9. *Bharat samvidhan ki Jaya ho*, *Bharat Mata ki Jaya ho* can be translated as: Victory to Bharat Constitution, Victory to Mother India. I have examined in greater detail the Hindu bias in India's Constitution and the link between the Constitution's Hindu bias and centralist bias in my Singh, 2005a.
10. Austin notes that at one stage of the debate on the issue of residuary powers, it led to communal polarisation "with Hindus claiming that residuary powers should vest in the centre and Muslims strongly holding the opposite view" (Austin, 2004: 196).
11. Lal was one of the members of the three-member Linguistic Provinces Commission in 1948, which had argued against the creation of linguistic states on the grounds that such states would harm the interests of Indian nationhood (Austin, 2004: 242). As a votary of strong centralisation, he reiterated his opposition to the demands

for the creation of linguistic states and said that he "strongly held the view that if a redistribution of provinces has to take place, it should be carried out on an administrative basis" (*CAD*, November 25, 1949, Vol. XI, 947). The Hindu nationalist organizations in post-independence India have almost always taken a similar position on the re-organization of states. Secular linguistic nationalism based in the different states of India is viewed, and viewed correctly, by Hindu nationalists as a threat to the consolidation of singular Indian Hindu identity.

12. Munshi, an early associate of Gandhi, became later on one of the founders of the right wing Swatantra Party and was president for many years of Bharatiya Vidya Bhavan, a publication house that promotes Hindu culture in India and abroad.
13. These "Hindu voices," Khilnani points out, had gone to the extent of demanding "that the Indian state should explicitly declare itself defender of the interests of the nation's Hindu majority" and that powerful Congress leaders like Sardar Patel and Rajendra Prasad had called for "the dismissal of Muslim state officials, and suggested that there was little point in the army trying to protect Muslim citizens" (Khilnani, 1997: 31). This distrust in the minority community officials was revealed again at another critical point in the history of independent India. During the anti-Sikh carnage in Delhi in 1984 after Indira Gandhi's assassination, the Sikh police officials in the Delhi police were disarmed and taken off duty.
14. The argument on the triangular relationship between Capital, State and Nation has been more fully elaborated in Singh, 1999.
15. For an earlier period, see Patnaik, 1986a and 1986b.
16. Conventionally, a country's foreign exchange reserves should be sufficient to meet its import needs for a period of three months (Prasad, 2005).
17. "Conditionality" refers to the practice of attaching conditions to loans setting out requirements for action by the recipient government without which assistance will be reduced or withdrawn (Killick, 1998).
18. I have explored the issue of Left alliance with regional nationalisms in Singh (2005b). See also Singh (2002, 1997 and 1991).

References

Archarya, J. (1993), *Nehru Socialism: Colonialism, Capitalism and Ideology*. Delhi: Indian Publishers Distributors.

Austin, G. (2004/1966), *The Indian Constitution: Cornerstone of a Nation*. Oxford: Oxford University Press.

Bains, A.S. (1996), Punjab Situation. P.V. Rao, ed. *Symphony of Freedom: Papers on Nationality Question.* 1st ed. Hyderabad: All India Peoples Research Forum.

Bajpai, R. (2000), Constituent Assembly Debates and Minority Rights. *Economic and Political Weekly* (*EPW*), XXXV (21, 22), May 27, 1779–1858.

Banerjee, A. (1992), Federalism and Nationalism. N. Mukarji and B. Arora, ed. *Federalism in India: Origin and Development.* Delhi: Vikas Publishing House.

Bardhan, P. (1984/1989), *The Political Economy of Development in India.* Oxford: Basil Blackwell.

Berbergolu, B. (1992), *Class, State and Development in India.* Delhi: Sage.

Bettelheim, C. (1968), *India Independent.* London: Macgibbon & Key.

Bhattacharya, M. (1992), The Mind of the Founding Fathers. N. Mukarji and B. Arora, ed. *Federalism in India: Origin and Development.* Delhi: Vikas Publishing House.

Blackburn, R. (ed). (1975), *The Explosions in the Subcontinent.* Harmondsworth: Penguin.

Byres, T. (ed) (1993a), *The State and Development Planning in India.* Delhi: Oxford University Press.

Byres, T. (1993b), State Class and Planning. T. Byres, ed. *The State and Development Planning in India.* Delhi: Oxford University Press.

Cassen, R. and Joshi, V. (ed.) (1995), *India: The Future of Economic Reforms.* Delhi: Oxford University Press.

Chakravarty, S. (1987/1989), *Development Planning: The Indian Experience.* Delhi: Oxford University Press.

Chandra, B. (1969), *The Rise and Growth of Economic Nationalism in India: Economic Policies of Indian Political Leadership 1880–1905.* Delhi: Peoples Publishing House.

Chandra, B. (1992), The Indian Capitalist Class and Imperialism Before 1947. B. Berberoglu, ed. *Class, State and Development in India.* Delhi: Sage.

Chattopadhyay, P. (1970), State Capitalism in India. *Monthly Review*, 21 (10), March, 14-39.

Chattopadhyay, P. (1992), India's Capitalist Industrialisation: An Introductory Outline. B. Berberoglu, ed. *Class, State and Development in India.* Delhi: Sage.

Constituent Assembly Debates: Official Report (*CAD*), 12 Vols., Delhi, 1946-50.

Desai, A.R. (1959), *Social Background of Indian Nationalism*. Bombay: Popular Prakashan.

Desai, A.R. (1984), *India's Path of Development: A Marxist Analysis*. Bombay: Popular Prakashan.

Desai, M. (1975), India: Contradictions of Slow Capitalist Development. R. Blackburn, ed. *The Explosions in the Subcontinent*. Harmondsworth: Penguin.

Government of India (1987), *Commission on Centre-State Relations: Report Part II*. Government of India.

Government of India (1988), *Commission on Centre-State Relations: Report Part I*. Government of India.

Grewal, J.S. (1990), *The Sikhs of Punjab*. Cambridge: Cambridge University Press.

Guhan, S. (1995), Centre and State in the Reform Process. *In:* R. Cassen and V. Joshi, ed. *India: The Future of Economic Reforms*. Delhi: Oxford University Press.

Gulati, I.S. (1987), *Centre-State Budgetary Transfers*: Bombay: Oxford University Press.

Harriss, J. (1989), Indian Industrialisation and the State. H. Alavi and J. Harris, ed. *South Asia*. London: Macmillan.

Jain, S.N., Kashyap, S.C. and Srinivasan, N. (ed.) (1972), *The Union and the States*. Delhi: National Publishing House.

Jalal, A. (1985), *The Sole Spokesman: Jinnah, the Muslim League and the Demand for Pakistan*. Cambridge: Cambridge University Press.

Jennings, I. (1953), *Some Characteristics of the Indian Constitution*. London: Oxford University Press.

Jessop, B. (1990), *State Theory: Putting Capitalist States in their Place*. Cambridge/Oxford: Polity Press/Basil Blackwell.

Joshi, S. and Josh, B. (1994), *Struggle for Hegemony in India, Vol. III, 1920–1947: Culture, Community and Power*. Delhi: Sage.

Khilnani, S. (1997), *The Idea of India*. London: Penguin Books.

Killick, T. (1998), *Aid and the Political Economy of Policy Change*. London: Routledge.

Majeed, A. (ed.) (1984), *Regionalism: Developmental Tensions in India*. New Delhi: Cosmo Publications.

Mitra, A. (1987), Will Growth and Centralised Fiscal Arrangements Do? I.S. Gulati (ed.) (1987).

Mukarji, N. and Arora, B. (ed.) (1992), *Federalism in India: Origin and Development*. Delhi: Vikas Publishing House.

Mukherjee, A. (1976), Indian Capitalist Class and the Public Sector 1930–47. *Economic and Political Weekly* (*EPW*), January 17.

Nandy, A. (1992), Federalism, the Ideology of the State and Cultural Pluralism. N. Mukarji and B. Arora, ed. *Federalism in India: Origin and Development.* Delhi: Vikas Publishing House.

Nayar, B.R. (2001), *Globalisation and Nationalism: The Changing Balance in India's Economic Policy 1950–2000.* New Delhi, Thousand Oaks, London: Sage Publications.

Omissi, D. (1994), *The Sepoy and the Raj: The Indian Army, 1860-1940.* London: Macmillan Press.

Patnaik, P. (1975), Imperialism and the Growth of Indian Capitalism. R. Blackburn, ed. *The Explosions in the Subcontinent.* Harmondsworth: Penguin.

Patnaik, U. (1986a), *The Agrarian Question and the Development of Capitalism in India.* Delhi: Oxford University Press.

Patnaik, U. (ed.) (1986b), *Agrarian Relations and Accumulation: The "Mode of Production" Debate in India.* Bombay: Oxford University Press.

Prasad, C.S. (ed.) (2005), *India: Economic Policies and Performance: 1947-48 to 2004-05.* New Delhi: New Century Publications.

Ramasubramaniam, K.A. (1992), Historical Development and Essential Features of the Federal System. N. Mukarji and B. Arora, ed. *Federalism in India: Origin and Development.* Delhi: Vikas Publishing House.

Rao, P.V. (ed.) (1996), *Symphony of Freedom: Papers on Nationality Question.* 1st ed. Hyderabad: All India Peoples Research Forum.

Santhanam, K. (1960), *Union-State Relations in India.* New York and Bombay: Asia Publishing House.

Sastri, K.A.N. (ed.) (1987/1957a), *A Comprehensive History of India, Vol. Two: The Mauryas and Satavahanas 325 B.C.–A.D. 300.* New Delhi: Peoples Publishing House.

Sastri, K.A.N. (1987/1957b), Minor States of the North, Monarchical and Non-Monarchical. K.A.N. Sastri, ed. *A Comprehensive History of India, Vol. Two: The Mauryas and Satavahanas 325 B.C.–A.D. 300.* New Delhi: Peoples Publishing House, 1957.

Sathyamurthy, T. (1995), *Industry and Agriculture in India Since Independence.* Delhi: Oxford University Press.

Sathyamurthy, T. (1996), Centralised State Power and Decentralised Politics, *Economic and Political Weekly*, March 30.

Sen, A. (1982), *The State, Industrialisation and Class Formations in India.* London: Routledge & Kegan Paul.

Sen, A. (1992), Modes of Production and Social Formation in India. B. Berberoglu, ed. *Class, State and Development in India*. Delhi: Sage.

Singh, K. (1984/1966), *History of the Sikhs Vol. 2*. Delhi: Oxford University Press.

Singh, P. (2005a), Hindu Bias in India's 'Secular' Constitution: Probing Bias in the Instruments of Governance. *Third World Quarterly*.

Singh, P. (2005b), Third Way in Indian Politics: Critiquing Centralist Indian Nationalism.

Singh, P. (2002), Political Economy of Nationalism: Minority Left and Minority Nationalisms vs. Mainstream Left and Majority Nationalism in India. *International Journal of Punjab Studies* (*IJPS*), **9** (2):287-98, July-December.

Singh, P. (1999), Capital, State and Nation in India: Reflections with Reference to Punjab. *International Journal of Punjab Studies* (*IJPS*), **6** (1): 85-99, January-June.

Singh, P. (1997), Marxism, Indian State and Punjab. *International Journal of Punjab Studies* (*IJPS*), **4** (2): 237–50.

Singh, P. (1993), Federal Financial Arrangements in India with Special Reference to Punjab. *Austrian Journal of Development Studies*, **9** (3).

Singh, P. (1991), The Coalition that will Realise a Goal of Indian Decentralisation. *Financial Times* (London), 3rd May.

Srinivasan, T.N. (2000), *Eight Lectures on India's Economic Reforms*. Oxford: Oxford University Press.

Political Economy of Tax Effort in North-Eastern States of India: A Case Study of Nagaland

3

B. Mishra, P.S. Suresh and *K.Z. Ovung*

1. Introduction

Demand for increased public expenditure due to enhanced political consciousness and implementation of public programmes with a mechanism infected with diseconomies are the two important forces among several others to increase pressure on the fiscal resources available with a state. Short-term measures, *viz.* dependence on federal transfers and resorting to overdraft evidently have their respective detrimental implications on fiscal health of a state. Thus the remedial approach pervasively suggested by the contemporary fiscal strategists to tackle the ever-increasing fiscal gap moves towards attaining an appropriate degree of financial self-reliance. In working out a developmental plan which implicitly takes into account the tax effort measures, a major question that always arises is how much tax and non-tax revenues can a country/state reasonably expect to raise and what sources should be tapped in order to meet the challenges of a volatile fiscal gap? No doubt, the fiscal philosophy of the government to mobilise a certain amount of resources in order to meet the ever-increasing demand for public expenditures, depends on the political ideology and the political leanings of the political party/ies in power. In a democratic set up, where the aspirations of the people get transformed into the plan policy programmes through a process of Voting, the government sometimes tries to transform these aspirations in the light of the political ideology/ies of the political party/ies in power. It may be added here that the formulation of economic policies (particularly taxation) do not emerge in vacuum. They are largely influenced by the political bias of the political party/ies in power. So, to what extent political ideologies or leanings of the political party/ies in power have been responsible for determining the absolute level of taxation in the states is an open question. Further, it may be added here that the fiscal philosophy of the government to impose and to carry on with certain level of taxation depends not only on the economic capacity of the people but also to a great extent on the societal needs, which are the by-products of societal value judgements. In a democratic set up, societal needs and value judgements are given a shape by the demand polity approach carried out by political institutions. The demand polity approach that aims at achieving popular sovereignty tries to articulate these societal value judgements through the political ideology/ies of political party/ies in power. What we intend to hammer at is the fact that taxation policies do not emerge in vacuum, but by and large, are mainly influenced by the political bias of the political party/ies in power.

Therefore, by taking into account political dimensions, a systematic analysis of tax determinants and comparisons may be illuminating for identifying the factors responsible for the slow pace of resource mobilisation programmes which has given rise to a explosive cycles of fiscal growth. We believe that the determinants' study would enable us not only to make more scientific projections of the tax revenues, but also to have a better understanding of the mechanism of changes that take place in tax revenues of the state.

2. Background of the Study

Most of the State Governments in Indian Federation face severe budgetary pressures with rising demand for expenditures. This may be attributed to the failures of the state governments to mobilise adequate resources from their inter sources to cope with their ever-increasing development works. As a result, the financial dependence of the States on the Union Government has been on the increase in recent years. We intend to accomplish this by analyzing fiscal position of Nagaland.

Nagaland is comparatively a background State, where agriculture is the predominant sector, providing means of livelihood to more than 85 per cent of the population. Though significant development has taken place in some sphere since its statehood, it has failed miserably in catching up the other North-Eastern States in terms of a minimum reasonable standard of living. The fiscal scenario of the state is by no means encouraging at all, where the State's Own Tax Revenue contributes hardly 8 per cent of the total tax receipts of the state. In a State like Nagaland, where the State's own tax revenue contributes no more than 2 per cent of the State's income and the aggregate Government expenditures constitutes about 110 per cent of the State's income, no doubt speaks about the volatile fiscal scenario of the State.

Thus, the overall picture that emerges is that, the tax generating capacity of the State of Nagaland does not cope with its increased public expenditure programmes, for achieving a desirable rate of economic progress. This exhibits clearly the low level of tax effort measures on the part of the State government in the overall scheme of resource mobilization for developmental purposes. As a result of this, economic backwardness has been the resultant outcome.

3. The Problem

The failures on the part of the government of Nagaland to mobilise adequate resources for the purpose may be attributed to the fact that rising level of taxation creates displeasures among the citizens and that the government may have chances of losing vote bank. To what extent, the failures of the state government to mobilise adequate resources for its development can be attributed to the political leanings or political ideology/ies of the various political parties that were in power from time to time remains an open question. It may be pointed out here that the State of Nagaland experienced the most political turmoil in the last three decades due to political instability which might have been due to the coalition politics in the formulation of the government. We intend to accomplish this by analysing the intricacies of the tax efforts of the State of Nagaland so as to ascertain the factors which have been responsible for its volatile fiscal scenario. The effects of ideological leanings of the parties in power is sought to be quantified in the framework of tax determinants analysis. Wherein, the effects of economic and political variables would be segregated since one of the major objectives of the study is to quantify the effects of ideological leanings of the parties in power on the changes of taxation over time. Ultimately, we believe, it is the quantum and level of taxation that the community looks to. Of course, political passion about the level of taxation runs high. But underneath the policy controversies, a vital question about the actual behaviours of the quantum taxation awaits dispassionate analysis. This is what has set out in this study.

All those points noted above provide a solid ground for the necessity and the desirability of undertaking an anatomy of political economy of taxation for the State of Nagaland. This, besides being essential for arriving at a proper assessment of the overall impact of the economic and political ideology on the level of taxation, would enable us to ascertain whether these factors have played any role in shaping and reshaping the trends and quantum of taxation over a period of time in the state. The present study is an attempt in this direction. The two major research questions that we have touched upon in this context are: to what extent the political ideology have got an impact on each item of taxation at different point of time in the State of Nagaland and, to what extent the economic factors have influenced each item of taxation in the state.

4. A Brief Note on Review of Literature

Though the present work is empirical in nature, we thought it imperative to provide a brief review some of the important works done in India and abroad on the substantive aspect of the problem at hand namely, the political economy of tax efforts.

A number of studies inquiring into the tax level determinants have been done in the international context, in order to generalize the differences in the tax levels in a cross-section of countries. Incidentally, almost all the past studies have employed the usual regression analysis approach using cross-section data to explain the functional relationship between the determinant variables and level of taxation. Williamson (1961) made a pioneering attempt to relate the difference in revenue shares in gross domestic product between the countries to their level of development as represented by per capita income. Plasschaert (1962) also analysed the factors responsible for determining the size of public revenue by following Williamson's method. Stephens and Schmandt (1962) in their analysis of tax determinants in United States made use of three variables, *i.e.* population size; density and median family income. The hypothesis that per capita income is the most important determinant of taxation is questioned in the context of developing countries by Hinrichs (1965). He advanced the hypothesis that it is the degree of openness as measured by import-GNP ratio which is the most important determinant of tax revenue in developing countries. Weiss (1969) used a sample of 66 countries covering the period 1958-63 to study factors affecting the government revenue share in less developed countries. Weiss used different socio-economic variables such as: urbanisation, literacy rate, percentage of people employed in agriculture, per capita income, openness and index of degree of mass communication, besides experimenting with a number of dummy variables to quantify the effects of various social, political and cultural factors on the level of taxation. Chelliah (1970) in his study on the trends in taxation, selected 30 developing countries for the years 1953-55 to 1966-68. Bahl (1971) developed a Tax Effort model in terms of three general determinants of taxable capacity, *viz.* the size of the foreign trade sector; stage of development and sectoral composition of income (the contribution of agriculture and mining). In order to overcome some of the deficiencies of the earlier studies, Nambiar and Rao (1972) made an attempt to study the determinants of revenue in developing countries by taking into account degree of monetisation as an additional variable along with other two usual variables (*i.e.* per capita income and degree of openness) from the earlier studies as the independent variables. Chelliah, Bass and Kelly (1975), in their study of tax ratios and tax efforts in developing countries for the year 1969-71, hypothesized that the average level of income, the degree of openness of the economy and the composition of GDP would each have a significant bearing on the determination of the taxable capacity of a country. Kolias and Makrydakis (2000) made an attempt to provide some additional evidence on the casual relationship between revenues and its determinants.

In Indian context, one of the most earliest studies was that of Nambiar and Rao (1972), where they made an attempt to study the tax performances and its determinants of some Indian States. By taking data for the period 1967-68, they employed a multiple regression equation to measure the impact of each independent variable on the total as well as on the individual taxes. Sarma, Rao and Radhakrishna (1973), in an attempt to identify the determinants of the individual taxes and their aggregate in the State of Gujarat for the period 1960-71, had experimented with a number of economic and demographic variables. Reddy (1975) made an attempt to study the determinants of tax efforts of the various State governments for the period 1963-1965. The study of Rao (1979) is an attempt at associating the changes over time in tax revenues with the ideological leanings and the stability of the parties in power for four States namely: Karnataka, Orissa, Kerala and West Bengal for the period 1951-52 to 1971-72. Desai and Ghuman (1984), in their study of tax efforts of the State of Punjab for the period 1973-75, considered four major economic variables to examine its determinants. Dwivedi's (1986) study presents an alternative method of measuring the tax performance of the Indian State governments known as 'taxable capacity ratio or adjusted tax ratio' approach. This method has been widely used in the IMF-studies of tax effort of developing countries. Bhat and Nirmala (1993), in their attempt to identify the main determinants of Tax Revenue with reference to 22 Indian States, adopted multiple regression model with ten explanatory variables. Bhat's (1997) study relates to the analysis of the determinants of public expenditure and tax revenue of India during 1960-61 to 1990-91. The study takes into account the political ideology of the political party in power along with the other economic variables to examine the determinants of public expenditure and taxation. With a view to test the influence of the change in political party in power, the study uses dummy variable, representing Congress and non-Congress regime.

5. Objective of the Study

The present study is an attempt to assess the overall impact of the political ideology on the level of taxation to ascertain whether this particular factor has played any role in affecting the level of taxation over a period of time in the state. The study takes into account a period of thirty-eight years to analyse the intricacies of the problem of taxation growth in the State of Nagaland.

In the framework of tax determinant analysis, an attempt is made to quantify the effects of ideological leanings of the political parties in power on the tax effort measures of the state. This particular exercise is carried out with the sole intention to segregate the effects of political variable and other economic variables. It is believed that the determinant analysis would enable us to have a better understanding of the mechanism of changes that take place in the tax effort measures of the state.

6. Methodological Issues

6.1. *Specification of Dependent and Independent Variables*

Since the main objective of the study is to enquire into the factors affecting the level of taxation, the data pertaining to state taxes as available in the state's budgets and the state government's various memorandums submitted to subsequent Finance Commissions are taken into account for undertaking the analysis. We thought it imperative to exclude all non-tax revenue items and centrally levied taxes in the state as these two categories of taxes do not come under the scope of our study. Thus, state own tax revenue are taken as the dependent variables in our study. The sets of independent variables that we have adopted in our analysis includes, the sectoral incomes originating in manufacturing sector, service sector and the residual sectors. We have not considered the agricultural sector income, as the income of the farmers is quantitatively negligible. The implicit logic in the selection of the above economic variables is that tax is usually being levied on the economic activities that are carried out in this sector. Besides sectoral incomes, the other factor that may be highly correlated to tax is the per capita income (Y) and consumer price index (CPI). In a democratic set up, it is the political process by which changes in tax base and tax rate in a given economy usually takes place. Therefore, in implementation of any economic policy issue as regards to taxation remains a logical offshoot of the political ideology/ies of the political party/ies in power. In order to ascertain the effect of political factors on the growth of tax revenue in the state, we preferred to use dummy variable by specifying the changes of the political parties in power from time to time. It may be mentioned here that the political ideologies gets translated into formulation of economic policy only when the government is stable. Ultimately, irrespective of their political ideologies, the stability consideration alone may guide the government in the state to take fiscal decision (Rao, 1979). For the purpose of quantifying the impact of parties in power on various taxes, *i.e.* Congress regime has been specified from 1982-83 to 1989-90 and 1993-2001. Similarly, the effects of changes of party in power have been quantified for non-Congress regime from 1963-64 to 1981-82 and 1990-91 to 1991-92. In order to quantify the stability consideration, it is thought proper to take the ratio of the number of ruling party/ies MLAs to total number of MLAs in the assembly for a particular tenure.

6.2. *The Model*

An attempt is made in this study to isolate the effects of various factors on tax effort of the State of Nagaland over a period of time by using the multivariate Linear Regression model. After examining various alternatives, we thought it more plausible to explain level of taxation as a function of sectoral incomes of the economy as given by:

$$AT = a_0 + a_1 MY + a_2 SY + a_3 OY \quad \ldots (1)$$

$$AT = a_0 + a_1 Yc + a_2 CPI \quad \ldots (2)$$

$$AT = a_0 + a_1 NSDP \quad \ldots (3)$$

where AT denotes Aggregate tax revenue, a_1's are estimates of parameters of exogenous variables for each equation separately,

Yc denotes per capita income, *MY* is income from manufacturing sector, *SY* represents income from service sector. Income from the remaining sectors is represented by *OY*, *CPI* stands for Consumer Price Index and *NSDP* denotes Net State Domestic Product. In equation 1, we have not considered the agricultural sector income, as the income of the farmers is quantitatively negligible.

For assessing the impact of political variable, we introduced a dummy variable in the empirical equations. The general form of the operational models used in this analysis runs as follows:

$$\overset{*}{AT} = a_0 + a_1MY + a_2SY + a_3OY \quad \text{... (4)}$$

$$\overset{*}{AT} = a_0 + a_1Yc + a_2CPI \quad \text{... (5)}$$

$$\overset{*}{AT} = a_0 + a_1NSDP \quad \text{... (6)}$$

$$AT = a_0 + a_1MY + a_2SY + a_3OY + a_4D \quad \text{... (7)}$$

$$AT = a_0 + a_1Yc + a_2CPI + a_3D \quad \text{... (8)}$$

$$AT = a_0 + a_1NSDP + a_2D \quad \text{... (9)}$$

Where *D* in the above equations represents Dummy Variable.

Individual Tax Revenue

The tax revenue of the state have been broadly divided into Income tax (other than Corporation) (IT); Professional tax (PT); Stamp and registrations (SR); State excise (ED); Sales tax (ST); Tax on vehicles (VT); Entertainment tax (ET) and Others (OT).

Models

$$IT = a_0 + a_1MY + a_2SY + a_3OY \quad \text{... (10)}$$

$$IT = a_0 + a_1Y + a_2CPI \quad \text{... (11)}$$

$$IT = a_0 + a_1NSDP \quad \text{... (12)}$$

$$IT = a_0 + a_1MY + a_2SY + a_3OY + a_4D_0 \quad \text{... (13)}$$

$$IT = a_0 + a_1MY + a_2SY + a_3OY + a_4D_1 \quad \text{... (14)}$$

$$IT = a_0 + a_1Y + a_2CPI + a_3D_0 \quad \text{... (15)}$$

$$IT = a_0 + a_1Y + a_2CPI + a_3D_1 \quad \text{... (16)}$$

$$IT = a_0 + a_1 NSDP + a_2 D_0 \qquad \text{... (17)}$$

$$IT = a_0 + a_1 NSDP + a_2 D_1 \qquad \text{... (18)}$$

Where, *IT* in the above equations refers to Individual Tax. The same steps follow for the other individual tax revenue too.

The number of equations may be exhaustive but they have the same exogenous variables or a combination of them. Some times the endogenous variables are estimated using the dummy variables D_0 = for non-Congress and D_1 = Congress regime. It may appear that all these equations might not be necessary for predicting or for using forecasting models of Nagaland State economy. After all, we either completely ignored eclectical method of introducing the substituting estimate of parameters of exogenous variables by known or assumed values or we did not intervene our econometric models with some other models that arbitrarily determines the estimates of exogenous variables.

6.3. *The Data Base*

The analysis is carried out by taking 38 years time period, *i.e.* from 1963-64 to 2000-01. The data are taken from the various sources like Annual Budget papers and Memorandums submitted to the various Finance Commissions from time to time by the Nagaland State Government. Necessary information on political variables has been collected from the various issues of electoral statistics of Nagaland published by the Directorate of Economics and Statistics of Nagaland.

7. Analysis and Results

The regression equations (1 to 18) mentioned above are used to estimate the determinants of taxation. Now we come to the empirical equations determining the aggregate tax, which are:

$$T = -152.436 + 3976.19Yc + .6635437CPI$$
$$(-.989832) \quad (8.760871) \quad (.42818)$$
$$R^2 = .93 \; DW = .951777 \; \text{... (1)}$$

$$T = 175.6211 + .0971655MY + .0130624SY + .015169OY$$
$$(2.38779) \quad (4.883697) \quad (1.48709) \quad (1.95759)$$
$$R^2 = .94 \; DW = .7132631 \; \text{... (2)}$$

$$T = 201.5326 + .0266377\,NSDP$$
$$(2.486874) \quad (18.7354)$$
$$R^2 = .91 \;\; DW = .673834 \;\ldots (3)$$

It is observed that all the empirical equations (1), (2) and (3) have the problems of serial correlation, although the estimates of parameters except (*SY*) in equation (2) are highly significant.

Economically speaking, all the variables employed as explanatory namely, *Yc*, *CPI*, *MY*, *SY*, *OY* and *NSDP* are responsible for the growth of state tax revenue. As expected, an increase in income (*i.e. Yc*) greatly influenced the growth of tax revenue. In other words, per capita income is the undisputed major determinant of state tax, whereas the rest (*CPI*, *MY*, *SY*, *OY* and *NSDP*) though they contribute positively to the growth of tax, their role are non-significant as indicated by the magnitudes of the estimates of parameters.

We have also estimated the determinants of tax with the introduction of dummy political variable to each of the three equations to assess the impact of political leanings on tax.

Determinants of Tax with the Introduction of Dummy (*D*)

$$T = 27.50977 + 39834.61Yc + .457016CPI - 227.25D$$
$$(0.08588) \quad (8.69154) \quad (.2861281) \quad (-.64255)$$
$$R^2 = .93 \;\; DW = .953108 \;\ldots (4)$$

$$T=897.447+.0926401MY+.0181005SY+.007717OY-1011.29D$$
$$(4.44784) \quad (5.56624) \quad (2.42961) \quad (1.142011) \quad (-3.75530)$$
$$R^2 = .96 \;\; DW = 1.20381 \;\ldots (5)$$

$$T = 824.6582 + .0257455NSDP - 904.1914D$$
$$(3.311757) \quad (19.06519) \quad (-2.622505)$$
$$R^2 = .93 \;\; DW = 1.02144 \;\ldots (6)$$

Equations (4), (5) and (6) are the empirical equations with the introduction of *D* (political variable). Equation (4) once again revealed serious autocorrelation but judging from the value of coefficient of determination, *i.e.* R^2, it is the best line of regression equation. However, except the t-value of *Yc*, none of the estimates of parameters are statistically significant and the equation probably is not viable for prognosis purpose. On the other hand, equations (5) and (6) though show some degree of serial autocorrelations, they are statistically highly significant. Therefore, we may suggest these two empirical equations for forecasting tax revenue of the state.

Once again, per capita income comes out to be the most important and major contributor to the growth of tax. From this result, we may infer that as expected, people pay more tax as this level of income rises and the question of tax evasion seemed to be negligible. The contribution of sectoral incomes to the growth of tax revenue appears to be very nominal though this contribution cannot be ignored. Another striking finding is that none of the parties in power is willing to initiate measures towards the growth of tax, that this contribution is negative as indicated by the signs and magnitudes of the estimates of parameters in all the three sets of empirical equations.

In order to reduce the severity trend effects on tax and to improve the seriousness of presence of autocorrelation, we have computed the transformed tax, *i.e.* T^* as a function of the same sets of exogenous variables and the results are:

Estimation of Transformed Tax (T^*)

$$T^* = -152.6919 + 39752.72Yc + .663208CPI$$
$$(-90.7593) \quad (75.938) \quad (38.6538)$$
$$R^2 = .99 \quad DW = 1.288071 \; ... \; (7)$$

$$T^* = 175.1272 + .0971568MY + .013067SY + .015159OY$$
$$(25.654) \quad (52.88) \quad (15.735) \quad (20.528)$$
$$R^2 = 1 \quad DW = 2.1155 \; ... \; (8)$$

$$T^* = 201.0396 + .0266375NSDP$$
$$(35.333) \quad (26.06)$$
$$R^2 = 1 \quad DW = 2.63737 \; ... \; (9)$$

As expected, equations (7), (8) and (9) gives a wonderful results that except little sign of presence of autocorrelation in equation (7), there was no serial correlation present in the other two empirical equations. Further, the estimates of parameters are all highly significant at a very low level of probability. We may thus suggest the use of these sets of variables with the transformed endogenous variable for prognosis purpose.

Income Tax Revenue

Now we come to Income Tax (I_t) with the exclusion of political variables from the model, these are:

$$I_t = -230.8641 + 14246.16Yc + .7020703CPI$$
$$(-2.34656) \quad (4.913976) \quad (.7091369)$$
$$R^2 = .84 \quad DW = .629603 \ldots (10)$$

$$I_t = -48.27643 + .0384722MY + .0131497SY - .0037081OY$$
$$(-1.95096) \quad (5.747499) \quad (4.449639) \quad (-1.423258)$$
$$R^2 = .96 \quad DW = .69288 \ldots (11)$$

$$I_t = -75.92413 + .0108461NSDP$$
$$(-2.127026) \quad (17.34378)$$
$$R^2 = .90 \quad DW = .835163 \ldots (12)$$

The estimates of the parameters of *Yc*, *MY*, *SY* and *NSDP* are highly statistically significant. But these equations have one drawback as shown by *D-W* statistics of each of them. Perhaps a modified model would have yielded a better result. On the other hand, it is not a serious drawback since we have been analysing a long time series data.

As expected, a rise in the per capita income leads to higher realization of tax, which is evident from the high magnitude of the estimate of the parameter of *Yc*. Although *CPI*, *MY*, *SY* and *NSDP* are all responsible for the growth of income tax, they are not that influential whereas income from the remaining sectors (*DY*) contributes nothing to the growth of income tax.

Next we come to the set of equations estimating excise duties, these are:

$$E_d = -65.85144 + 8410.158Yc + .378745CPI$$
$$(-1.407099) \quad (6.09849) \quad (.804228)$$
$$R^2 = .89 \quad DW = .54498 \ldots (13)$$

$$E_d = 31.82892 - .0168512MY + .0114016SY + .009059OY$$
$$(2.158132) \quad (-4.223815) \quad (6.473182) \quad (5.834109)$$
$$R^2 = .95 \quad DW = .841960 \ldots (14)$$

$$E_d = 26.74619 + .0061970NSDP$$
$$(1.37762) \quad (18.219)$$
$$R^2 = .91 \quad DW = .711587 \ldots (15)$$

From considerably large values of constant term, we might have preferably estimated (E_d) by trend variable alone, the other explanatory variables used in the model could possibly be considered as proxy of the trend variable.

Here again, *Yc* is the most dominant determinant of excise tax and the other contributory factors are *CPI*, *SY*, *OY* and *NSDP*. On the other hand, the role of *MY* as far as excise tax is concerned, is negligible beyond doubt.

Now we shall come to individual tax revenue where models are infused with political variables. We tried to estimate the individual tax with *Yc*, *CPI*, *MY*, *SY*, *OY*, *NSDP*, D_0 and D_1 as exogenous variables.

Income Tax (I_t)

$$I_t = -\ 1803.207 + 2376.828Yc + 23971.22CPI - 1.224083D_1$$
$$(-3.88941) \quad (2.806615) \quad (4.88989) \quad (-.781159)$$
$$R^2 = .96 \quad DW = 1.56478 \ \dots (16)$$

$$I_t = -\ 645.0469 + 715.8203MY + .039624SY + .0112270OY + .0022058D_1$$
$$(-1.977271) \quad (1.20203) \quad (4.574629) \quad (3.568302) \quad (.736687)$$
$$R^2 = .98 \quad DW = 1.88128 \ \dots (17)$$

$$I_t = 92636.88 + 145.9809MY - .7451093SY - 69.8844OY - 1850.478D_0$$
$$(3.74128) \quad (1.232027) \quad (-.257634) \quad (-1.34995) \quad (-2.15699)$$
$$R^2 = .56 \quad DW = 1.87780 \ \dots (18)$$

$$I_t = -\ 1397.152 + 2035.156NSDP + .0117731D_1$$
$$(-2.83190) \quad (2.321578) \quad (10.85957)$$
$$R^2 = .95 \quad DW = 1.778333 \ \dots (19)$$

All the explanatory variables namely *Yc*, *CPI*, *MY*, *SY*, *OY* and *NSDP* responsible for the growth of income tax during Congress rule government. Not only positive but *Yc*, *CPI* and *NSDP* are very prominent determinants during the same regime. On the other hand, *MY* is the only important variable determining income tax during non-Congress regime and the influence of *SY*, *OY* and that of non-Congress in power are not at all worth mentioning.

Next we shall examine the empirical equations for estimating the professional tax (P_t).

$$P_t = -50.27051 - 59.26953Yc + 4729.1927CPI + .0531355D_1$$
$$(-.614282) \quad (-.396491) \quad (5.465193) \quad (-.1920998)$$
$$R^2 = .97 \quad DW = 1.904633 \quad \ldots (20)$$

$$P_t = 2052.13 - 58677.86Yc - 10.09184CPI - 29.01502D_0$$
$$(2.26477) \quad (-2.44737) \quad (1.225669) \quad (-.1.978308)$$
$$R^2 = .54 \quad DW = 2.03309 \quad \ldots (21)$$

$$P_t = -42.61133 + 64.65625MY - .0022510SY + .0040605OY + .0030733D_1$$
$$(-.597789) \quad (.5038313) \quad (-1.20599) \quad (5.98883) \quad (4.763089)$$
$$R^2 = .98 \quad DW = 2.23065 \quad \ldots (22)$$

$$P_t = 2581.706 + .4358182MY - .0196307SY - .137084OY - 26.48629D_0$$
$$(3.98467) \quad (.6954501) \quad (-.048778) \quad (-.574327) \quad (-.66616)$$
$$R^2 = .52 \quad DW = 2.57801 \quad \ldots (23)$$

$$P_t = 50.85254 - 113.8613NSDP + .002831D_1$$
$$(.659783) \quad (-.8314099) \quad (16.72097)$$
$$R^2 = .97 \quad DW = 1.835305 \quad \ldots (24)$$

Contrary to earlier findings, *Yc* happened to be the most insignificant determinant of professional tax covering both the non-Congress and Congress regime. In other words, during non-Congress regime, *MY* is the only factor that nominally influenced the growth of professional tax and the role of non-Congress government in mobilising professional tax was negative. Whereas, *CPI* and *MY* are the most dominant explanatory variable during Congress regime, also the Congress government seemed to have contributed to some extent in the mobilisation of professional tax.

Next, we shall come to estimation of taxes realized from stamp and registration (*SR*). These equations are:

$$S_R = -\ 501.751 + 705.291Yc + 3578.547CPI - .174533D_1$$
$$(-1.69183)\quad (1.301918)\quad (.141139)\quad (-.1741145)$$
$$R^2 = .64 \quad DW = 1.69582 \ldots (25)$$

$$S_R = 16.37543 + 459.304Yc + .0461130CPI - .545549D_0$$
$$(1.71514)\quad (2.283979)\quad (.6695144)\quad (-1.05889)$$
$$R^2 = .68 \quad DW = 1.30176 \ldots (26)$$

$$S_R = -\ 116.7842 + 47.17969MY + .0168370SY - 7.258281OY - .000358D_1$$
$$(-.392801)\quad (.0881444)\quad (2.16272)\quad (.256661)\quad (-.124274)$$
$$R^2 = .78 \quad DW = 2.32875 \ldots (27)$$

$$S_R = 12.77271 + .001293MY - .0026218\ SY + .0032157OY - .3765354D_0$$
$$(1.551917)\quad (.344144)\quad (-2.840746)\quad (3.355068)\quad (-.928271)$$
$$R^2 = .86 \quad DW = 2.38384 \ldots (28)$$

$$S_R = -\ 436.8438 + 645.6035NSDP + .0017957D_1$$
$$(-153555)\quad (1.27719)\quad (2.87258)$$
$$R^2 = .65 \quad DW = 1.60442 \ldots (29)$$

It is quite evident that rise in income undoubtedly contributed enormously to the growth of revenue from Stamp and Registration in both the regimes. Nevertheless, rise in prices, *i.e.* *CPI* dominated over all other variables during Congress rule period also *MY* during the same regime emerged as an important determinant of Stamp and Registration. While *OY* is the most insignificant determinants during Congress rule *SY* appeared to be the weakest factor determining Stamp and Registration during non-Congress regime and none of the parties is responsible of the realization of revenue from the same source.

For the analysis of excise taxes/duties, we have two empirical equations:

$$E_d = -\ 114.9006 - .4762342MY + .02099SY + .3062773OY + 2.681831D_0$$
$$(-1.277637)\quad (-1.106652)\quad (1.998329)\quad (1.628994)\quad (.8607226)$$
$$R^2 = .67 \quad DW = 1.9381 \ldots (30)$$

$$E_d = 122.1532 + 5.03513NSDP - 4.143234D_0$$
$$(2.044502) \quad (1.79932) \quad (-3.78155)$$
$$R^2 = .64 \quad DW = 1.73276 \ldots (31)$$

It is interesting to find that *NSDP* is the most influential determinant of Excise Duty during non-Congress regime while *SY* and *OY* contribution was just nominal. On the other hand, *MY* role was negative in mobilising excise duty. The non-Congress government do initiated measures for the growth of excise duty while we could not report the performance of Congress government with regard to excise duties for lack of statistical reliability in the analysis.

Next, we shall be considering the empirical analysis of Sales Tax (S_t) by using the entire or some combinations of the same set of explanatory variables. The following are the empirical equations:

$$S_t = 499.4297 - 4.195313Yc + 12773CPI - 1.319529D_1$$
$$(.952306) \quad (-.004379) \quad (2.30338) \quad (-.744403)$$
$$R^2 = .74 \quad \text{DW} = .930752 \ldots (32)$$

$$S_t = 124.1826 + .012279Yc + .298912CPI - 35.30655D_0$$
$$(.354347) \quad (1.118832) \quad (6.67672) \quad (-2.207311)$$
$$R^2 = .87 \quad DW = 2.07947 \ldots (33)$$

$$S_t = 876.3578 - 531.5156MY + .0076788SY + .008885OY$$
$$(1.33788) \quad (-.450768) \quad (.447730) \quad (1.426248)$$
$$-.0009558D_1$$
$$(-.161221)$$
$$R^2 = .76 \quad DW = 1.05015 \ldots (34)$$

$$S_t = 228.4517 + .008769MY + 1.215745SY + .0196221OY$$
$$(.318601) \quad (.109673) \quad (2.719621) \quad (.8679891)$$
$$-46.92533D_0$$
$$(-1.461093)$$
$$R^2 = .59 \quad DW = 1.6339 \ldots (35)$$

$$S_t = 671.0781 - 222.2656NSDP + .0051385D_1$$
$$(1.261461) \quad (-.235138) \quad (4.395715)$$
$$R^2 = .72 \quad DW = 1.065329 \ldots (36)$$

Here, in all the equations the coefficient of determination, *i.e.* R^2 ranges from .59 to .87 that means all these equations except equation (35) have fitted well. The equation (32), (34) and (36) have some moderate type of serial correlation, as we have mentioned earlier, due to seasonal or cyclical variation of the time series data, there is always the possibility of serial correlation in the disturbance term. Since it is an accepted fact, probably we should not worry about the problem.

In case of equation (32) where there are three parameters estimates namely, *Yc*, *CPI* and D_1, neither the estimate of parameter of *Yc* nor D_1 are statistically significant, whereas, the estimate of the parameter of *CPI* is statistically significant. At least we expected the estimate of parameter of *Yc* if not that of D_1 also to be statistically significant. Equation (33) is the line of best fit (regression line) obviously. Here, the estimates of the parameters of *CPI* and D_0 are statistically significant. Again the estimate of parameter of *Yc* is not significant yet t-value suggests that it is significant at 10 per cent level of significance. Though equation (34) is also the best fit it has some serial drawback regarding the test of significance. The t-value of all the estimates appeared to be not significant. Therefore, there is some doubt about the reliability of the estimates of parameters. Also we can see here D_1 is not contributing much in the estimation of Sales Tax. The equation (35) has the R^2 = .59 and the *DW* statistic showed that there is moderate serial correlation problem. Here, the estimate of parameter *SY* is highly significant and the other estimates of parameters, namely *MY* and *OY* are not significant even at 10 per cent level of probability. But the estimate of parameter of D_0 is significant at that level of probability.

Lastly, equation (36) has R^2 = .72 which means that 72 per cent of the total variance is explained by the equation. Although to our surprise we found that the estimate of parameter *NSDP* is not statistically significant, the estimate of parameter of D_1 is very highly significant. From this equation, we can have a general guess that the political dummy variables are important explanatory variable so as *CPI*.

As mentioned elsewhere, we expected *Yc* to be contributing positively in the realization of Sales Tax but during Congress rule, it was contrary to our expectation instead *CPI* emerged the most dominant determinant. On the other hand, the role of *MY* and *NSDP* as well as *Yc* are rather poor during the same regime. As far as non-Congress regime is concerned, all the economic variables are equally responsible for the growth of sales tax but once again, it was found that none of the party in power contributed to the growth of sales tax.

Empirical Analysis of Vehicle Tax (V_t)

$$V_t = \underset{(2.97000)}{192.8848} - \underset{(-2.05444)}{268.3887Yc} + \underset{(6.575223)}{4972.375CPI} - \underset{(-2.393058)}{.5784731D_1}$$

$$R^2 = .95 \quad DW = 1.805326 \quad \ldots (37)$$

$$V_t = \underset{(3.60041)}{306.3594} - \underset{(-2.77029)}{424.3789MY} + \underset{(.688790)}{.0015347SY} + \underset{(4.38674)}{.003550OY} \underset{(-.3137211)}{-.000241D_1}$$

$$R^2 = .95 \quad DW = 2.18262 \quad \ldots (38)$$

$$V_t = \underset{(2.70017)}{256.2861} - \underset{(-2.12893)}{359.041NSDP} + \underset{(9.091281)}{.0018961D_1}$$

$$R^2 = .90 \quad DW = 2.07304 \quad \ldots (39)$$

The equation (37) is probably the best fit among all these equations. First it has $R^2 = .95$ and $DW = 1.805$ which means that it has explained 95 per cent of the total variance and there is no serial correlation problem at the same time. Also, we are satisfied with the test of significance results as given by the t-statistics. All the estimates of the parameters namely *Yc*, *CPI* and D_1 are statistically significant. Probably, this equation (37) can very well be used for prediction purpose. Similarly, equation (38) also explains 95 per cent of the total variance also *DW* statistics, which is 2.2182 definitely showed that there is no autocorrelation. Here, excluding the estimates of parameters of *SY* and D_1 all other estimates of parameters namely that of *MY* and *OY* are highly significant. Equation (39) again is the regression line of best fit with $R^2 = .90$ and $DW = 2.0730$ which implies that there is no serial correlation. It is also a line of best fit from the other angle. If we look at the t-statistics of the two estimates of the parameters of *NSDP* and D_1, they are highly significant. Therefore, again we say that this equation can be used for prognosis purposes.

It is quite surprising that we do not have any information about vehicles tax during non-Congress regime because the results are not presentable in our thesis. Once again, *CPI* is the most important determinant of vehicles tax while *SY* and *OY* though positive, they are nearly non-significant determinants during Congress regime. This time, *Yc*, *MY* and *NSDP* are not at all worth mentioning in the determinants of vehicles tax as the signs of the estimates of parameters are not only negative but to a considerable magnitude. Also, the Congress governments have a poor performance as clearly indicated by the signs and magnitudes of the parameter estimates.

Finally, we come to the estimation of Entertainment Tax (E_t) using the combination of the set of explanatory variables. The equations are:

$$E_t = 32.05603 - 12.31336Yc + 22.8945CPI - .059351D_1$$
$$(4.09003) \quad (-.860082) \quad (.276256) \quad (-2.24046)$$
$$R^2 = .84 \quad DW = 1.8872 \ldots (40)$$

$$E_t = 156.9658 + .008928Yc + .4575099CPI - 17.43549D_0$$
$$(.304594) \quad (.5532911) \quad (6.949711) \quad (-.739950)$$
$$R^2 = .86 \quad DW = 1.28767 \ldots (41)$$

$$E_t = 32.05994 - 19.48731MY - .0001587SY + .000671DY - .000279D_1$$
$$(3.46650) \quad (-1.170394) \quad (-.65557) \quad (.7638949) \quad (-2.240468)$$
$$R^2 = .87 \quad DW = 1.887233 \ldots (42)$$

$$E_t = 93.64649 + 6.990328MY + .1318215SY - .7556381OY - 8.029297D_0$$
$$(.172776) \quad (2.69523) \quad (2.082303) \quad (-.666847) \quad (-.427579)$$
$$R^2 = .89 \quad DW = 1.99100 \ldots (43)$$

$$E_t = 28.44739 - 15.54443NSDP - .000088D_1$$
$$(3.05049) \quad (-.938107) \quad (-4.310637)$$
$$R^2 = .76 \quad DW = 2.341412 \ldots (44)$$

The equation (40) has $R^2 = .84$ and *DW* statistics, *i.e.* 1.887 both are quite up to our expectation. Only one snag of this equation is that the estimate of parameter of D_1 is the only highly significant whereas the other important economic variables, *viz.* *Yc* and *CPI* are not statistically significant. Since D_1 is a political dummy variable, we should not give much stress upon as we suppose to do in the case of economic variables. Nevertheless, in this equation political influence is dominating over the other economic forces. Coming to equation (41) it has $R^2 = .86$ and *DW* statistics = 1.287. The former is an indicator of line of best fit but there is some problem of serial correlation as shown by *DW* statistics. Here, the estimate of parameter of *CPI* is statistically significant whereas the estimates of parameters of *Yc* and D_0 are not statistically significance. Equation (42) also is a regression line of best fit where $R^2 = .87$. *DW* statistics suggest almost no autocorrelation present. Only the estimate of parameter of D_1 is statistically significant whereas the estimates of parameters of *MY*, *SY* and *OY* are not significant that makes the equation a weak proposition for using it for prediction. As usual, equation (43) is also a line of best fit with $R^2 = .89$. *DW* also showed that there is no serial correlation of the disturbance term and the estimates of parameters of *MY* and *SY* are highly significant whereas the estimates of parameters of *OY* and D_0 are not statistically significant. Therefore, this equation still could be used for the purpose of prediction. Finally, 76 per cent of the total variance is explained by the regression equations (44) with *DW* statistics, *i.e.* 2.341 showed that it has absolutely no problem of autocorrelation. Only the estimate of D_1 is very highly significant whereas the estimate of parameter of *NSDP* is not significant.

Here is very striking important information for us that we have to explain with caution, specially the political dummy variable. In all these equations, the estimate of parameter of D_1 is significant (as indicated by t-value) but not that of D_0. Now the question is whether D_1 (Congress) is the more reliable agent for explaining or estimating entertainment tax as indicated by estimates of parameters. This is a matter, which sometimes lead us to explain the nature of non-economic variables in an economic model.

Coming back to the economic interpretations of the results, *CPI* still dominates over all other determinants during Congress rule and is more or less the lone important determinant of entertainment tax; whereas, all the economic variables (except *OY*) are positively contributing to the entertainment tax during non-Congress rule. It is obvious that political leanings have negative impact in the realization of tax from this source of revenue.

8. Conclusion

To draw up the summary, an increase in income and a change in prices seem to have contributed more prominently on the growth of tax revenue of the state over the years. On the other hand, political factor has negative impact on the variations of aggregate tax revenue in the state. Likewise, the impacts of both the non-Congress and Congress regimes, on the growth of the constituents of tax are rather dismal.

We may thus infer that the decision pertaining to additional taxation seems to have been guided essentially by stability consideration. The possible contradictions between the ruling parties at the Centre and in the States and a sense of insecurity caused to the non-Congress government in the State therefore restrained them from going in for higher tax efforts irrespective of their ideological position. For that matter, even the Congress government with a slender majority put in lower tax effort. Thus, on the whole, ideological leanings of the parties in power or a change of government from non-Congress to Congress do not seem to make any systematic difference to the tax revenue determination in the State of Nagaland.

References

Bahl, R.W. (1972), A Representative of Tax System Approach to Measuring Tax Effort in Developing Countries. *IMF Staff Paper*, XIX, 87-119.

Bahl, R.W. (1971), Regression Approach to Tax Effort and Tax Ratio Analysis. *IMF Staff Paper*, XVIII, No. 3, 585-87.

Bhat, K. and Nirmala, V. (1993), Political Economy of Tax Revenue Determination in Indian States. *The Indian Journal of Economics*, LXXIII, No. 290, 385-89.

Bhat, K.S. (1997), Political Economy, Public Expenditure and Tax Revenue in India, *The Indian Economic Journal*, 44, No. 1, 111-14.

Chelleah, R.F., Bass, H.J. and Kelly, M.R. (1972), Tax Ratios and Tax Efforts in Developing Countries. *IMF Staff Paper*, XXII, 190-91.

Chelleah, R.F. (1970), Determinants of Tax Ratios in Developing Countries. *IMF Staff Paper*, XVIII, No. 2, 256-94.

Coondo, D. and Mukherjee, R. (1989), Measurement of States' Taxable Capacities, Ninth Finance Commission Methodology, *EPW*, XXIV, No. 37, 2080-81.

Desai, A.H. and Ghuman, B.S.(1984), Aspects of Financing State Plans with Reference to Punjab. *Financing of State Plans: Problems and Prospects*, New Delhi: Sterling Publishers, Pvt. Ltd., 115-23.

Dwivedi, D.N. (1986), On Measurement of Tax Effort of Indian State Governments. *The Indian Economic Journal*, 33, No. 4, 127-28.

Fisher, G.W. (1970), Taxes and Politics: A Study of Illinois Public Finance. *The Journal of Finance*, 25, 735.

Hinrichs, H.H. (1965), Determinants of Government Revenue Sharing Among Less Developed Countries. *The Economic Journal*, LXXV, 549-54.

Kollias, C. and Mukherjee, S. (2000), Tax and Spend or Spend and Tax: Empirical Evidence from Greece, Spain, Portugal and Ireland. *Applied Economics*, 32, No. 5, 72-75.

Lotz and Morss (1970), A Theory of Tax Level Determinants for Developing Countries. *Economic Development and Cultural Change*, 18, 238-41.

Nambiar, K.V. and Rao, M.G. (1972), Determinants of Revenue in Developing Countries. *Anvesak*, 2, 42-47.

Nambiar, K.V. and Rao, M.G. (1972), Tax Preference of States. *EPW*, VII, No. 21, 1036-37.

Oommen, M.A. (1987), Relative Tax Effect of States. *EPW*, XXII, No. 11, 466.

Plasschaerts (1962), Taxable Capacity in Developing Countries. *International Bank for Reconstruction and Development Report*, No. EC-103, Washington.

Rao, M.G. (1979), Ideological Factors, Political Stability, and Tax Revenue Determination: A Case Study of Four States in Indian Federation. *Public Finance Quarterly*, XXXIV, No. 1, 115-26.

Reddy, K.N. (1975), Inter State Tax Effort. *EPW*, X, No. 50, 1916-24.

Roe, A.R. (1968), The Government Revenue Share in Poorer African Countries: A Comment. *The Economic Journal*, 78, 479-81.

Sarma, A., Rao, M.G. and Radhakrishna, R. (1973), Gujarat's State Tax Revenue: Growth, Responsiveness, Determinants and Projection. *Anvesak*, III, No. 1, 55-57.

Stephen, G.R. and Schmandt, H.J. (1962), Revenue Patterns of Local Governments. *National Tax Journal*, XV, No. 4, 436.

UNCTAD (1970), Objective for the Mobilization of Domestic Resources: Mobilization of Resources for Development (Mimeographed).

Weiss, S.J. (1969), Factors Affecting the Government Revenue Share in Less Developed Countries. *Social and Economic Research*, Indica Jamaica, 356-64.

Williamson (1961), Public Expenditures and Revenue: An International Comparison. *Economic and Social Studies*, XXIV, 43-47.

The History of Food Security Policy in India with Reference to Orissa and Kalahandi: An Integrated and Universal Approach Towards PDS

4

Bhabani Shankar Nayak

Introduction

The history of political economy of food and food security as a public policy of contemporary times in India is invariably open to diverse, sometimes contradictory interpretations, depending on the outlook, approach and ideology of the research scholars and perspective of the policy-makers. Perhaps, this is not true in case of Kalahandi district of Orissa—one of the poorest, most underdeveloped districts of India despite nature's generosity. It is a fact that Kalahandi district exports food and the per capita availability of food is higher than the other districts of Orissa. Yet, paradoxically, even in a good harvest year, malnutrition is endemic in Kalahandi. Reports of starvation deaths from the district and the State of Orissa, is a permanent coverage of newspaper column's each year leaving little doubt that Public Distribution System (PDS) has failed by and large to provide food security to the people.

The PDS has crossed 64 years of working as a public policy in a welfare state like India but the problem of hunger, starvation, malnutrition, poverty and food security of the poor and vulnerable sections of the society by cheap food is in question. Nevertheless, no time limit has been fixed for combating food insecurity and to solve all the above problems, which are rampant in the state of Orissa and Kalahandi in particular. The PDS that started earlier to solve the above problems by maintaining price stability of food and food products in the market and at the same time to provide food security to the poor through Fair Price Shops (FPS) failed to provide the umbrella of food security to the poor now.

Because the policy of PDS is regarded as the financial burden for the Central Government, the reduction of food subsidy became the primary motive that led the government to target the system with less food subsidy in budgetary allocation. In this way, the government is trying to dismantle the system forgetting the problem of food insecurity.

Even after more than four decades of Green Revolution, with the multiplication of food production, the goal of food security remains elusive. The PDS is influenced by the policies of government regarding production, procurement, storage, buffer stock, pricing and subsidies and the distribution mechanism of foodgrains. The paper focuses on the history of food security and the policy of Public Distribution System (PDS). It also attempts to analyse the distributional aspect of PDS and the factors that influence PDS.

The subject matter of this monograph is about the history of food security through "Public Distribution System in India with reference to Orissa and Kalahandi" in particular. It attempts to understand the causes for the failure of PDS to deliver food to the poor and vulnerable section of the population in Kalahandi district where production of food crops is higher than the other districts of Orissa. In case of the State of Orissa, FCI godowns are overflowing with stocks (three times more than buffer stock norms) and often rotting but majority of people of the state are food insecure. The paper intends to highlight the failure of state to provide food to the poor and government's wrong policies and lack of institutional support and concern for food security. It also argues for the Universalization of Public Distribution System on the basis of consumer needs irrespective of poor and rich to end hunger and starvation.

Meaning of Food Security

Food security means the availability of food at all the times, access to all the persons in terms of quantity and quality which should be nutritionally adequate, that should be acceptable within the given culture and food habit. It is indicated by physical and economic accessibility of food. The physical access to food depends on production, procurement, storage, buffer stock and supply of food whereas the economic access to food demands purchasing power of the consumer. In India, PDS as policy covers all the above items necessary for food security. The policy of PDS has been made primarily with the objective of providing food security to the poor and simultaneously fixing remunerative prices to the producers. In fact the latter function was better served in course of the implementation of the PDS. This was done in order to prevent farmers to resort to distress sale due to the weak bargaining power and monopoly market functionaries and also to their demands. The government through procurement operation provided Minimum Support Price to the producer to save the producer from market exploitation and to boost production as well. It also helps the government to build buffer stocks to face the scarcity situation. On the other hand, consumers suffered from food insecurity due to lack of purchasing power.

The huge network of PDS is a major instrument of Government of India's food and economic policy for ensuring food security to the poor. The system is designed to help both the producers and consumers of foodgrains. It helps the producer by procuring the foodgrains by providing Minimum Support Price (MSP) and ensuring the distribution of it to the consumers along with other essential commodities at affordable and subsidized prices throughout the country.

As a policy of government, PDS in India is 64 years old. Over these years, there have been important changes in the scale and scope of public distribution. Nevertheless for most of this period, the need for a system of delivery of cheap food was not questioned. Rather, in the 1990s under the regime of orthodox economic reform and structural adjustment, the objective of expenditure reduction took priority over the welfare objectives such as the objective of providing food security to the poor. By characterizing the existing universal PDS as inefficient, more leakages, less benefit to the poor, and mal-administration, the government shifted its operation to target orientation and revamped orientation of PDS.

History of Public Distribution System and Food Security in India

(i) *Origin of PDS and Food Security*

The PDS of foodgrains dates back to the years of World War-II and the Great Famine 1945. It was introduced to maintain the morale of the people in the context of war mobilization and scarcity of food. Thus, it started as an emotional issue meant for the benefit of the common man. Subsequently, it became an essential aspect of the economic structure, to meet the scarcity condition of essential commodities and fight the rising prices of foodgrains in favour of the vulnerable section of the society. In this way, it was first introduced as an emergency measure during the war for the benefit of the common man.

PDS in India continues as an essential plank of economic policy of the country even after independence. The policy on the food security of the fledgling Indian State had two essential components, *viz.* the policy of increased agricultural production and the policy of food distribution system. The first was clearly a vital component of the modernization agenda of the Indian State. In thought it also expressed an anti-imperialist impulse in its rhetoric of self-sufficiency and self-reliance. The second was more unambiguously a part of its welfarist orientation. Thus, increased agricultural production and an efficient PDS were seen as important components of an overall strategy against food insecurity.[1] Over a period of time with the beginning of the planning era, the system was assigned a significant role to bring efficiency and equitable distribution of the available supplies of foodgrains at reasonable price. Gradually, in its working, the system evolved many measures in relation to procurement such as: foodgrains price control, their procurement, building of buffer stocks through Food Corporation of India (FCI) for stabilizing foodgrain prices and an even below of the supplies movement control through zonal system, fixation of producers price to support their income. It also evolved policies towards the distribution such as providing a protective umbrella to the vulnerable sections of the community by distributing foodgrains at concessional prices through a network of Fair Price Shops. In the course of its functioning, the system evolved mechanism to impose procedures and enforce a price discipline in the foodgrain market for the consumers.

The PDS in India is made possible by a subsidy from the Government of India. While the food subsidy was negligible until the end of 1960s, it has increased steadily since. By the end of the mid-1990s, it was more than 50,000 million, which is 3 per cent of the total government expenditure of the Central Government budget and about 0.5 per cent of the Gross Domestic Product (GDP).[2]

(ii) *Stages of its Development*

The development of PDS till today can be divided into four phases according to its organization, coverage and structure:

Phase-I : Origin to 1960

Phase-II : 1960 to 1978

Phase-III : 1978 to 1991

Phase-IV : 1991 to present.

The first phase of PDS had a restricted coverage, the second phase was marked by major organizational changes and expansion of PDS, the third phase was influenced by the growth of domestic production which allowed for a sustained expansion of PDS and the fourth phase was characterized as the weakening of PDS with the beginning of the targeting approach during the period of structural adjustment and economic reforms.

Phase I: Origin to 1960

With the outbreak of War in September 1939, the prices of foodgrains in India tended to rise. It became difficult for the common man to purchase food from the market. In addition, the severe cyclone in October 1942 damaged the rice crop in Bengal and Orissa, the two major rice producing pockets of the country. Consequently, the food shortage became acute by the end of the 1942. To meet the exigencies, a comprehensive scheme of foodgrain distribution through price control and rationing, internal procurement and planned movement were undertaken by the government. The focus of the government during this period was mainly to control food price. The issue of supply of foodgrain did not as yet draw as much attention and thus no control was imposed either on supply or on the movement of foodgrain. The system grew from initial seven cities to 13 cities in 1943, 103 cities and town in 1944 and 711 cities and towns in 1946. Rationing was abolished in 1947, at the recommendation of the Second Procurement Policy Committee, but was reintroduced in 1950 as a welfare measure with the onset of planning (Swaminathan, 2000).

In the 1950s PDS was extended to certain rural areas (these were mainly areas viewed as food deficit regions), although the coverage was mainly in urban areas. As the study indicates the foodgrain distributed through PDS declined during the 1950s and through to 1960s (Swaminathan, 2000). Further, for most of this period, the quantity distributed through PDS was greater than the quantity procured domestically, and PDS thus depended on the imports of foodgrain, primarily under US Public Law 480 (PL-480) regime. In a way the PDS in this period acted as an instrument of price satiation and became a countervailing force against private traders who were interested in exploiting the situation of scarcity to acquire more and more profits.

Phase II: 1960-78

The year 1961 began with large supplies under PL-480. A new contract was signed under which the American Government promised to give 16 million tonnes of wheat and one million tonnes of rice for the next four years. Even during this period, the major objective of the distribution system was maintenance of price in the open market.[3] At the same time in the 1960s, there were major changes in the organization of food policy in India. In response to crop failures, food shortages, and price fluctuations, it was decided to make PDS a permanent and universal programme. New organizations, the Agricultural Prices Commission (later renamed as the Commission of Agricultural Costs and Prices or CACP) and the Food Corporation of India (FCI) were set up in 1965. The experience during 1961-64 was summed up by the Dandekar Committee[4] as follows: "The prices of domestic grains in general, continued to rule considerably above the price at which imported grains were being issued through the Fair Price Shops. Under the circumstances, one might say that the policy, succeeded in achieving its second objective namely, to protect the poor and vulnerable sections of the population from the relative high prices of domestic food-grain. As mentioned earlier, there were established sufficiently, large numbers of Fair Price Shops all over the country. Imported foodgrains were available through these shops at a fixed price considerably below the prices of domestic foodgrains. They were available to anybody who needed them at that price, and they were available insufficient quantities."

The drought of 1965-66 and 1966-67 provided a strong impetus for the expansion of PDS. Foodgrain distributed through PDS grew to more than 10 million tonnes in 1965. During the period of 1965-68, PDS depended heavily on import of food-grains, which peaked at 10 million tonnes in 1966. For the proper distribution of foodgrains in different regions, "Fair Price Shop Scheme"[5] was started as a component of Public Distribution System. During this phase, the PDS remained an 'ad hoc' programme, with no clear role defined for it on a continuous basis. It was only through experience, and action based on contingencies that PDS began to function. Thus, for example, in 1970-71, due to a good crop in 1970-71 agricultural seasons, supply position was relatively good and the open market price was low. Therefore the off-take from the PDS declined. This resulted in full stocks in government godowns. During the drought of 1972-73, the distribution of foodgrain in PDS picked up again.

Phase III: 1978-91

By the Fifth Five-Year Plan (1974-79) a major role for PDS was envisaged in ensuring supplies of essential goods of mass consumption to the people at reasonable price particularly to the weaker sections of the society. By the Sixth Five-Year Plan (1980-85) PDS had to come to stay as a permanent feature. It played a key role in the maintenance of stability in prices, reduction of fluctuations and achieves equitable distribution of essential consumer goods. The expansion of PDS to cover all areas was an important point of action under 20-Point Programme during emergency. Further, a scheme for supply of foodgrains at special concessional price to the people in areas covered under Integrated Tribal Development Programme (ITDP) was implemented. An elaborate arrangement for procurement operation and distribution through the PDS outlets were worked out which involved a certain amount of government subsidy. Further, procurement was linked with the policy of providing a Minimum Support Price to the farmers.[6]

Thus, by Seventh Plan, the PDS in India had close links with food security for the vulnerable sections of the population and it also had policy implications regarding budgetary support for food subsidy and food price policy.[7]

During this period, the criticism that PDS was urban biased become less relevant. Particularly, during the 1980s the PDS covered both urban and rural areas. Between, 1971-1991, the number of Fair Price Shops tripled to over 400,000 with greater part of increase going to rural areas. By 1990, the FCI handled about the 45 per cent of the commoditized grain trade, the rest being controlled by private traders. This phase is marked by the growth of comfortable buffer stocks and this provided the basis for the large-scale expansion of PDS as well as other employment generation programmes like RLEGP, NREP, JRY and FFW, etc. by Eighth Five-Year Plan (1990-95).[8]

Phase IV: 1991 to Present

The rhetoric of cutting down subsidies has been strong in the period after 1991 and major changes in food policy have been motivated by the goal of expenditure reduction. Since 1991, the emphasis of Central Government was therefore to reduce food subsidy. The Government of India's Economic Survey (1992-93) stated that "it was decided to have a phased withdrawal of food subsidies by targeting PDS." On the other hand, there was also an agreement as advocated by Bhagawati and Srinivasan (1993) for even a total abolition of food subsidies "in order to reduce fiscal deficit."[9] It was also viewed that this would help in control of inflation.

As a consequence, changes in the policies occurred. The Revamped PDS (RPDS) in 1992 and Targeted PDS (TPDS) in 1997 were launched. From a universal delivery, it was shifted to targeted approach specially directed to people living the Below Poverty Line (BPL). During this period, there was the narrow price difference between PDS issue price and market price. The hike in the issue price of PDS resulted in the fall in the purchases and low off-take from PDS. The introduction of TPDS resulted in the fall in the distribution. There was a fall in the amount of foodgrains distributed through PDS from 20.8 million tonnes in 1992 to 14 million tonnes in 1994. Thus, due to the fall in the distribution and off-take, there was a rise and excessive holding of stocks. In comparison to procurements and stock, distribution was very less. Although the distribution of foodgrain through PDS has risen in last few years, it remained below the peak of 1991. So, in the words of Madhura Swaminathan (2000), "instead of reforming the system so as to make it more effective, the specific solutions offered by Central Government in the post-1991 period of so-called 'Structural Adjustment' have led towards further dismantling and weakening of the delivery system."[10]

Over the period 1998-2001, the government reduced allocation of essential commodities under PDS. According to the Policy of TPDS, consumers were divided into two categories such as, BPL (Below Poverty Line) and APL (Above Poverty Line). Dual price mechanism was followed in PDS for the above two categories. For BPL consumers, issue price was less and allocation more, whereas for APL consumers, the issue price was relatively high and allocation was less. This also resulted in the low off-take leading to sharp increase in the stock and stock holding cost. It had an adverse impact on food subsidy bill and the poor consumers also because poor people were more dependent on PDS items and they spent more of their income on food items than the rich. So, the poor are paying more and are worst sufferers of the hike in the issue price and government is also spending more in the food subsidy because of stock holding cost.

History of PDS and Food Security in Orissa

The history of PDS of the country and its policies vary from State to State. Each State has its own specific conditions and thus, the origin and development of PDS in Orissa is linked with its socio-economic conditions.

PDS existed in Orissa even before the British era in different forms. It has been stated that "in pre-colonial India, there are countless, examples of monarchs providing free Kitchens and gratuitous relief measures in times of famine, as also tax remissions and loans."[11] In the writings of the Mauryan strategist Kautilya in his *Arthashastra* (Economics) which contains the passages instructing the emperor on methods of counteracting the effects of famine in his kingdom which includes the distribution of goods, seeds on concessional terms, sharing of the royal food stocks, commandeering private stocks for public distribution, shifting population to other regions and even encouraging temporary migration to friendly neighbouring kingdoms.[12]

In the colonial period, PDS started with three pronged strategy, *i.e.* price control, rationing and procurement.

(i) *Price Control*

Orissa was all along a surplus State in the rice and the scarcity was not felt till 1940. There was a scarcity of food due to the failure of the rice crop in Orissa during 1940-41 coupled with the difficulties in obtaining rice from the Central Government as the war broke out and as there was also a large-scale purchases of foodgrain by the British Government for the army posted in India. As a result, prices of wheat rose sharply. Thus, the government suddenly entered into the foodgrain market with price control measures for fulfilling large consumers in general and the needs of the army in particular. Thus, soon after the outbreak of the World War-II, with the enactment of the Defence of India Rule in September 1939 and the subsequent passage of the Essential Supplies Act in May 1940, the Provincial Governments were empowered to exercise control over prices of the foodgrains. And again the Government of India issued notification on 5th December 1941 fixing the Maximum Wholesale Price of wheat/rice and asked the other provincial governments to enforce this control order in their geographical areas. The Government of Orissa implemented it. Thus, public distribution of food started in Orissa with price control measures. The Government of Orissa, accordingly, issued various control orders in the State, such as, fixing maximum statutory prices for all major foodgrains, issuing fair price lists, publishing whole sale price bulletins and forming Price Advisory Committees. However, no maximum prices was fixed or enforced in the State in respect of paddy and rice which consisted of major foodgrains in the State. But these control measures were haphazard in character. In April 1942 when the Government of India issued the wheat control order to regulate inter-provincial movements of wheat, the State government responded to it but there is no restriction on its rice movement and stock (Mishra, 1985).

In addition, the Food Department was constituted at the Centre in December 1942, to integrate all control activities with regard to procurement, distribution and movement of food-grain on all India basis (Mishra, 1985). Orissa cooperated with the Centre and participated in the working of the basic plan as a surplus State. But during the period of "Modified Free Trade Policy" which operated in Eastern India to unearth the hoarded supplies of rice, the rice traders from Bengal took advantage of the situation as there was no control imposed by the government on the movement and stock of rice. Bengal traders captured Orissa supplies of rice at a higher rate and the price in Orissa rose almost to Bengal level. This is evident from the study of Bhagabat Mishra (1985) which indicates that the harvest price of rice in Orissa, on an average rose by 50 per cent every year from 1941-42 to 1943-44 and the discrepancy in the prices in Orissa and Bengal increased. As a result of this, the poor consumers in Orissa were hard hit and there were some starvation deaths during 1943-44.[13] The State Civil Supplies Price Enquiry Committee reported that "although Orissa price went up to a little less than two-thirds of Bengal price, it was beyond the purchasing capacity of the common man in Orissa and the result was that a large number of people died in 1943-44 due to starvation and malnutrition as they could not afford to purchase."[14]

Faced with the above state of affairs the Provincial Government of Orissa, on the recommendation of the Food Grains Policy Committee of 1943 imposed statutory price control on rice and wheat. It promulgated the Hoarding and Profiteering Prevention Ordinance in October, 1943. Subsequently, in July 1944, the Consumer Goods (Control and Distribution) Order was issued under which the ceiling prices of the foodgrains were fixed by Orissa Government.

Thus, in spite of all drawbacks, for the first time the State Government of Orissa entered into foodgrain market through the price control measures which was the first step towards a food policy.

(ii) *Rationing*

After price control measure, the second step in the growth of PDS in Orissa was introduction of rationing during the War period. This measure was conceived of when shortages were severely felt and prices of major foodgrains touched unprecedented heights and the policy of price control was inadequate to meet the situation. The foundation of rationing on all India basis was laid down when the Foodgrains Policy Committee of 1943 that recommended the introduction of rationing in all major foodgrains. It was stated that "the main objective of food rationing is not to reduce consumption but to distribute short supplies in an equitable manner...when supplies are ample, rationing is necessary for effective mobilization of resources against emergency, but when supplies are short and irregular, a closely controlled rationing is even more necessary to ensure a fair distribution to all."[15]

Thus, as a consequence of production shortfall and abnormal rise in prices, rationing was introduced in Orissa towards the end of 1943. It consisted of rice and wheat whereas the inferior cereals produced in the State were not rationed. This policy continued even after independence. But its coverage was not like the British system of war rationing which covered the entire population (Mishra, 1985). Indian rationing system was an urban phenomenon and covered only one-eighth of the total population. Thus a large section of the rural population remained outside the narrow rationing purview. This affected the poorer sections of the State even as the market purchase was the only alternative for the rural poor. In spite of the difficulties, the administrative machinery of the war time rationing was considered essential to continue the system in the State of Orissa. It was a part of all India scheme of equitably distributing the available supplies.[16]

In this way, rationing was the second step towards the development of the public distribution of foodgrains in the State with all its difficulties.

(iii) *Procurement Operation*

Faced with the scarcity of food and inflation during the war period, the government realized the futility of price control and rationing without any control over supply of foodgrains. Thus, in order to control supply, procurement of foodgrains was considered essential. This was the third aspect of PDS in Orissa; it consisted of procurement of foodgrain during World War-II.

Since the harvest of the rice crop in 1943, the government of Orissa procured more than 10 per cent of the total produced paddy by means of monopoly procurement. The monopoly procurement aimed at directing the flow of all rice and paddy sold in the wholesale market into the hands of the government. The system of monopoly procurement was voluntary in character under which the stocks offered by the producers and stockists were purchased by the government. The producer's prices of rice and paddy were fixed by the Government of Orissa for the whole of the crop year. The procurement operation was carried on through one or more of the purchase agents appointed by the government in the primary markets of both paddy and rice. The Director of Civil Supplies closely supervised the entire procurement operation in the state.[17]

The private channel in marketing and procurement of rice and paddy also existed. But no private trader was allowed to buy or sell more than 10 maunds of rice and paddy under the provision of Food Grain Control Order of 1940. It also further provided that no licence holder was entitled to hold a stock of more than 10 maunds of rice and paddy at any time unless he was a procurement agent or sub-agent of the government.

Besides all these things, strict regulations were also enforced by the State Government on the movement of foodgrains from one part of the State to the part. The export movement from one part of the State to another part and export movement from two border districts, *viz.* Balasore and Mayurbhanj was completely prohibited for 1943. All this facilitated the Government to have a procurement machinery to command over the market surplus of paddy and rice in the State. In this way, during this time, Orissa was not only a surplus State in the country but also contributed its mite to the War period procurement drive for working of the public distribution of food in the country.

(iv) *The Graingola System (Village Food Bank)*

Another important landmark in the history of development of PDS in Orissa, in the post-War years was the starting of the Graingola system for distributing foodgrains in rural areas (Mishra, 1985). It was undertaken mainly to help the rural poor who belonged to the farming community in the lean months of the year. The scheme emphasized the organization of Grain Banks in rural areas. It was felt that in an underdeveloped and pre-dominantly non-monetised economy with frequent production shortfalls and transport bottlenecks, credit was mostly required for consumption purposes and transactions were often made in kind. Under such circumstances, it was felt that it would be difficult to extend the facilities of institutional credit either by the Commercial Banks or by the Cooperative Societies. To benefit such farmers, the All India Rural Credit Survey Committee (1951) suggested the organization of Grain Banks in the rural areas. The Committee opined that "in relatively underdeveloped areas, especially...backward and tribal areas, the organization of Grain Banks should be undertaken."[18] Subsequently, the Food Grain Enquiry Commission (1957) also realized the need for such a system and it recommended the setting up of graingolas by village panchayats and cooperatives in order partly to relieve scarcity conditions in the lean session in the rural areas.[19] Accordingly, the Graingola System was introduced in the rural areas during the period of the Second Five-Year Plan (1956-61).

The main function of this scheme was to provide paddy loans to the members every year out of the society's stock gathered during harvesting period. The allotment of paddy from the scheme was both for the agricultural production and consumption at the time of their need. In other words, the scheme was intended to provide credit in "right form," in the "right time" and at the "right place."[20]

Prior to such a move at all India level the Graingola Scheme was first introduced in Orissa in the year 1951-52. Its main objective was to store paddy in the golas (bank of food, storage place), which could be lent out to the needy farmers at a moderate rate of interest. And for the operation of the system the government constructed graingola buildings in the Gram Panchayat headquarters and the government also provided interest free loans for the above purpose. According to the Government of Orissa, it worked successfully from fifties till mid-sixties. It was stated that "by supplying grains at a moderate rate of interest for the purpose of agricultural operations and consumption by poor farmers the scheme has counteracted to a great extent the usury of village Mahajans. It enabled thousands of cultivators every year to escape the stifling effects of rural indebtedness. Its scope and beneficial effects on the rural economy are indeed immeasurable."[21]

But its decadence started from the year 1966-67 when large number of graingolas became defunct. Firstly, the government money was not sanctioned regularly for the function of graingolas. Further construction of Graingolas was stopped and damaged ones were not repaired. Secondly, the repayment of paddy loans from the Graingola Cooperative Societies were very irregular, the overdues increased and in majority of cases the loans were not recovered. Thirdly, it lacked supervision and lack of accountability and the faulty organization was also responsible for the failure of the scheme.

Present PDS in Orissa

As mentioned earlier, the PDS Policy in the country was revamped in 1991. A Targeted PDS was introduced in which the poor were divided into two categories as such: Below Poverty

Line (BPL) and Above Poverty Line (APL). This Policy was adopted by the Government of Orissa as well. Thus, upto the 1991, under PDS, rice, sugar, wheat and kerosene was being distributed among all the ration card holders throughout the State, both in urban as well as in rural areas. All the citizens who either held land and or office were provided PDS items according to the size of the family and accordingly the quantity of every PDS item allotted to the family was written over it. After the introduction of TPDS, PDS became vague in Orissa since June, 1997. It became more vulnerable and by April 2001 the PDS card holders were segregated into BPL and APL. Dual issue price was followed for all the PDS items to the APL and BPL households. Subsidized food items under PDS like sugar were not available to APL families. Since the majority of the poor were categorised under APL, they were deprived of the benefits under BPL. Thus, in reality the families under APL were deprived of the benefits which were for those deemed as BPL. In this sense, the ration card issued to the APL holders did not offer much benefit. Thus, the existing ration cards have become meaningfully invalid. The identification of BPL and APL families so identified by the DRDA in the rural areas have been found to be erroneous and partisan resulting in anomalies wherein when "some have's have managed to put their name in BPL list whereas some haven't have failed."[22]

Thus, over a period of time, PDS in Orissa crossed its many phases with new experiments. It has now culminated into a stage of consumer segregation and dual price mechanism. By targeting and streamlining the system in actuality many poor consumers were excluded from the system whereas many non-poor were included. In fact when more than 48 per cent of the population are under the poverty line, to target some of them has resulted in a great deprivation of the poor.

Food Security in Kalahandi

(i) *History of Kalahandi and its Underdevelopment*

Kalahandi district was under Maratha domination in mid-eighteenth century, before kings ruled it and when the Nagpur Kingdom lapsed to the British, that suzerainty was also naturally extended to Kalahandi in 1863. During the British rule, the Kings of Kalahandi enjoyed a relationship of amiable subordinancy with the British rulers and helped them to suppress a few nationalist activities like Kandha rebellion.[23] The district came into existence when the former princely State of Kalahandi was merged with Orissa in 1948. But its ruler resisted merger of the district with Orissa and was the last to sign the merger in V.P. Menon's presence on 15th December 1947, complaining to the last of coercion. Thus, the district finally came under the State of Orissa.

The history of underdevelopment in Kalahandi can be traced back to the both the day of princely rule and colonial rule of Britishers. During the days of princely rule, the district was a vast, inaccessible State with extensive jungles and a largely aboriginal people. The system of administration was almost of a primitive nature where the rulers were all in all. The rulers through their oppressive administration exploited the subjects by high taxation. Even, the landless people and labourers were liable to pay cess called "Sukhabari." The local rulers were responsible for collecting tax from the cultivators of the village on behalf of the king. And the officials, teachers, clerks and traders who migrated from coastal belt to assist the kings exploited the people of the district. During the colonial rule, these coastal elite continued their presence in the district to help British rule and exploit the tribals as well. Thus, the people of the district, during both princely rule and colonial rule, had suffered a dual domination and exploitation. It is described clearly in the Report of the Orissa State's Enquiry Committee (1939) headed by Harekrushna Mahatab of the Congress Party.

Even after the independence of India and formation and reorganization of State of Orissa, Kalahandi remained underdeveloped. The coastal elites and higher caste people of the district continued their monopoly over the society and dominated the economy of the district. The middlemen among local tribal's people and the coastal elite have a decisive voice in the district who have exploited for their personal benefit, the development resources and programmes. Thus, historically like pre-independence era, the people of Kalahandi have faced the same dual domination and exploitation after the independence. These middlemen and coastal elite continue to play a vital role in the political process of the district and provide the socio-political base for both the major parties of Orissa like the Congress and Janata Dal despite the reservation of seats in State Legislature and in Parliament for the Scheduled Castes and Tribes who are the largest population in the district. But the Scheduled Caste and Scheduled Tribe members of both in State Assembly and in the Parliament are the passive participants in the political process and have been content to have only a minor say in the distribution of development resources.

The passivity of the tribal politicians of Orissa in general and Kalahandi in particular is attributed to several factors, including the sharp divide between the coastal, developed eastern region and the hilly backward western part of Orissa. The subservient position to which Scheduled Caste and tribal politicians have been relegated by all political parties and the absence of education added to the problem. Kalahandi had also experienced its own political history where the elected candidates belonged to Ganatantra Parishad and its ideological successor, the Swatantra Party. In this respect, until the 1980s, there was a convergence between the factors of voting in the State of Orissa as a whole and in Kalahandi, where the latter consistently voted against the political current of Orissa.

The landownership in Kalahandi district was in hands of few, the agrarian structure of economy was feudal and lack in initiative to exploit the rich natural/mineral resources of the district caused aggravation to the situation of underdevelopment of Kalahandi.

Orissa twice experienced acute famine in 1965-66 and 1988-89, when Kalahandi was among the most affected areas, but little is known about the impact of famine there, except that relief centers were opened to supply cooked food.[24] The 1988-89, scarcity occurred due to crop failure in general. During this famine, it is said that the rate of death was 81 persons per square mile. The severity of famine was indicated by the suspension of land revenue.[25] After independence, Kalahandi suffered drought in 1954-55, 1965-56 and 1974-75. It has been estimated that during 1965-66 drought, 55 per cent of population depended on free kitchens but during 1974-75 drought, the Drought Prone Areas Programme was launched. The District Gazetteer informed that the landless agricultural labourers were the worst sufferer. Even the landowners suffered a lot due to drought, as they could not reap a harvest nor could they do the manual labour.[26]

In this way even after independence, Kalahandi district became synonymous with death and destitution throughout the country. Hunger, poverty, drought, distress, sale of property in Kalahandi district attracted nationwide attention, which covered the columns of daily newspapers.

(ii) *Socio-economic Profile of Kalahandi*

Kalahandi district is located at South-Western region of the Orissa. It lies between 19° 3′North to 21° 3′North Latitude and between 82° 20′East to 83° 47′East Longitude. It covers an area of 8,364 square kilometres with 13,34,000 of population, which adds 3.64 per cent to the State population. The density of population is 168 per square km. It has 2,068 inhabited and 137 uninhabited villages (2,205 total number of villages). The pace of urbanization is very low with 2 Sub-Divisions, 7 Tehsils, 13 CD Blocks, 1 Municipality, 2 NACs and 273 Gram Panchayats (2001 Census Report). The home of SC/ST population is predominantly in the hill ranges of the Eastern Ghats, which cover virtually the entire eastern and southern areas of district and remain largely inaccessible to this day. The district constitutes of 17.01 per cent SC, 28.88 per cent ST, 93.09 per cent rural and 6.91 per cent urban population. The percentage of marginal, semi-marginal, small, medium, landholding population is more in the district and the large landholding population in the district is very less.[27] This indicates the land ownership pattern of the district where few people have major landholding in the district. The district has seven small-scale industries. The district has total 37.68 per cent of main workers with 35.66 per cent rural and 2.02 per cent urban workers. It has 7.39 per cent total marginal workers with 0.07 per cent urban and 7.32 per cent rural workers. The unemployment situation in the district is

54.93 per cent of total population with 50.11 per cent in rural and 4.82 per cent in urban areas. The district has 7.62 lakh hectares of cultivable land, 5.27 lakh hectares of forest, hundreds of perennial streams and rivers, rich deposits of bauxite, graphite and manganese, precious and semi-precious stones. Although agriculture is not developed as only 16.97 per cent of net area sown is irrigated, it is the principal occupation available and in 1991, approximately 84 per cent of working population of Kalahandi was dependent on it for a living with 45 per cent of these being agricultural labourers. The climatic condition of the district is extremity with 1,378.2 mm normal and 1,291.8 mm actual rainfall. In spite of the above problems, during the year 2000-01, the production in the district was of 51,81,757 quintals of paddy, 973 quintals of wheat, 11,158 quintals of maize, 13,228 quintals of ragi, 9,784 quintals of mung, 6,793 quintals of biri (Blackgram), 10,040 quintals of kulthi, 2,702 quintals of til, 1,5388 quintals of groundnut, 560 quintals of mustard, 41 quintals of potato and 5,03,455 quintals of sugar cane in the cultivable net area of 348 thousand hectares of land.[28]

(iii) *Food Security and PDS in Kalahandi*

For the first time a strategic approach to provide food security through PDS was taken by the Prime Minister P.V. Narasimha Rao on 18th August 1995, under the programme known as Long Term Action Plan (LTAP). One of the major steps in the LTAP was the strengthening of PDS and also the village level credit institutions like LAMPS.

It has been estimated that there are only 5,172 Fair Price Shops (FPS) working in all KBK districts against the requirement of 7,301 FPS as of 1998. All the six LAMPS in Kalahandi district have been "running on losses due to the low level of business coupled with low recover, contributory loss from PDS business and inadequate margins relating to input distributing business."[29] Again sixty-one out of 80 blocks in KBK districts are ITDP/ DPAP and are supposed to be covered under RPDS. The RPDS has not been launched as yet in these areas. The failure of all the above schemes for food security of the people of Kalahandi is attributed to the financial crisis of the State as reflected in the

Governor's speech in Orissa Legislative Assembly when it was mentioned that the ITDP/DPAP and LTAP has not taken off because of the financial crisis. In this way PDS and its functioning in the district is in serious doubt. The following factors as mentioned in the Report by the Ministry of Food and Consumers Affairs, Department of Food Supply and Consumer Welfare are responsible for the failure of PDS.

The District Manager, Orissa State Civil Supplies Corporation Ltd. (OSCSC) of Kalahandi district stated in April 1999 that due to non-receipt of the release of orders in time and non-cooperation of FCI authorities, full quantities of foodgrains could not be lifted. He had also stated in May 1998 that FCI and Orissa State Warehousing Corporation (OSWC) authorities were not giving the stock on 100 per cent weight and this fact had been intimated to the concerned quarters but the shortage could not be realized. And the delivery system adds to the problem of distribution of foodgrains under PDS in the district.

Due to the factors discussed above, PDS in Kalahandi district in particular but over all in the State failed to provide food security to the poor and vulnerable sections of the society. The PDS and other welfare schemes were put aside by the officials of the state. Thus, the failure of distributional machinery by the officials results in the food insecurity of the people and the highest yielding district 'Kalahandi' experiencing "hunger amidst plenty."

Conclusion

The PDS in India which started in the form of price control and rationing during the War years came to stay in one form or the other. In course of time it became an essential part of the welfare policies and economic structure of the country. In 1960s, PDS was a price support programme to the producer and subsidy programme for the consumer as a response to the foodgrain shortage. Till the 1970s, its main emphasis was on price stabilization and rationing was confined to the urban food deficit areas. But, in the early 1980s, the welfare dimension of PDS gained importance and its coverage was extended to the rural areas as well. Thus, by the Sixth Five-Year Plan, PDS had come to stay as a permanent feature of the country's public policy arena to achieve food security. It played a vital role in maintaining price stability and reducing fluctuation in supply in the market and aimed at equitable distribution of essential goods. The period during 1974 to 1991 was marked by the expansion of PDS with comfortable growth of buffer stocks and major food trade was controlled by the FCI.

In spite of a large network of procurement and distribution channels, it has been seen that there is persistence of hunger, malnutrition, vulnerability and poverty in Orissa. The objective of PDS was to provide essential consumer goods at cheap and subsidized affordable price to the consumers so as to insulate them from the impact of the rising prices of these commodities and maintain minimum nutritional status of the population has failed. The government policy of resorting to levy purchases of a part of marketable surplus from the traders, millers and producers at procurement price (fixed somewhere between Minimum Support Price and the open market price) benefited the middlemen and large farmers. The procured foodgrains, which was stored at FCI, seldom reached the PDS network of FPS for distribution to the consumers. Building of buffer stocks to meet uneven periods was the outcome of the PDS policy.

The Kalahandi district of Orissa is the example where per capita availability of foodgrain and production was more in comparison to other districts of Orissa but the rate of poverty and number of starvation deaths were also more in the district. Thus, it is being proved that production alone would not help in solving the problem of food insecurity. As long as the structure of power and authority remained unaltered, mere availability of food is insufficient condition to solve the problem of food insecurity. The poor are food insecure as they lack the capacity to exercise command over food.

In case of Orissa and particularly in Kalahandi district, the working of PDS revealed certain interesting facts. It found that PDS failed to meet even the partial requirement of the consumers. It is marked that neither TPDS nor RPDS was able to solve the problem of food insecurity. Because the government tried to shift the responsibility without giving any administrative support for the implementation of the policy, the policies have not served the poor and not enabled them to combat food insecurity. The system suffered from red-tapism, curruption, inefficiency, poor delivery system and even financial crunch resulting in there not being a single FPS in many areas of Kalahandi district. In some parts where FPS does exist, items are not available or are being sold in the private market. There is a low off-take of foodgrains from the PDS outlets, not because there is a scarcity of foodgrains or less need of food but due to the lack of purchasing power in the hands of the consumer. It can be said that as a result, PDS does not exist in the district and the tribals are in acute food crisis.

The policy of food distribution is linked the way in which procurement and storage of food is done. Procurement in Orissa is based on channeling of stolen rice and black-marketing from the PDS. Further, the major procurement of FCI is from millers and traders, which is actually rice recycled through black-marketing. Thus, the procurement has no doubt a bearing on the small farmers who are the major producers of foodgrain. In fact, there is an anomalous position where the total milling capacity available in the district is far less than the target for procurement. So, target procurement only encourages black-marketing. At the same time there is distress sale of paddy due to no procurement from the farmers in spite of there being space in FCI godowns. Thus, the focus of procurement policy in Orissa has not kept in view the real objectives of providing food security to the poor.

The off-take from PDS has diminished because of introduction of TPDS, RPDS. This has resulted in massive storage, more than the buffer stock norms, which lead increase in expenditure on the carrying cost of FCI. The Government of India's food subsidy increased substantially from Rs. 2,000 crore in 1987-88 to Rs. 7,500 crore in 1997-98 and further to Rs. 12,010 crore in 2000-01 (the Budget Estimate for 2001-02 has been put at Rs. 13,670 crore). However, it is observed that despite mounting food subsidy bill, the system failed to translate the macro level self-sufficiency with mounting food subsidy into household level food security for the poor, because a large amount of food subsidy covered up the expenditure of the FCI carrying cost, and storage maintenance cost.

The NSSO, 52nd Round revealed that the poor spent a large percentage of their earnings on food. Thus, with a universal approach the poor would be more benefited as the major consumers of food in any case. Many scholars have argued that PDS items should be universally distributed and the targeted approach of the government be abandoned. In Kalahandi district link with the Food for Work (FFW) and Employment Generating Programmes have been suggested to increase the purchasing power of the people. It has also been recommended that PDS items be distributed in accordance with the consumption requirements of the consumers. In doing so, poor would access food and the pressure of storage and procurement problem would also be solved. The problem of dual price mechanism, one for Above Poverty Line (APL) and another for Below Poverty Line (BPL) would also become redundant.

Lastly, it can be mentioned that the policy adopted by the government to combat food insecurity is inextricably linked with the policy of production, procurement and storage. The entire emphasis of the PDS in Orissa and Kalahandi district has been towards satisfying the millers, traders and large farmers along with the bureaucrats and not guided by the consumption needs of the poor and undernourished. This has led to an extremely anomalous situation with the warehouse having large stock of foodgrains while the majority of poor continued to suffer from food insecurity. Thus, an integrated and universal policy orientation and approach towards PDS can solve the problem of food insecurity.

Notes

1. Gopal, Jayal Niraja (2001), *Democracy and the State*, New Delhi: Oxford University Press, 42.
2. Jos Mooji, "Negative Policies: A Study of three Government Interventions in Andhra Pradesh," September 2002, for more *see*, www.livelihoodoptions.info/papers/wp181web.pdf.
3. *See*, Suryanarayana, G. (1985), *PDS in India*, Chugh Publication, Allahabad, India for more discussion and clarity.
4. Dandekar Committee was set up to study the working of the Fair Price Shops in India, submitted its report in 1966.
5. *See*, Suryanarayana, G. (1985) for the discussion about the Fair Price Shop Scheme, which renamed as PDS.

6. *See*, Swaminathan, Madhura (2000), *Weakening Welfare: The Public Distribution Food in India*, Leftword, New Delhi.
7. Venu Gopal, K.R. (1992), *Deliverance from Hunger: The PDS in India*, Sage Publication, New Delhi, India, 221.
8. *See*, Bapna (1990).
9. Bhagawati, J. and Srinivasan, T.N. (1993), *India's Economic Reforms*, Government of India, Ministry of Finance.
10. Swaminathan, Madhura (2000), *Weakening Welfare: The Public Distribution of Food in India*. Here, she argued how Central Government in order to dismantle the system, made changes in the principles underlying policy and objectives of PDS. The second feature of policy change is to increase the issue price of PDS. Thirdly, reduction in the supply of food to the distribution system, and fourthly, cutting back the coverage, 78-79.
11. Alamgir, Mohiudin (1980), *Famine in South Asia*, Oelgeschlager, Gunn and Hain Publisher, Inc. Cambridge Press, 54-56.
12. Kautilya (1987), *The Arthashastra* (eds.), L.N. Rangarajan, Penguin Books, New Delhi, 130.
13. Mishra, Bhagabat (1985), *Economics of PDS in Foodgrains*, Ashish Publishing House, New Delhi, 49-50.
14. Government of Orissa, (1969), *Radhanath Rath Committee Report on State Civil Supplies*, Price Inquiry Committee (Cuttack), 28.
15. Kirby Report on Rationing Scheme in India as quoted by H.N. Chatterjee in his work "Price Control and Rationing in India," Calcutta (1998), 98. Hence he described about the origin and development of price control and rationing and its rationale for an efficient food policy.
16. Mishra, Bhagabat (1985), *Op. cit.*, 56-58.
17. *Ibid.*, 63.
18. Government of India (1954), All India Rural Credit Survey Committee Report, Vol. II, 455, Bombay.
19. Government of India (1957), Foodgrain Enquiry Committee Report, Ministry of Food and Agriculture, Dept. of Food, New Delhi, 101-02.
20. Mishra, Bhagabat (1985), *Economics of PDS in Food Grains*, Ashish Publishing House, New Delhi, 84.
21. Annual Administrative Report on the Working of Panchayats in Orissa (1957-58). Department of Political and Services (G.P.), Government of Orissa, 11.
22. PDS in Orissa: A Report, Food Panchayat, Organised by Vandana Siva, 30th May, 2001, 1.
23. Kandha is the name of a tribal caste, which is the major population in the district. This Kandha caste people revolt against the Kulta

(a higher Tribal caste like Brahmins) cultivators in 1882 that is known as Kandha Rebellion.

24. *Ibid.* and *See District Gazetteer*, 1980, Government of Orissa.
25. Bhatia, B.M. (1967), *Famine in India*, Asia Publishing House, Bombay, 79. *See* R.S. Rao (1995).
26. *District Gazetteer*, 1980, Government of Orissa, 142.
27. *See*, *Economic Survey* 2001-2002. Annexure-23.
    See, *District Statistical Handbook*-Kalahandi-1997: 2-10.
28. All the data about Kalahandi District collected from the following sources: *District Statistical Handbook*-1989-90, 1997, Kalahandi. Economic Survey 2001-2002, Govt. of Orissa.
29. *The KBK Scheme* (1996), Government of Orissa, 12-13.

References

(A) Books

Acharya, K.C.S. (1983), *Food Security System of India*. New Delhi: Concept Publishing Company.

Agarwal, N.C. (1961), *Food Problems in India*. Bombay: Vora and Co.

Ahmed, Ehtisham; Dreze, Jean; Hills, John and Sen, A. (1991), *Social Security in Developing Countries*. Oxford: Clarendon Press.

Alderman, H. and Paxon, C. (1995), Do the Poor Insure? A Synthesis of the Literature on Risk and Consumption in Developing Countries. Bacha, E. ed., *Economics in a Changing World*, St. Martin's, New York.

Ananda, S. and Hariss, C. (1990), Food and Standard of Living: An Analysis Based on Sri Lankan Data. J. Dreze and A. Sen, eds., *The Political Economy of Hunger*, Vol. 1. Oxford: Clarendon Press.

Ananda, S. and Ravi Kanbur, S.M. (1991), Public Policy and Basic Needs Provision: Intervention and Achievement in Sri Lanka. J. Dreze and A. Sen, eds., *The Political Economy of Hunger*, Vol. 3. Oxford: Clarendon Press.

Anjaria, J. and others (1946), *Price Control in India*. Bombay: Popular Book Depot.

Bajpai, Nirupam and Sachs, Jeffrey D. (1999), Fiscal Policy in India's Economic Reforms Jeffrey D. Sachs, Ashutosh Varshney and Nirupam Bajpai, eds. *India in the Era of Economic Reforms*. New Delhi: Oxford University Press.

Bansil, P.C. (1992), Agricultural Statistical Compendium, Vol. 1 (ed.), Foodgrain Part-II, Techno-Economic Research Institute, Delhi.

Bapna, S.L. (1988), PDS and Food Security in India, Centre for Management in Agriculture (C.M.A.), Monograph, I.I.M., Ahmedabad.

Bapna, S.L. (1990), Food Security Through the PDS: The Indian Experience. D.S. Tyagi and V.S. Vyas eds., *Increasing Access to Food: The Asian Experience*. New Delhi: Sage Publication.

Bapna, S.L. (1990), *Issues in Food Security and PDS*, C.M.A., I.I.M., Ahmedabad.

Barr, N. (1987), *The Economics of Welfare State*. London: Weidenfeld and Nicolson.

Bhagawati, Jagdish and Srinivasan, T.N. (1993), Public Distribution System. *India's Economic Reforms*, Ministry of Finance, Government of India.

Bhalla, G.S. (1994), Policy for Food Security in India. G.S. Bhalla ed., *Economic Liberalization and Indian Agriculture*, Institute for Studies in Industrial Development, New Delhi.

Bhatia, B.M. (1970), *India's Food Problem and Policy Since Independence*. Bombay: Somaiya Publications.

Bhatia, B.M. (1983), *Institutions and Incentives in India's Food Security Structure: A Study in India's Food Policy*, Asian and Pacific Development Centre, Malaysia.

Birla Institute of Scientific Research (1980), State in Foodgrain Trade in India: Study of Policies and Practice of Public Distribution System. New Delhi: Vision Books.

Braun, J. Von; Bouis, H.; Kumar, S. and Pandya-Lorch, R. (1992), *Improving Food Security of the Poor: Concept, Policy and Programmes*, IFPRI, Washington, DC.

Brown, L.R. and Eckholms, E.P. (1975), By Bread Alone. Oxford: Pergamon Press.

Brown, M. (1944), *India Need Not Starve*. Bombay: Orient Longman.

Byres, Terry J. and Crow, Ben (1983), *The Green Revolution in India*, The Open University Press.

Chandrasekhar, C.P. and Ghosh, J. (2002), Poverty and Food Security in the Book, *The Market that Failed: A Decade of Neo-Liberal Economic Reforms in India*. New Delhi: Left Word Books.

Chatterji, R.N. (1948), *Price Control and Rationing in India*. Calcutta: Chatterji and Co.

Chellaiah, Raja J. and Sudarshan, R. (1999), Food Security and the Poor. *Income, Poverty and Beyond: Human Development in India* (ed.), New Delhi: Social Science Press.

Chopra, R.N. (1981), *Evolution of Food Policy in India*. New Delhi: Macmillan.

Currie, Bob (1993), Food Crisis, Administrative Action and Public Response: Some General Implications from the Kalahandi Issue, Ph.D. Thesis, University of Hull, UK.

Currie, Bob (2002), *The Politics of Hunger in India: A Study of Democracy, Governance and Kalahandi's Poverty*. Delhi: Macmillan India Ltd.

Dantwala, M.L. (1961), *India's Food Problem*. Bombay: Asia Publishing House.

Das, Ojha Ghanshyam (1987), *Organisation and Management of Public Distribution System*. New Delhi: Mittal.

Dogra, Bharat (1987), Empty Stomach and Packed Godowns: Aspects of the Food System in India. *The Author*, New Delhi.

Dreze, J. and Sen, Amartya (1990), *The Political Economy of Hunger*. Oxford: Clarendon Press.

Dreze, J. and Sen, Amartya (1993), *Hunger and Public Action*. India: Oxford University Press.

Dreze, J. and Sen, Amartya (1995), *India: Economic Development and Social Opportunity*. Delhi: OUP.

Gupta, A. (1969), *Public Distribution of Foodgrains in India*. IIM, Ahmedabad, India.

Gupta, Bhupesh (1965), *Why this Food Crisis*. New Delhi: C.P.I. Publication.

Kabra, K.N. (1990), *Political Economy of Public Distribution of Food in India*. New Delhi: Ajanta Publications.

Lappe, F.M. and Collins, J. (1986), *World Hunger: Twelve Myths*. New York: Grove.

Lipton, M. and Maxwell, S. (1972), The New Poverty Agenda: An Overview. Discussion Paper-306, University of Sussex, Institute of Development Studies, U.K.

Millick, S.C. (1974), Marketing of Rice in Orissa, Unpublished Ph.D. Thesis, O.U.A.T., Bhubaneswar, Orissa, India.

Mishra, Bhagabat (1984), *Economics of PDS in Foodgrains*. New Delhi: Ashish Publishing House.

Mooji, Jos (1998), Real Targeting: The Case of Food Distribution in India, Institute of Social Studies, Working paper series No. 276.

Mooji, Jos (1999), *Food Policy and the Indian States: The PDS in South India*. New Delhi: Oxford University Press.

Omved, Gail (1975), *The Political Economy of Starvation: Imperialism and World Food Crisis*, Socialist Education Trust.

Radha Krishna, R. and Rao, K. Hanumantha (1994), *Food Security, Public Distribution and Price Policy*, UNDP Studies on Human Development in India, Discussion paper, Session-4, New Delhi.

Sainath, P. (1996), *Everybody Loves a Good Drought*. New Delhi: Penguin Books.

Suryanarayana, G. (1985), *PDS in India*. Allahabad: Chugh Publication.

Swaminathan, Madhura (2000), *Weakening Welfare: The Public Distribution of Food in India*. Delhi: Leftword Books.

(B) Articles (Journals, Periodicals and Newspapers)

Bidwai, Praful (1996), Need for Universal not Targeted PDS. *The Times of India*, Bangalore, 2nd August.

Chandrasekhar, C.P. and Ghosh, J. (1997), TPDS: Is it Getting More Food to the Poor? *Business Line*, 22nd July.

Datt, Ruddar (1999), Effectiveness of PDS as a Provider of Food Security. *The Journal of Labour Economics*, Vol. 42, No. 3.

Dev, S.M. (1998), PDS: Impact on Poor and Options for Reform. *EPW*, 29th August.

Editional (2001), *People's Democracy* (A Weekly Organ of CPI (M), *Hunger Amidst Plenty*, Vol. 25, July.

Mooji, Jos E. (1994), PDS as Safest Net, Who is Saved?, *EPW*, 15th January.

Parikh, K.S. (1994), Who Gets How Much from PDS: How Effectively does it Reach the Poor?, *Sarvekshana*, Vol. 17, No. 3.

Pattnaik, Prabhat (1977), Some Reflections on Employment and Unemployment, *Indian Journal of Labour Economics*, Vol. 40, No. 4.

Pattnaik, U. (1996), Export Oriented Agriculture and Food Security in Developing Countries and India. *EPW*, Special Issue, September.

Pattnaik, U. (1997), Political Economy of State Intervention in Food Economy. *EPW*, May 24.

Prasad, Achana, Hunger and Democracy. www.ambedkar.org.

Prasanna, R. (2001), Something is Rotten. *The Week*, 26th August.

Venu Gopal, K.R. (1986), Food Security for Whom? An Indian Question (mimeo), Centre for Policy Research, New Delhi.

(C) Reports, Seminars and Discussion Papers

Annual Report 1993-94, Ministry of Civil Supplies, Government of India.

D.E.S., Bhubaneswar, Orissa (2002), Statistical Outline of Orissa, Government of Orissa.

D.E.S., Bhubaneswar, Orissa (2001), An Economic-Cum-Purpose Classification of the Orissa Government Budget, Govt. of Orissa.

D.E.S., Bhubaneswar, Orissa (2002), Districts at a Glance: 2002 Orissa, Government of Orissa.

Economic Intelligence Service (CMIE), *Monthly Review of Indian Economy*. July 2001 and January, February, March, April, May 2002.

Economic Research Foundation, New Delhi (2001), Union Budget 2001-2002 and PDS, www.kisanwatch.org.

Economic Survey 2001 and 2002, Ministry of Finance, Government of Orissa, Directorate of Economics and Statistics, Bhubaneswar, Orissa.

Government of Orissa (2001), Food Supplies at a Glance, Market Intelligence Wing F.S. & C.W.D., Government of Orissa.

Government of Orissa (2002), Report on the Activities of the Food Supplies and Consumer Welfare Department for the Year 2001-2002, Food Supplies and Consumer Welfare Department, Govt. of Orissa.

Nanda, S.P. (2001), Nanda Committee Report on the Distress Sale of Rice, May 2001, Govt. of Orissa.

National Nutrition, Ministry of Bureau (1993), Nutritional Status of Rural Population.

National Sample Survey Organisation (NSSO) (1990), Utilization of PDS: NSS 42nd Round (July 1986-June 1987). *Sarvekshana*, Vol. 13, No. 4, Issue-43.

NSSO (1997), A Note on Nutritional Intake in India, NSS 50th Round (July 1993 to June 1994). *Sarvekshana*, Vol. 21, No. 2, Issue-73.

NSSO (1997), Consumption of some Important Commodities in India, NSS 50th Round 1993-94.

Panda Commission Report on Starvation Deaths (2001), Government of Orissa.

Planning and Coordination Department (1985), Indicator of Economic Development of Orissa 1980-81 to 1983-84, State Planning Machinery, Government of Orissa.

Planning and Coordination Department (1987), A Hand Book on Implementation of 20-Point Programme in Orissa, P & C Department, Government of Orissa.

Planning Commission (1991), Ninth Five-Year Plan (1997-2002), Vol. II, Govt. of India, New Delhi.

Report of the National Commission for Women (1993), Revamped PDS in the Context of the New Economic Policy (mimeo.), New Delhi.

Report of the Study Team on Fair Price Shops (1996), Ministry of Food and Agriculture, Government of India.

Social Watch—India Report 2001, Withering of the Welfare State, www.cysd.org.

The Indian Economic Survey: 1995-96 to 2001, *An Alternative Economic Survey*, Delhi Science Forum.

(D) World Web Sites

www.expage.com/gacompass49/.

www.planningcommission.nic.in/mta-9702/mta-ch8-pdf.

www.CPIML.org/Pgs/orgns/liberation/2001/2001oct/food-sec.htm.

www.planningcomission.nic.in/SP0121.pdf.

www.Pib.nic.in/feature/beyr2000/fmar2000/f010320001.html.

www.Corpwatchindia.org/news/PND.jsp?articleid=1823.

www.Pd.CPIM.org.

www.orissagov.com/ecosurvey/prices/prices6.htm.

www.blonnet.com.

www.alfa.nic.in/dsdeb/ds/11/ses4/03240297.htm.

www.kisanwatch.org.

www.cysd.org/cepra/SWArchive/socialwatch.01.doc.

www.vshiva.net/report_14May2002.htm.

www.nird.org/deputyd.htm.

www.dsharma.org/hunger/wayout.htm.

www.ambedkar.org/gail/Rottingfood.htm.

www.bhu.ori.nic.in/ola/we034.pds.

Sericulture and Community Development in the Context of Globalization: An Empirical Evidence of a Village

5

Eswarappa Kasi and *R. Siva Prasad*

I

Introduction

Developmental efforts in the last decade have not been as successful as expected in a majority of the developing nations. Except in a few newly industrialised countries, in all the other developing nations poverty has been on the rise, economic growth has slowed down, employment faltered and inflation is on an upward swing. Consequently, the general levels of living are low for a majority of the people in these economies. These low levels of living are manifested in the form of low incomes, inadequate housing, poor health and low productivity, etc.

A greater portion of the population of developing nations depends on agriculture, the primary sector, for livelihood, for the simple reason that the first priority is for food and clothing. However, the productivity levels in the agriculture sector are low. This is not only because of pressure on land but agriculture in these nations is also often characterised by poor organisation, limited capital and investment. Hence, the developing countries are directing all their development strategies on the productivity levels in rural areas.

Countries like China and India have already shown that agricultural practices should be integrated with animal husbandry, dairying, fisheries, horticulture and sericulture to generate more income for each household. In India nearly 76.3 per cent of the population is living in rural areas and 68.8 per cent of it constitutes agricultural population. Indian agriculture is primarily rain-dependent. Rain-fed agriculture supports 40 per cent of the total cultivated area (Sandhya Rani, 1992). India has a net sown area of over 140 million hectares of which only 41.2 million hectares are under irrigation and irrigation facilities in general are inadequate. Therefore, agriculture is still a gamble and at the mercy of the monsoons. The rain-fed areas are frequently afflicted by periodic droughts, soil erosion, crop fluctuation and other related problems. To overcome drought problems and to improve the status of farmers, the Government of India has given high priority to major irrigation projects in the Five-Year Plans. So with a view to improve the drought prone areas, the Government of India has devised and implemented such projects as are helpful for economic development, rural upliftment, eradication of poverty and unemployment (Narasaiah and Jayaraju, 1999).

Indian policy-makers and planners have evolved measures to abolish unemployment and poverty. Moreover, they have realised that the employment opportunities created must be productive enough in ensuring minimum income and standard of living to the poor. Therefore, the discovery of productive employment opportunities under integrated rural development assumes vital importance for the economic development of India. In fact, Indian agriculture now is no longer confined to the cultivation of traditional crops alone. Farmers are encouraged to take up activities in non-farm sectors such as animal husbandry, poultry, fisheries, social forestry, sericulture, etc. (Ghosh, 1988).

In spite of limitations, it can be said that Indian agriculture is on threshold of entering into a stage of development characterised by a shift from traditional technology to modern technology, in which capital requirement and purchased inputs occupy large share (Hanumappa, 1986). Much of the success of the new programmes will depend upon the ability of the workers to act as growth promoters. In this context, sericulture with its vast potential for employment generation in rural areas plays a vital role in alleviating rural poverty and unemployment.

Now, in India sericulture has become the most promising rural activity due to certain reasons like minimum gestation period, less investment, maximum employment potential and quick turnover for the investment. Sericulture as a whole, by its very nature of activity, creates large-scale employment and income generation opportunities in the rural and semi-urban areas accelerating the economic growth of these areas.

Sericulture as a Development Strategy

In its long history, sericulture in India has experienced many ups and downs. However, during the last 30 years, India has made tremendous progress in the production of mulberry silk for which there is an increasing international demand. There is tremendous scope for the expansion of its production in the country. In recent years sericulture has achieved enormous progress in evolving suitable mulberry varieties and techniques to bring about new silkworm races suitable for tropical climatic conditions. With the evolution and introduction of more productive silkworm races, the productivity has increased and sericulture has become a highly remunerative activity. Attracted by these advantages many more farmers have taken up sericulture and the industry has spread to almost all the States in India (Narsaiah, 1992).

Karnataka has been the leading producer of mulberry silk accounting for more than 50 per cent of its production in the country and is now regarded as the "Silk Bowl of India." Andhra Pradesh comes next to Karnataka in producing mulberry raw silk. In Andhra Pradesh, sericulture has proved to be a money-spinner for many middle-class families. Except for Hyderabad district, almost all the districts in the State have taken to sericulture activity. In 1956 mulberry cultivation in the State was only in 1,212 hectares and it went up to 90,800 hectares by the end of 1993-94 (Department of Sericulture, Government of Andhra Pradesh, 1993-94).

Once confined to a few pockets in Anantapur and Chittoor districts bordering Karnataka, sericulture has caught up in such a big way that in just 10 years time the State of Andhra Pradesh has come to rank next only to Karnataka, the premier State of silk. Although almost all districts in the State have taken up sericulture, the main concentration of mulberry silk production is in the four Rayalaseema districts, *viz.* Anantapur, Chittoor,

Cuddapah and Kurnool, of which Anantapur, followed by Chittoor, stand first and second in the entire State in producing mulberry raw silk. At present these two districts show enormous growth rates in sericulture development in Andhra Pradesh. Chittoor has been ambitious of achieving first rank in the production of mulberry raw silk in Andhra Pradesh. If the present tempo of growth were maintained, it would not be a surprise if it achieves its desired aim long before. Chittoor has distinction of introducing new breeds of bivoltine like "Swarnandhra" and "Jica." Kuppam is one of the regions that is growing quite fast and occupies a prominent place in the sericulture map of Chittoor. The village Kotha Indlu, the study village, has the distinction of adopting these new varieties of bivoltine seed and also new techniques and methods of mulberry cultivation.

"Development" represents an increase in the capacities of a society to organize for its own objectives and carry out its programmes more effectively. The essential element here is organization. Anthropologically speaking, when one society is developed and another underdeveloped, the former is, by comparison with the latter, able to make much more complicated decisions and do more complicated things. It is widely assumed that an improvement in development implies an improvement in satisfaction or welfare. The fact is that some forms of development under some circumstances improve performance while other forms of development do not (Belshaw, 1977).

Anthropologists find themselves uncomfortable in the movement back and forth between micro field studies and macro interpretations that are increasingly necessary. More than any other social scientist they are aware of the gap between general theory and broad interpretations on the one hand, and empirical, down to earth interpretations on the other (Belshaw, 1977).

S.R. Charsley's *Culture and Sericulture* (1982) dwells on the significance of livestock industry and sericulture in the development of communities. It is not only a case study of silk industry of south India but it also offers a very good example for considering the role of social anthropology in development. Increasingly, anthropological interpretations of comparative development have been sought when economic ones prove insufficient. This book is a thorough study of a local community through an industry, its structure, it policies and their implementation. It is able to offer an anthropological interpretation of development and suggests ideas on the part of anthropology in development.

Realising the importance of social dimension of development, an international committee recommended the following items to constitute the indicators of development: health, including demographic conditions; food and nutrition; education, including literacy and skills; conditions of work; employment situation; aggregate consumption and savings; transportation; housing, including household facilities; clothing; recreation and entertainment; social security; and human freedoms (UNRISD, 1972).

Morris D. Morris (1979) emphasised on the welfare dimension to development, by adopting life expectancy, infant mortality, and literacy as the three most universal and important components of development. Basing on them he had developed 'Physical Quality of Life Index' (PQLI) as a composite indicator of development. United Nations Development Programme (UNDP) developed another index of development called Human Development Index (UNDP, 1990).

Early in the sixties Seers (1972) emphasized that development was basically a normative concept, synonymous with improvement, and its objective was creating appropriate conditions for the realization of full potential of human personality. He, therefore, stressed that development was to be understood and measured in terms of the satisfaction of certain basic needs, *viz.* reduction in poverty, unemployment and inequality, and not through growth in GNP or per capita income. The most important requirement for the realization of the potential of human personality was the satisfaction of the food requirement. There were also other basic necessities like clothing and shelter. Another basic necessity, without which personality could not develop, was a 'job'. To be chronically dependent upon another person even for food was incompatible with self-respect for a non-senile adult.

Realization of human potential also requires adequate educational levels, especially literacy, participation in government and belonging to a nation that is truly independent, both economically and politically. As under nourishment, unemployment and inequality dwindle, the educational and political aims become increasingly important objectives of development (Seers, 1972).

Quite a few liberals and Marxists hold the view that development is related to the relative participation of the deprived groups, who are the marginalized and powerless groups in a society, in the socio-political process. Thus, development is expected to free these sections from all forms of dependency—social, cultural and political—in order that their full potentials as human beings are fully brought out for their blossoming. Thus mobilization of the poor and their participation in socio-political process becomes an important feature of development (Pye, 1960; Palmer, 1980).

D.L. Narayana's book, *Economics of Sericulture in Rayalaseema* (1979) is an elaborate study of sericulture in the four Rayalaseema districts of Andhra Pradesh. It gives a detailed account of the economics of sericulture, the problems of sericulture and also the scope for its development.

D.V. Ramana's *Economics of Silk Industry in India* (1987) gives a picture of the sericulture activity during the eighties and covers both agricultural and industrial aspects. The author discusses the role of sericulture in economic development and the status of sericulture and silk industry in the world. He also presents an analysis of the economics of sericulture bringing out its importance in terms of income and employment generation.

The book *Sericulture, Society and Economy* (1993), edited by Hanumappa, is a volume of ten research papers by scholars engaged in studying the importance of sericulture to the economy and society. Hanumappa presents sericulture as an economically rewarding enterprise. He says that sericulture, consisting of several sets of activities, offers immense scope for social scientists to explore the interface that sericulture has with economy and society. These essays offer an insight into the processes by which rural development is taking place. The emphasis is mostly on the income, output, socio-economic aspects of reeling, etc.

In *Sericulture in India*(1992), Narsaiah examines in detail the growth of sericulture in India. This book contributes significantly to a better understanding of the strengths and weaknesses of sericulture operations. It also offers some useful practical suggestions to overcome the various current problems and hindrances faced by the industry, and to ensure overall development.

There are some studies on the problems and prospects of sericulture development. In the paper titled "Problems and Prospects of Sericulture" (1977), Periaswamy discusses many problems of sericulture, commencing from mulberry cultivation to cocoon production. He suggests some techniques and measures to overcome these problems. He also gives an account of the status of sericulture in China, the leading country in mulberry silk production.

According to Cahill (2002), Globalisation has a long history. He mentioned that the beginning of a global system of trade can be traced back to 1492 when Christopher Columbus presented himself at the court of the Spanish Queen Isabella and King Ferdinand. He further viewed that Columbus has obtained financial help for his expedition which resulted in the discovery of the 'new world.' It has led to the rivalry between Spanish empire, British and Dutch, and inaugurated an era of colonialism that opened up most of the world to the Western European powers and endured until the twentieth century (Cahill, 2002: 154).

Cahill (2002) opined that the proponents of globalisation argue for its novelty on two counts. The first is that the sophistication of modern technology means that distances have been considerably reduced. The explosive growth in communications technology made to move production from the rich world, where workers have good welfare entitlements, wages and conditions of work, to the poor world where labour costs are so much lower. It permits the global financial system to transmit trillions of dollars each day on foreign exchange markets.

The rise of the multinational corporations is an associated phenomenon. Globalisation means that multinational corporations are attracted to poor world economies because of their low labour costs which go hand in hand with poor social welfare (*ibid.*: 154-56).

Free markets are the second distinctive feature of the contemporary globalisation as felt by Cahill. Free markets are being introduced throughout the world because of the belief that this represents progress of humankind. Free markets ideology has led to economic modernisation (*ibid.*: 157).

There are three models of globalisation which seem to dominate and are clearly distinguishable. Globalisation is the emergence of world systems—usually economic or political systems. These systems are thoroughly developed in the work of Wallerstein. Wallerstein is considered to be the leading exponent of 'world systems theory,' though he himself did not see the object of his study in terms of 'globalisation.' Globalisation as a dual process where the world becomes a single place (Robertson 1992; quoted in Milton, 1996: 143-44).

There is the idea that globalisation is the creation of a particular kind of social condition as a direct consequence of modernity (Giddens, 1990; quoted in Milton, 1996: 144). Giddens defined globalisation as, 'the intensification of worldwide social relations which link distant localities in such a way that local happenings are shaped by events occurring many miles away and *vice-versa*' (1990: 64; quoted in Milton, 1996: 150-51). Globalised social relations flow inevitably from institutionalised ways of acting.

For Giddens, this intensification of social relations takes place in four dimensions: the world capitalist economy, the nation-state system, the world military order and the international division of labour (1990: 71; quoted in Milton, 1996: 151). He has rightly criticised both world systems theory and international relations theory as having produced only partial models of globalisation, since they each concentrate on only one of the four dimensions: the capitalist economy and the nation-state system respectively. It could be rightly argued that Gidden's model is nothing more than an integration of these two images of the world system (Milton, 1996: 151). The four dimensions of globalisation correspond to what he identified as the four institutional dimensions of modernity: capitalism, surveillance, military power and industrialism (1990: 55-59; quoted in Milton, 1996: 151). Capitalism has to do with relations among people, specifically between the owners of capital and the providers of wage labour. Industrialism has to do with relations between people and the material world; it is the production of goods through the use of machines (1990: 55-56; quoted in Milton, 1996: 151).

For Giddens, modern institutions enable social relations to operate over distances in time and space that would have been inconceivable in a pre-modern world. For instance, money as a store of wealth and a measure of credit and debt 'provides for the enactment of transactions between agents widely separated in time and space.' It is thus what Giddens called a disembedding mechanism, in that it lifts transactions out of a particular context (Giddens, 1990: 24; quoted in Milton, 1996: 152). Modern means of communication have lifted discourse out of local contexts and enabled it to technology. It has freed agricultural production from the seasonal constraints that operate in specific locations. It is now possible to guarantee the supply of any commodity at any time (Goodman and Redcliff, 1991: 96; quoted in Milton, 1996: 152).

Objectives

In view of the above, the present paper tries to look at the following objectives:

- To find out the role of women and different caste groups in sericulture.
- To understand the role of development programmes, and its impact on sericulture activity.
- To examine the impact of globalisation on sericulture activity and the living standards of the villagers.

Methodology

This paper is based on the data collected from Kotha Indlu village of Chittoor district in Andhra Pradesh during the year

1999-2000. This study is a qualitative micro-level study of a sericulture village. The primary data was collected through a structured household schedule, informal interviews using detailed checklists, key informant interviews, case studies and observation from all respondents in the village. Quantitative information with regard to the technological development, landholding, demographic aspects, cropping patterns, irrigation systems were collected by using household schedules and District Statistical Hand Book. Secondary data and information are collected from the annual reports of the Department of Sericulture, Andhra Pradesh, the studies and reports brought out by the Central Silk Board, Bangalore, Institute of Social and Economic Change (ISEC), Bangalore, National Institute of Rural Development, Hyderabad, and Central Sericulture Research and Training Institute, Mysore.

II

Location and People

Kotha Indlu is situated in the Kotha Indlu Panchayat of Kuppam Mandal in Chittoor district, about 15 kilometres from Kuppam, the Mandal headquarters. It is a multi-caste village inhabited by Balija, Vanniar, Scheduled Castes and washermen castes. The Balija are the dominant castes in this village. They are dominant politically, economically, educationally and also numerically. While the Balija occupy the highest position in the local caste hierarchy, Vanniar, Chakali and the SCs occupy the subsequent positions in that order. Vanniar, who are a backward caste, are competing with the Balija economically and educationally, though they are weak numerically and politically. Next to Balija, the Scheduled Castes are numerically higher than Vanniar and Chakali. The total population is 274 formed by 50 families. On the basis of landholdings, the residents of Kotha Indlu are classified into marginal, small, medium and large farmers, and the landless. In Kotha Indlu the number of small farmers forms the majority. The next bigger group is the medium farmers. The numbers of large and marginal farmers are quite few, while the landless are almost insignificant. The crops cultivated are paddy and ragi, which are the staple crops and they constitute the staple diet of all communities. Commercial crops like flowers and groundnuts are also grown in the village. Floriculture is specially found among the Balija farmers, while all the castes raise groundnut crop in their lands. Though sericulture occupies the second position after agriculture, it is the major source of income for the farmers in the village. Cattle, goat, sheep, buffaloes and donkeys are the major livestock in the area. Several varieties of grass along with stocked paddy straw maize stalk, groundnut and *bhoosa* are used as fodder. Poultry is widely prevalent in the village and only the SCs practise piggery. The village is very well connected by road and it has good transport facilities. The sericulture farmers use the tillers, tractors and bullock carts to transport their produce to the towns. The village has telephone as well as postal facility. This village has an upper primary school and a high school. It also has a ration shop under the public distribution system to supply the necessary commodities to the needy people at concessional rates. In Kotha Indlu village people give more importance to rituals. Rituals are associated with all their activities. The president of the Gram Panchayat is from the Scheduled Caste community. In fact, this (Panchayat) seat was reserved for the Scheduled Castes in the last elections held for the local bodies on rotatory basis. There is a farmers' club in the village, which takes care of their problems both in the society and outside. The village thus shows an organic unity with less of factional polities.

Sericulture Activity in the Study Village

Kotha Indlu village is located in Chittoor district, about 15 kms from Kuppam, the Mandal headquarters. There were 50 households in the entire village. Majority of them belonged to marginal, small and medium land owning categories. For 39 households the main economic activity is sericulture along with agriculture or horticulture, while 10 households practise only agriculture and horticulture. In Kotha Indlu the houses are scattered with the dwellings situated within agricultural fields. Kotha Indlu is predominantly agricultural with a majority of men and women being engaged in farming (which includes mulberry cultivation).

All the sericulture farmers have irrigation facilities for their mulberry gardens. Sericulturists have about 83 per cent of their cultivated land, other than mulberry, under irrigation. Even among the sericulturists, a few from SC families have only conventional open wells, which usually go dry during summer. Non-sericulturists, on the other hand, have only about 24 per cent of their land under irrigation. Availability of irrigation evidently is a contributing factor in opting for mulberry cultivation and silkworm rearing. A point to be noted here is that the quantity of water available for cultivation is crucial for the farmer to decide whether to take up sericulture (mulberry cultivation and rearing) or other agricultural activities. Thus, if well water is available, the farmer would take up sericulture; but if canal irrigation is at hand, he may prefer cultivation of paddy or sugar cane.

Kotha Indlu consists of Balija (Naidus), Vanniar, Chakali (washer man) and Scheduled Castes (Malas). Traditional occupation of Chakali caste was washing clothes, and now after adoption of sericulture they have stopped indulging in their traditional calling. Balija are traditionally an agricultural caste, while the SCs were agricultural labourers. Balija, Vanniar, Chakali and the Scheduled Castes have predominantly taken up sericulture. A Balija woman, who is from a landless family and whose husband goes for agricultural labour, has taken 0.75 acres of irrigated land on lease from a relative and has taken up sericulture. It is more economically viable to carry out silkworm rearing if land is also available for mulberry cultivation. Buying mulberry leaves makes the rearing process costly and much less profitable (as well as relatively uncertain in terms of finding right type of leaves at the right time) for which reason the number of people buying mulberry leaves for rearing silkworms is extremely small. There are one or two who buy leaf from the neighbouring village sericulturists during times of shortage, especially during summer when their wells go dry. In Kotha Indlu, most of the rearers also own land, even if it is just about half an acre or even less, which is usually sufficient to manage a moderately profitable silkworm rearing activity.

It is interesting to know that a woman from Balija caste brought sericulture to Kotha Indlu. In 1977 Konda Chellamma got married to Ramakrishna, her mother's brother's son, who was a teacher in Kotha Indlu. Her parents were practising sericulture in Srinivaspuram, which is near Kolar in Karnataka. Through her parents she learnt all the methods, practices and techniques of sericulture. After she moved to her conjugal home, she started practising sericulture. In that way sericulture enterprise has taken its birth in Kotha Indlu.

In the beginning the villagers and her relatives in Kotha Indlu ridiculed her. Their reluctance to adopt sericulture in the beginning was due to their apprehension about the success of the crop with which they have no familiarity. Further, the cropping pattern was tuned mainly to grow use value goods like paddy, ragulu, groundnut, etc. Besides, they were reluctant to accept this crop as a woman introduced it who was not known to them. However, Chellamma was not deterred by others opinion as she received complete backing from her husband. As a daughter of sericulture household, she felt very happy that she could perform all the tasks by herself. She started growing mulberry garden and raising silkworms. After witnessing her success in sericulture and seeing the profitability, slowly people in the village started adopting sericulture.

Adinarayanappa, who is Chellamma's father's brother's son and who migrated to Kotha Indlu, his mother's natal village, after his marriage, is the second man in the village who adopted this crop. This he did after he closely followed the sericultural activities of Chellamma, who encouraged and assisted him in switching over to sericulture. Here, we can see how kinship has influenced the people to grow mulberry and practise sericulture. After Adinarayanappa, people in the village realised that this crop yields good economic returns and could change their life style. Later, others also started growing mulberry in Kotha Indlu. Now, nearly all the villagers are practising sericulture.

After noticing the rising income levels of the new sericulturists, others started raising mulberry in their irrigated lands. In the beginning they adopted M-5, S-5 and S-1 varieties of mulberry and now they have adopted the improved varieties of mulberry like S-13, S-36 and V-1, locally called resham kaddi (sericulture sticks). They believe that good variety mulberry will yield quality leaves, which, in turn, will lead to good sericulture harvest as well as good income. However, most of the SC farmers and the marginal farmers from the Balija and Vanniar castes still have traditional M-5 mulberry gardens, as they could not afford to switch over to improved varieties as it involves costs. Thus, the motivating factors that turned the farmers to take up sericulture in Kotha Indlu are good returns and favourable conditions.

Silk Worm Rearing

Silkworm rearing is an "art," as said by one key-informant. It is really true in the sense that it needs skilled personnel. This activity needs people who have knowledge about their surroundings. People in Kotha Indlu have learnt techniques and have mastered silkworm rearing through observation, participation and also through their elders. Now, department of sericulture in Kuppam has arranged training programme in Mysore for the local farmers. Three people from Kotha Indlu have availed this training.

Case Study 1

Seeda Bhagyamma aged 43, stays along with her husband, Ramachandrappa, in a pucca house in Kotha Indlu. She has two sons and both of them are going to school studying in 9th class and 6th class. Bhagyamma studied up to 5th class and she looks after both her household work as well as sericulture work. She is a very active and hard-working person, according to the Convenor of the "farmers club" in Kotha Indlu. But she does not have a separate rearing house and is rearing silkworms in the dwelling house only.

It was quite interesting to hear about the selection of Bhagyamma for the training. She said, once she accidentally went to the cocoon market in Kuppam with her husband to know about cocoon market. During the auction of cocoons, officials of the Department of Sericulture announced that they wanted to take women from sericulture households for training in Mysore under women's training programme. Ramachandrappa gave his wife's name from Kotha Indlu village. There are about 20 women from Kuppam region who went with officials of the Department of Sericulture to Mysore.

Training was given for a period of three days. In the beginning, Bhagyamma was a bit afraid because this was her first experience to go out without her husband. Her colleagues however, enabled her to get maximum knowledge in the art of sericulture. In those three days, they were taught about mulberry cultivation, silkworm rearing (pulugulu penchadam or mepadam), disinfecting of sheds and application of fertilisers, besides taking precautions on health. She also came to know about the techniques/methods like maintenance of garden, use of nets, upkeep of rearing-house and plantation methods.

Bhagyamma after the training now feels that she could alone do any kind of sericultural activities by herself. Earlier she used to help her husband. Sometimes, now, she also goes to the market. She said that ever since the training programme, she periodically receives *Annadatha*, a monthly Telugu magazine, that updates her knowledge about sericulture.

Cropping Pattern

Tube wells and dug wells are the major sources of irrigation. The command area under tube wells is greater than the area under dug wells. The cropping pattern reveals that, besides mulberry, groundnut, ragulu and paddy dominate the other crops in the village.

Dairy

Sericulture also makes its contribution to the dairy enterprise and adds to the income of the sericulturists in Kotha Indlu. Its by-products form good cattle feed and hence, the sericulturists are able to maintain more number of milch cattle than the non-sericulturists. This is evident from the fact that per household income from milch cattle is far higher among the sericulturists than that of the non-sericulturists in the study village. Cattle are a source of FYM, an important component from mulberry cultivation.

Sericulturists in Kotha Indlu give priority to mulberry over paddy, groundnut and ragulu. Among the non-sericulturists, priority is given to groundnut, ragulu and potato. Some progressive farmers practice both mulberry on one side and paddy and potato on the other. It is evident that because of the higher returns that mulberry promises, the concentration is more on sericulture.

According to one key informant, sericulture farmers in Kotha Indlu get better income in sericulture because of high yields when compared to the other agricultural activities like groundnuts, paddy, ragulu, etc. One interesting feature in the village is that most of the sericulturists apply samrani and *agarbattis* (incense sticks) in rearing house, believing that it makes worms to eat more leaves and thereby grow in size and give good yield. In this village sericulturists are raising 5-6 crops in a year. Per crop they get around Rs. 9,900 for one acre of mulberry garden. The following case illustrates the comparative picture of crop yield in Kotha Indlu.

Case Study 2

Konda Adinarayanappa, aged 52, has a wife and two children, a son and a daughter. Son has studied up to 10th class and daughter is in the 5th class. Adinarayanappa studied up to 5th class. He had his education in Srinivaspuram. He looks after both sericulture as well as agriculture and manages other activities in the village as an ex-president of the Panchayat.

Adinarayanappa stated that sericulture yields in the village were responsible for encouraging the farmers to grow more silk-worms. He has 5 acres of wetland and 4 acres of dry land and has been practising agriculture from the beginning. He used to produce paddy, ragulu and groundnut earlier and now mulberry. In sericulture, he gets Rs. 9,900 per crop and he uses 200 DFLs per crop. Quantity of cocoons he gets is 90 kg per crop. Average price per kg of cocoons is Rs. 110 (110 × 90 = 9,900). Following Table shows the comparative yields of different crops in the village:

Table 1

Comparative Returns from Different Crops

Sl. No.	Details of crop	No. of crops in a year	Annual income per acre (in Rs.)	Expenditure (in Rs.)	Net income per acre (in Rs.)
1.	Groundnut	One to two	7,500	5,243	2,257
2.	Ragulu	Two to three	12,000	3,600	8,400
3.	Paddy	Two to three	20,500	6,075	14,175
4.	Mulberry	Five to six	49,500	21,500	26,000

Sericulture has been playing an important role in the life of the sericulture farmers in Kotha Indlu. Kinship is an important factor, which plays a crucial role in the establishment of sericulture and also in its cultivation. Kinship also influences the neighbour sericulturists to practice sericulture. Socio-cultural factors also have an influence on sericulture in Kotha Indlu village.

Development Programmes in the Village

People in Kotha Indlu village are practicing agriculture much before the entry of sericulture and it was their main activity. Agricultural farmers are mostly dependent on seasonal rainfall. Good rainfall makes them happy to cultivate their crops very enthusiastically. Because of uneven rainfall, farmers are looking towards Government for help. Government asked them to change their cropping pattern and to think about alternative crops. In this context, it is important to note that the Governmental programmes played a key role in promoting sericulture. Developmental programmes made them feel comfortable to practice sericulture and it also made them to think about their future, their children's education and other things.

Sericulturists in Kotha Indlu are quite happy about the returns they are getting. They felt that due to the developmental programmes their returns have slightly improved. This prompted more people to practice sericulture in the village. Sericulturists in Kotha Indlu have availed Bivoltine programme, Adarana Scheme, CMEY, DWCRA and Catalytic Special Area Development programme and other development programmes.

Under **Bivoltine** programme in the study village (Kotha Indlu) two sericulturists were selected and are given assistance to raise mulberry plantation and to construct rearing-house. After this they started practising bivoltine silkworm rearing. Both these progressive sericulturists were shown in the local Television coverage along with the Department of Sericulture personnel, which was held in Kuppam in January 2000. Following this, three more also have taken up rearing of bivoltine silkworms.

Under **Adarana** programme, Department of Sericulture provided chandrikas to the sericulturists who come under this scheme. Four sericulture farmers got pesticides under Adarana scheme in Kotha Indlu. They felt that because of this scheme, they could minimise their losses and it helped in improving their yields. However, they complain that sericulture officials are not properly distributing these pesticides to the needy sericulturists.

Under **CMEY** scheme, 4 to 5 people form into an association and register their name as youth organization (Yuva Sangham). In Kuppam, Nehru Yuva Sangham is getting the loan under CMEY. Under this, they bought chandrikas and constructed a shed to keep the chandrikas. The only difference between other programmes and CMEY is that only unemployed youth are eligible to take up CMEY scheme. In Kotha Indlu, Nehru Yuva Kendra also applied for CMEY scheme and is awaiting its award.

DWCRA programme was initially launched as a pilot programme in 50 selected districts with UNICEF co-operation to strengthen the women's component of poverty alleviation programmes. In selecting these districts, priority was given to those with low female literacy and high infant mortality rate so that the most backward sections of the rural population could derive the benefits first. The primary thrust was the formation of groups of 10-15 women from poor households at the village level for delivery of services like credit, skill training and infrastructural support (in the form of chandrikas) for self-employment.

Groups of poor women assisted through a package including subsidies, training for skill upgradation, group revolving fund (Rs. 15,000), group work centres and special extension staff. Each group is given a one-time grant of Rs. 15,000 as revolving fund contributed equally by the Government of India, the State Government and the UNICEF, for infrastructure, purchase of raw materials (Chandrikas, Nets and Thattalu), etc.

In Kotha Indlu, DWCRA group plays an important role in assisting sericulture farmers. In this village there are about 9 DWCRA groups, which are participating in the development of sericulture. DWCRA groups made people more coherent towards their work and further helped them to cultivate sericulture.

Case Study 3

Salla Krishnaveni, aged 28, lives with her husband, mother-in-law and three children. She studied up to 10th class in Kotha Indlu. She got married to her father's sister's son, Subramaniam, who studied up to Intermediate and was working as a Vidya Volunteer in Chandam village, near Kotha Indlu. Krishnaveni has been practising sericulture for seven years. She is the leader of DWCRA group by name Bharatha Matha. It was started in the year 1998. They meet once in a month and each one of them pays Rs. 30 or more. After the meeting, one person would go to bank and deposit the money.

Krishnaveni says that sometimes they go to private grainages like Purnima grainage in Krishnagiri and Gopikrishna grainage in Bangalore. But they also go to the Government grainage in Kuppam. She feels that because of sericulture women got economic freedom and could spend money to meet their needs. Women in Kotha Indlu also felt that because of sericulture and DWCRA groups their social status has improved. Women participate in the programmes like Janmabhoomi, Shramadanam, etc. as members of particular DWCRA group. In the 11th Janmabhoomi programme, they constructed a school building in the village with the amount collected from each DWCRA group.

Under **Catalytic Special Area Development Programme** proposed by the Central Silk Board (Bangalore), the following programmes are undertaken by the Department of Sericulture, Kuppam:

Drip irrigation: By using drip irrigation system one can cultivate mulberry with less water in regions of water scarcity.

Government is giving subsidy to sericulturists to follow drip irrigation system. Subsidy is 40 per cent of the total cost of the project. In the study village, one progressive sericulturist by the name Venkatachalam was selected under the Drip Irrigation scheme and he has availed this facility and adopted bivoltine sericulture. The criterion for selection of the sericulturist is that he should have suitable land in one particular area.

Case Study 4

Venkatachalam aged 43, is a progressive sericulturist in Kotha Indlu. He has his mother, wife and two sons living with him. His eldest son, who is 13 years old, is studying in 8th class in Tirupati. Venkatachalam studied up to 6th class. According to the Convenor of the Farmers' Club, Venkatachalam plays a key role in the village politics and other activities and is a very hard-working person, and keeps himself always busy.

Venkatachalam has two acres of wetland and 5 acres dry land. In dry land he cultivates groundnut, Ragulu and Jowar, which are mostly rainfed crops. In irrigated land, he is cultivating mulberry, flowers and paddy. He has one acre of mulberry garden, where he is following drip irrigation system. Because of this, he says, he is saving water, which is sufficient for another crop. Earlier when he was bringing cross breed DFLs, he faced scarcity of water for the mulberry garden. After so much of thinking, he approached the Department of Sericulture, where they gave him the idea of drip irrigation.

Department of Sericulture officials explained him about all the benefits of drip irrigation method. He has immediately accepted their suggestion and consulted the company, which installed the drip irrigation to his mulberry garden. Because of drip-irrigation he could save water and now he is cultivating flowers along with sericulture. After this system of irrigation was installed, sericulture officials from Chittoor visited him and selected him as one of the bivoltine mulberry rearers in Kuppam region. Under bivoltine programme, he got "Swarnandhra" seed, which is a new bivoltine seed developed by the Andhra Pradesh Sericulture Research Training Centre in Hindupur.

Swarnandhra gives good yield to farmers and the duration of crop is also less, within 18-20 days a farmer can get the crop. This is still in the testing stage and it will take minimum one year for it to become popular all over Andhra Pradesh. Already, scientists from Central Silk Board, Bangalore, visited these farmers and the cocoons are taken to Mysore for further research. Venkatachalam feels that it is all because of drip irrigation system that it became famous in the village. He informed that the returns are also very high, as one kg of cocoons fetch Rs. 250 and 100 DFLs will yield 70-85 kg of cocoons. However, he got 65 kg for the first crop and 68 kg for the second.

Supply of mini-kits, chemicals, pamphlets, wire-nets, etc. and construction of rearing sheds: Under CADP (Catalytic Area Development Programme) the Government has constructed rearing shed for some beneficiaries. The following case study of Mohanram gives an account of benefits enjoyed by a beneficiary under CADP.

Case Study 5

Mohanram, who is aged 36, studied up to intermediate and his wife, aged 28, is an illiterate. He has two children, studying; in class 2 in Kuppam. His parents, brother and his family live with him. His brother is doing some cloth business in Bangalore. He has 7 acres of wetland and 2 acres of dry land. In wetland besides mulberry, he is cultivating paddy, flowers and potato, whereas in dry land he cultivates groundnuts and ragulu. According to the Convenor of Farmers' Club, Mohanram is one of the progressive sericulturists in the village and he is one of the Swarnandhra seed rearers in the village.

Mohanram has two acres of mulberry garden and Department of Sericulture selected him under CADP for constructing a rearing shed. They sanctioned him an amount of Rs. 50,000 for R.C.C. roof (pai kappu) construction through a commercial bank. Before construction of rearing shed, he was rearing in his dwelling house and was getting reasonable yields. After construction of rearing shed, he started getting better yield for every crop.

Productivity Club, the most recent offshoot of the extension methods, is very much in consonance with the organization of quality circles in Japan and some European countries. Each Productivity Club consists of 10-15 members. In India, Andhra Pradesh, the second largest producer of silk, has established Productivity Clubs in its sericulture areas and Chittoor district is no exception in this regard. The main objective of the Productivity Clubs is to establish a Voluntary Association of local reelers, twisters and weavers so as to establish business links among themselves directly and reduce dependence on silk yarn traders of selected areas. Productivity Clubs are expected to increase the awareness of productivity and quality parameters in relation to their profitability. Its aim is to assist people in the upgradation/introduction of new technologies and discuss and sort out their problems with banks, Government departments, etc. Sericulturists in Kotha Indlu are planning to start their own Productivity Club.

Productivity Club acts as a gateway for introducing new technology among the sericulturists and members of the club act as models for others. Participation in the Club is voluntary and club works on democratic principles. These Clubs are in operation in the neighbouring villages already.

III

Findings and Conclusion

Kotha Indlu is a home for families that have consistently been progressive. The chief factor for such a change is primarily attitudinal. If there are any political and economic factors behind the growth, it is only due to the positive attitude of the people in absorbing such factors.

There are some social taboos in Kotha Indlu. For instance, women are restricted in the name of purity and pollution. The literacy rate of women is far less than that of men. Adult education programme is almost non-existent. In Kotha Indlu the lower caste people are not allowed into public places like temples. The patterns of landholdings, distribution of labour, appropriation of loans are all based on caste.

From time immemorial, women are involved in almost all sectors of the silk industry. Women are favoured because of their nature, patience, and hard work they are employed in a mulberry garden or silkworm rearing or in a grainage or in a weaving centre, etc. However, their work has not always been recognized or rewarded.

In a growing enterprise like sericulture, problems are bound to be many and sometimes unavoidable. The problems faced by sericulturists mainly relate to the insufficient financial support from the Government agencies, climatic hazards, wide fluctuations in cocoon prices, and also, to some extent, inadequacy of extension services.

The sericulturists in Kotha Indlu are also facing problems of rearing sheds, lack of awareness, low female literacy, absence of Non-Governmental Organizations in the area, etc. There are no formal banking services for capital generation and economic organization, except DWCRA groups. The ratio between land, labour and organization is based on caste and other social factors than economic factors.

To overcome these problems and to make this enterprise more attractive, the following suggestions are made:

- There is a need to introduce new varieties of mulberry, which have been found viable with regard to the quality and quantity of leaf by the research institutes.
- The sericulturists must be encouraged to rear bivoltine variety of silkworm rather than multivoltine silkworms to obtain better income.
- More farmers may be motivated to take up sericulture on a large scale through co-operative farming.
- Irrigation facilities have to be bettered and enhanced by encouraging farmers to adopt drip irrigation.
- To meet the growing demand for DFLs more grainages should be opened and care must be taken to supply good quality layings through them.
- Stifling units can be established both by the Government and private entrepreneurs to preserve the cocoons for longer periods to overcome the problem of fluctuations in cocoons prices.
- Necessary equipment for rearing silkworms may be supplied to the sericulturists at subsidized rates.

- Improvement and enhancement of infrastructural facilities will definitely promote the further growth of sericulture.
- Crop insurance may be considered with subsidized premium rates, to give the sericulturists a sense of security.
- Training and extension centres have to be established at mandal levels to educate the farmers in reducing the incidence of diseases and to get higher cocoon crops.
- Efforts should be made to put the fortunes of this labour intensive activity on sound lines by establishing regional organizations for stabilizing the silk prices.

References

Belshaw, Cyril S. (1977), The Contribution of Anthropology to Development. Hari Mohan Mathur's, ed., *Anthropology in the Development Process*. New Delhi: Vikas Publications House Pvt. Ltd.

Cahill, Michael (2002), *The Environment and Social Policy*. London: Routledge.

Charsley, S.R. (1982), *Culture & Sericulture*. New York: Academic Press.

Eswarappa, Kasi (2001), Development and Change due to Sericulture: A Village Study in Chottoor District, an Unpublished Thesis submitted to University of Hyderabad, Hyderabad, India, for Award of M.Phil. Degree.

Gosh, Alok (1988), *Indian Economy, 1988-89: Its Nature and Problems*. Calcutta: The World Press Private Ltd.

Government of Andhra Pradesh (1993-94), A Note on Implementation of National Sericulture Project in A.P. (Summary and Progress), Dept. of Sericulture, Hyderabad.

Hanumappa, H.G. (1986), *Sericulture for Rural Development*. Bombay: Himalaya Publishing House.

Hanumappa, H.G. (1993), *Sericulture Society and Economy*. Bombay: Himalaya Publishing House.

Milton, Kay (1996), *Environmentalism and Cultural Theory: Exploring the Role of Anthropology in Environmental Discourse*. London: Routledge.

Morris, D. (1979), *Measuring the Condition of the Worlds Poor: The Physical Qualities of Life Index*. New York: Pergamon Press.

Narasaiah and Jayaraju (1999), *Sericulture: Its Place in National Economy in Indian Silk*, Vol. 42, May.

Narayana, D.L. (1979), *Economics of Sericulture in Rayalaseema*, Technical Cell, S.V. University, Tirupati.

Palmer, Monte (1980), *Dilemmas of Political Development*. Itasca: Peacock Publishers.

Periaswamy, K. (1977), Problems and Prospects of Sericulture. *Indian Silk* Vol. XVI, No. 6, October.

Pye, Lucian (1966), *Aspects of Political Development*. Boston Little: Braun and Co.

Ramana, D.V. (1987), *Economics of Sericulture and Silk Industry in India*. New Delhi: Deep & Deep Publications.

Sandhya Rani, G. (1992), The Triumph of Sericulture in Andhra Pradesh *Indian Silk*, Vol. XXX, No. 9, January.

Seers, Dubley (1972), *What are We Trying to Measure*, IDS, Reprints Brighton, Institute of Development Studies.

UNRISD (1972), Contents and Measurements by Mr. D.U. Mc Granham, C. Richard Proust, N.V. Sovani and M. Subramanyam. New York: Praeger Publishers.

United Nations Development Programmes (1990), *Human Development Report*. New York: Oxford University Press.

Venkata Narsaiah, P. (1992), *Sericulture in India*. New Delhi: Ashish Publishing House.

Institutional Reforms for Sustainable Irrigation Management

6

Mamata Swain and *Deepak Kumar Das*

Introduction

In India starting from the very inception of planning and in subsequent Five-Year Plans a major chunk of plan outlay has been meant for irrigation development to increase agricultural productivity and to improve the standard of living of the rural masses. Nearly 30 per cent of public investment is earmarked for development of irrigation infrastructure as irrigation is a critical and vital input required for agricultural production. However, from early 1980s investment in irrigation projects has decelerated due to fiscal compression. Irrigation development holds the key to agricultural growth as availability of irrigation water triggers the use of other yield stimulating inputs like high yielding varieties of seeds, chemical fertilizer, farmyard manure and also induces farmers to adopt advanced agricultural techniques and improved agronomic practices. Irrigation increases agricultural production and farm income by enhancing crop yield, diversifying the cropping pattern in favour of remunerative cash crops and increasing the cropping intensity (Bharadwaj, 1974, 1990; Dhawan, 1987, 1988). Due to capital intensive nature of irrigation development, major and medium irrigation projects in India have remained fully state owned, state funded and are departmentally managed by a hierarchical bureaucracy in a centralized and top down approach.

Irrigation has played the key role along with application of fertiliser and high yielding varieties of seeds in ushering in green revolution in India during 1960s and made India self-sufficient in foodgrain production. Nevertheless, a scrutiny of process of irrigation development in India reveals that the overall performance of irrigation sector is sub-optimal, inefficient and inequitable, falling far short of expectations. In spite of massive investments made in irrigation projects, the physical as well as financial performance of irrigation sector is observed to be quite dismal. The agricultural productivity from irrigation commands has not increased appreciably. The yield-increasing potential of irrigation is rarely achieved. The estimated benefit-cost ratio or the internal rate of return is never realised. As regards the financial performance of irrigation projects, leave aside the capital costs of irrigation projects, even revenue receipts from sale of water hardly cover the recurrent operation and maintenance (O&M) expenses. The political economy of water pricing stands on the way of rationalising water rate structure. As a result water rates are highly subsidised to woo the rural electorate. Irrigation sector is, thus, unable to generate resources internally required for the operation and maintenance of irrigation structures.

On the other hand, due to general resource crunch and fiscal compression, budgetary allocation for O&M has been squeezed. On top of it, nearly 80 per cent of O&M expenses are meant for meeting salary bills of the employees and establishment expenditure. Therefore, an insignificant amount is left for works component and actual repair and maintenance of physical structures. Thus, due to paucity of finance and in the absence of proper maintenance the conditions of irrigation structures have deteriorated significantly causing system inefficiency, which is a matter of grave concern. Irrigation planners and executives are worried that huge investments made in the creation of irrigation potential have become virtually infructuous. The irrigation projects have become economically unviable. The sustainability of the created irrigation structures is in jeopardy.

In the wake of liberalization, privatization and globalisation Government is changing its stance and attempting to determine water rates based on market forces and to withdraw the subsidy. But water users who have been used to get water at a very nominal price are reluctant to pay higher water charges unless there is improvement in quality of irrigation service. To improve the irrigation system performance the government has to increase the water rate, whereas the farmers will pay the increased water rate only if there is improvement in quality of irrigation service. Thus, irrigation sector is confronted with a vicious circle and a deadlock situation (Jairath, 2001; Swain, 2002). As an escape from this impasse and to make the vicious circle a virtuous one, during the last one decade most of the state governments in India have undertaken profound institutional and financial reform measures in irrigation sector.

Prior to 1980s irrigation in India was mainly considered as a technical enterprise aiming at construction of hardware like dams, reservoirs, weirs, barrages and canals. The software component or the socio-economic aspects and management part of the system has been grossly neglected. Mere provision of irrigation facility to land does not ensure enhanced agricultural production. The productivity impact of irrigation is critically dependent on the way water is applied and utilised. The quality of irrigation service in terms of adequacy, timeliness, equity, dependability and convenience in its supply remarkably determines the yield from irrigation commands. For obtaining optimum yield, water should be provided in time and in adequate quantity according to the crop water requirement of plants at its various growth stages, as water stress affects crop yield adversely. Irrespective of the location and size of the farm, water should be allocated equitably among the head reach farmers and tail reach farmers and also large farmers and small farmers. For proper crop planning, farmers need to know in advance the timing and quantity of water supply. Water should be provided in a dependable, predictable and convenient manner without any uncertainty in its quantum of delivery and timing. Quality in irrigation service should be maintained over time and should be stable and sustainable in the long run. In the new agricultural technology, proper water management holds the key to increase agricultural productivity.

To establish such an improved water delivery system and for optimal utilisation of scarce water, new trends advocate much more active participation of the water user in all aspects of irrigation water resource development and management, which include planning, design, construction, operation, maintenance, on-farm development, rehabilitation, modernization, water distribution, financing, resource mobilisation and collection of water rates (Wade, 1987; Chambers, 1988; Ostrom *et al.*, 1993; Meinzen-Dick *et al.*, 1997; Balland and Platteau, 1996; Vaidyanathan, 1994 and others). Now there is a worldwide consensus based on experience, experimentation and research studies that for long-term sustainability of irrigation infrastructure, crafting appropriate institutional arrangement is as important a job as is good engineering. It is stressed that the water users have an important role in water resources management more importantly at the tertiary or downstream part of the canal system. Specifically the water users can better manage the operation and maintenance of canals, distribution of water among farmers and collection of water rates. During the last decade most of the States of India like Gujarat, Maharashtra, Karnataka, Andhra Pradesh, Tamil Nadu, Bihar, West Bengal and Orissa have initiated profound reform measures in irrigation sector under the economic restructuring programme mostly under the mandate of donor agencies like World Bank, Department for International Development (DFID), UK; European Commission, etc. These states are putting emphasis on farmers participation in irrigation management and encouraging the farmers to form Water Users Association (WUA) or Pani Panchayat (PP). The state governments are implementing the Participatory Irrigation Management (PIM) programme in a mission mode. Internationally also many countries all over the world are broad-basing their PIM programme. Pioneers in PIM are The Philippines, Mexico, China, Japan, Egypt, Turkey, Sri Lanka, Chile, Columbia, Morocco (Meinzen-Dick *et al.*, 1997; Johnson *et al.*, 2002).

In other countries the key background conditions that paved the way for initiation of PIM programmes leading to the turnover of management of irrigation systems to WUAs include: national financial crisis, political will of the ruling party to place the irrigation sector on a sound economic footing, progressive deterioration of irrigation infrastructure due to deferred maintenance (Johnson *et al.*, 2002). In Mexico, the Irrigation

Management Transfer (IMT) programme was implemented due to political will at the highest level of the government. In 1989, with a new administration in office, comprehensive water management was recognized as a top priority issue, the National Water Commission (CNA) was created and a national policy on privatization took off. In Colombia it was the National Planning Department who in 1991 submitted the Land Reclamation Programme 1991-2000. In Turkey, a budgetary crisis led to a squeeze on financial allocations to the state water resources agency and provided the initial impetus. In Argentina, a programme to modernize the entire economy, which began in 1990 with the privatization of large electricity utilities, led to the turnover of water management to the provinces. In The Philippines the National Irrigation Administration (NIA) embarked on an ambitious programme in 1974 to increase rice production. A provision of this policy was for subsidies for the O&M of systems to be gradually phased out over a five year period at which time NIA would be directly dependent on collections from farmers for its O&M expenses.

As a matter of fact, Participatory Irrigation Management through Irrigation Management Transfer to farmers is now regarded as the most appropriate mechanism to bring about efficient utilization, equitable distribution and sustainable irrigation service. In India, during 1990s, systematic institutional and organizational changes have been brought about to increase farmers' participation in irrigation management through formation of Water Users' Association (WUA) or Pani Panchayats either under externally assisted economic restructuring programme like Water Resources Consolidation Project (World Bank), system rehabilitation programme (European Commission), irrigation infrastructure development (Japan Bank for International Cooperation), PIM in lift irrigation projects (Department for International Development, UK) or through state government initiative.

Rationale for Farmers' Participation

The poor performance of irrigation systems in India has been mainly attributed to its bureaucratic management paradigm devoid of water users participation, who are actually the end users of irrigation water. Now there is a growing realization that in a bureaucratically managed canal irrigation system, it is extremely difficult on the part of irrigation agencies to provide dependable irrigation service catering to the needs of numerous marginal and small farmers having fragmented landholdings scattered over extensive irrigation commands. Due to not only rigid procedures followed in a bureaucratically managed system, which lacks flexibility but also interference of influential powers, the irrigation engineers are unable to take appropriate and timely decisions based on field conditions. Further, the absence of adequate information on local resources and local socio-economic conditions, specific responsibility and downward accountability, the irrigation executives are under no pressure to accomplish their job catering to farmer's need.

It is now emphasized that the farmers who are the end-users of irrigation water and sons of the soil should participate in its management. Farmers have sufficient information and more knowledge on their local resources like land and water. As the entire farmer community has right to use irrigation and nobody can be excluded from its use; it is a common pool resource. Therefore, in the management of irrigation, the existing social capital like local knowledge, skill, community network and kinship ties should be utilized. As irrigation service is intended for benefits of the farmers, their views should be given due importance in the decision-making process in irrigation management. As a matter of fact it is difficult on the part of irrigation agency to look into the individual problems of numerous farmers and supply irrigation service catering to each farmer's specific needs. Therefore, it is felt necessary to delegate management of the irrigation system from appropriate level to Water Users' Association for example tertiary system in major and medium irrigation projects or entire minor/small irrigation system. It is contemplated that democratization and decentralization of irrigation management and empowerment of water users will undoubtedly bring about improvement in irrigation service by substantially reducing transaction costs of getting accurate information, negotiation and enforcement of contract cost (Baland and Platteau, 1996). Moreover, in the changed decentralised irrigation management system the irrigation executives and technocrats can devote their time for effective management of main canal system and other technical matters in which they have competence and comparative advantage.

In the era of liberalization, delicensing and decontrol, which has started in India since 1991, its impact on irrigation sector is obvious. There is a growing realization that the unnecessary bureaucratic control in management of irrigation system at tertiary levels should be reduced to improve irrigation efficiency and to check corruption and rent seeking behaviour. As the farmers have better knowledge of their eco-environment and field conditions, they can manage the irrigation system more efficiently and effectively which is truly a common pool resource. Usually the farmers believe that the canals belong to the government and they are the beneficiaries of the system. They do not have any role and responsibility in upkeep of the physical structures. In the changed institutional context irrigation will be considered as a common pool resource and will be managed by the farmers community (Sengupta, 1991; Singh, 1994) and its maintenance and sustainability will be the responsibility of the WUAs.

As a matter of fact, in agriculture cooperative efforts are necessary, as there are several externality effects. If farmers at head reach use excess water, tail-enders face water scarcity; if there is pest attack in one's field, the neighbouring field is affected. Therefore, a rational economic response is to internalize such externalities by making coalition or forming an association. As irrigation is a common pool resource characterized by non-excludability and rivalry in its consumption (Meinzen-Dick *et al.*, 1997), rational action on the part of each water user in isolation will give rise to free rider problem and will result in Hardin's (1968) 'tragedy of the commons.' Therefore, there is a need for forming Water Users' Association for efficient, equitable and sustainable use of water.

Benefits and Costs of PIM

Benefits and costs of participation to two major stake- holders, *i.e.* farmers and irrigation agency have been indicated by several authors (Singh, 1991; Maloney and Raju, 1994; Svendsen *et al.*, 1997), which are as follows:

Benefits to Farmers

(i) Better water management at the tertiary level.
(ii) Farmers' flexibility in use of water, choice of crops and land use.
(iii) More crop production and more income.
(iv) Optimal use of water in agriculture.
(v) Ensuring equity in water allocation.
(vi) Helping resolve disputes on water distribution.
(vii) Encouraging community responsibility for the management of assets.
(viii) Forum for facilitating effective communication between farmers and government departments.
(ix) Better collection of irrigation fees.
(x) More economic use of water, less wastage.
(xi) Better maintenance-reduction in the cost of irrigation.
(xii) Encouraging collective management of agricultural input supply and marketing of agricultural produce.
(xiii) Less water logging because of careful use of water.
(xiv) Less opportunity for corruption.
(xv) Better mutual trust and understanding between farmers and officers.
(xvi) Sense of ownership.
(xvii) Scope for securing water right for agriculture sector.

Costs to Farmers

(i) Higher costs, increased water rates.
(ii) More time and effort required to manage.
(iii) Less disaster assistance.
(iv) No assured rehabilitation assistance.

Benefits to Irrigation Agency

(i) Improved relations with client farmers; less mistrust.
(ii) Reduced complaints on inequitable distribution of water between head reach and tail end.
(iii) Increase in irrigation efficiency, job satisfaction.
(iv) More time to attend to technical matters and using their expertise.
(v) Less bothering about unauthorized outlets, obstructions and maintenance problems.
(vi) Improvement of credibility of the irrigation agency and irrigation officers.
(vii) Better collection of water rates and saving on maintenance cost.

Costs to Irrigation Agency

(i) Reduced bureaucratic and political influence.
(ii) Uncertainty over agency role.
(iii) Reduced opportunity for rent seeking.
(iv) Reduced control over water resources.
(v) Reduced O&M staff levels.

It is apparent that for the major stakeholders, *i.e.* water users and irrigation agency the benefits of PIM outweigh the costs. Therefore, it can be construed that PIM is a win-win strategy for both the farmers as well as the irrigation agency and should be encouraged to improve quality of irrigation service.

Evolution of PIM in India

In India the concept of PIM has evolved gradually through three distinct phases (Maloney and Raju, 1994: 16). In 1980s the concept was in its nascent stage limiting to **farmers' participation** through their representatives. It was felt then that in the decision-making process of irrigation development, the views of farmers should be taken into account and they should be consulted in planning, development and management of the system. However, mere farmers' representation in scheme level committees could not yield much result. In the latter part of 1980s, it was realized that farmers couldn't have many stakes in irrigation management without a formal structure/forum to express their views. Therefore, the catchword became **farmers' organization.**

In various states like Andhra Pradesh, Tamil Nadu and Maharashtra thousands of outlet associations/chak committees had been formed only in pen and paper but actually most of them became dysfunctional after a short period. By this time the concept of PIM received due importance after the Water Resources Management and Training (WRM&T) project of Government of India supported by United States Agency for International Development (USAID) was initiated. Motivating farmers to foster Water Users' Associations was an essential feature of action research programme taken up by Water and Land Management Institutes (WALMIs) in eleven states of India (INCID, 2003). The publication of the Ministry of Water Resources, Government of India titled "Farmers' Participation in Irrigation Water Management" in 1991 provided the status of the erstwhile existing WUAs. By early part of 1990s it became apparent that the concept of farmers' participation in few activities is not sufficient. Therefore, a radical concept of **farmers' organization and system turnover (FOT)** has evolved in which it is envisaged to entrust the WUAs with the responsibility of operation and maintenance of minor/distributary, allocation of water among farmers and collection of water charges from water users. The National Irrigation Management Policy formulated in 1995 also states that unless farmers are actually involved in the O&M and maintenance of irrigation system, the objective of increased utilization and production from irrigated command area is difficult to realise and recommends to involve farmers in various aspects of management of irrigation system particularly in water utilization and collection of water rates.

During late 1990s most of the State Governments in India (Andhra Pradesh, Gujarat, Maharashtra, Madhya Pradesh, Orissa and others) have taken policy decision to introduce Participatory Irrigation Management and turning over the management of tertiary segment of the canals like minor/sub-minors/distributaries to Water Users' Associations (Maloney and Raju, 1994; Jairath, 2001; Hooja *et al.*, 2002; Brewer *et al.*, 1999). Thousands of WUAs have been formed and they are entrusted with the responsibilities of operation and maintenance of the tertiary units, distribution of water among water users and collection of water rates. In some states the irrigation agency will make bulk sale of water volumetrically to WUA at distributary/minor head and retailing of water to farmers will be the responsibility of WUA. In some other states the responsibility is limited to decision-making of crop planning, water distribution and tertiary system maintenance and participation in water rate fixation.

Andhra Pradesh has legislated Farmers' Management of Irrigation Systems Act in 1997. Government of Orissa has enacted Orissa Pani Panchayat Act in 2002. Madhya Pradesh and Rajasthan have promulgated laws based on Andhra Pradesh model. In Uttar Pradesh and Maharashtra membership of WUA is mandatory for water users. In Andhra Pradesh and Orissa more than ten thousand Pani Panchayats have been formed due to the political will of the party in Power. The target is to cover the entire irrigated command area under Pani Panchayat scheme within a couple of years.

Water Policy Environment

Water is a prime natural resource, a basic human need and a precious national asset. Therefore, it is stressed that planning, development and management of water resources need to be governed by national perspectives. In India the first National Water Policy was adopted in 1987. As regards PIM, this policy envisages that 'Efforts should be made to involve farmers progressively in various aspects of management of irrigation systems, particularly in water distribution and collection of water rates. Assistance of voluntary agencies should be enlisted in educating the farmers in efficient water use and water management.' Recently the National Water Policy, 2002 has been enunciated. The new policy is more explicit in emphasizing the need for farmers participation in irrigation management and broadly outlines a Participatory Approach to Water Resources Management as follows:

> Management of the water resources for diverse uses should incorporate a participatory approach: by involving not only the various government agencies but also the users and other

> stakeholders, in an effective and decisive manner, in various aspects of planning, design, development and management of the water resources schemes. Necessary legal and institutional changes should be made at various levels for the purpose, duly ensuring appropriate role for women. Water Users' Associations and the local bodies such as municipalities and gram panchayats should particularly be involved in the operation, maintenance and management of water infrastructures/facilities at appropriate levels progressively, with a view to eventually transfer the management of such facilities to the user groups/local bodies.

As irrigation is included in the state list of Indian constitution, irrigation policy, law, act, rules and regulations differ from state to state. In this paper we are describing the Indian scenario with special reference to Orissa.

In Orissa, the first State Water Policy was adopted in 1994. The State Water Policy of Orissa follows the principles enunciated in the National Water Policy, 1987 and aims at promoting citizen participation in all aspects of water planning and management and handing over of operation and maintenance of irrigation systems to the users in due course. Orissa Water Resources Policy is implemented by the Department of Water Resources. Subsequent to the declaration of the National Water Policy in 2002, a draft Orissa State Water Policy has been formulated, which has not yet been finalized.

Pani Panchayat Programme

In this section we briefly discuss the salient features of the Participatory Irrigation Management Programme or the Pani Panchayat Programme which is under implementation in the State of Orissa since 1996. Recognizing the need for systematic involvement and participation of farmers in irrigation management, initially in 33 irrigation projects covered under the Orissa Water Resources Consolidation Project (OWRCP) funded by World Bank, PIM process was launched and christened as Farmers' Organization and Turnover (FOT) programme. Steps have been taken to motivate farmers to form Water Users' Associations and to turn over the operation and maintenance of the downstream part of the canal system to WUAs (Swain and Kar, 2000). The major functions of the WUAs are to operate and maintain the distributary/minor canals, to ensure equitable water distribution among the WUA members, to advise the department on main system operation and ultimately with gaining experience to collect irrigation fees in due course. In OWRCP area the implementation of FOT programme has been entrusted to Water and Land Management Institute, Command Area Development Authority, Nabakrushna Choudhury Centre for Development Studies and some local Non-Governmental Organizations. Since 2000 Pani Panchayat scheme is being implemented by the personnel of Department of Water Resources in non-OWRCP areas as well.

Orissa is one of the pioneering states to legislate the Orissa Pani Panchayat Act in 2002. Pani Panchayat is a three-tier organization for medium irrigation project and four tiers for major irrigation projects as indicated below:

(i) WUA/Pani Panchayat at primary level consisting of several chak or outlet committees.

(ii) Distributary committee at secondary level (major projects) is a federation of all the WUAs/Pani Panchayats under the distributary.

(iii) A project committee at project level is a federation of all distributary committees for major projects. Similarly for medium irrigation projects, a project committee at project level is a federation all the WUAs/Pani Panchayats.

(iv) A state level committee is constituted by the Government with presidents of the project committees not exceeding ten.

A Pani Panchayat/Water Users Association is an association of all persons owning land within a hydrologically delineated portion of the command area ranging in size approximately from 300–600 ha in case of major/medium/minor irrigation project. It may be in respect of minor or sub-minor or direct outlets from the main or branch distributary of the project. In case of minor flow or lift irrigation, the area is limited to project command area when the project command area is less than 300 ha. At the lowest level, outlet (chak) committee is formed electing three farmers, one from head reach, one from middle reach and one from tail reach of the outlet. An elected representative from among the outlet committee members (called chak leader) of each chak committee is a member of executive body of Pani Panchayat. The president, secretary and treasurer of the Pani Panchayat are elected out of the executive body of concerned Pani Panchayat. It may be mentioned that all the water users are members of general body of the Pani Panchayat. The details of organizational structure of farmer organization is given in the following figure.

For successful implementation of PP Programme, the implementation process is divided into several phases, *viz.* (1) Preparation, (2) Assessment, (3) Organizing, (4) Joint Management and (5) Turnover. The sequencing of various Pani Panchayat activities is as mentioned below:

(i) Delineation of Pani Panchayat Boundary.
(ii) Motivation of farmers regarding advantages of PIM.
(iii) Identification of villages, collection of village maps.
(iv) Collection of Irrigation Record of Rights.
(v) Preparation of beneficiary list and beneficiary-wise landholding.
(vi) Selection of contact farmer.
(vii) Conducting Participatory Walk Through.
(viii) Socio-economic baseline survey.
(ix) Collection of membership fees.
(x) Opening of bank account.
(xi) Conduct of election.
(xii) Training of accounts procedure to office bearers of WUA.
(xiii) Hydraulic testing.
(xiv) Discussion on Memorandum of Understanding.
(xv) Joint management.
(xvi) Handing over of the system for final turnover.
(xvii) Motivation of farmers for On Farm Development Work.

Pani Panchayat (PP)	General Body (All Water Users within the PP Boundary) Executive Body (All Chak Leaders within the PP Boundary) (Non Voting Members: One officer from DOWR (JE) and one officer from DOA (JAO) nominated by the Government)
Distributory Committee (DC)	General Body (All Presidents, Secretaries & Treasurers of PP) Executive Body (Maximum 9 persons elected from GB of DC) (Non voting members: Officers not below the rank of Executive Engineer of DOWR and DAO of DOA are permanent invitees to the executive body meetings nominated by the Government)
Project Committee (PC)	General Body (All Presidents, Secretaries & Treasurers of DC) Executive Body (Maximum 9 persons elected from GB of PC) (Non voting members: Officers not below the rank of Executive Engineer of DOWR and DAO of DOA are permanent invitees to the executive body meetings nominated by the Government)
	STATE LEVEL COMMITTEE

Constituted by the Government with such number of Presidents of Project Committee considered necessary but not exceeding ten and Equal number of Government Officials and Professionals not exceeding ten nominated by the Government

(JE: Junior Engineer, DOWR: Dept. of Water Resources, DOA: Dept. of Agriculture, DAO: District Agril. Officer, JAO: Junior Agricultural Officer)

Fig 1: Structural Arrangements of People and Government Participation.

As envisaged in the Orissa Pani Panchayat Act, the principal objectives of Pani Panchayat shall be 'to promote and secure distribution of water among its users, adequate maintenance of the irrigation system, efficient and economical utilization of water to optimize agricultural production, to protect the environment, and to ensure ecological balance by involving the farmers, inculcating the sense of ownership of the irrigation system in accordance with the water budget and the operational plan.'

Also, in the Act it is mentioned that the major functions of Pani Panchayats will be as follows:

- To prepare a cropping programme suitable for the soil and agro-climatic condition with due regard to diversification.
- To prepare a plan for the maintenance of irrigation system in the area of its operation at the end of each crop season and carry out the maintenance works with the funds of the PP.
- To regulate the use of water among the various pipe outlets under its area of operation according to the warabandi schedule.
- To promote economy in the use of water allocated.
- To assist the revenue department in the preparation of demand and collection of water rates.
- To resolve disputes between the water users.
- To raise resources.
- To conduct regular water budgeting and to conduct annual audit of its accounts and periodical social audit, as may be prescribed.
- As per the latest figures available from Department of Water Resources, Government of Orissa, the progress of Pani Panchayat scheme in the state by September 2004 is indicated in Table 1 and Table 2.

Table 1

Achievements of Pani Panchayat Programme in Orissa

Types of Irrigation Projects	Created Irrigation Potential (Lakh ha)	PP Programme Area	No. of PPs Formed (Lakh ha)	Area Covered Under PP (Lakh ha)
Major & Medium	11.90	7.08	1,112	5.03
Minor	3.64	3.64	1,233	2.07
Lift	2.17	2.17	8,675	1.97
Total	17.71	12.89	11,020	9.07

Table 2

Taking over of O&M of Irrigation Commands by PPs

Types of Irrigation Projects	No. of PPs Formed	No. of PPs Taken over	Taken over Command Area (Lakh ha)
Major & Medium	1,112	696	3.21
Minor	1,233	755	1.19
Lift	8,675	6,867	1.57
Total	11,020	8,318	5.97

Data on progress of PIM in Orissa reveals that so far 11,020 PPs have been formed and irrigation management has been transferred to 8,318 PPs and the taken over command area is 5.97 lakh ha out of total command area of 17.71 lakh ha. Thus, the data reveals that the PIM programme in Orissa is in expanding stage.

Constraints in Operationalizing PIM

Crafting a new institution in the management of irrigation infrastructure is obviously a difficult task. Changing the mindset and ingrained attitude of farmers and officials of water agency is not so easy. Therefore, while motivating the farmers to form WUAs and implementing various activities of FOT programme many problems are encountered in the field, which act as impediments to the formation of Pani Panchayat and their sustainability in the long-run. Some major constraints in organizing farmers as experienced by the authors in implementing Pani Panchayat programme in Baghua and Hiradharabati medium irrigation projects in Orissa during 2002-2004 are discussed in the following sections.

(i) *Intra-village and Inter-village Conflicts*

The inegalitarian production relations, community divisiveness, caste antagonism and class differential observed among water users in a village or within a WUA have significant implications for the formation of WUA and its sustainability. If the inter-village and intra-village socio-economic and cultural conflicts are severe, it is very difficult to organize Pani Panchayat. The conflicts of interests and lack of collective efforts on the part of water users are major hindrances in implementing Pani Panchayat activities. Peasant agriculture is most often confronted with the problems of a heterogeneous and hierarchical society having several caste and class cleavages. There are also political differences. The farmers having different political affiliations naturally have differences of opinion. Therefore, the more homogeneous the farmer community, the easier it is to form farmers association.

It is a fact, that it takes a long time to change peoples' attitude and to create awareness about the importance of forming a unified association for better water management. Implementing personnel must have the patience and perseverance to overcome such systemic and endemic problems in organizing farmers. Learning by doing approach should be followed to determine the model and modalities of organizing Pani Panchayat depending on the socio-economic conditions, psychology and cultural heritage of the farmers in the locality.

As the boundaries of Pani Panchayats/WUAs are determined on hydraulic basis, *i.e.* minor/sub-minor, most of the Pani Panchayats cover more than one village. If historically the villages coming within the boundary of a single Pani Panchayat have hostile relationship for some reasons or other, this may pose as a serious setback in forming WUAs.

(ii) *Election of Farmers' Representatives*

At the time of election of leaders of chak committee, executive committee of Pani Panchayat and of Project committee, many problems crop up. Water users having different political affiliations reveal their differences in interest and opinion. Political differences result in formation of separate groups within a particular Pani Panchayat/WUA or among Pani Panchayats/WUAs. Though the election procedure under Pani Panchayat Programme has no provision for role of any political party, the unwanted political interference during implementation process does spoil the very purpose of the programme, *i.e.* organizing water users for a common cause and facilitating farmers' participation in the operation and maintenance of canals and distribution of water with united team spirit. The political interference creates separation walls among the water users. In fact, the degree of political interference has an important bearing with the successful achievement of objectives of Pani Panchayat. Less political interference implies more smooth and easier formation and functioning of Pani Panchayat/WUAs.

The election of office bearers of Pani Panchayats should be fair and no money and muscle power should be used to persuade/pressurize the farmers to cast vote against their conscience. Success of any democratic institution depends on an enlightened and informed electorate. Therefore, the water users should be made aware of the details of the Pani Panchayat programme like the objectives and benefits of forming WUA, its structure, the organizing procedure, functions, rights, duties and responsibilities of different stakeholders, incentives for forming Pani Panchayat etc. The different clauses of Pani Panchayat Act, 2002 and the Memorandum of Understanding between the Department and the Pani Panchayat/WUA for handing over of the irrigation system to the Pani Panchayat/WUA should be explained to the farmers in simple terms for their understanding. If they have any doubt in any clause, it should be clarified immediately. The farmers should be apprised of the need for forming Pani

Panchayat/WUA for better operation and maintenance of canal minors/sub-minors, equitable water distribution between head reach farmers and tail-enders, adoption of common cropping pattern preferably remunerative cash crops and above all for getting sustainable quality irrigation service.

One of the important constraints that affects the process of formation and sustainability of Pani Panchayat/WUAs is lack of confidence of water users in the credibility of office bearers of Pani Panchayat and/or local leaders. Unless the office bearers and leaders are honest, dynamic and farmer friendly, the very purposes of the programme may not be successful. The role of the office bearers of WUAs like president, secretary and treasurer is very much crucial for obtaining the intended benefits of Pani Panchayat programme. They should have strong commitment for the cause of farmers' benefits and they should be honest, efficient and corruption free.

The executive committee should meet regularly to take decision on water management issues. The general body meeting should be convened and all decisions and actions taken need to be informed to the water users. No room should be left for arousing suspicion in the minds of water users regarding misuse of administrative and financial powers.

Utmost care should be taken that the rural elites do not capture power. In the words of Bardhan (2002: 202-03): 'After all, the logic behind decentralization is not just about weakening the central authority, nor is it about making governance at the local level more responsive to the felt needs of the large majority of the population. To facilitate this, the state, far from retreating into the minimalist role of classical liberalism, may sometimes have to play certain activist roles: enabling (if only as catalyst) mobilization of people in local participatory development; neutralizing the power of rural oligarchs; providing supralocal support in the form of pump-priming local finance; supplying technical and professional services toward building local capacity; acting as a watchdog for service quality standards, evaluation and auditing; investing in larger infrastructure; and providing some coordination in the face of externalities across localities.' Therefore, local accountability mechanism should be strengthened. In the Pani Panchayat Act of Orissa, 2002 there is a provision to recall the president of a Pani Panchayat if he is not responsive to farmers' needs and misuses his power and position.

(iii) *Physical System Inefficiency*

Due to resource constraint, most of the irrigation projects suffer from several physical system inefficiencies. Many irrigation structures like head regulators, outlets, cross drainage works, village road bridges, falls are in deteriorated and derelict conditions. Unless the faulty structures are renovated, rehabilitated and become fully operational, there is little hope that farmers will come forward to take up the responsibility of operation and maintenance of an inefficient system. Hence it is imperative that irrigation structures be kept fully operational so as to facilitate smooth implementation of turn over of irrigation system to farmers. In the modernization and rehabilitation of irrigation infrastructure, Pani Panchayats should be involved.

Before turning over the minor/subminors to Pani Panchayat for operation and maintenance, the project authority should conduct a proper hydraulic testing of the irrigation system in the presence of Pani Panchayat executives and farmers. The water users of the concerned WUA should be satisfied that the canal is discharging the designed volume of water and water is proportionately distributed in different reaches of the canal without any tail-end deprivation.

(iv) *Information, Education, Training and Incentive*

The water users should have thorough knowledge of various aspects of PIM programme such as the process of forming WUA, its structure, short-term and long-term benefits, functions, rights, duties and responsibilities of Water Resource Department and WUA. The water users need to understand and appreciate the goals and objectives of the programme. However, in some cases, farmers wrongly infer that it is a process of privatization by which government wants to get rid of the problem of distribution and operation by simply handing over the system to the farmers. In some other cases, farmers feel that operation and maintenance of irrigation structures is the task of irrigation staff and the department is shifting its responsibility and unnecessarily exerting extra pressure on the farmers without any additional benefits. These types of numerous misunderstandings stand on the way of smooth formation of WUAs. Hence, farmers should be made aware of the pros and cons of the PIM programme in its right perspective.

Farmers will come forward to form WUAs and will be ready to take up the additional responsibility, if they are convinced that the benefits due to participatory management will exceed their costs of participation. As most of our farmers are not educated and lack vision to comprehend the future benefits due to participation, special care should be taken while motivating the farmers. They are to be convinced that the benefits due to participation will be substantial, tangible, quick yielding and sustainable over a long period of time. Otherwise the farmers will not evince interest in a programme introduced and implemented through a government directive. The Department of Water Resources, Government of Orissa has declared many incentives for forming Pani Panchayat, which include annual maintenance grant and prizes for better functioning of Pani Panchayats. If 75 per cent of water users within the boundary of a Pani Panchayat become members of the Pani Panchayat, then grant-in-aid at the rate of Rs. 100 per hectare multiplied by the command area of the Pani Panchayat is allotted to the concerned Pani Panchayat every year. Government of Orissa has increased the per hectare water rate for *kharif* paddy (Class I irrigation) from Rs. 39.54 paise to Rs. 100 in 1998. Farmers are extremely reluctant to pay the increased water rates and have vehemently protested the arbitrary increase. Therefore, Government of Orissa has declared that nearly 40 per cent of the water charges collected from water users will be given to the concerned Pani Panchayat as O&M grant. Every year the DOWR is awarding prizes to the best Pani Panchayats of the State. These incentives have induced the farmers to form PPs to avail of the financial benefits. For sustainability of PPs, the performance of its governance structure and its functional efficiency in attaining the objectives need to be monitored and improved upon from time to time by applying a learning by doing approach.

Capacity Building for PIM

The WUAs will be able to operate and maintain the minors/sub-minors provided their personnel have the expertise, technical know-how and do-how to manage the irrigation system. Being aware of the need for capacity building, Government of Orissa is providing appropriate managerial and technical training to office-bearers of PPs and farmers through Water and Land Management Institute, Orissa.

The identified trainings for office-bearers of PPs are:

Technical: O&M, inventory and asset management, preparation of estimates, procurement, quality control, crop planning, water management, crop water requirement, preparation of canal operation plans, water scheduling and budgeting.

Legal: Awareness of the law and legal provisions and procedures, dispute resolution.

Financial management: Accounting, audit and social audit, raising resources, levy and assessment.

Administrative: Conducting of meetings, recording minutes/proceedings, communication and negotiating skills, conflict resolution and conjunctive management with the irrigation agency/government.

Irrigation officials as well as field staff should, also, be trained from time to time to imbibe the right mindset, attitudinal change and technical expertise required for participatory irrigation management. Before taking over the O&M of irrigation system, during the joint management phase the office-bearers of PPs should take keen interest to clarify their doubts and strengthen their knowledge and skill in operation and maintenance of tertiary segments of canals. There should be good relationship and mutual reciprocity between the departmental irrigation engineers, field staff and office-bearers of PPs with the common objective of improving quality of irrigation service for benefits of the farmers.

Given the low literacy rate in Orissa, mass awareness programme through print media and television has been taken up by the Government of Orissa to convince the farmers regarding the importance and utility of PP in improved water management.

WALMI has been identified as single source consultancy service provider to carry out Mass Awareness Campaign on "Pani Panchayat." In this context, WALMI is also providing posters, pamphlets, resource persons and technical know-how for the "Pani Panchayat Fortnights" observed in the State from time to time. A good number of district level Pani Panchayat launching workshops have been conducted in the State. Further one video training module on Pani Panchayat for awareness campaigning amongst the farmers has been developed. The Pani Panchayat programme is further boosted by telecasting Oriya tele-serials on Pani Panchayat through *door darshan* with the active collaboration of WALMI, Orissa.

Monitoring and Evaluation

Systematic M&E with modern tools and techniques during the process of implementation of PIM helps in rectifying the mistakes and fastens the process of turn over and improves the functioning of WUAs (Das, 2000). M&E procedure can be either goal oriented or multi-perspective. Goal-oriented M&E is based on official targets and, even if it is carried out through a participatory approach, tends to be primarily quantitative. On the contrary, a multi-perspective M&E (Vermillion, 2000) is based on the assumption that the values and interest of different stakeholders should be taken into consideration in M&E with the help of various technical, socio-economic, agricultural and environmental indicators in the pre- and post-PIM situation measured in quantitative or qualitative terms.

Monitoring

Monitoring of different aspects of project implementation is to be carried out as follows:

(i) *Performance Monitoring*

To track the use of project inputs and production of outputs and to identify delays and problems.

(ii) *Financial Monitoring*

To monitor the correct use of funds, disbursements and internal cash flow and assess cost-effectiveness.

(iii) *Diagnostic Studies*

To understand why implementation and sustainability problems have occurred and propose solution.

(iv) *Mid-term Assessment of Project Performance*

To assess the overall progress of the project in order to identify key issues and required changes.

(v) *Monitoring Operations, Maintenance and Sustainability*

To assess the capacity of the project to continue delivering intended services and benefits throughout its planned economic life.

Evaluation

For evaluating the impact of PIM data need to be collected on technical, agricultural and socio-economic indicators of irrigation system performance in pre- and post-PIM situations with the objective to examine the following factors:

- Achievement of programme goals and objectives.
- Satisfaction of other participating agencies regarding their relations with the PP.
- Community satisfaction with the performance of PP.
- Effectiveness of coordination with other agencies.
- Effectiveness and efficiency of monitoring and evaluation.

The following arrangements need to be examined:

- Financial administration and control.
- Overall efficiency and effectiveness of the PP's management.
- Procedure.
- Effectiveness of beneficiary participation in O&M of irrigation projects.

Apart from goal-oriented activities, a multi-perspective M&E involving multiple stakeholders and multiple indicators should be carried out to identify the areas where the restructured institutions need strengthening. Number of methodology for multi-perspective M&E based on several stakeholders and multiple indicators as developed by Das, Mangaraj & Acharya (2003, 2004) has been applied for Orissa. Several indicators have been taken into account which include process indicators, outcome indicators and impact indicators, which may be expressed either in quantitative or qualitative terms. In this perspective collected opinion of various stakeholders regarding the performance of PPs are aggregated to obtain the composite information on performance of PPs. These studies and other evaluation studies in limited projects in Orissa unveil that though Pani Panchayat Programme has benefited farmers in some projects, still it is observed that additional strengthening of the institutions in the following aspects is required for ensuring sustainability:

- Marketing of produce.
- Agricultural support services.
- Continued support for Pani Panchayat and field personnel need to work directly with Pani Panchayat to ensure they are effective.
- Resource mobilisation.

It seems these aspects have been well recognised by Government of Orissa and necessary interventions have been made.

Furthermore detailed M&E studies based on Vermillion (2000), Das, Mangaraj and Acharya (2003, 2004) and the indicators described by Nelson (USBR) should be carried out in different types of irrigation projects for true understanding of the impediments in implementation of PIM and sustainability of PPs.

Conditions for Success of PIM

Though several state governments in India have taken policy decision to encourage farmers' participation in irrigation management and attempts are under way to motivate farmers to form WUAs, the farmers' response in this regard is not up to the satisfaction. The success of any organization depends on some fundamental factors as mentioned below:

(i) Felt needs.

(ii) Common interest.

(iii) Collective effort.

(iv) Effective leadership.

(v) Bureaucratic commitment of the agency involved.

(vi) Political will of the party in power.

(vii) Financial viability.

(viii) Enabling policy and legal environment.

(ix) Effective role of change agents.

(x) Agriculture is the major source of income and commercialised.

(xi) Land tenure security.

(xii) Benefits due to participation are tangible, substantial and guaranteed.

(xiii) Existence of indigenous community organizations.

Some of the above factors are also highlighted in review of worldwide experience with water users' organizations (Meinzen-Dick *et al.*, 1997; Johnson *et al.*, 2002) as critical factors that influence the likelihood of success of devolution programmes.

It is often argued that state sponsored programmes meet with failure due to its top down approach to solve localized grass-root problems. The local problems in natural resource management like water and land should be resolved through local initiatives and peoples' participation. In case of irrigation management the farmers should themselves feel the necessity of forming an organization or association to improve the situation. There should not be any imposition from above. The change should be spontaneous and demand-driven based on bottom-up approach.

Moreover, the farming community should perceive that the Pani Panchayat/WUA would serve their common interest. There should not be disproportionate distribution of benefits among farmer groups. If the group of water users is small and homogeneous, conflicts are less. It is not mere felt needs and common interest that will foster WUAs, more importantly majority of water users should strive collectively to set up WUAs.

For motivating and organizing the farmers there should be effective leadership. Capable, efficient, honest, trustworthy farmers should be elected as office-bearers of Pani Panchayats.

The irrigation bureaucrats should be committed to the cause of organizing farmers to form WUA and to decentralize and delegate power to them. The political party in power should provide all out support for implementing the programme successfully. In Andhra Pradesh and Orissa the success of PP is solely due to the initiative taken by the ruling party under the dynamic leadership of the concerned Chief Minister.

There should be necessary amendment of irrigation rules and acts to incorporate the role of WUAs in irrigation management. There should be clear policy guidelines to implement PIM. For adjudicating the conflicts within and among WUAs there should be special water courts. Spain has established a special system of water courts for adjudicating water conflicts. Specialized water courts tend to work better than the regular courts, since the former are often clogged with pending cases and unfamiliar with water issues.

There should be well-defined water rights of WUAs. Rights to water are actually a bundle of rights. These include:

(i) Rights to use the resource.

(ii) Rights to derive income from a resource.

(iii) Rights to change a resource.

(iv) Rights to transfer the resource to others.

Not all of these rights must be involved in a rights allocation and registration scheme. For example, rights to use and to derive income from a resource could be specified initially, while rights to change the resource and to transfer it could be kept in abeyance until at later stage. Moreover, it is not necessary to assign water rights to individuals.

Furthermore, the WUA should be financially viable by raising its own resources from different sources. The WUAs need to have reliable sources of income; otherwise they can hardly be sustainable. Different categories of income to WUAs are:

- Sale of water.
- Sale/leasing out common property resources.
- Fees and contributions.
- Commercial operations.
- Maintenance contracts.
- Subsidies and grants.

The role of change agents in fostering WUAs is very important. Change agents are roles coming from outside the government-service provider-farmer chain of responsibility (Johnson *et al.*, 2002). These include local and international consultants, international banks, bilateral funding organization, UN agencies, local and international research organizations, NGOs, including WUAs. Acting in this role, change agents bring in new ideas, evidence of successes and failures elsewhere, pragmatic action plan, robust research findings, and perspectives and values that may challenge local orthodoxy and inertia. To be effective, international change agents should collaborate and work with local change agents to provide technical support, new ideas, legitimacy, methodologies and financial assistance for strengthening the restructured institutions steering them in right direction.

In general, the more commercial the agriculture, the easier it is for farmers to pay actual costs of delivering irrigation supplies and to pay for higher quality service. Countries that are seriously interested in institutional reform must also support well-designed agricultural development programmes.

Bardhan's (2000) empirical study of 48 indigenous irrigation communities in South India reveals that cooperative behaviour in an irrigation community is by and large negatively related to inequality of landholding, to urban or market connections, and positively to duration of access to water, monitoring by guards, and in some cases to social homogeneity, small group size, proportional cost-sharing rule, and collective hostile relation with other villages over water.

Sustainable WUAs require an enabling legal and administrative environment, strong political will with clarity of objects, accountable partnerships, and incentives. Empowerment of water users through capacity building, adequate resource mobilisation, appropriate incentives with timely monitoring and remedial actions can go a long way in strengthening the WUAs. The sustainability of a WUA clearly depends upon internal factors: farm size, location, social stratification and heterogeneity; and external factors such as the institutional environment, legal framework, financial and technical assistance, land reforms, agricultural policies and markets. To ensure effectiveness and sustainability of decentralised irrigation management an integrated and comprehensive reform is necessary.

Suggestions

As discussed in the main text, the ultimate success and sustainability of WUAs depends on some fundamental factors like common interest and collective efforts of water users, effective leadership of office bearers of WUAs, political will of the party in power, bureaucratic commitment of irrigation executives, governmental patronage, legal support, financial viability of WUAs and catalysing role of change agents. However, while introducing an institutional change in the management of an infrastructure, which is a crucial and vital input for agricultural production and a common pool resource, a careful and cautious approach should be followed. A few suggestions are made for propagating and implementing PIM through formation of Pani Panchayat/WUAs and Irrigation Management Transfer:

- As far as possible the formation of Pani Panchayats/WUAs should be spontaneous and demand-driven. The WUAs should be endogenously created, based on felt needs, common interest and collective effort. The existing social capital like social network, kinship ties, community solidarity should be used to foster WUAs. The approach should be voluntary, bottom-up and flexible.
- Successful implementation of the PIM programme requires involvement and cooperation of all stakeholders that include: farmers, government, personnel of Department of Water Resources, Department of Agriculture, Department of Revenue and the implementing NGOs. Political will of the party in power along with cooperation

of opposition party and bureaucratic commitment are highly essential for decentralising irrigation management. The role of change agents both external and internal is important in fastening the process.

- The dilapidated irrigation system should be improved and the canal should be rehabilitated and renovated to discharge the designed quantity of water and make proportionate distribution of water. There should be a proper hydraulic testing of the canal in the presence of water users. A fully operational and fault-free irrigation system should be turned over to WUAs for its upkeep.
- The organizing efforts should be closely integrated with physical improvements to ensure that the farmers are committed to maintaining the improvements.
- Farmers' representatives should not misuse their power. Department of Water Resources must support the group decision in their internal affairs and refrain from interfering.
- Commitment and active interest of top policy-makers and irrigation executives is essential in overcoming bureaucratic inertia and resistance to PIM programme.
- As the PIM process is very complex, no detailed blueprint solution or road map for achieving the changes can be laid down. In fact, the process requires experimentation, negotiation, adaptation to local circumstances and time. It is emphasized that it may take a long period to achieve attitudinal changes needed at all levels for true success of PIM programme.
- WUAs are concerned about legal complexity due to emergence of free riders and anti-socials. Sufficient legal support should be given to WUAs for tackling such situations.
- The WUAs often demand a minimum period of warranty from Water Resources Department and working agencies for the physical work done in terms of workmanship and quality.

- Regular monitoring and evaluation of PIM programme is necessary.
- Appropriate managerial, financial and technical training should be imparted to office-bearers of WUAs/Pani Panchayats to build their capacity to manage the irrigation system efficiently. Irrigation officials as well as field staff should, also, be trained from time to time to imbibe the right mindset, attitudinal change and technical expertise required for PIM.
- There should be downward accountability of irrigation officials to client farmers.
- WUA should have proper legal status and clear water right. The water resource department should supply canal water as entered in the Memorandum of Understanding/ Agreement between the WUA and the department.
- There should be a regulatory body to adjudicate any conflict or breach of contract between WUAs or between WUA and the department. Water courts may be established to render justice in time.
- The WUAs should be multi-functional. Along with the management of water, WUAs need to facilitate timely supply of good quality agricultural inputs like improved seeds, fertilizer, farmyard manure and farm implements at reasonable prices. The WUAs may also take up other allied activities like transfer of technology through effective extension services, marketing of agricultural produce and agro-processing for value addition; so that agriculture can be a profitable and paying enterprise.
- Decentralisation of irrigation management should be accompanied with agricultural intensification programme to increase agricultural productivity. Land reform measures should be undertaken to recognize/record tenancy contracts, so that tenants who constitute an important segment of peasantry can become members of WUA and receive the benefits of farmer participation in management of water resource.

References

Baland, Jean-Marie and Platteau, J.P. (1996), *Halting Degradation of Natural Resources: Is there a Role for Rural Communities?* Oxford: FAO and Clarendon.

Bardhan, Pranab (2002), Decentralization of Governance and Development. *Journal of Economic Perspectives*, Vol. 16, No. 4, 185-205.

Bardhan, P.K. (2000), Irrigation and Co-operation: An Empirical Analysis of 48 Irrigation Communities in South India, *Economic Development and Cultural Change*, Vol. 48, No. 4, 847-65.

Bharadwaj, K. (1974), *Production Conditions in Indian Agriculture: A Study Based on Farm Management Survey*. London: Cambridge University Press.

Bharadwaj, Krishna (1990), *Irrigation in India: Alternative Perspectives.* ICSSR Research in Economics, Second Survey, Monograph-3.

Brewer, J.S.; Kolavalli, S.; Kalro, A.H.; Naik, G.; Ramanarayan, S.; Raju, K.V. and Sakthivadivel, R. (1999), *Irrigation Management Transfer in India: Policies, Processes and Performance.* New Delhi: Oxford and IBH Publishing House.

Chambers, Robert (1988), *Managing Canal Irrigation: Practical Analysis from South Asia.* New Delhi: Oxford.

Coward, E. Walter (1980), *Irrigation and Agricultural Development in Asia: Perspectives from the Social Sciences.* Ithaca: Cornell University Press.

Das, D.K. (2000), Participatory Irrigation Management with Special Reference to Orissa. M. Swain and G.C. Kar eds., *Farmer and Local Participation in Irrigation Management*. New Delhi: Commonwealth Publishers.

Das, D.K.; Mangaraj, B.K. and Acharya, R.C. (2003), Multi-Perspective Monitoring and Evaluation of PIM (Pani Panchayats) in Orissa: An Analytical Approach, Proceedings of Tenth National Water Convention, Ministry of Water Resources, Govt. of India. 339-48.

Das, D.K.; Mangaraj, B.K. and Acharya, R.C. (2004), Performance Monitoring of Irrigation Management Reform (Pani Panchayat) in Orissa: A Multi-perspective Approach, 45th Technical Annual, Institution of Engineers (India), Orissa State Centre, 425-31.

Dhar, Bonani (2001), *UP Water Sector Restructuring Project: Social Assessment*, World Bank Report.

Dhawan, B.D. (1988), *Irrigation in India's Agricultural Development: Productivity, Stability and Equity*. New Delhi: Sage.

Dhawan, B.D. (1987), Productivity of Irrigated Farming: Survey Evidence from Three States. *Journal of Indian Water Resources Society*, Vol. 7, No. 3, July, 23-37.

Gooneratne, W. and Hirashima, S. (1990), *Irrigation and Water Management in Asia*. New Delhi: Sterling.

Govt. of India, Ministry of Water Resources (1987), *National Water Policy*.

Govt. of India, Ministry of Water Resources (2002), *National Water Policy*.

Govt. of Orissa (1994), *State Water Policy of Orissa*.

Groenfeldt, D. and Sun, P. (2004), Demand Management of Irrigation Systems through Users' Participation (mimeo).

Gulati, A. *et al.* (1994), Major and Medium Irrigation Schemes: Towards Better Financial Performance. *Economic and Political Weekly*, Vol. 29, No. 26, June 25, pp. A72-A79.

Hardin, Garrett (1968), The Tragedy of the Commons. *Science*, No. 162, December.

Hooja, Rakesh; Panagare, G. and Raju, K.V. (eds.) (2002), *Users in Water Management*. Jaipur: Rawat.

INPIM (2003), *Report on Participatory Irrigation Management*. New Delhi.

Jairath, Jasveen (2001), *Water User Associations in Andhra Pradesh*, Centre for Economic and Social Studies. Hyderabad and New Delhi: Concept.

Johnson, Sam H.; Svendsen, Mark and Gonzalez, Fernando (2002), *Options for Institutional Reform in the Irrigation Sector*, presented at the International Seminar on Participatory Irrigation Management: 21-27 April, Beijing.

Maloney, C. and Raju, K.V. (1994), *Managing Irrigation Together: Practice and Policy in India*. Sage: New Delhi.

Mitra, A.K. (1992), Joint Management of Irrigation Systems in India: Relevance of Japanese Experience. *Economic and Political Weekly*, Vol. 27, No. 26, June 27, A-75-A-82.

Mitra, A.K. (1996), Irrigation Sector Reforms: Issues and Approaches. *Economic and Political Weekly*, Vol. 31, No. 13, Mar. 30, A-31-A-37.

Palacios, Enrique V. (1999), *Benefits and Second Generation Problems of Irrigation Management Transfer in Mexico, EDI Participatory Irrigation Management Case Studies Series, World Bank*. The Orissa Pani Panchayat Act, 2002.

Ruth, Meinzen-Dick; Mendoza, Meyra; Sadoulet, Loic; Abiad-Shields, Ghada and Subramanian, Ashok (1997), Sustainable Water User Associations: Lessons from a Literature Review, A. Subramanian,

N. Vijay Jagannathan, Ruth Meinzen-Dick eds., *User Organizations for Sustainable Water Services*. World Bank Technical Paper No. 354.

Sengupta, N. (1991), *Managing Common Property: Irrigation in India and the Philippines*. Sage: New Delhi.

Singh, K. (1994), *Managing Common Pool Resources: Principles and Case Studies*. Delhi: OUP.

Singh, K.K. (ed.) (1991), *Farmers in the Management of Irrigation Systems*. New Delhi: Sterling.

Svendsen Mark and Ashok Gulati (eds.) (1995), *Strategic Changes in Indian Irrigation*. New Delhi: ICAR; Washington DC: IFPRI.

Svendsen, Mark; Trava, Jose and Johnson III, Sam H. (1997), *Participatory Irrigation Management: Benefits and Second Generation Problems*, Economic Development Institute, World Bank.

Swain, Mamata (1998), Water Rate Fixation in Major and Medium Irrigation Projects in Orissa: Issues and Problems. *Water and Energy International*, Vol. 55, No. 2, 63-72.

Swain, Mamata and Das, D.K. (1999), *Emerging Trends and Reforms in Irrigation in India: A Perspective of Orissa*. New Delhi: MD.

Swain, Mamata and Kar, G.C. (eds.) (2000), *Farmer and Local Participation in Irrigation Management*. New Delhi: Commonwealth.

Swain, Mamata (2002), Turning over Irrigation Management to Farmers: Prospects and Constraints. *Kurukshetra*, Vol. 50, No. 8, 4-10.

Swain, Mamata (2003), Farmers' Organization and Turnover Programme: Some Lessons from Orissa Model. *Kurukshetra*, Vol. 51, No. 12, 42-48, October Annual Issue.

Vaidyanathan, A. (1994), Better Resource Management for Poverty Alleviation. *Economic and Political Weekly*, Vol. 31, No. 23, June 8, 1397-1404.

Vaidyanathan, A. (1999), *Water Resource Management: Institutions and Irrigation Development*. New Delhi: Oxford.

Vermillion, L. Douglas (2000), Guide to Monitoring and Evaluation of Irrigation Management Transfer, The Japanese Institute for Irrigation and Drainage (JIID), Tokyo.

Vermillion, L. Douglas (2002), Current Issues and the Need for Monitoring Evaluation: Visit Note on PIM Programme in Andhra Pradesh; Users in Water Management. Rakesh Hooja, Ganesh Pangare, K.V. Raju (eds.) Jaipur: Rawat Publication.

Wade, Robert (1987), *Village Republics: Economic Conditions for Collective Action in South India*. Cambridge: University Press.

The Right to Development in India and Government Intervention through Collective Action

7

S.S. Rath

Introduction

The United Nations adopted the Declaration on the Right to Development in 1986, signifying for the first time that the international community had accepted the right to development as a new human right. There was no consensus about that right at the time. In 1993, at Vienna, at the second UN World Conference on Human Rights, a new consensus emerged which was supported by all the states including the United States. This consensus was enshrined in the Vienna Declaration, which, reaffirmed the 'right to development,' as a universal and inalienable right and an integral part of fundamental human rights. Article 1, paragraph 1, of the Declaration states: "The right to development is an inalienable human right by virtue of which every human person and all people are entitled to participate, contribute to and enjoy economic, social, cultural and political development, in which all human right and fundamental freedom can be fully realised." The article spells out three principles: first, there is a human right called the right to development which is inalienable; second, there is a particular process of 'economic, social, cultural and political development in which all human rights and fundamental freedoms can be fully realised,' and third the right to development is a human right by virtue of which 'every human personal and all people' are entitled to 'participate in, contribute to and enjoy,' the particular process of development.

State and the Market

The emphasis of development theory shifted from GDP, to real per capita GDP, to human development index, to reduction of poverty, unemployment and inequalities, to economic freedom, to sustainable development and now to interdependent development. Policy emphasis shifted from price mechanism and market forces with no safety nets for those who are put to disadvantage by these forces, to government intervention for planned rapid development, protecting those who get marginalized and removing poverty, unemployment and inequalities. Once again the emphasis has shifted to market driven forces but along with state playing the role of facilitator and providing safety nets for those who are put to disadvantageous positions, thereby preventing the market failures. In case of markets the emphasis shifted from market failures to non-market failures to new cases of market failures and to institutional failures. However, the challenges are unending. Now, when knowledge has become the most powerful engine of economic development, it has been realized that 'people are not poor because they are poor but because of poor policies' (Meier, 2000). Markets, process and incentives have been the central issues of the policies but now emphasis has shifted to 'get institutions right: IMF's Loan conditionalities and World Bank's structural adjustment tending led to the adoption of the policies of liberalization, de-regulation, privatization, other macro economic reforms and stabilisation programmes. All such market friendly policies have contributed in their own way to correct the distortions, but these policies lacked emphasis on infrastructure, human development, poverty alleviation, employment generation, protection of environment, financial regulation and quality of governance.

Economic development is concerned with improvement in standard of living of human beings and neglect of people at the bottom of the ladder would indicate a failed economy (Sen, 1984). However, markets by their very nature are discriminating towards the poor and there is need for enhancing opportunities for the poor in the markets. There is strong causal relation between good governance and better development outcomes

(Kaufman *et al.*, 1999). Through political stability, effectiveness, rule of law and reduction of corruption, etc. good governance contributes a lot. In fact, corruption may even threaten the entire reforms process and economic reforms are to be designed and implemented in a way that incentive for illegal behaviour and corruption are minimized (Broadman and Recantini, 2000).

The developing countries have faced significant dilemmas of choosing their development strategies with optimum blend of the State and the Market. It is worth noting that India had adopted the approach of the middle path since the early stages of development in the 1950's in the framework of Mixed Economy, where both the State and the Market are to co-exist. However, India has not been able to project the uniqueness of its development strategy and work out an optimum blend of the State and the Market realizing efficiency in resource allocation and also high growth. Being carried away by the recent waves of globalisation and marketisation many countries including India have shown the tendencies of marginalizing the State without redefining the role and the functions of the State in the changing environment. The result of all this has been the emergence of a weak state and mis-directed market forces which tend to distort fairness in the distribution of benefits of growth among the different segments of the community. There is growing evidence on the increase in gap between the rich and the poor, increase in the levels of poverty and destitution, frustration in the empowerment in the weaker sections of the society.

Neither state-led economic growth nor political efforts at redistribution and poverty alleviation have proved to be enormously successful in India. State capacity to push either the Korean type of high economic growth or the Chinese type of radical poverty alleviation was, simply, missing. The more this understanding of past failures speed into the gestalt of India's political class, the more they embraced "market-oriented" solutions to problems of development. A moment of reflection, however, suggests that past failures could have been interpreted differently, with different implications for policy change. For example India's leader could have embraced the model of East Asian "developmental states," or (less likely, but not totally out of the question) a more genuine social democratic model that was an adaptation of what has been tried in some such Indian States as West Bengal and Kerala. The fact that they did not do this, in turn points to other pressing factors that have put pressure on India's new economic choices: the "liberalizing" trend is consistent with dominant interests and ideas, both within India and abroad.

In spite of its socialist flourish, India's statism provided a framework for the emergence of a largely capitalist economy in India. The more that Indian capitalism has matured over the last few decades, the more; it has become difficult for India's leaders to maintain anti-capitalist political positions. Even India's communist parties now accept "market realities" and seen to attract private investors.

It is important to note that, in spite of commitment to economic liberalization, by global standards India's political economy still remains quite static: for example, public enterprises remain very significant; tariffs have come down but are far from negligible; the role of foreign investment in the economy is minimal; numerous laws govern capital movement in and out of the country; and variety of labour laws make the economy anything but a model of "flexibility." We are neither endorsing nor criticizing this state of affairs; what we wish to underline instead is that, over the last two decades, India's leaders have sought to "liberalize" the statist economy that they inherited. This "liberalization" while real, has also been limited.

Democracy and Economic Performance

India's leaders have nearly always put political goals ahead of economic ones; thus India's economic politics often reflect, not only an economic calculus but also such underlying political considerations and ruling ideologies, interests of the economic elite, concerns of political stability, and of course, the needs of the leaders to gain and maintain democratic power. Any full discussion of state-market interactions in India thus must begin by focusing on the changing nature of the Indian state and democracy itself, and then moves to an analysis of the impact of chosen policies.

A proto-democratic colonial inheritance and a democratically inclined cohesive, mass-nationalist movement thus provided institutional preconditions for the emergence of democracy in India. As this democracy consolidated during the Nehru era, however, it also developed characteristics that made it difficult for India's political leaders to pursue their social and economic goals. Although the colonial bureaucracy that sovereign India's leaders inherited was a fine professional force, it was mainly a "law and order" bureaucracy, not well suited to implement the ambitious development goals of Indian leaders. A major overhaul of the bureaucracy was contemplated but never really pursued, mainly because the well-trained civil servants were indispensable for governing the new state. When faced with the cruel choice of state as an effective agent of political order or as a successful facilitator of economic development, India's leader opted for the former. A longer trend, however, was also born namely, prioritizing political needs over economic ones and thus initiating what would eventually become a substantial gap between the state's capacities and its developmental ambitions. Another significant political development concerned the evolution of Indian federalism. Soon after the nationalist struggle was won and India had gained sovereignty, its numerous ethnic groups started to demand a greater share of power within the new state. These struggles came to a head in the late 1950s, when a reluctant Nehru agreed to a linguistic reorganization of Indian federalism. This decision again, probably wise, helped to accommodate ethnic demands and create a more stable political unit. At the same time, however, the central state cost some of the power that it needed to pursue its developmental agenda. To the extent that the developmental ambitions of India's leaders found institutional expressions (such as Planning Commission), these were nearly all at the centre. By contrast lower level governments were mainly "machines," with significant powers and resources. Although India's central state continued to be quite powerful in relation to its constituent federal units, a federal reorganization also dictated the state's overall capacity to pursue a coherent developmental agenda.

The freedoms available under Indian democracy—such as free speech, free press, the ability to conduct public action, and the ability to hold elections—allowed the citizens to exercise their rights in many ways that are not available in other non-democratic, developing economies. To an extent, these actions of the public in turn influence government policies and ultimately, economic development.

Persistent poverty and low quality of life has always been a problem associated with India. Prior to independence, the majority of the people lived in poverty, devastating famines occurred periodically, and social indicators of well-being (such as literacy and mortality rates) were abysmal.

Despite much rhetoric and higher growth rates, the governments during the last two decades obviously have not been able to make any major progress in reducing poverty in India. One-third of India's population still lives below the poverty line, and many of those living above the poverty line are far from leading a life where their basic needs are adequately satisfied. Over one-half of Indian children below the age of four are still moderately to severely malnourished, and high infant mortality rates registered little progress during the 1990s. Basic educational attainment is still denied to about half of India's population: over two-thirds of Indian females and one-third of males were illiterate in the early 1990s. Furthermore, India is one of the few countries in the world to have had a low female-male ratio of 927 females per 1,000 males in the early 1990s—a ratio that illustrates its severe and persistent gender inequalities.

Land inequality in India is not as high as that in many other parts of the world. Yet the failure to implement land reforms in a poor and still highly unequal country such as India is another example of India's larger state failure. In India, three quarters of the population (and most of the poor) still live in rural areas, and control of lands largely undergrids the political and social organization of rural society. Land ownership in rural areas is therefore still a good indicator of well-being; conversely, landless people are much more likely to be poor. Unequal landholdings, insecure tenancy rights, absentee landlords, lack of access to land, and a situation where land ownership still equals power continues to characterize most Indian states today. The carrying out of land reforms is difficult for any state to accomplish, because restructuring social relations to benefit the poor at the expense of the rich is opposed by the powerful. Nevertheless, land reforms have been carried out by some Indian states, thereby illustrating that this is both possible and beneficial. Re-distributive interventions such as land reforms are best carried out by strong states that have well-organized ruling parties with a commitment to poverty reduction and effective governments also at the local levels.

Since independence, the Indian State's spending on education and health, in particular, has remained below recommended international norms; and allocations to these sectors have been fairly stagnant for the last decades. Under funding of health and education has resulted in the under provision of facilities, inadequate maintenance, lack of resources and supplies at the facilities, high ratio of pupils to teacher and patient to health facilities, and increasing inequalities between richer and poorer regions, with the expected result on social indicators. The dismal functioning of the public services is exacerbated by lack of accountability in the education and health sectors. Local governments—the institutions that could ensure accountability of service provision on a daily basis—are not empowered to take action to enforce job performance of local civil servants, such as school teachers or health care workers.

The Constitution of India, in its various Articles, gives a prominent place to the development of the human factor. The preamble of the Constitution itself is a recognition of this fact. The Articles of the Constitution relating to 'Fundamental Rights' and 'Directive Principles of State Policy,' among others, lay down that the State shall make an effective provision for the development of human resources. Articles 38, 39, 42, 44, 45, 46, 47 and 48 of Part-IV of the Constitution are directly relevant to the development of human resources. Growth with social justice was adopted as the basis for development planning in India. India ranks 115th out of 162 countries in terms of the UNDP's Human Development Index (HDI) and is classified in the group Medium Human Development with an HDI of 0.571 in 2001.

India's comparative position on Human and Gender Development is listed in Table 1. Though the overall index on gender-related development has improved in 2001 as compared to 1992, it is still low in comparison to the country's human development level (Report of NIPFP on Gender Diagnosis and Budgeting in India, December 2001).

Table 1

India's Global Position on Human and Gender Development

Country	Human Development Index		Gender Development Index		Gender Employment Measure	
	1998	2001	1992	2001	1992	2001
Norway	0.933	0.939	0.911	0.937	0.752	0.836
Australia	0.927	0.936	0.901	0.935	0.568	0.738
Sri Lanka	0.704	0.735	0.660	0.732	0.288	0.308
China	0.594	0.718	0.578	0.715	0.474	0.321
Indonesia	0.637	0.677	0.591	0.671	0.362	@ 0.362
India	0.439	0.571	0.401	0.533	0.226	@ 0.240
Pakistan	0.483	0.498	0.360	0.466	0.153	@ 0.176
Nepal	0.343	0.480	0.310	0.461	0.315	—
Bangladesh	0.364	0.470	0.334	0.459	0.287	0.309
Mozambique	0.246	0.323	0.229	0.309	0.350	@ 0.428
Ethopia	0.227	0.321	0.217	0.380	0.205	—
Niger	0.207	0.274	0.196	0.260	—	@ 0.120

Note: @ related to 1999.
Source: Human Development Reports, 1995, 1999 and 2001.

The 2002 Human Development Report presents a disappointing picture of India's position in the global arena. It shows in particular that India ranks 124th in the world. India's Human Development Index—a statistic that is compiled on the basis of life-expectancy, literacy and GDP—is estimated at 0.577. This compares with higher HDI of 0.942, which is held by Norway, 0.939 of USA, 0.933 of Japan and 0.928 of UK. Hong Kong has a HDI of 0.888 and Singapore 0.885. Even compared to other developing countries, which have an average HDI of 0.654, India stands lower.

Conclusion

Article 8 of the Declaration on the Right to Development states that "effective measures should be undertaken to ensure that women have an effective role in the development process."

The 1995 Beijing Platform for action asserts that all members of society should benefit from a "holistic approach" to all aspects of development: growth, equality between women and men, social justice, conservation and protection of the environment, sustainability, solidarity, participation, peace and respects for human rights. One of the benefits of using human right approach to development is that it focuses attention on those who lag behind others in enjoying their rights, and requires that positive action be taken on their behalf. Throughout much of the world women experience discrimination with regard to the right to food, the right to education and the right to health. The Beijing Platform for action noted that "lack of food and inequitable distribution of food for girls and women in the households, inadequate access to safe water, sanitation facilities and fuel supplies particularly in rural and poor urban areas, and deficient housing conditions, all over-burden women and their families and a negative effect in their health." To counter this inequality the Beijing declaration proclaims, "it is essential to design, implement and monitor, with the full participation of women, effective, efficient and mutually reinforcing gender sensitive policies and programmes at all levels that will foster the empowerment and advancement of women." Literacy of women is an important key to improving health, nutrition and education in the family and to empowering women to participate in decision-making in society.

The ongoing economic reform process should be reappraised and revitalized to give the entire national development efforts a more human face. The eradication of poverty and unemployment must be the abiding goal of our development policy and programmes.

References

Ahluwalia, Isher Judge (1985), *Industrial Growth in India: Stagnation Since the Mid-Sixties*. Delhi: Oxford University Press.

Bardhan, Pranab (1998), *The Political Economy of Development in India*. Oxford: OUP.

Broadman, H.G. and Recantinis, Francesa (2000), *Seeds of Corruption: Do Market Institutions Matter?* World Bank Research Paper No. 2368, June.

Dreze, Jean and Sen, Amartya (1995), *India: Economic Development and Social Opportunity*. Oxford: Cearendon Paperbacks.

Kaufman, Daniel; Kraay, Aart and Zoldo-Labaton, Pablo (1999), *Government Matters*, World Bank Policy Research Paper No. 2196, October.

Meiler, G.M. and Stiglitz, J.E. (ed.) (2000), *Frontiers of Economics Development*. Oxford University Press, New York.

NIPFP (2001), *Report on Gender Diagnosis and Budgeting in India*. December.

Sen, Amarty K. (ed.) (1984), Poor Relatively Speaking. *Resource, Values and Development*. Oxford: U.K.

UNDP 1995, 1999, 2001 and 2002. *Human Development Reports*.

World Bank (1997), *India: Achievements and Challenges in Reducing Poverty*, Statistical Appendix, Washington.

Brain Drain and Scientific Diaspora: Prospects and Implications Back Home

8

Sadananda Sahoo

The idea of brain is based on particular conception of work. When we talk of brain drain we usually link it to the people who are highly skilled or professional. Brain drain is self- contradictory. What we called brain drain depend on the one side of the phenomena and at a particular time. In fact the circulation of brain is an age-old phenomenon. It is only after Cold War, people associate brain drain with the migration of skilled professionals from poor or third world countries to the first world.

Loss of highly skilled workers as well as top intellectuals by way of migration is however not a phenomenon that only affects developing countries. Britain complains that USA has stolen their best Nobel Laureates. In fact, the British Royal Society coined the term "brain drain" to describe the outflow of scientists to the United States and Canada in the 1950s and early 1960s. There was a massive migration in the 1960s primarily of British, German and Canadian scholars to the United States. Beginning in the late 1960s, the brain drain came to be associated with the flow of skilled individuals from the developing world to Western Europe and North America. 'OECD countries like Canada, UK and Germany too face loss of human capital through migration. But their problem is of different order. However, the scale is smaller and the loss is offset by the presence of equally skilled workers in the country' (Goswami, 2002).

'The brain drain is having a significant negative effect on most developing countries, although a few have coped successfully with the problem. Seventy-nine per cent of

1990-91 Ph.D. recipients in science and technology from India and 88 per cent of those from China were still working in the United States by 1995. By contrast, only 11 per cent of South Koreans who earned science and engineering doctorates from American universities in 1990-91 were still in the United States in 1995. Ph.D. recipients in the United States from Taiwan also tend to return to their country of origin. I will revisit the reasons for this success in South Korea and Taiwan (Shinn, 2002).

It is true that countries in North America and Europe today are overwhelmingly the net beneficiaries of the brain drain. The United States attracts most of the skilled workers from other countries. The following statistics will provide a clear picture of higher study in USA.

Table 1

Percentage of 1990-91 Foreign S & E Doctoral Recipients from U.S. Universities who were working in the United States in 1995, by Country of Origin

Country	Foreign S & E Doctorates	Per cent working in the United States
Total	**13,878**	**47**
China*	2,779	88
India	1,235	79
Japan	227	13
South Korea	1,912	11
Taiwan	1,824	42
England	142	59
Germany	177	35
Greece	240	41
Canada	417	46
Mexico	194	30

* The high rate of Chinese students is attributable to a one-time granting of permanent residence status in the United States (Chinese Students Protection Act) following China's response to students' demonstrations.

Note: Includes foreign doctoral recipient with temporary visa status at the time of receipt of degrees in 1990-91 (not permanent residents).

Source: NSF, 1998.

Recent Policy Initiatives in OECD Countries to Attract Foreign Talent

Canada (Quebec Province): The provincial government of Quebec is offering five-year income tax holidays (credits) to attract foreign academics in IT, Engineering, Health Science and Finance to bring employment in the provinces' universities.

European Union: As a follow-up to the Bologna Charter on education, efforts are under way to harmonise educational certification and qualification systems among member states in order to encourage greater student mobility within the EU.

Finland: The government has taken steps to encourage the enrolment of foreign scientists in Finland, including from Asia.

France: Several recent measures seek to facilitate the temporary migration of foreign scientists and researchers. In 1998 the government established an agency, EduFrance, with a budget of FRF 100 million to attract a greater number of students to France, particularly from Asia and Latin America.

Germany: The government seeks to increase foreign student inflows through grants and fellowship schemes. In addition, it launched a programme to issue 20,000 immigration visas to fill IT job vacancies. In the second quarter, only one-third of the visas had been granted, mainly to people from India and Eastern Europe who were hired by small firms.

Ireland: The shortage of skilled workers, especially in IT, has led to government campaigns in 2000 and 2001 to attract foreign workers as well as former Irish emigrants. Government-sponsored job fairs have been held in Canada, the Czech Republic, India, South Africa and the United States. In addition, work visas were introduced in 2000 specifically to allow the entry of highly skilled workers in areas where shortages exist in Ireland (MacEinri, 2001).

Japan: The government seeks to double the number of foreign students through the use of scholarships.

United Kingdom: In 1999 the UK government launched a major campaign to increase the number of international students in higher education from 19,800 to 248,000. The strategy is based on (i) a promotional/marketing campaign;

(ii) streamlining of visa procedures and rules on employment for foreign students; and (iii) special scholarships for top achievers.

United States: The US Congress has temporarily increased the annual cap on the number of temporary visas granted to professional immigrants under the H-1B visa programme whose statutory limit in 2000 was set at 195,000 visas per year until 2003.

Reasons for the Brain Drain

The causes of the brain drain do not vary significantly from one developing country to another. Migration specialists identified two important factors such as "push" and "pull". The importance of the individual factors varies over time and from country to country.

The "Push" Factors

Unfavourable socio-economic and political environment often push people to search for better environment.

Experts who have studied the brain drain point to a basket of economic reasons for causing or exacerbating the problem. As daily living conditions become more difficult, many professionals will look for opportunities elsewhere. A country with a weak economy, high unemployment, low wages and considerable poverty is a prime candidate for a major brain drain. Low salaries for professionals are often cited as the major culprit.

A related concern is the matter of professional opportunity, benefits and development. This includes issues such as training and research opportunities, moral and job satisfaction and human resource and management policies. Institutions that do poorly in these areas are more likely to lose staff to the brain drain. Most developing countries do not have particularly friendly working environments, healthy budgets, clear policies and generous research funds. The relative lack of involvement of professionals in the decision-making process also made them professionally suffer.

Some of the problems are seemingly mundane. Professionals become discouraged if they cannot afford to live in decent, albeit modest, housing. Poor supervision and limited career advancement opportunities add to the frustration.

One should not underestimate the lack of psychological satisfaction that many professionals encounter in their working environment in the developing world, including Ethiopia. If they conclude that they cannot accomplish what they were trained for, they become frustrated. Lack of access to professional literature and minuscule research budgets add to the problem. Dr. Yoseph Hassen Mengesha reported that the research environment in Ethiopia has deteriorated in recent years, partially due to the brain drain. You have a vicious cycle whereby professionals depart the country due in part to limited research opportunities and then those who leave, contribute to the problem by reducing the number of scholars who are able to conduct research.

None of these "push" factors is easy to solve and they afflict all developing countries to some extent. The ones that could be ameliorated by huge amounts of money will be especially difficult to deal by the poor countries.

The "Pull" Factors

In most cases, these are the reverse sides of the "push" issues. If the economy is weak and wages are low in the country losing skilled personnel, the economy tends to be strong and wages high in the gaining country. This is certainly the situation in North America and Europe. In a relative sense, it is even true for many developing countries that lose large numbers of professionals each year to North America and Europe but gain from less developed and poorer countries.

Beyond a peaceful political environment and high standard of living, perhaps the most important attraction of countries like the United States and Canada that are net beneficiaries, is the opportunity to exercise fully one's professional training. Career advancement and job mobility are usually predictable. More attention is given to human resource policies, supervision and training. Nations that benefit from the brain drain generally attach a higher importance to the development of knowledge than to losing countries. Institutions such as hospitals and universities usually have functional and up-to-date equipment and well-stocked libraries. Internet connectivity is nearly always complete and funded research opportunities numerous. Benefit packages for health care, life insurance and retirement are more common and generous. There even tend to be fewer bureaucratic frustrations in the developed countries.

Some gaining countries, including the United States, have visa policies that encourage the brain drain. The United States has the Diversity Immigrant Visa Programme, better known as the DV programme, that is intended to encourage the immigration of underrepresented nationalities to the United States.

Brain Drain is a Loss or Gain?

The conception of brain drain is changing from time to time. In the colonial time (after 16th century) there had been so much geographical exploration by Europeans. Once they knew other parts of the world they wanted to colonize them. It took about five centuries to consolidate the colonization process. The Europeans colonized Asia, Africa and America. Europeans who thought themselves modern wanted to civilize the colonized people. Thus they invited 'brains' (professionals in medicine, science and engineering, etc...) to civilize the savages in colonized countries. During this time, brain was not associated with brain drain. Once the colonization ended, things got changed. During this stage there were empires, colonies, etc. The colonized countries had set up their own institutions and train the manpower.

The next phase is the 'Cold War' stage, which started after World War II. This lasted till 1989. No more any group was called savage. But initially few and later many professionals found better career opportunities elsewhere, thus they migrated to the countries such as Europe and USA. This created a vacuum in certain areas. Thus it was termed as 'brain drain'. There was free flow of brains from one society to the other. Brain from Third World went to the First World to study, practice etc. in the area of medicine, engineering, and other disciplines. These brains may not return to their land of origin. During this time 'nation state' emerged.

Thus the idea of brain drain is an anachronism. It is matter of convenience that you work in India or somewhere else. The next stage is 'Global Age' which started after 1990s. During this age, no one talks of brain drain. It does not support the idea of brain drain. Today, the BPO (Business Outsourcing Process) industries even utilize brains available anywhere in the world. Brain drain is no more just associated with physical migration. With the advancement of technology, one can use brains from any parts of the world.

Brain drain refers to professional technical people (IT, Medicine, Engineering etc.) and academic people such as lawyer, nuclear physicists, etc.). India is the 6th largest scientific manpower in the world.

There are certain thing which can be taken into consideration, *i.e.* if the loss of brain is permanent we call it as brain drain and if it is temporary we cannot call it brain drain. A loss at present is a gain in future. Many IT experts of India can come back and contribute to India. The reality of loss is that the loss remains within one society. If one country loses, the other country gains. Loss or gain can be measured only in terms of national or global terms. Countries may lose or gain, region may lose or gain, and corporation may lose or gain. As a whole there is no definite answer to this question. There can be answer only at the point of departure or destination.

In fact the main point is individual, who makes decision independently to migrate other country. If hundreds and thousands of people make such decision, it will affect the nation. Individuals are rarely anti-national or pro-national. He/she looks at particular perspective. But this affect if it is in large number.

Brain drain can be seen as problem from the Third World point of view at a particular period of time. But then how can Third World countries balance it? The empirical evidence point out to a very unequal distribution of world resources in science and technology that mimics large disparities in per capita income across nations. Rich countries spend more (as a share of GDP) in science and technology than middle income and poor countries. However, there are some significant outliners such as China and

India whose ratios of spending in science and technology (S & T) to GDP are significantly higher than the international average corresponding to their income per capita levels (Solimano, 2002). These international differentials in resources devoted to S & T is correlated with the observed outflows of scientists and technology experts from developing countries/transition economies to the U.S. and other OECD countries where they find more resources (including better pay) to carry out their scientific research and technology work. Here comes the nation-state, patriotism and diaspora. The three are interrelated. The conception of diaspora can help in minimizing the disparities between rich and the poor countries. Many of the underdeveloped and Third World countries are now working out strategy to utilize their diaspora brainpower.

Human capital and talent is an inescapable feature of globalization. The expansion of the knowledge economy and the rapid pace of technical change accelerated the international mobility of human capital and talent. Human capital flows can take several forms and include the international circulation of scientists, information technology experts, intellectuals, artists and entrepreneurs. The traditional "brain drain" which was a kind of permanent and irreversible outflow of human capital co-exist with cycles of emigration and return of national talents ("brain circulation"). Thus, for developing countries, the emigration of domestic talent need not be always a permanent loss (Solimano, 2002).

Most of the scientific activities and entrepreneurial ventures have a growing international network today. Resourceful people always search for opportunities wherever they are available. The advances in telecom and internet made the communication between people crossing geographical boundaries. The similar development also made people link with each other who are of same origin, same identity, same culture. Often the development brought out by these technologies made people to exploit the resources outside their country.

T.K. Oomen conceptualized brain drain in following terms:

(i) Types of brain which migrate.

(ii) Exporting countries' capacity to absorb (India can spare physicians not nurses. But we don't care if nurses migrate but we bother when doctors migrate.'

(iii) Quantum of investment is in training of doctors and physicians but not on nurses. Therefore we don't bother if nurses migrate. It is not a matter of sparability but matter of investment.

(iv) Destination and motivational aspect. Migration is also motivated by professional consideration such as peer group, quality of life, laboratory and professional colleagues.

(v) The quantum of material return. If my father sends me and state sends me there is difference. Investing party has a claim. Capitation fee is a lump sum. Professional courses demand heavy capitation fees.

How does Diaspora Addresses these Issues?

What are the economic consequences of the international mobility of human capital and talent? Who gains? Who loses? Sometimes back, the answer was that definitely the sending countries were the loser. But today, it has taken new mode. The human capital that a country loses to other country forms a very resourceful diaspora. There can be more gain if a country can make use of their resources. If large number of a country's people migrate and send money and know-how, and scientific knowledge to their home country, it is favourable for the country.

In the process of migration, there will be more trained people for a country. These migrant professionals often acquire the best skills and knowledge to benefit their respective countries.

In a world without barriers to the movement of people across nations, individuals should be expected to migrate from places where their productivity (and income) is lower to places where their productivity is higher, regardless of national borders. "In a time of porous borders, e-mail and overnight flights to anywhere, talent that flies away hasn't disappeared. Russian scientists do lab work in the U.K., while New Zealand's engineers raise bridges in Canada. Cuban doctors treat patients in South Africa, and South Africans teach English school children. The smartest Chinese and Indians go where they please; nearly a third of all scientists and engineers from developing countries currently serving in the United States, Japan and Europe" (Margolis, 2004).

Options for the Developing Countries: Policies, Voluntary Actions and Other Informal Networks

Since 1960s the brain drain has been identified as a problem, hence something against which policies had to and, supposedly, could react and struggle through voluntaristic decision-making. Until the late 1980s, these national or international policies have focused on countermeasures, either to prevent/regulate flows of skills or to cancel their negative effects through taxation. Though their design had often been thoroughly studied, they failed to bring feasible or effective solutions (Meyer *et al.*, 1997). Today, it appears that these repeated failures are mainly due to the partially wrong underlying theoretical assumptions on which these policies were based. They basically referred, indeed, to human capital approach where the skilled person is conceived as resulting of prior investments (Gary Becker). Accordingly, the two ways to counter the loss of human capital is either to restrict the flows through authoritative or negotiated decisions or to evaluate its monetary cost and get financial compensation. It simply could not work because, in fact, the human capital approach reflects but a small part of the phenomenon.

For the past two decades, the sociology of science and technology has brought new understanding of the process of knowledge creation, transmission and application. It insists on the collective nature of such a process, emphasizing the role of scientific communities (Robert Merton, for instance). They show that these are socio-cognitive communities, not only social or institutional ones (Thomas Kuhn's paradigm). They demonstrate that this socio-cognition is very specialized and thus enacted in local—not easily duplicable/replicable—conditions, involving partly collective tacit knowledge built through daily group practice and requiring the individual's abilities and activities only make sense and generate results with regard to the human and non-human entities to which he/she is linked (Michel Callon and Bruno Latour's actor-network theory).

The migration of professionals from India and China to developed countries is very significant. The best intellectual infrastructure of these two countries is lost to developed countries like the United States, Great Britain, Japan, and other European countries. These groups are largely comprised of highly skilled professionals; therefore highly educated members belong to the prime-age workforce (18–40 years old). These people are also those who have the capacity of being high earners.

Policies to stem the outflow of human capital and entrepreneurship require action at several fronts: national governments of developing countries need to give a greater priority and devote more resources to science, technology and knowledge generation at home recognizing its pay-off in enhanced productivity, competitiveness and long-run development. Less bureaucracy and more friendly policies to business creation help also to stem the outflow of entrepreneurial talents. Developed countries in turn can increase the transfer of knowledge to LDCs and redefine foreign aid priorities towards science and technology in developing countries.

The return varies from country to country, poor economies suffer particularly hard from the emigration of domestic talent.

The last decade has seen an increase in the international mobility of highly skilled, talented individuals (*i.e.* human capital) in response to the expansion of the knowledge economy accompanying globalization.

The topic of human capital mobility and brain drain has remained somewhat dormant in the academic and policy literature in the last two or three decades after being actively debated in the 1960s. Two views dominated the positions of that time: one was the "internationalist view" championed by Harry Johnson. The alternative view was the "nationalist view" exposed by Don Patinkin and others.

What can developing countries do to revert the outflow of human capital? How to increase their share in the process of global generation of knowledge? How to improve the world distribution of resources for science and technology?

The *Newsweek* had a special report on the return of professionals to their home country (Margolis, 2004). The report documented the cases of some of the well-known professionals and entrepreneurs who returned to their homeland and started their work. The report said that sending workers abroad does not mean squandering minds. For many countries, Diaspora talent is the key to success.

Diaspora as a Resource

Most persons who have studied the brain drain phenomenon have concluded that it is not realistic to expect a significant percentage of those who left their country of origin to return many years later (Shinn, 2002). Most are now married, have established families, have children in school and become accustomed to their new lives. Philip Emeagwali stated it starkly when he noted that "an African professional will not resign from his $50,000 a year job to accept a $500 a year job in Africa." Only after African economies become much stronger and the political situation improves substantially will it be possible to think in terms of significant numbers of returnees to the continent. These are the factors that have been so important in the ability of countries like South Korea, Taiwan and Ireland to attract professionals back. They have, in addition, established policies to foster domestic investment in innovation and research and development.

But there are some persons who, for family or other reasons, are prepared to make the move. 'Dr. Meera Sethi reported that the International Organization for Migration has a small programme for reversing the brain drain through selective return migration. IOM helps African countries identify priority skill needs and then matches those needs with qualified nationals living outside the country. Between 1983 and 1995, IOM helped to return to Africa 2,565 the most urgently needed professionals. IOM has undertaken a project in cooperation with the government of Kenya to return Kenyan professionals to assist with its development programme. Known as Migration for Development in Kenya, some 320 professionals have already returned. The Director of IOM recently announced that the organization is prepared to replicate the programme in other African countries (Shinn, 2002).

Countries that wish to encourage the return of professionals need to offer special incentives if they hope to achieve any success. A similar programme for professionals and scholars might include payment of relocation expenses, free or subsidized housing, tax relief, loans and salary supplements for the first few years. India's Resurgent India Bund (RIB), PIO card and several benefits for NRIs and PIOs often directed for this purpose. In addition, it would engender considerable resentment among those persons of similar qualification who never left the country and would not be eligible for the incentives.

An increasing number of developing countries are considering their highly qualified citizens abroad as a potential asset for national development. Renewed policies are consequently being developed in order to recover these expatriated talents. Besides the repatriation—return option generally enacted in these policies with variable success, a second one has recently emerged: the diaspora option.

The diaspora option is the most recent policy that has come under full implementation with regard to migrations of highly qualified human resources. As a brain gain strategy it differs from the return option in the sense that it does not aim at the physical repatriation of the nationals living and working abroad. Its purpose is the remote mobilization of the diaspora's resources and their association to the country of origin's programmes.

DIASPORA CONTRIBUTIONS WORLDWIDE

Australia

Successful expatriates remain an important part of national life, write Michael Fullilove and Chloe Flutter (2004). Relatively speaking, this group is prosperous, well-educated, well-connected, highly employable and, crucially, well-disposed to Australia. The group is also highly mobile: rather than turning their backs on Australia once and for all, expatriates these days are more likely to move back and forward between Australia and other countries as opportunities present.

Given our small population, the rollcall of Australians in top international positions is impressive. They head up businesses such as McDonald's and British Airways; they edit leading international newspapers; they run international organizations and cultural institutions and teach at the world's best universities. Together with other expatriates, they constitute our worldwide web of ideas and influence.

It is time to take this group seriously. The existence of a large community of overseas Australians is relevant to a wide range of issues facing this country and needs to be considered. It also relates to the question of our national identity, and the face we show to the world.

Many people have assumed that Australians are resentful of expatriates, or at least of the high-profile variety—that we suffer from foreign poppy syndrome. Our opinion polling indicates, on the contrary, that most resident Australians are remarkably positive about expatriates. Furthermore, they are generally comfortable with the idea of a large number of Australians living overseas. Forty-four per cent of respondents to our survey believed this phenomenon was good for the country, compared with only 22 per cent who thought it was bad. Sixty-three per cent of respondents agreed that expatriates benefit Australia by building networks and projecting our image offshore; only 24 per cent thought the numbers represented an alarming brain drain.

This goodwill on the part of residents towards expatriates is matched by their offshore cousins: we were struck by the strong sense of "Australian-ness" expressed by most of our expatriate interviewees. One example was the academic who sent his postal ballot to Australia by courier to ensure that it arrived in time to be counted.

In our new report, we argue it would be appropriate for Australian institutions, both public and private, to reach out to expatriates and capitalise on their talent and goodwill.

Research indicates that emigration can have positive effects on the home country, by influencing trade and investment flows and connecting local organizations to international developments.

Studies have pointed to the influence of Chinese emigrants on investment that flows back to China and Taiwan, or the role played by Indian software engineers as middlemen between American and Indian businesses.

In Australia's case, the diaspora is not a first-order economic issue, but it is one that deserves consideration. And while it is difficult to make policies for a population that does not live within the national borders, it should not be completely beyond our wit.

There are a number of steps Australian institutions should take. Our national leaders should follow the lead of their international colleagues who articulate the value of their diasporas and draw them into the mainstream of national life.

The Government should also take a more co-ordinated approach to engaging with our expatriate community. Many Australian diplomats use their contacts with expatriates creatively to further the national interest. It would be useful, however, to make this an explicit aim of the Department of Foreign Affairs and Trade, and to establish a co-ordinating unit within the department to capture the experiences of different posts and distribute best practices throughout the system.

The Government should also explore methods of involving our overseas citizens more fully in our democratic processes. It is, of course, appropriate that a balance be struck between the right to vote and the principle of electoral legitimacy, which requires that elections should be determined by those with a stake in the outcome.

At the very least, the current complicated arrangements for enrolment and voting should be reformed and advertised widely in an effort to raise significantly the number of expatriates who actually vote.

However, if Canberra should take the lead on this issue, it is not a matter for Government alone. There are also opportunities for businesses to take advantage of expatriates' international experience; and for non-profit organizations to tap the generosity of the diaspora.

In recent years, a national conversation on the diaspora has begun, with reports published and more are on the way, including from a Senate committee of inquiry.

The task now is to build on these early steps and create a truly global community of Australians.

Taiwan

In the 1970s, Taiwan was poorer country seen primarily as a source of cheap manufacturing labour for most U.S. multinationals. Accordingly, Taiwan exhibited a classic first-world-third-world relationship with the West: while capital and technology resided chiefly in American, European, and Japanese corporations, chcap labour was found in Taiwan. In contrast, Saxenian explained, by the 1990s Taiwan had become one of the world's most sophisticated manufacturers of semiconductors and personal computer and third in the world after the U.S. and Japan in IT hardware production. Saxenian showed data indicating that currently Taiwan is the leading producer of laptop computers and is moving quickly in China also.

Saxenian explained that a common reaction to Taiwan's growth during the past thirty years has been to analyze how the region moved from cheap labour in the 1970s to world leadership in IT manufacturing by the 1990s. Among other reasons, Saxenian explained, the key role policy-makers played in creating a bridge.

African Scenario

In general, all the African countries suffer from the brain drain. African countries like Nigeria, Ghana, South Africa and Kenya are struggling with the same challenge. A few African countries such as Botswana and Mauritius seem to be minimally affected by the brain drain. David H. Shinn (2002) mentioned that 'More than 2,000 Nigerian doctors work in the United States even though there continues to be a critical need for health professionals in Nigeria. About 10,000 Nigerian academics are employed in the United States alone. There reportedly are more Sierra Leonean doctors living in the Chicago area than in Sierra Leone. An estimated 600 Ghanaian doctors work in New York City, catering with about 20 per cent of its requirement.

More than 1,000 professionals left Zimbabwe for other countries in 1997 alone. There are more African-born scientists and engineers working in the United States than there are in Africa.' How can such a loss be balanced? It can only be done through Diaspora's looking back to home.

'In a paper delivered two years ago before an Addis Ababa Conference on the brain drain, Dr. Meera Sethi, the International Organization for Migration representative in Ethiopia, noted that Africa lost a third of its professionals to the developed countries between 1960 and 1987. An estimated 23,000 academics and 50,000 middle and senior management personnel leave the continent each year. More than 40,000 Africans with a Ph.D. now live outside the continent. Dr. Sethi concluded that almost half of those who left Africa did so to study abroad while nearly 30 per cent sought professional development. Less than 7 per cent left for political reasons. Looked at another way, Dr. Dejene Aredo of the Addis Ababa University faculty of business and economics estimates that 20,000 professionals leave Africa annually. For every 100 professionals sent overseas for training between 1982 and 1997, 35 failed to return to the continent. The largest migratory flows are from Egypt, South Africa, Nigeria, Kenya, Ghana and Ethiopia' (Shinn, 2002).

The financial cost of the brain drain for Africa is huge. The International Office for Migration estimates that about 300,000 professionals from Africa live and work in Europe and North America. Approximately 100,000 expatriates from the West at an annual cost of $4 billion are employed to help make up for the loss of professionals from sub-Saharan Africa. This expatriate labor force is considerably more expensive than the Africans they have replaced, although many of their salaries and benefits are paid by foreign governments as part of grant aid programmes. African countries have, nevertheless, invested scarce capital in training their nationals. The cost of training, for example, a non-specialized doctor in a developing country is about $60,000 and for a paramedical specialist about $12,000. When these individuals emigrate from the continent, wealthier nations usually reap the benefits of training provided by poorer nations (Shinn, 2002).

Engaging the African Diaspora

'For the first time, the African Union has invited Africa's Diaspora (those who trace their roots back to the continent) to actively take part in the region's development. Heads of state who met for the African Union extraordinary summit in February agreed to amend the organization's charter to "encourage the full participation of the African Diaspora as an important part of the continent...." This followed active lobbying by members of the diaspora seeking recognition as agents for the continent's development (Mutume, 2003).

In the absence of formal structures, African Diaspora groups have generally relied on *ad hoc*, disparate and small-scale programmes to assist in the development of the continent. Despite this, many have been able to help build schools, hospitals and roads, run training programmes, supply books and computers to deprived schools and establish scholarships to assist students.

But they operate outside the sphere of mainstream development agencies, even though they may be working towards the same ends. "Africa must develop a collective strategy for engaging the diaspora," noted US Ambassador to Nigeria Howard Jeter (Mutume, 2003). He said there have been no meaningful attempts to engage the diaspora and no institutional connections exist. "Few African-Americans know about NEPAD. Why should that be?" asked Ambassador Jeter, in an address to the Nigerian Institute of International Affairs in November. He observed that Africa is not utilizing African-Americans as a primary political constituency in the US. "Are African-Americans really being encouraged to do business with Africa? I don't think so." As Africa begins to map out a strategy to engage those in the diaspora, such questions need to be asked, he said (Mutume, 2003).

South Africa

With the reintegration of South Africa into the international community, the data reflect, that emigration has increased and immigration has decreased (Kaplan and Meyer, 1997). This reintegration of South Africa into the world economy represents several challenges in terms of international competition. Therefore, South Africa cannot afford to lose its valuable human resources especially highly qualified professionals. This concern is reflected in newspaper articles discussing the brain drain phenomenon, for example the *Cape Argus* (03-03-98) reported that more than 6,855 South Africans including doctors, engineers and computer experts emigrated in 1997, the *Cape Times* (12-01-98) reported that South Africa is losing skilled medical research personnel to especially the United Kingdom and the United States of America.

SANSA: A Response to the Brain Drain

South Africa has a large skilled diaspora. According to Kaplan and Meyer (1998), there are approximately 21,485 graduates from the major universities (Cape Town, Witwatersrand, Natal, Rhodes and Stellenbosch) in South Africa who are living abroad. This skilled diaspora is spatially concentrated, with 58 per cent of all graduates located abroad in six countries. A little less than half are located in the UK, USA and Australia (Kaplan and Meyer, 1998).

In the light of the above-mentioned statistics, the idea of utilizing South Africa's diaspora has potential. This gave rise to the idea of setting up a network of skilled expatriates interested in contributing to South Africa's development.

SANSA was thus initiated for this reason. SANSA aims at establishing links between, mostly but not exclusively, highly skilled (ex) South Africans living abroad and South Africa (Kaplan and Meyer, 1998; Kaplan, 1996).

SANSA hopes that this network will allow expatriates to make meaningful contributions to South Africa's economic and social development by :

(i) receiving South African students in their laboratories or training programmes,

(ii) participating in training or research with South African counterparts,

(iii) facilitating business contracts and

(iv) initiating research and commercial projects, etc. (Kaplan and Meyer, 1998).

It is also important to go beyond just the setting up of the network, but ensuring that it is self-sustainable. From the Colombian experience it is learned that for the South African network to be sustainable, political and administrative commitment is needed. Well-planned technical resources are also needed to ensure proper connection between network members.

Kenya

Shinn (2003) at the Kenya Medical Association recently warned that emigration of medical professionals is threatening the very existence of the country's health services. The Association said that low pay is forcing about 20 doctors to leave Kenya each month to take better positions in other countries. Kenya now has only 600 doctors and 70 dentists in the public sector to treat 28 million Kenyans. The Kenya Medical Association argued that this brain drain has contributed to a general deterioration in medical services for the masses. Increasingly, medical care and health facilities are only available to the wealthy.

Ethiopia

For starters, several persons who have looked at the brain drain phenomenon have observed that prior to the 1974 revolution virtually all Ethiopians who attended university in the country remained at the completion of their work and the vast majority of those who studied overseas returned to Ethiopia. According to one study, only one Ethiopian physician was working outside the country as recently as 1972. The brain drain has not always been a problem in Ethiopia. The environment created during the Derg government as a result of political persecution and the Red Terror was a major turning point. It caused a significant emigration of highly skilled Ethiopians that continues to the present day, although the reasons for the exodus have changed somewhat.

Statistical information on the Ethiopian brain drain tends to be anecdotal, confusing and sometimes conflicting. There are no reliable, long-term macro statistics for documenting the problem. The anecdotal information since 1974 is, however, consistently depressing, especially in the areas of science, engineering and medicine. Dr. Dejene Aredo reports that of the Ethiopian students officially sent abroad for study between the 1968-1969 and 1995-1996 academic years, 35 per cent failed to return to Ethiopia. A study of four government organizations, including Addis Ababa University, indicated that out of every 100 professionals sent overseas for training between 1982 and 1997, 35 did not return. Among female professionals in this group, the number was 43 out of 100. Those trained in medicine were the least likely to return and the higher the level of education, the greater the probability remained in their adopted country.

Dr. Seyoum Teferra, who is with the Addis Ababa University, faculty of education, has investigated the brain drain as it impacts institutions of higher education. In one study he found that out of 135 Ethiopian academic staff who were teaching at AAU in the early 1970s, almost half of them had left Ethiopia by the mid-1980s. The Academic Vice President's annual report for the 1983-1984 academic year noted that more than 300 academic staff had been sponsored for study leave in previous years. Only 22 of them or 7 per cent returned to the university. Another report done in 2000 stated that of the 600 AAU academic staff who were sent abroad during the previous 20 years for further studies, only 200 had returned. The AAU department of mathematics alone lost 17 of its staff. They all have a Ph.D. and they all currently teach in American universities.

Dr. Yoseph Hassen Mengesha, associate professor of physiology at AAU, compiled one of the most thorough accounts of the impact of the brain drain on Ethiopia. In a paper he gave earlier this year to the 38th Annual Medical Conference of the Ethiopian Medical Association, he reported that 50 per cent of all Ethiopians who went abroad and completed their studies have not returned home in the past 10–15 years. During that part of the Derg era from 1980 to 1991, 22,700 Ethiopian students went abroad and only 5,777 or about 25 per cent returned to Ethiopia. A staff of twenty from the faculty of physics went abroad for study in the 1970s and 1980s. All twenty remained outside the country. Between 1980 and 2001, nine physiologists from the faculty of medicine went overseas for additional training; only three returned.

In another survey of all disciplines at AAU, covering the period from the 1981-82 to the 1996-97 academic years, out of 898 staff who went abroad 563 or 63 per cent returned. Interestingly, of those who left AAU and the Ministry of Health between the 1968-69 and 1995-96 academic years to study medicine in the former Soviet Union and Eastern Europe, 79 per cent returned to Ethiopia. On the other hand, between 1980 and 2001, 85 academic staff in the faculty of medicine took positions overseas, leaving only 121 on the faculty in 2001. The primary destination for health professionals is North America, Europe, Australia, South Africa, Botswana and the Gulf States.

The Gondar Medical Science College reported in 2000 that during the previous three years it lost 25 specialists and general practitioners to private clinics and foreign employers. This left the college with 90 instructors—down 40 per cent from its requirement. The departure of medical personnel forced the college to close five departments. The dean of the medical school commented that higher pay offered by private clinics, employment opportunities in other African countries and Gondar's isolation from Addis Ababa were the major reasons for the loss. I visited the medical schools in both Gondar and Jimma last year and can attest to the fact that they are suffering enormously as a result of the departure of skilled medical staff.

Dr. Yohannes Kebede, public health specialist at the Ministry of Health, explained at the 38th Annual Medical Conference earlier this year that Ethiopia trained 2,491 general practitioners between 1988 and 2001. He estimated that one-third have already left the country seeking better employment opportunities in North America, Europe and South Africa. He listed 1,366 physicians working throughout Ethiopia in 2001. This works out to about one physician for 47,000 persons. By comparison, in 1996 there were 1,483 or nearly ten per cent more, physicians in the country. Ethiopia can ill afford this continuing loss of trained medical personnel.

It is clear from this anecdotal information that the brain drain has had and continues to have a significant negative impact on Ethiopia's ability to fill highly skilled positions in all fields of specialization. The result is particularly severe in medicine, the sciences and engineering. Although the magnitude of the problem seems to have decreased since the fall of the Derg, it continues to be sufficiently serious as to merit urgent attention.

Ethiopian North American Health Professionals Association (ENAHPA) is a distinguished organization that is dedicated to transferring medical skills, services and equipment to Ethiopia. The establishment in the African Diaspora of additional groups like ENAHPA could make an important, positive contribution to the economic and social development of the continent (Shinn: 2002).

An Ethiopian Web journal (2004) describes:

> Of the estimated 3.6 million Africans who live in Europe and North America over 100,000 are highly qualified professionals. The World Bank estimates that Africa loses 50,000 executives and 23,000 university graduates every year looking for greener pastures compounding the huge intellectual loss that is brought about by the HIV/AIDS scourge.

Partly to make up for this brain drain, Africa is paying about 4 billion dollars of its development assistance to hire foreign experts on whom it is increasingly dependent in many fields. This undoubtedly is a fairly high cost to an already impoverished continent. The word is that African nations will have to learn to manage and achieve development goals through the transfer of relevant skills and financial resources of their nationals in the diaspora.

The International Organization for Migration (IMO) is one organization, which continues to assist, encourage and mobilize African countries on issues of migration. It has recently adopted a new and improved program to encourage the transfer of vital skills and resources from the African diaspora. Professionals could return to their homeland on a temporary basis or even relocate permanently either to complement local initiatives or to create them.

There is growing recognition that the African Diaspora is a key strategic asset in building its capacity. African intellectual, economic and political assets abroad are a vast reservoir yet to be tapped to achieve the common vision of development. Already, the African diaspora are Africa's biggest aid donors. Remittances account for substantial contributions to increasing number of African nations: in 1999 remittances from migrant workers amounted to 4.1 per cent of GDP in Nigeria, 4.2 per cent in Egypt, 6.4 per cent in the Comoros, and an impressive 16.7 per cent in Eritrea.

In Ethiopia we were hovering in the range of 1.2 per cent of GDP for the years 1996 to 2000. This figure could be higher since most of the money flows through unofficial channels to avoid exchange rate restrictions, high taxes and tariffs, and bureaucratic requirements or because of poor and unavailable financial services. Experts tell us the potential is much higher, if only we could tap it.

There are an estimated one million Ethiopians living abroad today, mostly in the Middle East, Western Europe and North America. Ethiopia Economic Association estimates that 9.4 billion Birr in remittances was transferred in 2002-03, and only about half of it came thru official channels like banks, money orders or the post office. In Addis Ababa there are at least 46 informal local agents (sometimes specialized by regions of transfer). The remittances support families, build schools, finance small clinics and are nothing to scoff at.

The potential for Birr remittances is put at about 17.5 billion and, if fully accessed it could more than bridge the resource gap that exists in the country because of shortfall in domestic savings.

If the skilled livings in the diaspora were permitted to open dollar accounts locally and if the price and hassle of acquiring land were reasonably surmountable, a lot more dollars and skills could flow in maybe even eventually displacing development aid. The cost of land in Addis Ababa does not have to compete with New York City. Home for the family is a primary consideration of any professional who wishes to return with skills and money.

It could help if capital markets were allowed to operate providing an exit strategy for investors who for whatever reason need to cash in and get out. And skills inventory has to be compiled and properly matched with the skills deficit. While we are at it we could do away with the exit visa requirement altogether and revisit the issue of dual citizenship. Ethiopia is not in good company with Cuba and North Korea when it comes to exit visas.

The government has been slow in understanding and appreciating the importance of remittances, although the foreign office has established a directorate for expatriate affairs to encourage professionals to return, contribute and invest in Ethiopia.

Nigeria

David H. Shinn (2002) made an interesting account of the Nigerian Diaspora. Nigeria has a special assistant to the president for the diaspora. More than 2,000 Nigerian doctors work in the United States even though there continues to be a critical need for health professionals in Nigeria. About 10,000 Nigerian academics are employed in the United States alone. There reportedly are more Sierra Leonean doctors living in the Chicago area than in Sierra Leone. An estimated 600 Ghanaian doctors work in New York City, about 20 per cent of its requirement. More than 1,000 professionals left Zimbabwe for other countries in 1997 alone. There are more African-born scientists and engineers working in the United States than there are in Africa. Senegal created a Ministry of Foreign and Diaspora Affairs. Ghana changed its laws to allow dual citizenship to make it easier for the diaspora to return.

Increasingly, African countries, non-governmental organizations, and continental organizations like the African Union and the New Partnership for Africa's Development (NEPAD) Secretariat are seeking new ways to reverse the outflow of African talent.

What are the meaning and the future of the diaspora option in a global knowledge society? Does it make sense to reply on national based intellectual co-operation when communication has become pervasive and multilateral? Why would a scientist wish to collaborate with an expatriate when there are options to collaborate with any fellow scientists in any parts of the world? Meyer and Mercy Brown (2002) study found that it is 'the effectiveness of the links created by a Diaspora/network compared to other possible, virtual, ones.'

Today, there is huge information and it is becoming increasingly difficult to get access to the relevant and useful and translatable into action. This is what the diaspora network provides to its members and users, be they abroad or at home. Technically, through its databases or information system, it focuses on the information, which is useful, especially for building partnerships. Socially, through a common identification, it acts as a community of knowledge and interests breaking the anonymity which hampers consistent interaction, and as a social network setting up the confidence which is known to be crucial connection, the network and its members may expect support from Nation-State entities such as a social network setting up the confidence which is known to be crucial for human transactions and undertakings.

Scientific Diaspora

Recent literature (Meyer, J.B. and M. Brown, 1999) has identified 'scientific diasporas.' These diasporas maintain attachment to their home countries, create knowledge networks of nationals belonging to a certain scientific field that work or study abroad.

A main purpose of these networks is to connect professionals and scientists scattered around the globe who are interested in maintaining contact among themselves. In addition, they are also interested in helping to promote the scientific and economic development of their home countries. These networks may have a link with national governments or be fully independent. Several networks such as Chinese Scholars Abroad (CHISA), The Colombian Network of Engineers Abroad (Red Caldas), The Global Korean Network, The Silicon Valley Indian Professionals Association (SIPA), and several others. 'Scientific knowledge generation taking place in the world to networks, in principle, de-link the contribution of scientists to their physical residence in the home country and thus can be an interesting vehicle or transforming developing countries' (Solimano, 2002).

Indian Diaspora as Brain Bank

The emergence of a worldwide computer software industry has enabled electronically skilled emigrants to disseminate their skills back home. The expansion of the software industry in Bangalore, India, has made possible for Indians educated in the United States, often holders of green cards, to start their own firms in India rather than take lesser positions in Silicon Valley. As a result, governments no longer complain of a brain drain. Late Prime Minister of India, Rajiv Gandhi, had captured the mood when he had said that he regarded Indians abroad as a bank "from which one could make withdrawals from time to time."

Anjali Sahay (2003) argues that in the case of the Indian Diaspora, migration of people has not resulted in 'Brain-Drain' but 'Gain' because:

(i) Brain drain from India in the period 1990–2000 did not hamper the economic development and growth within India.

(ii) Indian Diaspora in the United States did not significantly add to the growth rate in the United States for the given period as compared to other diasporas.

(iii) Members of the Indian Diaspora (NRIs and PIOs) have significantly contributed towards the growth and development in India.

(iv) Financially powerful and politically well-connected Indian Americans have contributed towards improving Indo-American relations, thus overall contributing towards 'gain' to the country.

Dr. R.A. Mashelkar (2004), Director of CSIR, observed that today things have changed back home too. About the Scientific Indian Diaspora, he observed, 'It certainly appears technological creativity and productivity, just like scientific creativity and productivity lies in the abilities of a relatively small number of individuals. We have lost them to the Western world so far. For instance, the cream from the IITs went abroad. We comforted ourselves by saying that if we lost a small number, it didn't really matter. But we didn't realize the implications of Lotka's law—that they were the ones who made a huge difference to the economies abroad. We didn't realize that when we lost one per cent of our top talent, we also lost 90 per cent of the intellectual energy.'

He said that this occurred because we had nothing to offer to these creative people. But the situation has changed over time. He observed, 'Why are foreign companies, some with budgets higher than India's R & D budget, moving their R & D to India?' There are several reasons. First, the cost of R & D here is a fraction of that in the developed world. Last year, the entire spend of India's R & D was US $5 billion, less than the R & D budget of one company like Pfizer alone. A dollar in India delivers so much more. Indian advantage is not just the cost but cost-competence. I heard a presentation by the chief executive of a German software company in Bangalore. He showed the ideas generated per employee in the Indian unit were, on the average, three and a half times higher than in units elsewhere.

Second, there is world-class technical manpower. India has over 250 universities, 1,500 R & D units, several IITs and engineering colleges. India has the world's largest chain of public-funded R & D institutions.

Third, the shortage of R & D personnel in some emerging hi-tech areas in industrialized countries. The companies have to bridge that demand-supply gap by external outsourcing.

The fourth reason is R & D in industries such as biotech, microelectronics, pharmaceutical, InfoTech and new materials has become highly science based. The costs of R & D here also increasing phenomenally. To put one new drug molecules in the market takes Rs. 30,000 crore. Moving to highly skilled but lower-cost countries like India is one solution.

He observed that we have plenty to offer now. As Indian industry becomes globally competitive, it will require people with skills, which have to be globally benchmarked and globally sourced. There will be enhanced competition among institutions, among both Indian and foreign industrial R & D centers, to seek the best brains.

Another implication of India's emergence as a global R & D hub is linked to India's positioning in the comity of nations. Just imagine around one-third of the new knowledge of major firms around the world being produced in India.

Take this fact along with the crucial dependence of the world's big economics on this new knowledge production centre has huge social, cultural, political, economic and strategic imperatives.

The Reverse Trend

The media is full of stories of Indians returning from the US to work with IT, BOP and other technology-related firms. There's a quieter reverse exodus that has gone unreported, but is just as significant. For years, Indian academia has seen its brightest talents move westward, striking at the root of the much vaunted education system that has created the skilled manpower that's snapped up by the thousands by the Microsofts and Sun Microsystems.

But that is changing, quietly yet dramatically. The IITs, in particular, are striking back. Today, when people apply to us, they come with opportunities. They know they are globally connected, so they demand quality. We now have the confidence that we can meet these demands, says N. Sathyamurthy, Dean Faculty Affairs, IIT Kanpur.

"Faculty agrees that when it comes to research funding, it matters little which country you are in. Beyond the seed capital, you have to write proposals to various agencies and earn your own grants, says Avinash Agarwal, who joined IIT in '01" (Zachariahs, 2004).

In another related observation, Peter Drucker (2004), an eminent American economist, who has predicted in the early fifties how computer technology would one day thoroughly transform business, has said India is becoming a powerhouse very fast. "The medical school in New Delhi is now perhaps the best in the world. And the technical graduates of the Indian Institute of Information Technology in Bangalore are as good as any in the world. Also India has 150 million people for whom English is their main language. So India is indeed becoming a knowledge center," said Peter Drucker in an interview to the latest issue of *Fortune Magazine* (2004). The return migrants might have sense this trend too.

There are also some international scenario, which facilitates trigger return of Indian professionals to the mother country. Since September 11, 2002, some 35,000 expatriate Indian Information professionals returned to India.

The exodus of Indian engineers mostly to the United States costs India $2 billion annually, according to a recent U.N. study (Krishnadas, 2001). "Rich nations have been opening their doors to developing-country professionals at a high cost to the home countries," the U.N. study warned. Based on the $15,000 to $20,000 average total cost of providing a university education in India, the country loses as much as $2 billion a year in technical investment.

The migration nevertheless offers countries like India some indirect benefits. "In a global market, people with the right skills will naturally migrate to the high-tech, high-wage frontier, whenever it is," said Nancy Birdsall, special adviser to the Administrator of the U.N. Development Programme. "But we do see signs that when countries create the right conditions, including openness to new investment and new ideas, they can recapture some of what they have lost. The Indians in Silicon Valley are an important part of Bangalore's success" (Krishnadas, 2001).

The loss of professionally skilled human capital is not all bad news if the diaspora can help in facilitating the development in the home country. China is much ahead of India and it has taken prompt action to address the issue, while India's response to the problem is not yet clear. China effectively networks its skilled professional outside and reaps the benefits. They are successful in utilizing the skills of the professionals staying abroad through various ways. The Indian Government has also several policies, but they are not functioning effectively. For example the Scientific Pool Scheme of Council for Scientific and Industrial Research (CSIR) has become almost non-functional (Khadria, 1999: 160). The 'National Register' of Indians abroad was drawn up which totaled 16,000, of this 40 per cent were scientists (Dutt, 1984: 141). This kind of effort at the institutional level has not been taken in proper spirit. Rather most of these are on paper now.

However, some experts say: "Unlike earlier brain drain the recent brain drain to these developed countries, especially to the US will be mostly to India's advantage" (Basu, 2000: 74). The reason, according to Basu, is that "many of these people are plugging back at least some of the money into India, to start companies and for collaborative work. More importantly, there have been large flows of knowledge back to India through these individuals" (Basu, 2000: 74). This brain drain may also serve as a *safety valve* for reducing unemployment in many developing countries like India.

In a recent study on the fiscal impact of Indian immigration to the United States, Dr. Mihir Desai of Harvard University and his colleagues Dr. Devesh Kapur and Dr. John McHale found that 'one million Indians in the United States account for only 0.1 per cent of the total Indian population, they earned the equivalent of 10 per cent of India's national income' (Goswami, 2002). India can tap these vast resources through systematic planning.

Important Role of the Diaspora

Many Indian professionals are not prepared to return permanently to their country of origin but, at the same time, would like to contribute to India's development. The question arises how will they play most effective role? India diaspora can and should be important partners in the development process. They are numerous and many of them are highly skilled. Some have capital to invest. The sooner that Indian diaspora, the Indian government, non-governmental organizations, the international donor community and the private sector appreciate this fact, the faster India can take advantage of this resource. It is important, however, that the Indian government, perhaps assisted by various other agencies, draw up a strategy for making the best use of the skills and knowledge in the Diaspora.

In today's environment, the role that information and communication technology and virtual networks can play can also be tapped. They are ideally suited to a talented diaspora that wants to make a positive contribution. These networks can link Indian professionals overseas with their counterparts back home. Many other countries, for example, Thailand has initiated a reverse brain drain project that is designed to identify and attract experienced. Thai professionals in the diaspora are to participate in mission-oriented projects without requiring them to uproot and return home. India's CSIR made a good attempt which needs further intensification.

Grass-roots initiatives in South Africa and Latin America now link their researchers to their respective diasporas. Ghanaians in the diaspora created a Ghana Association of Distance Learning and Computer Literacy. It has the full support of the government of Ghana and colleagues in Ghana. This same group also established non-profit organizations to solicit financial and in-kind assistance to support activities in elementary and secondary schools.

The Information Communication Technology Task Force of the United Nations has launched the Digital Diaspora Network for Africa in a joint undertaking with Digital Partners, a non-profit organization in Seattle, Washington and CERFE of Rome. The project is intended to promote development in Africa by creating a network of experts and entrepreneurs in computer technology who are members of the African diaspora in Europe and North America. The United Nations Development Programme and the United Nations Development Fund for Women are promoting similar programmes to encourage African development.

Migration is a phenomenon, not a problem. Without efforts to share wealth more evenly, migration will only increase. In this matter, no short-term and obvious solutions exist. Traditionally, such footloose talent has been seen as a liability—so many beautiful minds flushed down the brain drain. But that concept is changing. Now many experts speak not of a drain but of brain *gain*.

References

Fullilove, Michael and Flutter, Chloe (2004), Forget the Brain Drain, a New Global Community of Australians is Emerging, November 17, 2004 http://www.smh.com.au/articles/2004/11/16/1100574465158.html? from=storylhs&oneclick=true.

Herbert, Ross and Guy, Trish (2003), Using Digital and Social Networks to Tap the Diaspora (Solimano, A., 2002).

Krishnadas, K.C. (2001), Brain Drain Hurts Developing Nations, U.N. Reports, http://www.eetimes.com/story/OEG20010719S0088.

Mashelkar, R.A. (2004), The Brains Drain Back. *The Indian Express*, 3rd January 2004, 9.

Mutume, Gumisai (2003), Reversing Africa's 'Brain Drain': New Initiatives Tap Skills of African Expatriates, *Africa Recovery,* Vol. 17 #2 (July 2003), 1 http://www.un.org/ecosocdev/geninfo/afrec/vol17no2/172brain.htm

Sahay, Anjali, Brain Drain or Gain: Case Study of the Indian Diaspora, (Ph.D. Thesis), October 8, 2003 http://www.odu.edu/al/crgs/crgs events/2003-2004/asahay braindrain.htm.

Sahay, Anjali (2004), Reversed Brain Drain and Remittances, Capitalethiopia.com, April, http://www.ethiopiandiaspora.info/articles.asp?id=44.

Shinn, David H. (2002), Reversing the Brain Drain in Ethiopia, delivered to the Ethiopian North American Health Professionals Association on November 23, 2002 in Alexandria, Virginia http://chora.virtualave.net/brain-drain8.htm

Zachariahs, Candice (2004), Reverse Swing: IITs are in for some Brain Gain, *Economic Times*, 12th January 2004, 10.

PART II

GLOBALIZATION, ENVIRONMENT, TRIBAL ISSUES IN DEVELOPMENT

Sixth Schedule of the Indian Constitution: A Boon or a Bane for Tribal Development?

9

Samantha Syiem

Introduction

In the wake of the failure of the government to initiate any participation among the people and to implement the programmes effectively, I will look and question at how the Sixth Schedule of the Constitution especially the role of the Autonomous District Council becomes a barrier to the development process of the State. I will also argue at, given the inexistence of the Panchayati Raj System, how the 'traditional' institutions, which are in one way not being recognised by the Constitution yet its existence is accepted by the Constitution makers therefore making way for the inclusion of the Sixth Schedule, could play a more major part in the development process. The chapter will also analyse the relationship and the overlapping of power between the two institutions that exist along-side each other from the time the Khasi Hills became part of the Republic of India.

Historical Context of the Sixth Schedule

Article 244(2) of the Constitution provides for a Sixth Schedule which shall apply to the administration of the tribal areas in the States of Assam, Meghalaya, Tripura and Mizoram. In this section, I will explain the historical context to understand why a separate schedule is being introduced specifically for this area. While the rest of India has been linked up with one another culturally and politically as part of the chain as it were, at one phase or the other, of history and religiously by the shared caste systemic values which did not penetrate the bulk of the areas in North-East, North-East India has had very short-lived ties with the rest of the country but has similar ethnic groups, social formations and in some cases stronger ties with South East and Central Asia. It was only through the colonial political control that sustained ties were created with the rest of the country without much social and cultural interaction. The Treaty of Yandaboo signed in February 1826 after the defeat of Burma in the First Anglo-Burmese War (1824-1826) was an important landmark in the history of the British colonisation of North-East India. The treaty provided for the renunciation of the Burmese claim over Assam, Manipur, Cachar, Jaintia and their neighbourhood. Assam was immediately annexed to the British Territory and later became part of Bengal (Gassah: 173). The dispute over the construction of road between Guwahati and Sylhet led to the Anglo-Khasi War (1829-1833) and on 11th February 1835, the British introduced the political agency with its headquarters at Sohra (also known as Cherapunji in East Khasi Hills). In 1874, Assam was separated from Bengal and became the Chief Commissioner's Province and Shillong became the Capital of the Province. Under the Government of India Act, 1935 the tribal areas were classified into Excluded, Partially Excluded and Frontier Areas. The Garo Hills, Mikir Hills and the British portion of the Khasi-Jaintia Hills other than the Shillong Municipality and Cantonment area were considered as Partially Excluded Area. The principle adopted in the selection of these areas was that where there was an enclave or a definite tract of country inhabited by a compact tribal population, it was classified as an 'excluded area'. Where, however, the tribal population was mixed up with the rest of the communities and the tribals were substantial enough in numbers, the area was classified as 'partially excluded' (Gassah: 41-42).

Sir Stanfford Cripps, member of the Cabinet Mission, suggested that a powerful committee should be set up to make proposals for the administration of the tribal areas. On the basis of this suggestion an Advisory Committee was set up on 24th January 1947 and the Advisory Committee further constituted a Sub-committee under the chairmanship of Gopinath Bordoloi which is known as the North-East Frontier (Assam) tribal and

Excluded Areas Sub-Committee. The report submitted by this committee appreciated the tribal courts and recommended that the tribal institutions should be retained as safeguards on land, forests, law, education and administration, this could be done through the establishment of District Council. In this report too, it took three factors into consideration for proposing a separate state scheme of administration of these areas which are ultimately called the Autonomous District. These factors are: (a) the distinct social customs and tribal organization of the different people as well as religious beliefs, (b) the fear of exploitation by the people of the plains on account of the latter's superior organization and experience of business, and (c) the fear that unless suitable financial provisions were made, the provincial government might not set apart adequate funds for the development of the tribal areas (*Ibid.*, 43).

Thus the District Councils were carved out under the Part A of the Sixth Schedule of the Constitution of India. The Assam Government enacted the Autonomous District Rules in 1951 and the Khasi Hills district was formed in 1952. It may be mentioned that it was only on the 21st January 1972 that a new State of Meghalaya was formed out of Assam comprising Khasi, Jaintia and Garo Hills districts.

Each District Council consists of thirty members who are elected from the single member constituencies on the basis of adult franchise and not more than four members are nominated by the governor, the members who are popularly known as MDC (Member of District Council).

The Sixth Schedule was therefore designed to confer a considerable amount of autonomy on the tribal people by giving them protection to retain their identity according to their own political genius, politically, socially and economically, through their elected representation and nominated members (Dutta, 2000: 10).

To sum up the activities undertaken by the District Councils, which are outlined in the Sixth Schedule of the Indian Constitution, are:

(i) The Autonomous District Councils look after matters pertaining to primary education (lower primary), which involves looking after the activities of the primary schools, their administration, day-to-day activities, payments of teachers, etc.

(ii) Activity based on forest, which is mostly managed by the ADC.

(iii) Taxation, that is, professional taxes are to be paid by all professionals including business and government employees to the ADC.

(iv) The councils look after activities in fisheries.

(v) Another major activity of the council is public works; it involves building of roads, bridges, pavements, footpaths, digging of ponds, etc.

(vi) Elaka administration, which involves an overall charge of the traditional Khasi organizations.

(vii) Trade and commerce.

(viii) Market regulation.

(ix) Transport.

(x) Control of grazing grounds.

(xi) Control over land resources (Dutta, 2000: 11-12).

As mentioned earlier the Sixth Schedule was introduced to maintain the district culture of the tribal people of the region and also to allow them to develop and administer themselves according to their own genius. Yet it was also found that the Sixth Schedule has further curtailed and reduced the powers and functions of the traditional institutions. Thus, these institutions have to face various changes with the onset of political modernisations and new administrative set-up in the post-colonial state. These new developments thus affected the powers and functions of the traditional chiefs and institutions. Most of their powers and functions were put under the control and supervision of the District Council and the traditional chiefs are now treated as its subordinate officers.

The loss of their powers created a lot of resentment on the part of the traditional chiefs. There are various cases which are being fought in the High Court and the Supreme Court by the traditional associations challenging the rights of administration of the District Councils on certain aspects. The most recent ruling of the District Council on the removal of the Syiem of Mylliem was met with various criticisms from various circles. The Syiem of Mylliem moved the High Court challenging the District Council and the ruling of the High Court went in favour of the Syiem. Such actions by the District Councils have given rise to comments by a noted social worker, Lamare, who observed that, "the removal of the Syiem duly elected through traditionally accepted variant democratic process without following or respect to accepted usages and process of tradition and customary laws, respected even by the alien ruler (British), raised a vital question as to whether the Sixth Schedule of the Indian Constitution works through a channel to preserve or destroy the Khasi identity or culture through preservation of Khasi traditional institutions, such as Syiemships that form part of an integral part of Khasi traditional democratic polity...."

Thus, with the introduction of the District Councils, the traditional arrangement of local self-government became complex with overlapping jurisdiction which I will discuss later.

Given the background of the District Council relationship with the traditional institutions, I will go on to examine how this relationship affect the development process at the village level.

District Councils: A Critique

In relation to the development activities, there are various constraints and deficiencies. Firstly, most of the District Councils have not yet taken over the charge of many of their functions as prescribed by the Sixth Schedule. Also, there is no provision in the development schemes and social welfare to the largest extent possible, the district council have failed to evoke the local initiatives and people's participation in the development activities. The Councils have hardly brought about social and economic changes in the area at all.

Secondly, even in areas where the District Councils could be involved in development work like in water supply by means of providing drinking wells, land reforms, primary education, village border disputes, environmental control, the councils have not been able to properly deliver the goods. There has not been any development activity that was taken up by the council in Mylliem as such. Primary education is one of the activities which the Council has to look after, especially their administration and day-to-day activities. The payment of the teachers is so badly politicised that it has now become a total failure. The teachers were not paid for months and there were allegations of misuse of government funds granted for schools development. The standard of education has rapidly fallen down and of late, the government of Meghalaya has decided to take over control of primary schools.

Thirdly, the most important subject is the duty of the District Council to the tribal people, *i.e.* the protection of the rights to an occupation of land and the resultant land tenure system. But as seen during the field work, the disturbing trend of *benami* where the non-tribals set up business by using a name of a tribal for ownership is becoming an issue of the day. The District Council would by law exercise power to check the unhealthy practices of *benami* but it does not seriously pursue the matter. The people of the village charged the District Council members with receiving attractive bribes from non-tribals in this regard.

Fourthly, most of the members of the District Council are party based politicians. To be member of the District Council is always seen as a testing ground for those aspiring to be members of Legislative Assembly. The members therefore show more allegiance to the party system than to upholding the tenets of customs and tradition; thus the interests of the people have always been overlooked and marginalized.

Fifthly, as mentioned before, the traumatic relationship between the Khasi states or 'Himas' and the District Councils seems to arise out of the 'whims and fancies' of the members of the District Council to suspend and remove any chief which do not seem to agree on flimsy ground. Under the provision of paragraph 3(i)(g) of the Sixth Schedule, it has been constitutionally empowered to make laws with respect to the appointment or succession of Chiefs and Headman. As such, there is a constant tug of war between the District Council and traditional institutions. This has risen primarily because of the 1959 Succession of Chiefs and Headman Act enacted by the District Council which gives overriding powers to appoint or dismiss any Syiem (Chieftain) or Rangbah Shnong (village Headman). The contention of the traditional institution is that the District Councils have no right to dismiss a democratically elected chieftain/headman. The District Council, on the other hand, says that they dismiss a 'Syiem' only on complaints of the electors and the people themselves and not of their own accord. Traditional institutions have always believed that the District Council has always engineered the dismissal of any Syiem who does not toe their line. This power clash inhibits the smooth functioning of governance at the grass-roots level.

The leaders of the District Councils are also not taking interest in plan formulation schemes, implementation or monitoring on various development programmes systematically. They were unable to play any significant role in strengthening the planning process at the micro level. Consequently, the Councils have neither been able to do anything of interest to involve the tribals in development activities either as beneficiaries or as decision-makers on any significant scale. When asked why hasn't there been any significant development work in Mylliem, given the fact, that the District Council gets its major source of funds from the taxes collected from Mylliem State 'Hima Mylliem,'[1] one of the District Council members replied that much of the money goes to paying the staff of the Council and as at present, there is a financial crunch in the Council! However, it is also seen that much of the major sources of funds for the District Councils come from the taxes collected at the tollgates, share of income from trade and commerce, income from professional tax and revenues from forests, shares on royalty on major and minor minerals and taxes from vehicles. The Council is also getting sizeable grants from the government but in spite of such grants no substantial work has ever been done by them. The only activities that the District Council is busy with are the appointment and suspension of Chiefs in the 25 Khasi States and the issuing of trading license. These two activities have often been seen as a major source of income of the District Council, which apart from the legal money that comes in, part of the finance is also earned from corruption and bribes and much of these bribes goes to the individual Member of the Council. Such activities could be done simply because as provided by the Sixth Schedule, the accounts of the district council are outside the purview of the Public Account Committee of the State Legislature. The absence of audit, therefore, leads the elected and appointed officials to political and economic corruption. Even though the State government gave major grants to the District Council, yet the State Government has no power to review or assess the working of these Councils except to approve their legislations by the government and to sanction loans and grants for development schemes. The District Councils are independent in their functions and they do not have to surrender the unspent balances of the grants to the State government.

At present, there is a strong feeling among the local intellectual sections that the District Councils have outlived their utility. They feel that the Councils were needed to preserve the unique culture and tradition of the tribes from the onslaught of the dominant culture of Assam when they were part of that larger State. However, since the new tribal State of Meghalaya has been created, they feel that the councils are no longer relevant as they subsist on getting trading licence to non-tribals and royalties from forests and minerals (letter to the editor *ST,* July 9, 2004 Michael Syiem's article, *ST,* February 10, 2004).[2]

Multiple Power Centers

The 73rd Amendment of the Constitution of India relating to Panchayati Institutions that was passed by the Parliament in December 1992 and brought into effect on April 24, 1993 is going to have an effect on the autonomous District in the states of Assam, Manipur and Tripura from the North-Eastern states. The 73rd amendment stipulates that, "Nothing in this part shall apply to the Schedule Areas referred to in clause (1) and the tribal areas referred to in clause (2) of Article 244."

Article 243 M(2) also says that "Nothing in this part shall apply to (a) the States of Nagaland, Meghalaya and Mizoram,

(b) the hills areas in the State of Manipur for which District Councils exist under any law for the time being in force."

Therefore, the 73rd Amendment was not imposed in Meghalaya, Mizoram and Nagaland because of the existing tribal institutions of governance and as such seeks to protect these institutions from being non-functional. In the case of Nagaland which does not even fall under the Sixth Schedule,[3] in place of District Councils they have Village Development Boards which formulate developmental schemes and programmes of action and is the implementing body of all development work within its area. Similarly, Mizoram has also made sufficient arrangement to administer the development programmes through Development Council without the existence of the District Councils.

To support the Central government's move on not including Meghalaya in the 73rd Amendment, the current Chief Minister of the state argued that he wants the government to strengthen the District Councils and that Panchayati Raj is not suitable as both the District Council and the traditional bodies are the accepted institutions. It was reiterated again in the meeting by the Minister of Panchayati Raj that Meghalaya, Mizoram and Nagaland will continue to have their existing tribal systems of administration, which they still enjoy and some special privileges under the Sixth Schedule (*Shillong Times*, 18th May 2005). If the government declared that the traditional institutions are accepted bodies and if according to the Chief Minister, the Panchayati Raj is not an alternative to it, then the question arises as to why the traditional institutions are not fully involved by the government to pursue its own course of development activities. The answer to this lies in the fact that there are no efforts made at all by the government or by the District Councils to involve the traditional bodies in the course of development. Similarly, there is no effort to enhance the capacity of these institutions that has socio-economic potentials even though the District Council's main duty is towards this end. Though the amount of money that these institutions generated from various sources of taxes and royalties from markets and toll gates in these areas is quite substantial to be able to carry out development work in their respective areas yet they could not do so because whatever activity that they undertake, permission has to be taken from the District Council. The District Council on the other hand takes a certain percentage of money from the traditional bodies and makes use of it for its own purpose excepting development work. To cite an example of this, the Syiem and his dorbar earns approximately 30 lakhs rupees every month from all the markets located within the 'Hima' (State) of Mylliem. The tax from the daily market in Shillong and from other weekly markets from the villages that fall within the jurisdiction of the Syiem of Mylliem generates this monthly income, these sources being the biggest revenue provider for the Syiem and his Council. But in spite of the amount of money that is generated every month, part of the money goes to the District Council. However, the District Council has no interest at all to start any development projects with the Hima leave alone allowing the 'Hima' (State) to start with one on their own.

While different authorities are sorting out their differences, the common man suffers from lack of governance; he does not know where the buck stops and who is accountable for any failure in the service system delivery. Mr. Kharbuli, an active social worker and a sitting Headman of one of the localities in Shillong, explained more on this point:

> I have said this often, that we have too many governments, the Syiem, the District Council, and the State Government. There are instances and circumstances that we don't go to the District Council or Syiem but to the State Government as such, so we don't understand whether we really need the District Council or not, it confuses us. When it comes to legal cases, the District Council is useful; as for such case we go to District Court. Even when it comes to development works, when we go to the District Council there is nothing they could do, so we have to go to the State Government, the District Council does not contribute anything in development, it's just a way to confuse us the people because there is always a clash of power. Sometimes when the State Government in power belongs to a different political party but that of the District Council is in another party, it just

> creates tension among us people, they want to divide us.... From the government the development schemes comes through the Headman, but from the District Council if it sees that the Headman did not support the member of the District Council then it will not come through the headman but goes through another way round, back door method. All this confuses us, they (District Council, State Government and Syiem) do not show that they are responsible at all for the welfare of the people and because of that there is no uniform development at all in our state. The Syiem has the money but his hands and feet are tied by the District Council yet on the other hand he is the one who has a say on land and on giving 'sanat' to the Headman, so you see, we have too many power centres.

Thus as seen, there is a plethora of governing authorities in Meghalaya. As stated before, there is a Dorbar Shnong or village level council. Above it, there is a Dorbar Raij or a council for a conglomeration of villages, and at the top is the Dorbar Syiem or the chieftainship that exerts overall control over two other councils. Apart from it there is the District Council which the people, especially the Khasis, felt is an imposition on their traditional governance systems, it was created by the Sixth Schedule of the Constitution without prior consultation with them. Then there is the State Government with its subsidiaries. However, the relationship between all the above power centres is contentious and the sufferer is the common man.

Because of these multiple power centres, there is a lack of accountability, and because of the lack of it there can be no responsibility and without responsibility, there cannot be proper implementation of projects, policies relating to development or otherwise. According to Sanjoy Hazarika (noted columnist), the heart of governance lies in three factors, which are: innovation and initiatives; combining resources and skills; review, monitoring and transparency. He suggested that if the government takes this approach and acts only as a support system and policy trainer then the role of the people is maximized through involvement and implementation (*Astha Bharati*, June 2004, Vol. 5, No. 4).

De-centralisation in Meghalaya: Alternative Proposals

The Constitutional Review Commission which sat on 2001 has this to say in its report on the system of governance in Meghalaya, and on the basis of its finding has recommended certain provisions:

> In Meghalaya, the District Councils are dominated by the tribal communities. The major tribes of the State are Khasi, Jaintia and Garo. Besides District Councils, there are traditional ruling systems, namely, the Syiems (rajas) of the Khasi Hills, the Dolois of the Jaintia and the Nokmas of the Garos. Of these three, the Khasi traditional polity was regulated under a three-tier system with the Durbar Shnong, *i.e.* Village Council presided by the Rangbah Shnong (headman) at the base, the Durbar Hima, *i.e.* State Assembly presided by the Syiem or the equivalent of a king at the apex. The Dolois of the Jaintia Hills and the Nokmas or traditional Headmen of the Garos are not as well organized as the Syiemships. There are at present competing systems of authority each of which is seeking to serve or represent the same constituency, and the system therefore requires streamlining as per the aspirations of the people. Trends towards militancy in the State can be discouraged through measures leading to self-governance. For this to happen, the traditional systems of governance will have to be included and given specific roles and opportunities instead of being marginalized.

As regards Meghalaya, the Commission makes the following recommendations:

(1) A tier of village governance to be created for a village or a group of villages in the Autonomous District Councils, comprising of elected persons from the traditional systems plus from existing village councils with not more than 15 persons at each village unit.

(2) At present, each of the Autonomous District Councils in Meghalaya consists of 30 seats. It is recommended that this number may be increased by 10 seats, *i.e.* to a total number of 40 seats. Of the 10 additional seats,

having regard to the non-representation of women and non-tribals, the Governor may nominate up to five members from these categories to each of the ADCs. The other five may be elected as follows:

- by Syiems and Myntris, from among themselves to the Khasi Autonomous Council;
- by Dolois from among themselves to the Jaintia Autonomous District Council; and
- by Nokmas from among themselves to the Garo Autonomous District Council (2001, Chapter 9, Part 9.29).

In the above instances, the first recommendation is not at all feasible, there are already Village Councils at the village level and there is no need to create another system. In my point of view, the village council needs to be more empowered in relation with executing development activities and funding of development work ought to be given to them, as these Village Councils are ultimately accountable to the people of their own village.

As seen above, the Constitution Review Committee suggested a tier of village governance within the Autonomous District Council, but a question arises as to why is there a need for a new tier when there is already an existing tier of governance within the traditional institutions. To include such Village Councils within the District Councils will probably give rise to another council that will be again plagued with nepotism, and corruption that we have seen happening in the Community Development Blocks.

With regard to the second recommendation of expanding the seats allotment in the District Councils from 30 seats to 40 seats, whereby from the additional 10 seats, 5 seats would be nominated by the governor and five should be drawn from the different Syiemships (in the context of Khasi Hills), the five seats to be allotted to the traditional rulers are very meager. As known, there are about 25 Syiemships in Khasi Hills alone which have their own Chief or Syiem. Therefore to be able to get their states representation in the District Councils the chiefs would be left fighting with each other for the seats, the review committee did not even take this into context while making this recommendation.

The whole object of the Review Committee is towards the same end and that is to bring all the powers of the traditional institutions under the District Councils by making the traditional bodies rely more and more on the District Council rather than devolving power to them.

However, one point is that the Constitutional Review Committee has recognised the existence of the third kind of authority apart from the State Government and the District Council and that is, the traditional institutions. It also recognizes the role of the traditional institutions especially in an effort to thwart off militancy and the role that it could play in ensuring self-governance. It also calls for streamlining their roles and functions which is very much needed if the traditional institutions assert their rights to have a more active role in the development process of their respective ' himas.' As in the words of Toki Blah, Director International Fund for Agricultural Development, North-East India, "the traditional bodies are strong in governance; they stand bereft of knowledge or basic skills in rudimentary jurisprudence. Strongly democratic by nature, they stand isolated from modern precepts of equitable franchise. Emphatically rustic, they contribute nothing to the economic requirements of the rural communities they serve. Ethnically homogenous, they languish in our inability to mobilize their inherent potentials."

Thus, it is seen that the State and the Central Government through their political hegemony have failed to recognize that economic development cannot be achieved if the people and the traditional administrative functionaries are not fully involved and their role in development is not taken into account. Due to the non-involvement of the people, the State Government could not utilize most of the economic development opportunities in the rural areas. Much of the schemes and projects implemented have hardly made much difference to the ordinary people as seen in the study made. There has been insistence from the Central Government that there should be a transfer of functions and funds from the State Government to the elected Panchayati Raj, this is exactly what is needed for the existing traditional administration institutions of Meghalaya.

While others like noted academician, Dr. B. Datta Ray, recognized the demerits of the Sixth Schedule as not only having failed to inspire the process of democratization of society, but, has developed an identity syndrome which retarded the democratic process in social and economic activities in bringing significant changes at the grass-roots levels. (Datta Ray in Karna, 1995: 20). He also on the other hand decried the traditional institutions as a semi-feudal set up in which most of them have lost their powers and has no role to play in the process of development. According to him, it also lacks basic principles of good governance like transparency, accountability, gender balance and people's participation (Editorial *Shillong Times*, June 15, 2004). Thus to him, the District Councils should be replaced by the Panchayati Raj system which he sees as better placed in matter of development functions and also it gives much hope for the meaningful participation of the people in social and economic development of the local areas at different levels. Gurudas Das too voiced the same concern and called for the 73rd Amendment Act to be implemented in the state and cautioned that it will directly impinge on the constitutional jurisdiction of the District Councils but it will not disturb or affect the tribal political ethos (Karna, 1995: 45). However, I do not see how the introduction of the Panchayati Raj system will not change the 'tribal political ethos', as it will be a new system which will totally replace the traditional system. The system will replace the party-less election of the traditional institutions into a party-based elections and this by itself will definitely have an effect on the socio-political scene at the traditional level. Even the Panchayati Raj itself is not free from constant meddling from politicians, in some states it has been so politicized by politicians that govern the State Governments in these states (*e.g.* Karnataka, Rajasthan and Tamil Nadu). As Dr. Naiar observed that 'politicians would not want their power and status to be reduced, bureaucrats would not want to work under local elected representatives' (*Kurukshetra*, Oct.–Nov., 1996: 96).

As we have seen, the District Council is not doing much in development, leave alone involving the people in the process of development when the District Council itself does not have a major role to play. However, various development workers have made various recommendations and suggestions on an alternative system to the Panchayati Raj. According to Toki Blah (Director, IFAD, NE India), rural development based on participatory model which will be people driven and not target driven, where the government department, NGOs, communities can become active stakeholders and where such development can be entirely owned by the people could be one of the alternatives to the Panchayati Raj system. According to him, this is entirely possible through the existing traditional institutions with or without the involvement and concurrence of the District Councils (editorial *ST*, July 26th, 2004). He cites an example of IFAD led project in two districts of Meghalaya, West Khasi Hills and West Garo Hills. In these projects community based organizations comprising the National Resource Management Groups and the Women Self-Help Groups were set up under the jurisdiction of the traditional institutions which are more effective as according to him the traditional institutions are not castes based, are classless and non-political in character (*Ibid.*). However, it could be taken into context that IFAD being an international organization with funding coming directly from the United Nations and where it is not accountable to the State Government could carry out development activities with or without the assistance from the State Government and on its own implementation designs. The work of the organization in itself is concentrated only in very few areas in the state and has not widen its target and scope in other areas of the state, this left the majority part of the state to depend on government led projects. There has not been any major development projects carried out by any international organization, World Vision has started work among the street children but its work is concentrated only in the urban area within the city of Shillong. Aus Aid has just started to set up its project office in Shillong and is working to prepare a framework for future access to funding towards the development of civic amenities such as sewage, drainage, solid waste and sustainability of drinking water in the city (Editorial *ST*, May 4, 2004). However for most of these activities it will liaise with different government departments which again will not be forthcoming in involving the community in any of its decision-making or implementation phase.

Apart from that, there is also a new organization that was formed under the name of Rajya Sabha Grass-roots Democratic Advisory Councils. This Council is seeking direct funding for development works from the Central Government. In January 14, 2004, the council held a grand 'Durbar' of all traditional states in Nongkrem (about 40 kms away from Shillong). Representatives from different parts of the states representing Syiem, Dalois (traditional bodies in Jaintia Hills) and Nokmas (Chiefs from Garo Hills) gathered together along with 50,000 people coming from different parts of the states, the meeting was considered as the largest gathering of traditional bodies in recent times and is termed as the largest people's assembly. The proposal for direct funding was presented in the Assembly by a member of a consultancy organization, who was in-charge of formulating the project. The Council has proposed a project known as an Integrated Village Development Project, whereby development plans will be prepared at the level of Syiemships and the passing of the plans will be held in an open forum in which it will go through three stages—Dorbar Heh (a conglomeration of all the Syiems, Dalois and Nokmas), then the Dorbar Syiem (at individual Syiemships levels) and lastly at the Dorbar Shnong (village level). It also brought out a tentative budget on how much each village will be getting for various development projects and for training personnel who will be managing the projects.

The project that the Council formulated draws criticism from some of the people who do not support the traditional institutions at all, from the government officers and from the District Council. The District Council sees such move as a power game. It even took a radical position to suspend all the Syiems if they support the spokesperson of the Council in contesting the general elections. This move by the District Council again has been criticised by even some sections of the people who are not in favour of the traditional organizations. Whereas others in the government departments see the move of the Council as having a political agenda especially as it was organized just before the general elections and also because one of the members of the council is an active member of a political party and a sitting member of the Rajya Sabha (Upper House of Parliament).

While members of prominent organizations fighting for the rights of Information, opined that the Council need not ask for direct funding from the Central Government anymore since many of the 'Himas' (traditional states) through the powers of the Instrument of Accession that the Syiems signed with the Government of India, unlike other former princely states of India who signed the Instrument of Merger and who received only a yearly pension from the Government of India, the Syiems are allowed to collect taxes from their respective himas. The tax collected is very substantial but however no development work has been taken up by the Syiem. The organization is in favour of making the Syiems accountable to the people by making them known the amount of money generated through various sources. The money thus collected and generated from different sources should be used for development work. Though these organizations did not bring any recommendation as to ways in which such development should take place.

Thus with the formation of the new State of Meghalaya in 1972, the State has no constitutional power to control and supervise the functioning of the District Council, as both institutions exist parallel with overlapping legislative powers within a single socio-political field. Thus this multiplicity of legislative authority has made the legal system too complex, particularly in relation to resource management, to undertake developmental activities. There have been debates over the years by political scientists and constitutional experts on this issue but not even the constitutional review committee which was represented by only one member from the North-East[4] could not come up with any solution to bring about an administrative structure conducive to economic development which might pave a way to an establishment of vertical administrative linkage whereby less overlap of power could be possible.

Village Councils: A Future Role

Given the fact that such overlap of power and functions can only be rectified by a constitutional amendment, case might take years to come through. Therefore the issue in hand is how to strengthen the existing institutions operating at different levels especially the ones working at the grass-roots level. One such institution that is very active and performs a variety of roles and functions at the grass-roots level is the Dorbar Shnong or the Village Council, which occupies the third tier in the traditional political set-up.

Though certain writers like John Harris and Apurba Baruah has refused to acknowledge that this institutions is old enough and they claimed to be 'an invented tradition which appears until the 20th century and is the creation of a small educated tribal elite about 1920s who were themselves responding to the early initiative of the British Colonial government to establish local government' (Harris, Crisis State Programme, Working Paper No. 13, 2002, London LSE, www.crisesstates.com). However, Helen Giri and Hamlet Bareh argued that village councils has been in existence long before the British came to the Khasi Hills, they both quoted a British official who had to attend a village *'Durbar'* or village parliament at Nongkhlaw in 1820, who said, "I was struck with astonishment at the order and decorum which characterises the debates...every speaker was fairly heard out. I have often witnessed the debates of St. Stephen's Chapel, but those of the Cossya (Khasia or Khasis) parliament appear to be conducted with more dignity of manner"[5] (Giri, 1996, quoted from *Memoirs of David Scott*, 1832: 52). Hamlet also states that the village dorbar was a 'social institution and was also known as dorbar blei, *i.e.* council of god.' Thus the dorbar has religious significance which fixed strict disciplinary rules, treating the durbar with contempt even result in excommunication.

The present-day 'Village dorbar' or *dorbar shnong* in a Khasi village is usually held once a year and when certain important matters comes up, the dorbar is held as many times as needed. It is also responsible for maintaining law and order and it does so by sanctioning some rules and regulations known as *adong shnong* by which residents of the village has to adhere strictly. Similarly judicial functions relating to crime and land disputes are often taken up by the 'dorbar shnong' but critical cases which cannot be dealt with by village councils were transferred to the *Dorbar Hima* in which case the Syiem and his council will decide upon it. Similarly it decides on fights, divorces, ex-communication of incestuous couples, boundary disputes and petty thieves. It also organizes functions like community feast during religious holidays, football matches, archery, and traditional dances. Over the years with the introduction of various governmental programmes and schemes, the council also works together with government agencies for implementing these schemes for development work. However, the relation between the village council and the government is often volatile marked with conflicts and tussle of authority.

The *rangbah shnong* who is the head of the *dorbar shnong* is a powerful decision-maker relating to the activities of the village. The State Government seems to be dependent on the *rangbah shnong* for information relating to household numbers, BPL households and permission for any developmental work is often given by the *rangbah shnong* and his council. Thus to sum it up, the *rangbah shnong* acts like a magistrate, a police officer and an administrator of the village, however he is an unpaid official for all the work he does.

Dorbar Shnong therefore enjoys a *de facto* legitimacy which it derived from its own community by acting as an arm of the state which has the system of coercion and patronage. This also is seen in the fact that their word is law within their own jurisdiction and is respected and obeyed even more than the edicts of the government (*ST* editorial, May 4, 2004). The fact that some of the localities in the city and the villages do not allow a policeman to enter the village until permission is sought from the *rangbah shnong* and proves the point that the *dorbar shnong* has an unwavering authority and influence.

But it is however no denying that over the years this institution has gone through a process of change and function in different ways as to what had been practiced during the 19th century. Traditionally, members of the founding clans of the village are usually reserved to occupy the high places in the durbar, but with time, education and knowledge of the bureaucratic machinery of the State Government seems to be the first criteria in choosing the headman, this is particularly true in the case of Mylliem. This is because, firstly, many men who belong to a certain clan originally from the village married outside their own village and most of the men who are *rangbah shnong* in Mylliem migrated from other villages to marry women from that village. Secondly, a person chosen to be a *rangbah shnong* would have to be literate,[6] this is necessary as the *rangbah shnong* has to deal with a lot of administrative functions of the village and also with the government.

In his study on "Ethnic Conflicts and traditional self-governing institutions: A study of laitumkhrah dorbar" Apurba Baruah shows that many of the durbars especially those located in the Shillong city are fast losing their traditional character and are incorporating more modern liberal democratic values into its functions. He cites an example of a dorbar in a locality of Shillong which issues notices to its residents on issues relating to inspection of trading licence of business houses in the locality. These types of notices issued by the *dorbar shnong* show that there is formalization of the system at present whereas some durbars have their own constitution concerning the administration of their own village and locality (Baruah, Working Paper No. 39, January 2004, London LSE www.crisesstates.com).

There have been critiques against the traditional institutions that they are lacking in accountability and transparency (M. Karlsson, Seminar Paper, Interpreting Adivasi Social Movements in South Asia, University of Sussex, 13). However, I will argue here that if these institutions are not legally recognised and if their role and functions are not spelt out clearly in the Constitution of India, there is no binding force which could make these institutions accountable and transparent in their work.

Similarly, other critiques of the traditional institutions often brought out the issue that the traditional institutions are not democratic enough, given that women are not allowed to participate or attend dorbars and as such the traditional institutions are not gender sensitive enough. But John F. Kharshiing, Spokesperson of the Federation of Khasi states,[7] opined that the traditional institutions are so flexible, non-formalized, and are based more on convention that the issue of women not being allowed to participate in the durbars can be bend. In fact it is noticed that some of the villages in Mylliem have opened up the Durbar doors to the women too. Similarly women representing 'Seng Khynthei' (women organizations) in the city also form part of the locality durbars. These instances show that there has been significant break with the tradition in the past. One of the reasons for this gradual change is the role that the educated elites have on most of the durbars and in most villages or localities people holding good positions or just serving for the government are often elected as President, Secretary of these *Durbar Shnongs*.

Therefore, if durbars could accommodate such changes then, as Apurba Baruah points out, there is an influence of constitutional democratic governance on tradition as various interpolations of constitutional procedures could be seen in the functions of traditional governance.

If these institutions, particularly the *dorbar shnong*, has a space to change and that the functions are not static but dynamic in character, then it could play a more prominent role in the development process of the village.

Therefore, in conclusion, I can say that given a plethora of authorities working parallel to each other which instead of generating efficiency in its role and function however gave rise to conflict amongst them, the effect of which led to the stagnation of development in the area. Because of the overlap of power that can be rectified only by a constitutional amendment, I believe that strengthening the village councils that represent the grass-roots will bridge the gap between the people at the village and the government and will ensure success in the development process. This could be done by involving the village councils in decision-making, implementation and evaluation of the development programmes, these will create a sense of participation, a sense of belonging and a sense of possession and ownership of the programmes, but most of all it will create a sense of responsibility and accountability for the people.

Notes

1. The word 'Hima' is used here to mean the Khasi State, *i.e.* Hima Mylliem means the State of Mylliem. However, other writers use the term 'hima' to also mean kingdom.
2. Also Toki Blah's article on Reforming Schedule Sixth, *Shillong Times*, Dec. 3rd, 2003.
3. Nagaland disagrees to be included in the Sixth Schedule as it maintained its right to secede from India.
4. P.A. Sangma, former Lok Sabha Speaker, represented the North-East in the Constitutional Review Commission.
5. This parliament was held to debate on the permission to be granted to the British to build a road passing through Nongkhlaw which will connect Sylhet and the Brahmaputra valley. The Nongkhlaw dorbar passed a resolution allowing the British to build the road, the effect of this is the beginning of the British colonization of the Khasi Hills which also led to the Anglo-Khasi War, 1829-33.
6. While some of the headmen in Mylliem hold good positions in the different department, there are others who have done till the secondary education.
7. The Khasi chiefs formed the Federation of the Khasi states in 1956 with the objectives: to preserve the rights and customs of the people, to act as an intermediary between the khasi states and the government, to act as a Supreme Court appeal for the Khasi in the country, to assume legitimate control of affairs relating to the Khasi states, to demand higher judicial powers and autonomous bodies (Constitution of the Federation of Khasi states, date not cited). However, the federation did not function for some years and was revived again in 1990.

References

Baruah, A., Ethnic Conflict and Traditional Governing Institutions: A Study of the Laitumkhrah Dorbar, January 2004, Crisis State Programme, Working Paper Series No. 1.

Blah, Toki, Reforming Sixth Schedule. *Shillong Times*, December 2, 2003.

Blah, Toki, Traditional Institutions and Urban Governance II. *Shillong Times*, May 4, 2003.

Datta Ray, B., A Case of Panchayati Raj in Khasi Hills. *Shillong Times*, June 15th, 2004.

Gassah, L.S. (ed.) (2000), *The Autonomous District Council.* New Delhi: Omsons Publications.

Harris, John, The State, Tradition and Conflict in the North Eastern States of India, August 2002, Crisis States Programme, Working Papers Series No. 1.

Hazarika, S., Governance: Approach Issues Innovatively with Pro-people Emphasis. *Astha Bharati*, June 2004, Vol. 5, No. 4.

Karna, M.N.; Gasa, L.S. and Thomas, C.J. (eds.) (1995), *Power to People of Meghalaya*, Indian Council of Social Science Research, North Eastern Regional Centre, Shillong.

Nair, K.V., With People's Participation. *Kurukshetra*, Oct.-Nov., 1996.

Report of the Constitutional Review Commission, 2001.

Syiem, Micheal, Less of Government the Better Government I and II. *Shillong Times*, February 9-10, 2004.

Adivasis Shining: Standing up to the Face of an Invasion of Aluminium Companies in Orissa*

10

Felix Padel and *Samarendra Das*

"India Shining" was used as a slogan in India's 2004 election. It backfired because most people's experience did not at all reflect the sense of prosperity implied in these words. The aluminium industry is at the centre of India's new vision of itself as a budding superpower, as laid out in a book written by India's President, *India* 2020 (Abdul Kalam 1998). But *behind the shining* this industry has a very dark side which few people know much about, destroying and polluting some of the world's best mountains, rivers and forests, and dispossessing thousands of indigenous people from their land and sustainable lifestyle (Wysham, 2001).

This paper focuses on tribal people's resistance to what is officially termed "development-induced displacement," and in particular, against the aluminium industry's escalating exploitation of their environment. The account and analysis we offer here of what is happening in Orissa examines the local situation as well as the foreign pressures behind it. In mining confrontations, indigenous communities meet the most powerful of vested interests: elements of the power structure which controls the world situation as a whole. This being so, it does not make sense to analyze a tribal movement without analyzing the forces which are imposing themselves over tribal people, which they are resisting for all they're worth.

As we write this paper, their movement is facing vicious repression by company thugs as well as police. On 27th March

* Based on a paper presented by Felix Padel at the Sussex University in March 2005.

2005 Sukru Majhi, a tribal activist in Kalahandi district, was run down on the new road to Lanjigarh by a vehicle that reversed over him and crushed his head to make sure of his death. Kucheipadar village in Kashipur is virtually under police siege now. On 25th May a journalist who had joined tribal demonstrators had his video camera smashed by the police at Tikiri, near Kashipur—part of a pattern to suppress the movement and prevent its expression: at least 6 journalists were filming the demonstrators from the side of the police. But essentially this movement is not against development: it is a movement to uphold Adivasis' most basic rights to their land and standard of living—rights written into the 5th Schedule of India's Constitution. A movement to assert people's right to choose their own path of development. For them, a dam or mining project which displaces them is no development at all. Quite the opposite: it causes a massive drop in their standard of living. In the words of Kishen Pattnayak—a political leader in the true Gandhian tradition, who was most influential on people's movements in Orissa and India as a whole, until his untimely death in September 2004:

> The first step of mining is displacement. In Orissa there is not a single successful story of rehabilitation by the government of displaced families, who otherwise have been surviving on the natural resources of the area by living peacefully since hundreds of years on their own land.

About 20 of Orissa's biggest mountains are now in the eye of the world's aluminium companies, because the bauxite that lies in a layer near their summits is classed as one of the world's best deposits of the raw material for aluminium. Two of these mountains are under immediate threat from mining projects which are also trying to build alumina refineries nearby: Bapla Mali from the Utkal project in Kashipur, which the movement has stalled for over twelve years, and Niyamgiri from the London-based Vedanta company in Lanjigarh, which is presently constructing a refinery despite a Supreme Court ruling which questions its legality. Local movements to stop these companies are recognized as among India's most important campaigns by social and environmental activists in India and abroad: the living edge of the global anti-capitalist movement, which activists everywhere could learn and take inspiration from.

Orissa has a strong tradition of people's movements, since the time of Gandhi and before. Gandhi took his symbolic *dhoti* style of dress from Orissa, among many other connections. During the 1940s, the tribal leader Lakhman Naik was executed for attacking a police station near Koraput during the "Quit India" movement, becoming a symbol of tribal people's struggle for justice. After Independence, when big dams started to displace Adivasis by the thousand, there were large movements to resist. These were quite ruthlessly suppressed by the police. Even their history is little known. In the case of the Upper Indravati project, involving 7 large dams, a strong local movement did not survive intense police suppression, with lathi-charges and arrests in 1992.

The network of big dams on Orissa's rivers was actually planned during British times with a view to powering aluminium plants. Mining also began then of coal and iron-ore in the mountains of north Orissa. These mines and the metal factories they feed have left a trail of devastation on mountains, forests, rivers and tribal communities. The tide started to turn in 1987 with the success of the Gandhamardan movement, which stopped bauxite being mined on a mountain range in west Orissa. Since then, other movements have stopped a missile firing range at Baliapal, a Tata steel plant at Gopalpur, and a Tata shrimp monopoly on Chilka lake, among others. But the present Orissa Government headed by Naveen Patnaik has staked much on a massive new wave of industrialization, based on mining, and striking deals with numerous mining companies, in the belief that exploiting the State's rich mineral resources will transform Orissa from poor to rich, and pay off its debts. In the Orissa Assembly on 4th Dec. 2004 Naveen Patnaik stated:

> No-one—I repeat no-one—will be allowed to stand in the way of Orissa's industrial development and the people's progress.

But who defines the people's progress?

Basically what is termed "development" in tribal areas of India, has become a mask for quite gross forms of exploitation and corruption. This is certainly how most of Orissa's Adivasis now see it, and any objective sociological analysis would have to conclude that they are right. As the leading journalist P. Sainath observes in his book "Everybody loves a good drought," huge amounts of money go for "tribal development," very little of which benefits tribal people at all. Most of it feeds various forms of corruption. As for big "development projects"—these have had a destructive impact on tribal people's lifestyle for several decades now. Big dams and factories which displace existing communities are the antithesis of development for nearly every *adivasi*: everything they valued is annihilated. In the tribal villages near Lanjigarh we are witnessing this right now: forest, rock formations, fields and villages systematically erased all around the refinery construction site.

"Development projects" in Orissa have dispossessed at least a million Adivasis since Independence—probably over 5 million. The largest numbers have been displaced by big dams. Of these Hirakud was the first, near Sambalpur in NW Orissa, where a huge dam in the 1950s displaced about 285 villages—at least 160,000 people—no proper statistics have been kept for any of these dams (Viegas, 1992). Its foundation stone was laid by the last British Governor of Orissa, and then again by Nehru himself. One of the main reasons for the dam was to provide power and water to an aluminium smelter nearby. Several of Orissa's mega-dams since then were also built to power aluminium plants—the State already has 2 of India's 6 aluminium smelters, and is planning 2 more (Hindalco and Vedanta) in a huge further industrialization near Hirakud. The Upper Indravati reservoir is the most recent big dam project to be completed, financed by loans from the World Bank in the '90s, and displacing an estimated 99, mostly tribal, villages—at least 40,000 people. It turned the river from its southward path to go north to join the Tel river, from where the Lanjigarh project is trying to take its water now: huge pipe sections have been placed ready for laying over a distance of about 50 kms.

But more are being planned for immediate construction. Right now work is about to start on a Lower Suktel dam project in Bolangir district, displacing at least 26 tribal villages. Already the authorities have tried to force people to accept advance compensation, though most have refused, and police beat up Adivasis in early May, when they were protesting against a *Bhumi Puja* for inaugurating the construction work on this dam. How can a Ritual honour the Earth (*Bhumi*) when Adivasis are dishonoured? A few days later on 11th May, Ho tribals from Chandia and other villagers staged a protest against a *Bhumi Puja* at "Kalinganagar" (Jajpur district), where the authorities are setting up a 4,000 sq km "industrial park," starting with construction of a steel plant by Maharashtra Seamless Steel. We have seen film footage which clearly shows the authorities disarming seated Adivasis of their bows and arrows, before attacking them with *lathis*, the event culminating in a woman run over by a truck and killed, and many arrests. Around 24 women were arrested and kept locked up for over 3 weeks, with their children, two of whom died.

The plan for a huge-scale integrated aluminium industry in Orissa goes back to the colonial era, and was outlined by the British geologist Cyril Fox in the 1920s—the mountain-top mines, the series of aluminium factories, the big dams tapping Orissa's hydro-potential to power these factories, and the rail links were all spelt out. Now, 80 years later, these dams have been built, the railway extended, and the leases for the bauxite mountains and sites for aluminium plants are matters of high-powered, mostly secret negotiations. However, since October 2004, Orissa opposition parties and press have exposed an extreme level of corruption in these negotiations, involving numerous legal irregularities and bribes paid by aluminium companies to senior members of the administration and Government. The promise is—Orissa is to get developed and rich fast. What isn't said is that the whole history of such projects in mineral rich areas, tends to suck their inhabitants into a vicious cycle of industrial poverty and dependency, where all the profit vanishes abroad and into the hands of an elite, along with the basic resource: a cycle known as the "resource curse" (Ross 1999). The mining and industrial areas in north Orissa and the neighbouring States of Jharkhand and Chhattisgarh are nearly all situated in what were once tribal areas of outstanding natural and cultural value. The majority of Adivasis get jobs with difficulty and at the lowest level in the hierarchy: labouring in conditions close to a form of slavery. What has their sacrifice achieved? How are we to understand what has happened to them, as sociologists, or historians, or simply as fellow humans? Are they "more advanced" now? Or has their former standard of living been degraded? And what has their sacrifice achieved "for the Nation"? Who has profited?

This is the age of corporate power, and companies wield an influence that's central to today's power structure. The rise of this kind of power in Orissa follows the course of the same phenomenon in Britain and America, and has been promoted everywhere by the World Bank among other agencies, which in Orissa works closely with the DFID (Department for International Development) of the UK Government. What's interesting in an Indian context is that British power in India was first established during the 17th-18th centuries by one of the world's first and biggest companies: the East India Company, which laid out the very system of administration which still defines the Government of India. How the EIC took power—the whole story of complex, legal and financial manipulation—bears a striking similarity to the increasing power which foreign institutions and companies have gained recently in India.

The modern story involves massive loans, which have demanded further loans to repay former loans, and these further loans have had hidden "conditionalities" attached, which have forced the "liberalization" process onto India. This has meant the removal of laws that protected individuals and restricted the activities of foreign companies. In particular, a law was passed in 1993 which eased foreign mining companies' rights to Indian mineral deposits. Orissa is India's heavily indebted State. It can only repay its loans + interest with massive further loans. Obviously, behind closed doors, the Orissa Government has been told the only way out is to open up their mineral assets to foreign companies. And in a way, perhaps this is why Orissa entered the debt trap—lured there by projects which created the initial phase and infrastructure for future foreign-controlled mining projects. The loans ensured it is the Government, and even more the people of Orissa, who bear the real cost, while foreign companies get the profits.

The present deals with foreign mining companies are part of the promotion—by WB economists as well as sections of the Indian Government and private sector—to promote FDI (Foreign Direct Investment). Yet the main profits from FDI go abroad (Woodward, 2001), and in mining, the foreign companies are actually gaining control of India's most precious of resources: the mineral deposits. In other sectors such as electricity and telecommunications, foreign companies such as Enron have pulled off notorious scams in India, and the evasion of responsibility for the Bhopal disaster by Union Carbide/Dow Chemicals shows the kind of dangers which foreign companies pose. But with mining companies the danger and exploitation is at an altogether different level, because minerals are "the starting point of value-creation" in world finance. They are also a non-renewable resource. From their natural placing in the earth they ensure the land's fertility. So the damage from mining them is irreversible, both for nature and for indigenous communities.

Companies are slippery customers to analyze sociologically, partly because they merge into each other, by owning shares in each other and staging take-overs, and also because key people at the top move in and out of senior positions in Government. From the Indian Government to the present Bush administration in the US, corporate heads have become top Government officials (and *vice versa*) through "revolving doors," and company interests dictate Government policy, to the extent that elections make increasingly little difference to any policy that involves important company interests. Adivasis have a comprehensive understanding of this, from meeting company power close to, at its rawest. A song from Kucheipadar, *Kompani Hawa*... ("Company Wind..."), summarizes the changes which "the company" has brought to Kashipur. The local people have seen many faces of "the company." They understand that when the Utkal consortium was first formed in 1993 it consisted of INDAL

(Indian Aluminium), Tata and Norsk Hydro (Norway's biggest company, specializing in dams, aluminium and fertilizer). Now the same consortium consists of Hindalco (= Aditya Birla) and ALCAN (Aluminium Canada): yet it is essentially the same, and the police and local Government acts as an extension of "the company," so complete is their support and co-ordination. In terms of the basic power structure and aim of exploitation, is not this almost exactly the same situation as when "the company" (meaning the EIC) was extending its power all over India?

Aluminium companies (here called al.cos. for short) are among the most powerful companies today. Their power is much less visible and known about than the oil companies, *e.g.* for their role in supporting America's wars. Yet they are probably as powerful behind the scenes, because they supply the "strategic metal" that is of greatest importance to the arms industry. For this reason, it is worthwhile trying to understand the aluminium companies that are invading Orissa, and their history here.

The first Orissa mountain to be sold for bauxite mining was the biggest, in Koraput district of south Orissa—Panchpat Mali ("Five-fold Mt."). This is mined by NALCO (National Al.Co.) —a public sector company set up in the 1980s. The Government tried to privatize it in 2003, but Nalco employees + a large section of Oriyas fiercely resisted this and for the moment it remains one of India's most profitable public sector companies, and "the pride of Orissa." Below the mountain, Asia's biggest alumina refinery reduces the bauxite to aluminium oxide. This is the Damanjodi refinery, which directly displaced 19 tribal villages—about 3,000 people, though it has indirectly affected many more. A rail extension then carries about half of this alumina to Vizag on the coast for export, and about half to Nalco's aluminium smelter at Anugul in central Orissa. The whole project involved collaboration with France's biggest al.co. Pechiney—now merged with Alcan. The power and water for the Damanjodi refinery comes from the Upper Kolab dam, which displaced at least 16,000 people from about 60 villages.

Nalco's profit comes from the quality of Orissa's bauxite, because it has a low in silica content, and can therefore be refined at a lower temperature than most other bauxite; and also from the low labour costs, relatively lax environmental standards, cheap electricity and water supply, etc. This is why other Indian and foreign al.cos. are competing for the other bauxite mountains: they stand to make a huge profit in Orissa because getting bauxite cheaply is the "starting point of value creation" for al.cos. All these mountains have an unusual massiveness—no sharp contours: the largest are 15-20 km in length, and sometimes several kms wide. They are flat on top, which is convenient for mining. Some are well-forested even on their summits, others are largely bare now, but nearly all have a ring of trees on the small cliff that runs around the summit. There is a lot of evidence that the high aluminium content of these mountains is a key factor in the outstanding fertility of Orissa's forests and agriculture, and that mining the bauxite reverses this fertility and sets in motion a process of desertification: bauxite no longer acts as a "sponge" at the top of the mountain, collecting and storing water during the rainy season for slow release through countless streams throughout the year.

The next mountain to be leased for bauxite mining was Gandhamardan in west Orissa, where BALCO (Bharat Al.Co.)—another public sector co.—tried to start mining in 1985. Here it was confronted by a strong movement representing an alliance of Adivasis, Dalits and a wide range of social activists, including devout Hindus, because this mountain is famous from the Ramayana, and there are two outstanding medieval temples on its sides, one of which was damaged by initial blasting on the summit. Basically, the local people blockaded the mining road up the mountain, which Balco had built. Environmental clearance had not been given, and the Ministry of Environment came down on the side of the activists: Gandhamardan is superbly forested from top to bottom, and it was clear that the streams which start from the mountain-sides would have been badly affected, and thousands of human lives over a wide area jeopardized. Balco built a colony of several hundred flats for its workers. These were never used. The jungle's taken them over. They stand as a symbol of misguided development, and a tribute to the strength of the Movement that stopped this project, and the hundreds of people who courted arrest and police beatings.

Women played a vital role too. When the men were in jail, the women at the blockade placed their babies in front of the police and mining vehicles and challenged them to run them over, since they would have no future if the mountain was mined. The vehicles backed off.

The next project to come up was the Utkal consortium in Kashipur, an isolated, mostly tribal block of Rayagada district. It was led at first by Indal, which was originally set up as a subsidiary of Alcan in the 1940s. The project faced stiff opposition from local villagers, mostly but not all Adivasis. This opposition in turn met vicious repression by the police along with towns-people who supported the project, believing it would make them rich. The Adivasis have for the most part remained remarkably non-violent, while police and town thugs have repeatedly beaten up Adivasi activists, or arrested them. The worst case took place in 1998, when a leader called Mangta Majhi from a small village called Ramibera, right on the site of the proposed alumina refinery, was abducted by police at night, who came, according to fellow villagers, in Indal company vehicles. They tied him up with two Dalit men from a neighbouring village—in such a way that they had to clean each other's backsides after defecating. In other words, humiliation was a key aim. Mangta was beaten up so badly in police custody that his face was a mess when he was released after a few days, and he died soon afterwards. Mangta owned some of the key land wanted for Utkal's refinery. The details of his abduction have never been brought to light, but they're important, because this was apparently the movement's first death. On 16th December 2000, Kashipur made world headlines when three more tribal people were killed by police firing into a crowd of protestors. The police had gone to Maikanch village to break up a meeting that was organizing a road blockade. Basically politicians and journalists had gone there the day before to try and stop the meeting, and probably to provoke a reaction. When they were driven off by the Adivasis with minor injuries, the politicians called in the armed police, who opened fire during the encounter.

Several little known facts are deeply significant surrounding the Maikanch firing. One is that the Utkal project had been made a centre-piece of the World Bank's "BPD" programme—Business Partners for Development: the idea for companies, Governments and NGOs to work together for development. The only Government that got heavily involved was Britain through the DFID. Within the month before the firing, the WB had organized local meetings with Kashipur leaders from the various communities and political parties. Feelings on both sides had been running high. At the same time a DFID-sponsored study by Ian Barney from Swansea had been studying the situation. Barney also visited Kashipur just before the incident, and described how he was threatened by local towns-people, who were armed, and made access to Maikanch difficult; and how he met local politicians (all three of the main parties had joined in support of Utkal), who spoke of the pro-mining lobby as "patriots," and the anti-mining tribals as "traitors" who were "anti-development" and "anti-Government." Immediately after the police firing the Utkal project was removed from the WB's BPD website without explanation.

An enquiry was held into the causes of the incident, which took about three years. We attended one of its sessions on 29th May 2002, in which an Adivasi woman and a Dalit woman appeared as witnesses, as well as a senior Utkal official. The two women kept their hands together in a Namaste/Johar supplication the whole time they were in the dock, in an obvious appeal for justice. It was amazing to see how the company lawyers tried to trip them up with devious questions, and how they tittered at their answer to the judge's question "Occupation?" which was "*Chaso*"—"cultivation"—implying: these people are just peasants. When excerpts of the report were made public in October 2003, they appeared to condone the firing, and to justify the project as a whole, while making token criticism of the police officers who took wrong decisions. In November 2004, after a lull of several years, police suppression restarted with a vengeance. Several Adivasis from key resistance villages were beaten up and arrested. Some are still behind bars. This was to try and stop the 16th December commemoration (which was attended by several thousand nonetheless), and to clear the ground for the Orissa Chief Minister to lay a foundation stone in January (which did not happen). The police have also been building a new post 2 km from Kucheipadar—one of the largest and best kept Kond villages we know, and which police have barely entered since the late '90s. On 8th June, Adivasi protestors in Guguput village blockaded the road and turned back company vehicles. A week later on the 15th police *lathi*-charged a meeting in the same village, and used tear-gas, a significant escalation, putting tribal villages on a par with big urban confrontations.

What happened to the consortium has been most instructive. Tata left first: it had faced similar protest movements against "development projects" elsewhere in Orissa. After the police killings Norsk also left: it had faced pressure from Norwegian activists over previous human rights abuses in Kashipur. As for Indal, it had been bought up by Alcan (its parent co.) and sold on to its rival HINDALCO (Hindustan Al.Co.). This company was formed by a collaboration between the American al.co. Kaiser and India's key industrialist Birla in the 1960s, building the vast Rihand dam in U.P. (another project disrupting thousands of sustainable village lives) to power a refinery and smelter at Renukoot. Kaiser has now gone bust, but Alcan remains one of the world's key suppliers, especially to US and UK arms companies, so has evidently taken Kaiser's place in relation to Hindalco. Alcan is now facing activist pressure in Canada from a protest group called "Alcan't in India!," who express solidarity with Orissa's Adivasi Movement, and have the undertaking of Alcan factory workers in Canada that they will refuse to take alumina mined in Orissa.

Meanwhile, 100+ kms to the northeast, another company has made swift preparations for a bauxite mine and alumina refinery at Lanjigarh: Vedanta, or Sterlite, headed by Anil Agarwal. As Sterlite, it bought up Balco in 2001. In Dec. 2003 it launched itself on the London stock exchange as a UK-based company called Vedanta Resources. Locally the project is now "Vedanta Alumina Ltd." While some villages of the local Majhi Konds, in the plains just north of Niyamgiri, refused all offers, several were persuaded to accept compensation in cash plus a concrete house in a newly built "colony" nearby—now named "Vedantanagar." In Jan.-Feb. 2004 the police came and ordered these out of their villages, giving them only a day or two, before moving them to this colony in trucks. Their villages were immediately bulldozed to clear a space to construct the refinery. As a woman said to us a few days later: they all bitterly regretted accepting compensation. They had lost everything they valued: the houses they or their forefathers had built, the fields they had worked all their lives—they would never grow their own food again—their livestock, "*amoro devata bi*"—"even our gods": the main deities of a Kond village reside in a group of *darni*-stones embedded in the centre, which had been bulldozed along with the rest.

As for the villages nearby that had refused compensation—when the Collector of Kalahandi district came to them some months before, and tried to persuade them to accept, he said they would get rich and drive tractors, and when they still refused he got angry and said their village would be destroyed anyway and he would never come there again. This Collector, Saswat Mishra, has played a key role in pushing this project through. The refinery site was inaugurated by a foundation stone laid by Orissa's Chief Minister, who came by helicopter along with Anil Agarwal, Brian Gilbertson, representatives of J.P. Morgan and other key foreign players. Agarwal is the head of the Sterlite-Vedanta group of companies, now resident in the UK where he is listed as among the richest of the rich. Gilbertson was the highest paid Chief Executive Officer of any company in 2003, when he left BHP Billiton to head Vedanta with Agarwal for several months, evidently to set it up in London. Another Director of Vedanta was Sir David Gore-Booth, an ex-British High Commissioner to India, which shows the kind of stakes involved. J.P. Morgan, one of the world's leading investment banks, played a crucial role in arranging the funding for the Lanjigarh project, which was also briefly advertized on the website of the DTI (Department for Trade and Industry of the UK Government) for its investment and employment opportunities—until a British activist questioned this, when the entry was withdrawn without explanation. It is also known that senior officials from the DFID in Orissa played a key role in bringing Vedanta to London.

Local Adivasi activists destroyed the foundation stone the next day, but the refinery site was soon defined by a big, Palestine-like wall several kilometres in circumference, which left the refusing villages just outside. Though they have held out against compensation, their condition by June 2005 had become desperate, surrounded by worksites which are eating into their land. Many of the villagers themselves are now breaking up the rock-formations under contractors, making them into stone chips for construction—their resistance undermined by severe and continuous pressures. They do not actually work inside the refinery site, where they say conditions are extremely harsh, and at least 100 labourers have been killed in "work accidents" that go largely unreported. Most of these labourers have been brought in from distant areas. The villagers are also certain that several human sacrifices have been performed on the construction site or mountain, of children kidnapped from nearby areas. Oriya anthropologists who have studied industrialization say that no big project gets under way in the State without at least one human sacrifice, which can be understood as part of a debased tantrism. Even educated people believe in its power. Proving this would be near impossible, of course. The "social fact" is that the local people are convinced this is so, and the extreme harshness of work conditions is agreed on by everyone concerned, as well as the violence of pro-company thugs based at Lanjigarh, who have beaten up non-violent Adivasi demonstrators on a number of occasions. This culminated in the killing of Sukru Majhi in March 2004: one of the most active of activists, who was run down near his own village of Kansari when he was returning from a meeting at Panimunda. This happened on the newly metalled road from Lanjigarh to Dhoikal and Muniguda. It is one of the best roads in the area now, but his death shows the true cost of such "development." Human sacrifice takes many forms.

Another form is evident in Balco's operations in Chhattisgarh, west of Orissa, where a refinery-smelter complex originally built in the 1970s with Soviet help is being rebuilt with direct London finance. Balco's centre is at Korba, named after the elusive Korwa tribe, who were displaced in large numbers to make way for this complex and the city which now stands around it. One of the main Balco mines is on Mainpat to the north (Surguja district), where a mountain 40 km in length is covered with mines in between the numerous tribal villages. Here the mining is done by hand, and the labourers are given no facilities for education. There is no electricity, and no compensation if they meet an accident. Balco is setting up a new mine near Kawardha in the west of the State, in an area of the greatest natural and cultural sensitivity, which has already displaced some families of the Gond and Baiga tribes. Everyone on Mainpat agreed, and so did workers at Korba, that their work conditions have got much harsher since Sterlite/Vedanta bought up Balco. This sale was notorious for its undervaluing of Balco's assets at about a tenth of their real cost. Also notorious have been Sterlite's tax evasions and siphoning its profits out of India via its holding company Twinstar, based in Mauritius, and insider trading on the Bombay Stock Exchange (Bidwai, 2001). This shows why the main population at Lanjigarh will never get rich from the project: it is streamlined for creating a profit in London. The whole history of such mining projects has been one of gross exploitation. Sterlite's history of financial manipulation shows that it is one of the sharpest practitioners.

The Konds at Lanjigarh feel overwhelmed. As Daising Majhi of Belamba village said in 2004, when construction had barely started: "They want to flood us out with money." This is the village now surrounded by construction work on every side. Numerous non-tribal activists have visited them and offered support in the past, but a number of these have been arrested or beaten up. Others support them from a distance.

A number of cases are now being investigated by the CEC (Centrally Empowered Committee) of India's Supreme Court in Delhi, which sent a team to Lanjigarh in Dec. 2004, and has ruled the project illegal on a number of counts, involving unauthorized clearing of forest land, etc. and though the company has gone slow on its mining preparations on top of Niyamgiri, the refinery is being built at full speed below. On

15th June, the CEC paid the Lanjigarh project a second visit, at which a large number of people raised objections and pointed out legal irregularities, in the presence of the Collector.

In Kashipur the tribal people are from three main groups: Konds, Jhorias and Pengos. Lanjigarh involves the Majhi and Dongria Konds. *Kuwinga* is Konds' own name for themselves. There is considerable evidence that they are the same people as the *Kalinga*, whom Ashoka slaughtered and enslaved so many centuries ago. Even from 19th Century Gazetteers it is clear that as Orissa's Rajas near the coastal areas came under British control they threw out large populations of Konds, in order to make their lands more "profitable". These joined the main concentration of Konds in central-west Orissa, where they number at least a million—Orissa's largest tribe. The Konds' main deities include Darni Penu, the "Earth Goddess," and Sora Penu, the "Mountain God".

Mountains are central to the Kond religion. In fact, Census officials asking Konds their religion often got the reply simply *Pahar*—Mountains, according to an anecdote in Gopinath Mohanty's autobiography. The big Mountains are always sacred places. Niyamgiri is the place of origin for thousands of Konds, both the Dongrias, who live in 200+ villages in the folds of the mountains, and the Majhis in the plains below. It is an interesting fact that the base rock of these mountains, below the bauxite layer, was named Khondalite by a geologist called T.L. Walker (Fox, 1923). Appropriate, since these mountains are central to Kond spirituality, while the Konds turn out to be the mountains' most important protectors. Living in close proximity, they understand that all their life comes from the mountains, and depends on them, via the streams that start from their sides, and the forest that clothes them holding the soil together. They rarely venture onto the mountain tops without good reason, and have a taboo on cutting timber there, which is why such excellent forest survives on this summit. But they come here for *pujas*, and the singing in trance of their *Bejunis* ("female shamans") on these occasions is beautiful and powerful beyond words.

So why all this fuss about bauxite and aluminium? The fact is, the history of the aluminium industry is inextricably linked with the history of big dams on one side, and the history of the arms industry on the other, and as a result has a vital connection with modern finance and speculation too. This means that sources of bauxite and potential plant sites involve a high level of political pressure by foreign governments behind the scenes. What's happening in Orissa is a classic case, following patterns set by the industry in Guyana, Surinam, Haiti, Jamaica, Guinea, Ghana, Sierra Leone, Brazil, Australia and New Zealand. In each case, local populations were promised that the industry would bring them great prosperity. In each case, it did not, because of controls kept by the al.cos. and their supporting Governments, involving highly subsidized water and electricity rates, a very low price fixed for the bauxite itself, and a system of creaming the lion's share of the profits off to the company directors abroad, and their associates. The reason for this clout is the close dependence of arms manufacturers on a constant, relatively cheap supply of aluminium.

In terms of what it really costs to produce it, including the exceedingly high human and environmental costs, aluminium should be priced far higher than it is. To give just one example of the many costs which are classed as "externalities" to the aluminium industry, and therefore not counted: a recent report by the Department for the Environment of the UK Government calculates the financial/environmental cost of one ton of carbon dioxide emissions at $56-223. It takes 20.6 tons of CO_2 to produce one ton of aluminium (if the smelter is coal-fired—5.6 if it is hydro). Multiplying the higher figure by 20 makes $4-5,000. Yet a tonne of aluminium is traded for about $2,000. Other "externalities" not calculated include the environmental cost of other, equally damaging smoke emissions from aluminium plants (including fluoride and fluorocarbons). Also the highly contaminated "Red Mud" that always pollutes the groundwater near a refinery, and in the Lanjigarh case, is actually planned for in such a way that it is bound to release such pollutants into the Bamsadhara river, right at its source below Niyamgiri. Also not counted is the cost of subsidizing water and electricity to aluminium plants. Without such subsidies (which means: costs taken on by local Governments, which actually fall on local communities), making aluminium is simply not profitable. This is one of the extraordinary yet basic facts about the industry which are revealed in a US policy document from the 1950s (Anderson, 1951), published for 50 cents—facts which have been well-concealed from everyone except top planners ever since—and Dewey's pamphlet is not available in a single British library. Aluminium's hidden history is thus a sordid and complicated tale of manipulated prices, and of unbearable costs falling on indigenous communities and their natural environment and basically destroying them.

Aluminium's "strategic" value to the arms companies—to America's "permanent war industry" in particular, which Eisenhower called its "military-industrial complex"—is obviously a key reason that these costs are hidden and transferred like this. And while Britain closed down most of its manufacturing industries during the Thatcher era, we have kept the arms industry—what's euphemistically called aerospace—as the basis of our economy, because it is the most lucrative and "strategic." We know that Balco had a contract (presumably inherited by Sterlite/Vedanta) to supply aluminium to India's nuclear weapons programme. As for Alcan, it is a key supplier to the UK (and US?) weapons industry. Vedanta Resources at Lanjigarh has obvious financial and Foreign Office backing from London. Probably the kind of supply it offers of cheap aluminium from India (even specifically from Orissa) has been planned for many years.

To summarize this connection between aluminium and arms very briefly: a little-known invention was made in 1901 that virtually defined the violent course of the 20th century: thermite. An alumina refinery separates aluminium oxide (Al_2O_3) from other minerals, using huge amounts of energy and water and causing great pollution. Al_2O_3 is a white powder, which is made into metal in a smelter. This is done by splitting the aluminium from its bonding with oxygen in molecules of aluminium oxide, by applying a tremendous charge of electricity. Supply of this electricity has been a main reason for the building of mega-dams from the first decade of the 20th century up to the 3 Gorges Dam in China and a big dam presently being constructed in Iceland. Thermite reverses this process: a bomb is packed with iron oxide and aluminium powder. When the fuse ignites, the aluminium leaps to the high temperature of its "heat of formation" to re-bond with oxygen, making the explosion very large: this was the basis of the First World War hand grenades, the Second World War incendiary bombs and napalm, and the "daisy cutters" used by American planes for "carpet bombing" from the Korean and Vietnam wars to Iraq. Aluminium is also basic to the technology of nuclear missiles.

Apart from actual bomb technology, the whole development of modern fighter planes took off with the use of aluminium alloys during the 1930s. Aluminium companies made huge profits from both World Wars, and became the centre-piece of America's "permanent war industry" from the start of the Korean War in 1950 till today. All the arms used in the Iraq war bring profit *via* the arms companies, to the al.cos. Since the First and Second World Wars, al.cos' profits soar when the military hardware is being used up fast. War is the al.cos' best business.

But alongside these military uses, and in effect subsidized by them, is the increasing use of aluminium in other industries: especially in building construction, car manufacture, and packaging. Aluminium is promoted as a "green metal" because a most insignificant percentage is recycled, while its reality is that it is one of the most highly polluting of all industries. The waste in the form of Red Mud released by Refineries (approx. one tonne for every tonne of alumina) is highly toxic and pollutes large areas, invariably infecting the groundwater. Smelters release some of the worst greenhouse gases, and poison surrounding areas with fluoride, which produces a terrible wasting disease in nearby villages. For this reason, both Orissa's existing smelters (at Hirakud and Anugul) are also opposed by local movements which seek to control their expansion or close them down. Both are being greatly expanded nevertheless.

Until around 1990, senior Government officials in both India and the USA wrote reports saying basically that aluminium consumption should be kept to a minimum, because of the high cost of producing it, in subsidies, as well as to the environment. Since then, there has been a reversal: an aggressive move to up consumption enormously in all uses. India is considered "backward" because its average consumption per person per year is less than one kilo, compared with around 30 kilos in the US!

These details are important for understanding the Orissa movement, to comprehend what exactly the Adivasis are up against. The power system they are challenging is not just the aluminium companies themselves, and parts of the Indian/Orissa Government determined to promote their projects, backing them up with tough force from the police, etc. It also involves much more hidden pressure from foreign governments and financial institutions, which are under pressure in turn to ensure a huge supply of aluminium at an advantageous price. In other words, what they are up against is a system of exploiting India's natural resources far faster and at a far greater cost than anything which even the East India Company devised. The whole process of "liberalization," from the point of view of Adivasis threatened by these mining, dam and factory projects, is a mask for destroying their land for outsiders to make a quick profit from its minerals or hydro-potential.

So when the WB and DFID call their programmes "poverty elimination," most people in Orissa can see that this is the opposite of what they are really promoting, even if it is made hard to understand how and why this is so. For many involved this is no doubt a self-delusion too, but if one analyzes the power structure as a whole, the grants for social welfare, etc. coming from abroad mask a really quite monstrous system of control and exploitation. When one examines the way the whole system of WB loans has worked, and the real reasons for constructing Orissa's big dams—far from eliminating people's poverty or raising Adivasis' standard of life, they have done the complete opposite.

So, again we come back to the point that for Adivasis, these projects are not development at all. If pushed to admit this, another strand of thought comes into play which justifies their displacement as a "sacrifice" they have to make "for the nation's progress." Essentially, this is the modern idiom of human sacrifice—the "price of progress" in an endless stream of modern "consumer durables"...until we destroy the whole earth? These assumptions have been particularly questioned by Kishen Pattnayak in the Indian context. We've been asking ourselves these questions recently, because those opposing these projects have sometimes been labelled "anti-development," and some of our own ancestors in the 18th and 19th centuries, played a leading role in the industrial revolution. A belief in industrial progress was virtually the guiding belief of their lives. So what has changed since then? And what does it mean now to support or oppose a programme of intensive industrialization?

The lifestyle we take for granted now, in towns and cities, is full of metals, and getting fuller: from vehicles of all kinds, to aluminium foil packaging our foods, to the highly complex uses of metals in laptops and mobiles. A lifestyle that our species probably cannot sustain for very long. The mines, factories and dams that feed it cause enormous pollution to water, air and earth, and a depletion of limited oil and mineral resources. India's water-table is going down everywhere, and the rivers that used to flow with such force are so dammed and polluted that in many places they have reduced to a slimy trickle of their former power. The trouble is, we are caught in a habit of wants and needs that is constantly growing, fed by companies' competition for profit.

By contrast, Adivasis' lifestyle has sustained their village communities for centuries. Their custom forbids taking too much from nature. Nothing is wasted. Pollution is almost non-existent. People take pride in living frugally and not having more than their neighbours. As one tribal elder said to us, from a small village near Phulbani, "We're all saints here. Where are the saints in your society?"

Yet, instead of giving tribal culture the respect it deserves, mainstream society tends to denigrate it: to look down on it, perceiving it through negative stereotypes—"primitive," "backward," "ignorant," "uneducated," "superstitious," "lazy," etc.—which tually turn the truth on its head. In many ways, in their understanding of nature and how to live sustainably,

Adivasis are a lot wiser and more advanced than mainstream society. This word "sustainable" is used a lot nowadays, but almost the only way of life that is really sustainable—over a period of over 2,000 years since Ashoka's time for instance—is Adivasi village life. When the word is used in development projects and especially in talk of "sustainable mining," the word loses its way and becomes a lie: the phrase "sustainable mining" began to be used from around 1999, when the world's 10 biggest mining companies met to launch a project they called "Mining, Minerals and Sustainable Development" (MMSD, part of their Global Mining Initiative), to see how the mining industry could "contribute to the global transition to sustainable development." The whole exercise has been basically an exercise in "greenwash"—the use of politically correct language to mask the truth. As it is generally used now, "sustainable mining" simply denotes a project that can sustain worthwhile profits for a number of consecutive years! The long-term vision—how to plan to live sustainably for the next 2,000 years—is completely absent from the corporate perspective, and there is a pervasive blindness to the fact that our limited resources are being permanently destroyed for the sake of short-term gain—to the fact that "*current forms of extraction, and the trend for ever-increasing extraction and consumption of mineral products is totally unsustainable...*" (Evans, 2002).

The Khondalite mountains in Orissa have stood for millions of years. The bauxite on their summits acts as a sponge to hold the monsoon rain and slowly release it during the year, feeding the streams and rivers, and releasing minerals that nourish the land's fertility. This is the mineral wealth of Orissa, as well as of neighbouring Chhattisgarh, which faces a similar situation: from its natural placing at the top of mountains, this mineral wealth constitutes a tremendous storehouse of fertility for the soil, supporting forests and fields for thousands of villages and a great wealth of wildlife. What kind of planning destroys all of this for ever for a few years' profit riding the world's currency markets? The mined-out and industrial areas of Orissa, Chhattisgarh and Jharkhand are virtual deserts. This devastation of nature and culture has all happened within the space of a few years.

The Konds viewing their mountains as *Devata*—what could be more realistic and logical? They understand that the mountains give life. Our scientists, company engineers, and political leaders have apparently lost this understanding. Even referring to the minerals in these mountains as "resources" to be "utilized" brings an ideological distortion. For those living near these mountains, they are not "resources" but quite simply the *sources* of life.

One stereotyped argument that is often repeated, which was first used against Verrier Elwin, is to distort any positive view of Adivasi society or idea that they should be allowed to remain in their villages on their own land, into the intention to "keep them in a museum"—"Do you want to keep them in a museum? How can we let them remain in their primitive state?" To understand the origin of this stereotype, one needs to see the role which anthropology played during British times. Many administrators and missionaries wrote books about the tribes of central India. The theoretical or ideological framework almost without exception is "evolutionist": they promote the idea that tribal society represents a "primitive stage of development." Modern anthropology rejects this view, and looks on tribal societies as no less sophisticated than mainstream society: more developed than us in many areas, less developed in others. The areas where tribal societies are more highly developed than us include a huge sensitivity and knowledge about relating to nature—in effect, the art of living sustainably. At the same time as they wrote their ethnographic volumes which defined tribal societies through negative stereotypes, anthropologists also set up museums which displayed tribal artifacts, and even lifesize models of tribal family groups (in Bhubaneswar museum for instance), which again emphasize the idea that Adivasis are "primitive." The museums "preserve" tribal culture by taking their tools, instruments and dresses from villages and placing them in museum cases to gather dust, where their life as objects of daily use simply dies. Everywhere, ethnographic museums have supplemented a political reality of systematically destroying tribal culture. In the US, countless such museums preserve beautifully the artifacts of tribal peoples who suffered genocide from the European settlers and soldiers. In Orissa, this process of death-by-museum continues today. Alongside the Damanjodi and Kolab dam development projects which dispossessed thousands of tribal families in Koraput district during the 1980s, the authorities paid for an ethnographic museum in Koraput town, to preserve a memory of the cultures they were destroying.

"Genocide" is not too strong a word for what is happening to Orissa's Adivasis: a slow death. Not literally the physical death of every individual, as happened in the paradigm case of America's or Australia's tribes. But a psychic death: technically, "ethnicide"—the killing-off of cultures. And without their culture, seeing the sudden confiscation of the land where their ancestors lived and the collapse of their communities, no longer able to grow their own food and forced to eke a living through degrading, exhausting coolie work for the very projects which destroyed their homes. Orissa's displaced Adivasis exist in a living death, witnessing the extermination of all they have valued. The fact that their artifacts and traditional hand-made, home-dyed bark-cloths are safe in museums adds insult to their loss: they too are preserved in a living death.

So "preserving them in museums" is part of the genocide. And their traditional lifestyle, which Adivasis everywhere now are risking their lives to maintain, is not primitive at all. It is highly developed and sustainable.

According to the Fifth Schedule of India's Constitution, it is the duty of the Government to uphold tribal people's rights to their land, and even when a "development project of national importance" has been determined upon, to consult with communities and compensate them properly. This has not happened, as Kishen Pattnaik pointed out, in even a single case. The Panchayat (Extension to Scheduled Areas) Act (PESA), passed in Dec. 1996 and based on the findings of the Bhuria Committee from 1993 to 1996, extended Panchayat rights in the Schedule 5 (*i.e.* tribal) areas of India. A key provision is that tribal land can only be acquired after proper consultation with the local Panchayats. This consultation process has been conspicuous by its absence in Kashipur and Lanjigarh.

The Samatha Judgement in 1997 was a victory in India's Supreme Court for Adivasis' Constitutional rights as against mining companies' attempt to acquire their land in collusion with State Governments. Several State Governments, including Orissa, have tried to deny its validity, although its main point of law is quite clear.

To summarize, the movement we are discussing should be understood as a vital expression of civil society against forced dispossession by the al.cos. In Kishenji's words:

> The politicians, social workers and pro-people intellectuals should start thinking in this direction: are mines a bane or a boon to the indigenous people? They must take a clear stand. Have they any evidence for the idea being propagated that leasing out mines to the companies will benefit and make the people and the state prosperous? Why will not the people resist such projects when there is no evidence supporting this propaganda?

In Kashipur, resistance is focused by the PSSP (*Prakrutika Sampad Surakshya Parishad*). On the whole their movement, like similar movements throughout central India, is scrupulously non-violent, despite facing extensive violence from police and company toughs. While the majority of those active in the movement are Adivasis, because they have the most to lose, and the very roots of their culture and way of life is threatened, large numbers of non-tribals are with them. It is instructive to witness how this support has been misrepresented by the Government and media. The Government has blamed certain NGOs for instigating the movement especially Agragamee, which has a base near Kashipur. Yet, people at the centre of the movement reject any role for the NGOs, and some even accuse Agragamee of dividing the movement, since it worked together with IFAD and the OTDP (Orissa Tribal Development Project) between 1988 and 1993, before blaming its partners for not consulting the villagers properly and leaving what turned out to be an IFAD-funded infrastructure for the entry of the aluminium companies.

But Government repression is tending to drive Adivasis in numerous areas of Orissa, as well as Chhattisgarh, Jharkhand, Bihar and Andhra Pradesh increasingly into the Naxalite camp. The underlying system of exploitation is so pervasive, and legal redress is so limited, basically because most police and lawyers are of the same class as the exploiters and gain a share of company largesse. The Naxalites or Maoists offer an attractive alternative to people who have suffered years of exploitation and humiliation, even though Naxalite/Maoist power structures are sometimes as hierarchical and disrespectful of people's sustainable lifestyle and traditional values as mainstream society. Like companies, they represent an arbitrary, unaccountable power. They also invite police retaliation. In a sense, if violent repression of the non-violent movements against industrial projects drives displaced people to follow the Naxalite-Maoist path, this makes it much easier for repressive elements in the State Governments to use greater violence to try and crush them. Already they claim many supporters of this movement as Naxalites to justify attacking them. Thus, police brutality is tending to drive non-violent movements into a more violent path. At present the main supporters of this largely Adivasi movement advocate non-violence. The *Samajvadi Jan Parishad* (Socialist People's Union), a political party founded by Kishen Pattnaik, which can be characterized as a true successor of Gandhi's movement, has been prominent in its support, which is articulated through articles in *Bikalpo Bichar*, a bi-monthly Oriya magazine of alternative thinking.

The enemy exploiting India's resources and oppressing the people now may still be foreign control, but it is not as visible as when the British ruled India directly. A foreign way of relating and valuing comes down to one single value: profit. The Company exists purely to make a profit. The effects of its actions on people are considered irrelevant. It represents a totally hierarchical, unnaccountable power, with no long-term safeguards at all. Its psychology, that of a psychopath. One significant contrast in the Indian context is the *Arthashastra*. Interestingly, that text does focus on the creation of wealth through mining, but insists that the State should own and control all important mines and not allow them to get into private hands. Mining companies play a crucial role in the creation of wealth out of minerals in the present world economy. Their's is the rawest exploitation, especially because their metal factories use exorbitant quantities of water and electricity from poor areas, at highly subsidized prices, and create exceptional pollution. Aluminium companies in turn supply the arms companies. During the 1920s, there was a widespread understanding that arms companies were a prime cause of the First World War and other wars. There was a move at the League of Nations to get the selling of arms for private profit banned. This was quashed by company lobbyists (Sampson, 1977). Where is this understanding now?

The aluminium companies form a cartel, in effect controlled by key financial institutions and Government heads, particularly from Washington and London (part of whose history is outlined in Stiglitz, 2002). As with mining enclaves all over the Third World, the Orissa Government has been made lavish promises of rapid wealth creation by foreign companies and Governments. Yet again, the promises are believed, and the people's interests are sold out. India's own mineral deposits are starting to come under a kind of foreign control that will not be easy to limit or control. This is the significance of the wave of protest currently sweeping across Orissa, where villagers are meeting a kind of repression they associate with the past horrors of British rule: "*You're our Government! How can you let this happen?*" The companies, with the backing of foreign Governments that depend on a constant supply of metals at the cheapest possible rate, know how to manipulate the rules and technologies to ensure that none of the main profit stays in Orissa, or only in the hands of an elite sold out to serve company interests. In Kishenji's words:

> Orissa has enormous mineral reserves. This is considered to be the biggest asset to increase the prosperity of Orissa. This is really a myth. Mining areas of Orissa have never been known for being rich or developed. Now the condition is becoming much worse.... A few national/multinational companies and their contractors and those ministers and officials helping these companies in unlawful, unethical manner become the owners of huge property. Orissa as a

> state is not going to get any benefit from this.... Overall the state and the people will suffer the loss, only a small class of rich people will be created. Rich will become richer, poor poorer. Mining is a curse to the indigenous people and the environment.

Orissa's movement to stop the al.cos. thus represents a real continuity not only with Adivasi Movements going back to the Santal Hul and Birsa Munda in the 19th century, but also with what is called India's Freedom Struggle. In fact, this is India's freedom struggle, on-going. Financially, India started to re-lose its Independence as soon as it began to get loans from the WB in the 1950s. At the end of the Second World War, Britain was in debt to India from the war loan. Within ten years, this situation had reversed: India had been persuaded to take big loans for dams and industry from the World Bank, etc. and its cycle of indebtedness had begun. The exploitation represented by foreign mining companies—as well as other companies taking up privatized electricity, telecom and water units, and covertly promoted by the DFID—is an extreme form, similar in essence to what happened under the EIC, and through similar legal and financial contortions. Obviously—not just in India. But the tradition of people's movements which India established in her struggle for independence gives this particular movement a significant place in the global movement against company power. Kashipur's Adivasis have started to understand that they have solidarity and support from many people in the so-called "developed" countries. They are the real heroes, facing the direst dangers, at the forefront of what's inadequately called "anti-globalization"—the movement to try and stop capitalism's further, insane excesses.

The power structures they face are basically the same as what Gandhi faced. When police open fire, and fire to kill, as at Maikanch and on many other tribal protests over the last 20 years, this follows the example set by General Dyer, giving his Gurkha troops the order to fire on the crowd in Amritsar in 1919—"to teach them a lesson." The movement's aims are similar to those of the *swadeshi* movement too: campaigning against foreign/outsider control and exploitation of "resources," which these people—like Gandhi—understand clearly are actually the sources of life. The scale of displacement for Adivasis is something far worse than anything before independence—dispossession from their ancestral land, like the bogus "treaties" that stole native Americans' land, and the Highland Clearances that cleared Scotland's remoter regions of their native clansmen in the 19th century: Cultural Genocide. The move to industrialize tribal areas involves a sacrifice of human life at many levels: a select number of violent deaths to "set an example" and instil fear, work deaths in the unsafe conditions on construction sites and in the aluminium factories themselves (at least 200 have died in the Damanjodi refinery's 20 years), and a living death for countless thousands of "displaced persons." And not least the sacrifice of future generations' quality of life. This is a movement to save us all from the brink.

References

Anderson, Dewey (1951), *Aluminum for Defence and Prosperity.* Washington: US Public Affairs Institute.

Bahuguna, Sunderlal (1986), A Voice from Gandhamardan. *The Sunday Statesman,* 27th April, 1986.

Bakan, Joel (2004), *The Corporation: The Pathological Pursuit of Profit.* London: Constable.

Barney, I.; Ota, A.B.; Pandey, B. and Puranik, R. (2001), *Engaging Stakeholders: Lessons from Three Eastern India Business Case Studies.* Swansea: Centre for Development Studies and Bhubaneswar: Resource Centre for the Social Dimensions of Business Practice.

Bidwai, Praful (2001), Balco's Privatization. *Alternative Economic Survey 2000-2001. 2nd Generation Reforms: Delusions of Development.* By Alternative Survey Group. Delhi: Rainbow Publishers, Azadi Bachao Andolan & Lokayan.

Caufield, Catherine (1997/1998), *The World Bank and the Poverty of Nations.* London: Pan (Macmillan).

Evans, G.; Goodman, James and Lansbury, Nina (2002). *Moving Mountains: Communities Confront Mining and Globalization.* London: Zed.

Fox, C.S. (1923), *Bauxite and Aluminous Occurrences of India.* Calcutta: GSI Memoirs, Vol. xlix.

Kalam, A.P.J. (1998), *India 2020: A Vision for the New Millennium.* Penguin.

Monbiot, George (2000), *Captive State: The Corporate Takeover of Britain.* London: Macmillan/Pan.

Moody, Roger (2005), Ravages through India: Vedanta Resources plc Alternative Report, Nostromo Research Report by Mines and Communities, London and India Resource Center, New Delhi.

Mosse, David (2005), *Cultivating Development: An Ethnography of Aid Policy and Practice.* London: Pluto.

Padel, Felix (1995/2000), *The Sacrifice of Human Being: British Rule and the Konds of Orissa.* Delhi: OUP.

Pattnayak, Kishen (2004), An Introduction to *Out of this Earth: Orissa's Indigenous Lifestyle and the Aluminium Cartel* by Felix Padel and Samarendra Das.

Philip, Viegas (1992), The Hirakud Dam Oustees: Thirty Years After. Enakshi Ganguly Thukral (ed.), *Big Dams, Displaced People: Rivers of Sorrow, Rivers of Change.* Delhi: Sage.

Rich, Bruce (1994), *Mortgaging the Earth: The World Bank, Environmental Impoverishment and the Crisis of Development.* London: Earthscan.

Ross, Michael Jan (1999), The Political Economy of the Resource Curse. *World Politics,* No. 51.

Sainath, P. (1996), *Everybody Likes a Good Drought: Stories from India's Poorest Districts.* Delhi, London: Penguin.

Sampson, Anthony (1977), *The Arms Bazaar: The Companies, the Dealers, the Bribes, from Vickers to Lockheed.* London: Hodder & Stoughton.

Sheel, Alok (2001), *Strategy Paper on Aluminium Tariffs for India*, Delhi: Rajiv Gandhi Institute for Contemporary Studies, Working Paper No. 23.

Stiglitz, Joseph (2002), *Globalization and Its Discontents.* London: Penguin.

Thakaran, Siby (ed.) (2002), *The Nowhere People: Responses to Internally Displaced Persons.* Bangalore: Books for Change.

Woodward, David (2001), *The Next Crisis? Direct and Equity Investment.* London: Zed.

World Bank Development Policy Review, 14 July (2003), *India: Sustaining Reform, Reducing Poverty.* Washington, Report No. 25797-IN.

Wysham, Daphne (2001), *Behind the Shining: Aluminium's Dark Side.* Washington: IPS/SEEN/TNI (unpublished MS).

11

Fortress Conservation and Accumulation by Dispossession: The Case of the Shoolpaneshwar Sanctuary in the Narmada Valley

Judy Whitehead

Introduction

The Sardar Sarovar Project, as the first stage in the much larger Narmada river project, has involved not only the construction of a large dam and an extensive canal system, but also the creation of the Shoolpaneshwar Wildlife Sanctuary. This involves a sizeable extension of the former Dumkhel Slothbear Sanctuary, from 5,300 to 68,000 sq. hectares. The sanctuary construction was included as a conservation adjunct to the dam, in order to meet the World Bank's environmental guidelines regarding biodiversity conservation. It is projected to displace an additional 38,000 to 40,000 people who are not covered by the Narmada Water Disputes Tribunal Award and are therefore not eligible for land compensation as are others in the submergence area of the dam. Like other parks, biosphere reserves and wildlife sanctuaries created throughout the world in the past twenty years, it has been driven by transnational conservationists' concerns about the extinction of endangered species. Conservationist organizations such as the World Wildlife Fund, the International Conservationist Union and the Sierra Club, among many others, argue that extensive wildlife corridors need to be constructed to prevent further species loss. Their requirement that conservation requires extensive and unpopulated wildlife corridors has led to the emergence of the term 'fortress conservation' to describe a strategy that appears to put species welfare above the social and individual rights of people to places previously inhabited by them.

Fortress conservation has led to a great deal of controversy between local communities, conservationists, the state and transnational organizations. Some conservationists go so far as to argue for the 'rewilding' of previously inhabited spaces, involving the loss of homelands and/or property for people residing in areas that 'trespass' on important animal routes. In a few years, the topic of fortress conservation has become the single most discussed issue on e-mail lists of environmental anthropologists and sociologists. The bibliographies on this topic are now in the hundreds.[1] Yet, few who have entered this debate, have noticed the link between accumulation by dispossession and the construction of wildlife corridors. Most social scientists, even those who have sided with community concerns about loss of territories to protected areas, have generally criticized the 'appropriative' character of modernist science and seen state policy or neo-colonial attitudes as the source of land dispossession by parks (Igoe, 2004; Kothari, 1998).

Yet, for the people who are to be displaced, whether their lands are appropriated for a park, a dam, or for mining or other industrial purposes, matters very little. What ties together these various forms of territorial dispossession is a common concept of space as a site of important 'resources', whether these are biological, mineral, or water. Furthermore, I would suggest that a concept of landscape as a space consisting of valuable resources could only occur in a social formation in which commodity relations have been previously generalized to the point where they are depoliticized and naturalized, taken as 'the norm' upon which further policy options are elaborated (Rubin, 1973). This is because non-commodity forms of property are generally embedded in kinship, community and/or and other social relations, falling under the generalized rubric of 'common property regimes' and do not make a separation between 'public' and 'private' property (Singh, 1986). The concept of 'public parks' acquires its salience in contrast to its normative other, private property, and as a means to stem the ecological crises which competitive capitalist accumulation sets in motion. Furthermore, seeing the modern state as the source of dispossession through parks ignores the role of the state in enabling and aiding the long-term reproduction of capitalism, which the latter's own competitive necessity for short-term profits has a tendency to preclude (Foster, 2003). In creating parks and biosphere reserves, forests and nature have been cognitively turned into 'natural resources,' objects to be protected from human destruction and open to tourist activities but closed to human settlement and production.

History of Parks

Far from being sources of 'natural wilderness', national parks are an invented tradition of the nineteenth century. As industrial capitalism emerged and grew, areas in Europe and North America that had formerly been seen as barren, infertile, or desolate wastelands came to be viewed, first by elite male tourists, as areas of sublime beauty where pure nature reigned (Cronon, 1996). The constructed nature of North American parks is shown by the fact that the first ones, Yosemite and Yellowstone, were created hard on the heels of the Indian wars, in which the prior human inhabitants of these areas were rounded up and moved onto reservations. Incidentally, this was a solution to the 'tribal' problem that was also espoused by a few British Forestry Department officials for Western India during the 1880s. As native North Americans were forced to move elsewhere, tourists could safely enjoy the illusion that they were seeing nature in its pristine, original state. Hence, the sense of peace and absence of violence within the boundaries of national parks was contrasted with the process of accumulation by dispossession of Indian lands that was marked by force and even genocide. To this day, for example, the Blackfeet of northern Montana and southern Alberta continue to be accused of poaching on the lands of Glacier National Park that were ceded by treaty only with the provision that they be permitted to continue hunting there (Cronon, 1996).

The idea that parks should preserve biodiversity, and not only function as recreational spaces, is the result of a recent phase of post-war environmentalism. This phase has been marked by the emergence of influential transnational organizations such as Greenpeace International, the Worldwatch Institute, the World

Resources Institute, the IUCN and the WWF. In recent years, these well-financed and highly professionalized environmental NGO have largely supplanted the more activist groups that dominated environmentalism in the 1970s (Jamison, 1996). They have also tended to steal the stage of global concern from local environmental groups that emerged in southern countries, and which are increasingly vocal in their opposition to Northern definitions of global environmental problems (*ibid.*).

The insertion of such organizations into a regime of transnational governance emerged during the Rio Summit on the environment in 1992, where the policy documents framing wildlife conservation choices of southern countries moved from the UN to the World Bank. Referred to as the UNDP Environmental Facility, biodiversity conservation's vast enlargement of national parks and wildlife sanctuaries is now being implemented by the World Bank and the International Monetary Fund. Today, national parks, wildlife sanctuaries and biosphere reserves cover 11.5 per cent of the globe's area, up from 5.6 per cent two decades ago. The philosophy underlining fortress conservation is that wilderness has to be large and continuous in order to allow animal movement, and that any and all human intervention is damaging to the preservation of diversity (Tomforde, 2003). Development projects funded by the World Bank now require the adjuncts of wildlife sanctuaries and national parks as part of their environmental guidelines. The implementation of 'fortress conservation' occurs despite the fact that most biodiversity hotspots throughout the world contain substantial number of human inhabitants, many of whom have been resident in such areas for long time periods and who depend on the common property resources of these regions. The knowledge interests of northern environmentalism are now being reformulated by corporate actors and the IFIs. They are imposed on national states that have been incorporated into the international global economy through various structural and sectoral adjustment programmes, including India after 1991. Not surprisingly, the greatest increase in protected areas has been in countries undergoing structural adjustment policies, some of them being among the poorest in the world.[2]

Protected Areas in India

In India, the major legal instrument relating to the appropriation of land for national parks, biosphere reserves and wildlife sanctuaries is the Indian Wildlife Protection Act of 1972, amended in 1991. It enables state governments to declare an eco-region as a sanctuary, except for those regions already consisting of reserve forests. However, even parts of reserved forests can be included in a sanctuary, if they are deemed by the government to have important ecological, faunal, geomorphological, natural or zoological significance. Wildlife sanctuaries are referred to as a Tier II Protected Area. This is because they are differentiated from national parks, in that no human habitation is allowed inside parks, while some human settlement is allowed within the buffer areas of the sanctuary, while core areas are to be uninhabited.

Restrictions on entry into sanctuaries are quite exclusive, as they forbid anyone except public servants on duty, people who have been permitted by the Chief Wildlife Warden to reside within the sanctuary, people who have immovable property within the sanctuary, people passing through the sanctuary along a public highway, and any dependents of any of the above persons. In addition, human activities within the buffer areas of the sanctuary itself are limited. No destruction of any wildlife within the sanctuary boundaries is permitted, no fires can be set in the forests, and all domestic animals residing in or within a 5-kilometre radius of the sanctuary, need to be immunized. Finally, the Chief Wildlife Warden controls, manages and maintains all sanctuaries and can take such steps as will ensure the security and preservation of wild animals in the sanctuary (GOI, 1991).

The declaration of a sanctuary is to be followed by an inquiry by the District Collector into existing land rights within the sanctuary. A claimant must submit his or her records relating to land ownership within two months of the public declaration of the sanctuary. If written records do not exist, then the Collector is empowered to appropriate that land for sanctuary purposes and to evict people living in that area. However, the 1894 Land Acquisition Act can also be used to appropriate land for a sanctuary, even if it is privately owned. In this case, however, compensation in either money or land, must be paid to the owner. Since 1971, 521 protected areas have been declared in South Asia, amounting to 6.7 per cent of the land surface of the subcontinent.

The Shoolpaneshwar Wildlife Sanctuary, declared as such in 1989, covers 608 square kilometres in the Rajpipla Hills and greatly enlarged the existing Dumkhel Slothbear sanctuary. Within the sanctuary's core area, which comprises 13 villages, no cultivation or habitation is allowed. This is why the local populations in the region, consisting mainly of Tadvi and Vassawa ethnic groups, regard its construction as a means of curtailing their right of access to forest resources and of appropriating land previously used by them for cultivation. In addition, even in the buffer areas, where some settlement and cultivation is allowed, they believe that the Forestry Department is trying to use harassment to force them to leave the area.

A few environmental anthropologists, working from the standpoint of small-scale communities, have dismantled the separation between nature and culture embodied in science, including the environmental discourse that sees 'nature' and 'wilderness' as somehow outside human social construction (Ingold 1996; Gisli and Pallson 1996). They argue that a concept of the landscape can provide a less ethnocentric perspective on how humans and environments interact within a total socially constructed region (Hirsh 1995: 2).

There has been a spate of recent anthropological work on landscape in recent years (Hirsch 1995; Basso 1996; Santos-Granero 1998; Escobar 1998; Dirlich 1998, etc.). With the exception of Durkheim and Mauss' early work on classification, the lack of concern with perceptions of landscape in the past is as striking as its present abundance in anthropology and sociology. With Hirsch and Williams, I agree that there is an implicit tension between the subjective position of place and the non-subject position of space. Place implies the local, the familiar, the here and now, and thus the insider's perspective, whereas space refers to the distant, the unfamiliar, the yet-to-come, or the outsider's viewpoint (Hirsch, 1995: 4-5). These contradictions between concrete place which is experienced and abstract space which is inexperienced emerged during the Renaissance period with the reinvention of 'perspectival maps' following the rediscovery of Ptolemy's classic work, *Geographica* (Harvey, 1989: 244; Brown 1977: 64). The abstract grid of such maps created an overview of landscape that was disinterested and objective, and which rationally ordered and positioned the objects within its 'field of view.' It thus produced an elevated, fixed perspective, one that was divorced from the direct and sensory, or the embodied experience of place (Harvey, 1989: 254). This abstract perspective reflected the growth of a modern, scientific concept of space: for the ideas of Galileo, Newton, Descartes and others led to the visualization of space, like time, as homogeneous, isotropic, isometric and indefinitely extended (Casey, 1996: 28).

As various maps that accompany the Shoolpaneshwar sanctuary plans suggest, wildlife conservation plans for the Rajpipla Hills are being constructed on the basis of the scientific perception that space is abstract and geometric. These maps position the sanctuary in terms of 'universal' coordinates of longitude and latitude, arranged on a grid, and differentiate towns and villages according to the type of forest around them and the amount and various species of wildlife. The series of five maps contained in the architects' plans display the region's geomorphology, its forests, the rainfall levels in the three zones of the sanctuary, and the location of the various endangered species, including barking deer, *sambar*, leopards, and sloth bears, and their corridors of movement.

The grid of the maps imposes a perspective that is visually ordered, distanced and objective, like other maps associated with post-Renaissance science, and are thus remote from direct, sensory experience (Harvey, 1989: 254). The eco-region is portrayed from the 'superior viewpoint' of the outsider. Their most striking aspect is the extent to which the familiar environment of the inhabitants—their towns, ethnic names, history of migrations, etc.—is downplayed. Few of the 108 villages inside the sanctuary area are noted, and these do not enter the discussion of sanctuary plans. The spatial ordering of the landscape, fragmenting its cultural totality and reordering it through the priorities of biodata, symbolizes the potential for future land appropriation. Abstract space becomes in this case a technology of accumulation by dispossession, since its imaginary landscape is a territory devoid of prior human settlement. Indeed, it is arguable that many cases of territorial accumulation and conquest have been legitimated partly through a concept of abstract space, while prior inhabitants have been either discounted or rendered primitive and hence undeserving of land ownership.

Recent Conflicts over the Shoolpaneshwar Sanctuary

Given the very different conceptions of place and space embedded in the interactions between the Forestry Department and the hill communities, and the relative power differentials between them, it is not surprising that complaints about the high-handedness of Forest Department officials have marked their dealings over the past century, nor that similar reservations against amendments to the Forestry Act and the Wildlife Protection Act of 1972 have been voiced. The recent conflicts between Tadvi, Vasawa, and the state government culminated in a demonstration of 5,000 people in Rajpipla in August 2000 that continues their resistance against threats of spatial and cultural erasure.[3]

The Shoolpaneshwar sanctuary was created in 1989 in response to conservationist demands to protect the wildlife that would remain in the region following the creation of the Sardar Sarovar Reservoir. India's Ministry of Environment and Forests view it as compensating for the forestland that the dam's reservoirs would submerge. But while 11,000 hectares of forest lie in the dam's submergence zone, the sanctuary has been allocated 61,000 hectares as an extension of the Dhumkul Slothbear Sanctuary. Since the beginning of its construction, local residents of the 104 villages inside the sanctuary have complained of harassment and intimidation by armed forest rangers. In fact, most of the residents possess written land deeds for at least a portion of the land they are cultivating. Hence, they believe that the Forest Department is trying to use harassment and intimidation to force them to move out of the buffer area of the sanctuary. Their complaints relate to the fact that they have not been allowed to hunt, enter the sanctuary with weapons, or light fires without permission. They have also been forbidden from frightening wildlife, 'poaching,' damaging trees, mining, collecting forest produce, fishing, trapping animals, or clearing land for cultivation. They have been increasingly restricted to cultivating only revenue lands, *i.e.* those for which they have written records. On the other hand, a young woman in Ganpiper pointed out an area cleared from the forest that she said was being farmed by a forestry department official with rice for his own cultivation. A particularly serious complaint relates to the fact that teak plantations have been positioned on some revenue lands in order to create wildlife corridors for the animals that are being introduced to the sanctuary. The first animal to be introduced was a panther in 1992, and was only removed after it had killed a village girl. Bullocks, seen by the Forestry Department as causing deforestation due to overgrazing, have frequently been confiscated while their owners are fined for using them for ploughing.

Widespread confiscation of bullocks, ostensibly because they were not immunized, led to a demonstration in Rajpipla on August 28, 2000. In a meeting after the rally, people demanded their right to control resources and land inside the sanctuary. The village representatives said that they appreciated the need for forest conservation. "But while the government has helped the timber lobby to clear-fell the forest, it was the tribal community which helped in protecting the forest," said Phulsingh Vasawa. Indeed, there was evidenced that the Central Pulp Mills of JK Industries had been extended a ten-year lease and continued felling bamboo in the sanctuary despite a Supreme Court order against commercial activities in sanctuaries. Phulsingh Vasawa went on to say that 'we are living in this forest for the past many generations and because of this sanctuary now we are called encroachers.' In interviews after the meeting, elders from various villages in the sanctuary asserted that not only were they caretakers of the environment, but that Tadvi and Vasawa ways of populating the landscape provide a better means of protecting the environment than the practices of the Forestry Department.

'After all,' they said, 'it is only near *adivasi* settlements where forests have not been felled indiscriminately.'[4] They argue that they must protect those areas where their ancestors once resided, and that their ancestors require them to treat the forest with respect, while the Forest Rangers live by the roadside and enter the forest only to get chickens or rivercrabs from the Adivasis. How can these two forms of knowledge compare and how can the Forest Rangers have the intimate knowledge of the forest that those living there possess?[5] They also complain that the Forest Rangers do not understand the balance and relations necessary between sanctuary animals, relations that are expressed in kinship terms. If they did, why did they allow leopards and panthers to increase so much that they are now threatening children and goats? In Adivasi narratives, knowledge of place and of social relations that include the animal world takes precedence over the science of conservation that includes and allows the commercial felling of forests, which the Vasawa see as the main reason for habitat loss.

In addition to open resistance, Vasawa and Tadvi in the Rajpipla Hills are reconstructing oral histories with the help of organizations such as Pariyavaran Suraksha Samiti. The Tadvis and Vasawas who inhabit the sanctuary area have sought to fill in and repopulate the landscape by stressing the kinship-based idioms of place and history. These idioms are rooted in a subject position in which space is not geometric/abstract, but populated and meaningful. Their relations to the landscape are, above all, symbolic ones. This reterritorialization of space has resulted in the emergence of a distinct and conscious sense of identity focused on the term Adivasi, rather than tribal. It centres on their culturally distinct relations to land, forest and landscape. As the movement against the dam has received setbacks in the Indian courts, concern for land and forest rights of the Adivasis of the region has correspondingly gained some momentum in the past few years.

In the Narmada Valley, these place-based interactions with the 'environment' are marked by descent, alliance and settlement patterns, so that an oral history of movement is mapped onto the landscape. These histories intersect with aspects of alliance and residence patterns in two major ways. Marriages of Tadvi and Vasawa are contracted between villages, with the primary rule being that villages should be exogamous. The kinship terminology, in fact, seems to reflect a Dravidian matrilateral cross-cousin marriage pattern, since the mother's brother's daughter is referred to by the term *bahu* which means marriageable woman, while the father's sister's daughter is referred to as *bhen*, or sister, *i.e.* as non-marriageable.

Table 1

Tadvi and Vasawa Kinship Terminology Compared with Gujarati Kinship[6]

English Equivalent	Tadvi and Vassawa[7]		Gujarati Upper Caste
Male Ego	Self		
Wife of Ego	Wife	Bibi	Vahu
Son of Ego	Son	Putra	Putra, Chokra
Daughter	Daughter	Chokri	Chokri
Son's wife	Daughter-in-law	Vahu	Vahu
Dau's husband	Son-in-law	Jamaya	Jamai
Wi's brother	Bro-in-law	Sala	Salubhai
Wi's sister	Si-in-law	Sali	Sarotri
Wi bro wife	Si-in-law	Bahu	Sarotri
Wi bro wife's dau	Cousin		
Ahu	Sato		
Wi bro wi's son	Cousin	Ala	Salubhai
Brother	Brother	Bhai	Bhai
Sister	Sister	Bhen	Bhen
Sister's hu	Bro-in-law	Jaith	Benevi
Si hu sister	Si-in-law	Numyund	Benvoi
Si hu sis hu	Bro-in-law	Bhai	———
Si hu sis hu sis	———	Bhen	———
Si hu dau	Cousin	Bhen	Boneki
Si hu son	Cousin	Bhai	Bhatija
Bro dau	Niece	Bhen	Bartiji
Bro son	Nephew	Bhai	Batrijo
Father	Father	Pita	Pita
Mother	Mother	Mata or Tai	Mata
Father's brother	Uncle	Kaka	Kaka

Contd...

English Equivalent	Tadvi and Vassawa		Gujarati Upper Caste
Fa bro wife	Aunt	Kaki	Kaki
Fa sister	Aunt	Phui	Fafu
Fa si hu	Uncle	Phua	Phoi
Fa bro dau	Cousin	***Bhen***	———
Mo si	Aunt	Mausi	Mausi
Mo bro	Uncle	Mama	Mama
Mo bro dau	Cousin	**Bahu**	———
Mo bro son	Cousin	Sala	———
Mo bro wife	Aunt	Maumi	Maumi
Mo father	Grandfather	Dada	Bapa
Mo mother	Grandmother	Dadi	Bapi
Fa father	Grandfather	Dada	Dada
Fa mother	Grandmother	Dadi	Dadi
Son's son	Grandson	Kaka	Bhikra
Son's dau	Granddaughter	Phui	Bhikri
Son's son's wife	———	Kaki	Bhikri
Son's dau's hus	———	Phua	Bhikra
Si son's son	———	Phoi	Bhikra
Si son's dau	———	Phua	Bhikra
Wi son's dau	———	Mausi	Bhikri
Wi son's son	———	Mama	Bhikra

Two major principles differentiate Tadvi and Vasawa kinship terminology from an upper-caste Gujarati pattern.[8] The latter tends to follow North Indian norms, while the former is similar to a Dravidian pattern. The first difference is that brides are usually taken from the mother's side, and often from the mother's brother's lineage or *faliya*. This is indicated by the term *bahu* which can also be translated as wife or eligible wife. It applies to the wife, the son's wife, the wife of the wife's brother, the daughter of the wife's brother, as well as to the mother's brother's daughter. The term *bhen*, roughly translated as sister, and therefore referring to a non-marriageable female, applies to the sister, the sister's daughter, the sister's husband's sister's daughter, to the sister's husband's sister's husband's sister, and, most importantly, to the father's brother's daughter. This indicates the presence of matrilateral cross-cousin marriage.

In regard to marriage relations, any exogamous village acquires brides from villages related to either the wife or the mother's side. In practice, this means that women married into a village tend to come from about 3 to 4 different villages and are often related. For example, in a village I stayed in, women came from Dev Mogra, Namgir and Moti Singloti. All women from the same village considered themselves sisters. This type of marriage pattern produced a series of alliances that extended throughout the Rajpipla Hills, as brides were always coming, or at least were thought of as coming, from the mothers' *faliyas*. As one Vasawa elder put it rather emphatically, 'These are the real boundaries of Vasawa society, not so much our villages.'[9] The fact that the wife's brother's wife and wife's brother's wife's daughter were also termed *bahu* or *vahu* provides for flexibility in an otherwise strict matrilateral cross-cousin marriage system for those elopements and free-choice marriages that sometimes occur. Elopements could usually be incorporated into its kinship terms, as women who did not belong to the wife's brother's *faliya* could easily be designated with the same term, *vahu or bahu*. In fact, there were several instances of in-marrying sons-in-laws, or *gher jamais*, in a village I studied, and I was told that this was not uncommon in other villages, since prospective husbands could not always afford the increasing bridewealth demanded of them. Although nominally patrilineal and patrilocal, there were instances in which both daughters and/or widows would inherit either their father's or husband's property. The major taboo that came into play was for men not to marry from within their own village or from their father's lineage. There were always possibilities for creating new alliances with other villages, and such possibilities were often strategized and discussed. For example, on one of my trips to a neighbouring village that had been prominent in the anti-Sanctuary movement, a 16-year-old girlfriend asked me to spread the word there about the honour, beauty and industriousness of the young ladies from her village.

The second way that alliance and residence patterns intersect with local histories is that rules for lineage exogamy applied not only to an existing village, but also to the previous areas of settlement.[10] Both Tadvi and Vasawa practice subsistence cultivation that combined ploughing, monsoon irrigation only, and some historical shifting of fields. Due to declining fertility, fields were moved and more forest land was taken under cultivation about once every fifty years. Periodically throughout history, villages and lineages therefore moved *in toto*. These moves would invariably be close to or adjacent to villages in which one's own patrilineal *faliya* or clan already had some presence. However, the previous settlement was still reflected in the naming of *faliyas*. Hence it was not only a patrilineal ancestor whose name was included in *faliya* surnames, but also the former place of residence, which became a kind of sub-clan name. This could have ironic overtones. For example, a group of two families who had moved to village X from near the SSP dam site because of a patrilineal connection and who had lost some of their land, mused whether their settlement name would be 'gas pump *faliya*,' since it was a gas station that had been settled on their old land.

Faliyas are exogamous not only according to present settlements, but also to preceding settlements, and the sub-lineage name became activated during periods of marriage negotiations between families. It is not present as part of an everyday ethnonym, nor as a fixed principle of descent. Rather, it helps to compose and recompose households through the marriage practices that establish relatedness. It tends to follow Dravidian kinship terminology that stresses clan endogamy and village exogamy (Trautman, 1993: 82; Dumont, 1993: 109). The period during which marriages were negotiated between October to January also became spaces during which lineage settlement histories were discussed, mapping settlement history onto the landscape through the idioms of marriage and descent. Such idioms not only naturalized kinship relations, but also socialized the landscape, providing concrete idioms of historical place in what the Forest Department viewed as an otherwise abstract space consisting of plant and animal resources.

The theme of people socializing the landscape through kinship classification is hardly a new one in anthropology (Durkheim and Mauss, 1904; Rosaldo, 1989; Connerton, 1989). However, such culturally-mediated idioms of place have often come into conflict with more abstract notions of space that are represented by the courts and are adjudicated through the legal definitions of property in space and territory (Hirsch, 1995). In such conceptions, space is geometric, objectifiable, possessed through idioms of individual ownership, and based on the notion of an abstract, scientific perspective (Harvey, 1989: 256). This geometric conception of space implies a radical separation between subject and object, so that the landscape constitutes the background 'environment' upon which human sensuous activity is carried out 'in the foreground' of one's social life. Such modernist conceptions imply a radical break between nature and culture, the environment and society, space and place (Hirsch, 1995; Williams, 1973). They also imply the construction of a landscape that can be depopulated, a knowledge that is radically unsituated, and a history that implies a process of hierarchical accumulation of land, resources, and in many cases, people.

In the past few years, the Tadvi and Vasawa communities in this region have attempted to interpolate their kinship-determined reckonings of place into the universalistic legal framework of the court system. In postcolonial India, the contrasts between place and space are highlighted in legal precept, since it is dominated by property laws that are of colonial provenance. In fact, the various laws circumscribing rights of hill communities to space, encoded within the various Forestry Acts from 1878 to 1972, and culminating in the Wildlife Protection Act, constitute place-based kinship narratives only as spaces of 'erasure,' both symbolically and practically (Lefebvre, 1991; Nala, 2001). Contemporary government-recognized rights of ownership are derived from the application of prior written deeds of a century ago. Since most Tadvi and Vasawa at that time lacked such written deeds, the means of acquiring them, or the political power that would merit territorial recognition by the colonial state, common and personal property resources in lands, forests and settlements were largely erased and cultivation in the forest—especially burning of forest cover—was termed 'encroachment.'[11] Indeed, subsequent attempts to improve this situation have been framed in terms of 'regularising' the encroachers and their rights to 'encroached' land. Often, however, they are still considered legally landless, although some states, *e.g.* Maharashtra, have attempted to address this question in the post-Independence period. The legal landscape of India's forest areas, like most of North America, was largely made to assume the emptiness of post-Renaissance landscape paintings and maps.

However, 40 forest villages in the Sanctuary have been omitted from this process, occupying a kind of legal limbo but considered part of the lands managed by the Forestry Department. Its villagers, nonetheless, are determined that their socially-inscribed relatedness to landscape be accorded equal recognition with other forms of property, arguing for their role as caretakers of the landscape, their knowledge of oral history which spans 20 generations, and the folk heroes who participated in the independence struggle and who are themselves remembered in terms of landscape categories.

In seeking to 'repopulate' the geometric concept of space with settlement histories, ancestors and rights, *adivasis* of the Shoolpaneshwar Sanctuary appear to be moving towards the trajectory of 'tribal' identity-formation, stressing the validity, even superiority of their ways of reckoning landscape and environment over those of the homogenizing state and market. This has involved reconstructing Tadvi and Vasawa history from the standpoint of the margins, reinserting the validity of the oral memory of resettlement into the discursive space of a homogenizing legal structure that replicates the abstract reworking of space.

Conclusion

It is uncertain today how the dialogue between place and space, and between local histories and fortress conservation will develop in the future. This depends, in large part, on whether the Indian courts will in the future begin to recognize the historical erasure of land rights of *adivasi* populations that was enabled through the Forestry Acts and the more recent Wildlife Protection Act. The difficulties of accepting 'oral histories' and 'kinship histories' by courts have seemed to rest on the fact that societies in which vital information is passed on mainly by word of mouth are often ones in which history, *per se*, becomes encoded in performance or kinship narratives: there is often NOT a separate 'oral history' in the way in which literate societies conceive of it (Cruickshank, 1992: 31). The recent case of Sri Pradip Prabhu *versus* the State of Maharashtra (1995) indicates some success for a strategy that asserts the unity and specificity of adivasi identity in relation to place, although this case did not challenge the concept of 'encroachment.'[12] Instead, it chose to argue its case in terms of rights recognized prior to 1978.[13] However, it did legally enshrine the prior rights of Adivasis to land in principle. Following this success, Vassawa and Tadvi Adivasis in one forest village in the sanctuary have filed a case in the Ahmedabad High Court, and Adivasis of Akkalkua and Akrani districts of Maharashtra have filed a similar case in the Bombay High Court, arguing that in Adivasi society the relationships between nature and the human world are symbolic and inclusive, in which each nurtures and conserves the other.[14] Here, legal references to 'cultural specifity' open up the possibility that in future other than written records should and will be recognized. The petitioners claim that cultural relations to place and environment should take precedence over commodified definitions of land-use and property, which have failed to record and recognize Adivasi traditions for the past century. A recent Maharashtra government committee has also recommended some legal recognition of such rights.[15]

While the future outcome of these new legal challenges is uncertain, it is clear that competing concepts of land-use, possession, and settlement history will be central to these interactions. This paper has tried to show how the construction of a sanctuary has functioned as a means of accumulation by dispossession (Harvey, 2003). This process is not simply a means to enable accumulation to continue, through privatization of land and other resources held in common and through the long-term protection of resources through conservation efforts. It also includes a process of differentiation, that occurring between the owners of capital and those who sell their labour-power. The process of differentiation involves divorcing self-sufficient 'producers from the means of production.' Marx saw this as one side of the process through which capitalism is extended. This is because the process does not require just the accumulation of physical assets: capital is not only property, but also a social relation. It also requires the 'annihilation of self-earned property, *i.e.* the expropriation of the labourer:'

> In themselves, money and commodities are no more capital than the means of production and subsistence are. They need to be transformed into capital. But this transformation can itself take place only under particular social circumstances that meet together: *i.e.* the contact....between two different types of commodity owners; on the one hand, the owners of money, and with it means of production and subsistence, who are eager to valorize their sum of values....by buying the labour power of others; on the other hand, free workers, the sellers of their own labour-power'.... Free workers, in the double sense, that they form neither a part of the means of production, as would be the case with slaves and serfs, nor do they own the means of production, as would be the case with self-employed farmers or factory owners. The workers are therefore freed from any means of production of their own.... (Marx, 1976: 846).

In other words, for capitalism to survive and grow, there not only has to be an increase in capital accumulation, but there also has to be 'free labour,' in the sense that there has to exist a group of people who have no ties to a subsistence base that lies outside the circuits of capital. In short, no alternative to working for wages for someone else. It is ironic that fortress conservation, in seeking to protect species loss, is also, perhaps unwittingly, becoming a part of the expansion of capital, a process that it often rhetorically criticizes.

This paper has also tried to show how the concept of abstract space is linked to processes of accumulation by dispossession through the construction of wildlife sanctuaries. Accumulation by dispossession involves a rearrangement of space, since it constitutes 'an annihilation of pre-existing property' and of customary ways of relating to landscapes and waterscapes. It is therefore accompanied by an erasure, or at least, a denigration of pre-existing ways of relating to such resources, which are often defined as 'uncivilized, wasteful, etc.' The concept of abstract space enables developers to maintain an objectified and external relation to the landscape, which becomes emptied of people, their history and entitlements. It is replaced by a quantifiable area consisting of commodifiable resources. Abstract space conceptually erases the ties of people to their landscapes, and hence complements the policy erasures of territorial dispossession that have been an unfortunate part of 'fortress conservation.'

Notes

1. Some of the standard references are:

   Kothari S., *et al.* (1998), *Communities and Conservation*, New Delhi: Sage Publications.

   Brockington Dan (2002), *Fortress Conservation: The Preservation of the Mkomazi Game Reserve, Tanzania*. Indiana Univ. Press.

   Igoe, Jim (2004), *Conservation and Globalization: A Study of National Parks and Indigenous Communities from East Africa to South Dakota*. Case Studies on Contemporary Social Issues. Thomson/Wadsworth, Belmont, California.

   Blaikie, P. and S. Jeanrenaud (1997), *Biodiversity and Human Welfare in Social Change and Conservation*, K. Ghimire and M.P. Pimbert (eds.), 46-70. London: Earthscan.
2. For example, in North America, 220 km^2 is under conservation, consisting of .5 per cent of the land mass. In eastern and southern Africa, by contrast, 2,689 km^2 is in protected areas, consisting of 11 per cent of the land mass.
3. Nala P. (2001).
4. Interview, Rajpipla, August (2001).
5. Interviews inside Shoolpaneshwar Sanctuary, August-September (1999).
6. I would like to thank Rasikh Bhai Tadvi and Ramji Nandria Vassawa for helping me identify and understand this kinship terminology.
7. The relevant terms for marriage patterns are emphasized in bold.
8. I would like to thank Radhika Desai for helping me with Gujarati kinship idioms.
9. Interview, Rajpipla, July 2001.
10. I would like to thank Swati Desai of the Paryavaran Suraksha Samiti for alerting me to this pattern.
11. An exception to this was the Chief of Sagbara, who was given the title of a minor rajah by the British. As discussed earlier, this chief was able to maintain a small contingent of troops and harass both

Marathas and British by controlling one of the passes on a major trade route between Taloda and Surat.

12. Writ Petition (Civil) no. 1778 of 1986, Pradip Prabhu *versus* State of Maharashtra, Judgement delivered March 7, 1995.
13. This has obvious parallels with the Delgamuukw land claims case in Canada 1997, which overturned a century of judicial dismissal of Native concepts of 'property' expressed through oral history and kinship. However, the latter case differs from the South Asian context in the fact that no treaties had previously been signed between the aboriginal peoples and the Canadian government in B.C.
14. In the High Court of Judicature at Mumbai, Civil Appellate Jurisdiction, Writ Petition of 2001, Vesta Dhama Pavra *et al.* versus State of Maharashtra.
15. Daud Committee Report on Resettlement and Rehabilitation of SSP Affected PAFs in Maharashtra, chaired Justice S.M. Daud (Retired), tabled July 2001.

References

Basso, K.H. (1996), Wisdom Sits in Places: Notes on a Western Apache Landscape. K.H. Basso & S. Feld (eds.), *Senses of Place,* Santa Fe: School of American Research.

Baviskar, A. (1995), *In the Belly of the River: Struggling over India's Narmada Valley.* Delhi: OUP.

Brody, H. (1981), *Maps and Dreams.* Vancouver: Douglas and McIntyre.

Brown, L.A. (1977), *The Story of Maps.* NY: Dover Publications.

Buckle, Major C. (1862), *Papers Relative to the Improvement of the Forest Revenue of the Punch Mahals, Selections from the Records of the Bombay Government, # LXXVII (NS),* 13.

Casey, E.S. (1996), How to Get from Space to Place in a Fairly Short Stretch of Time: Phenomenological Prolegomena. K.H. Basso & S. Feld (eds.), *Senses of Place.* Santa Fe: School of American Research.

Connerton, P. (1989), *How Societies Remember*, Cambridge [England], New York: Cambridge University Press, 1989.

Cronon, W. (1996), *Uncommon Ground: Rethinking the Human Place in Nature.* NY: Norton.

Cruikshank, Julie (1992), Invention of Anthropology in British Columbia's Supreme Court: Oral Tradition as Evidence in *Delgamuukw v. BC Studies*, Special Issue No. 95, 25-42.

Dumont, L. (1993), North India in Relation to South India. P. Uberoi (ed.), *Family, Kinship and Marriage in India.* Delhi: OUP, 91-113.

Government of India (1880). *Rewa Kantha District Gazetteer*. Bombay: Government of India Press.

Government of India (1880), *Gazetteer of the Bombay Presidency*. Bombay: Govt. Central Press.

Government of India (1863), *Papers Relative to the Improvement of the Forest Revenue of the Punch Mahals*. Bombay: Education Society Press, Byculla.

Government of India (1884-95), *Rajpipla Administrative Reports*. Bombay: Government of Indian Press.

Guha, S. (1999), *Environment and Ethnicity in Western India*. Cambridge: Cambridge University Press.

Hardiman, D. (1995), *The Coming of the Devi: Adivasi Assertion in Western India*. Delhi: Oxford University Press.

Hardiman, D. (1987), The Bhils and Shahukars of Eastern Gujarat. R. Guha (ed.), *Subaltern Studies,* Vol. 5. Delhi: Oxford University Press.

Harvey, D. (1989), *The Conditions of Postmodernity*. Oxford: Basil Blackwell.

Harvey, D. (2003), *The New Imperialism*. Oxford: Oxford University Press.

Hirsch, E. (1995), Introduction, Landscape: Between Place and Space. E. Hirsch and M. O'Hanlan (eds.), *The Anthropology of Landscape: Perspectives on Place and Space*. Oxford: Clarendon.

Igoe, Jim (2004), *Conservation and Globalization: A Study of National Parks and Indigenous Communities from East Africa to South Dakota*. Case Studies on Contemporary Social Issues. Thomson/ Wadsworth, Belmont, California.

Ingold, T. (1996), Article in G. Palsson and P. Descola (eds.), *Nature and Society: Anthropological Perspectives on the Environment*. London: Routledge.

James, C. Scott (1998), *Seeing Like a State: How Certain Schemes to Improve the Human Condition have Failed*. New Haven: Yale Univ. Press.

Jamison, A. (1996), The Shaping of the Global Environmental Agenda. S. Lash (ed.), *Risk, Environment and Modernity*. London: Sage, 224-45.

Kothari, A. *et al.* (1998), *Communities and Conservation*. New Delhi: Sage.

Lefebvre, H. (1991), *The Production of Space,* trans. D. Nicholson-Smith. Oxford: Blackwell.

Marx, K. *Capital,* Vol. 1, trans. Ben Fowkes. NY: Basic Books.

Nala, P. (2001), In the Spaces of Erasure: Globalisation, Resistance and the Narmada River. *Economic and Political Weekly,* June 2, 2001.

Palsson, G. (1996), Introduction in P. Descola and G. Palsson (eds.), *Nature and Society: Anthropological Perspectives on the Environment.* London: Routledge.

Rosaldo, R. (1989), *Ilongot Headhunting, 1883-1974: A Study in Society and History.* Stanford: Stanford University Press.

Santos-Granero, F., Writing History onto the Landscape: Space, Myth and Ritual in Contemporary Amazonia. *American Ethnologist,* Vol. 25, No. 2, 1998.

Shewan, Alexander (1891), *Land Alienations in Rajpipla.* Bombay: Govt. of India Press.

Singh, C. (1986), *Common Property and Common Poverty: India's Forest, Forest Dwellers and the Law.* New Delhi: Oxford University Press.

Sivaramakrishnan, K. (1999), *Modern Forests: Statemaking and Environmental Change in Colonial Eastern India.* Stanford: Stanford University Press.

Smith, D. *The Conceptual Practices of Power.* Toronto: Univ. of Toronto Press.

Trautman, T. (1993), The Study of Dravidian Kinship. P. Uberoi (ed.), *Family, Kinship and Marriage in India.* Delhi: OUP, 74-91.

Williams, R. (1973), *The Country and the City.* New York: Oxford University Press.

Cashing in India's Forests: Globalization, Reform and Medicinal Plants in Madhya Pradesh

12

Garry Fehr and *René Véron*

1. Introduction

The regulation of India's forests and forest resources recently has undergone significant market-oriented reform through a multitude of new government orders, programmes and projects at national-and state-levels. There has been a general shift from highly state-controlled low-value timber production to a more market-oriented extraction of high-value non-timber forest products (NTFPs), including medicinal plants. Furthermore, the Joint Forest Management (JFM) Programme has aimed at making forest management more participatory, and it should—at least in theory—have improved access to NTFPs for people living near the woods. At the same time, domestic and global market demand for "natural" remedies and medicines has increased manifold, and created new opportunities for India's underdeveloped medicinal plant sector, potentially perhaps also for poor Adivasi communities, the primary collectors of NTFPs.

This paper aims to illustrate how the interacting forces of markets and reform policies related to the NTFP and medicinal plant sector have impacted different social groups in rural Madhya Pradesh with a focus on the poor and the marginalised. With this sector and region-specific study, we hope to contribute to India's globalization and liberalization debate without falling into the trap of gross over-generalizations. Forest resources obviously constitute only a part of the income of the rural poor, including Adivasi communities, and they are affected by macro- and meso-level factors other than forest-related policies too. Therefore, we have made an attempt to link globalization and reform to a holistic livelihoods approach that allows putting forest-based income sources of the rural poor into context with other socio-economic activities and opportunities, as well as with various meso- and macro-level changes. Section 2 describes this theoretical approach. As the study furthermore tries to make links between policy and market changes at the macro level and livelihood dynamics at the micro level, research was conducted at different spatial scales. Qualitative studies starting from two purposively selected villages in the Mahakoshal region of southern Madhya Pradesh have been supplemented with policy-maker interviews and secondary data. Section 3 provides an outline of the methodology and methods applied.

The empirical part of the paper starts in section 4 with an account of the global and national NTFP and medicinal plant sector, as well as of related policy changes at the national and state levels that have been implemented since the early 1990s. In part stimulated by growing global demand for alternative medicines, India's medicinal plant sector has become more vertically integrated. Trade in NTFPs has been liberalized, and the production of medicinal plants has attracted central government subsidies. Section 5 presents a case study on *safed musli* (Chlorophytum borivilianum)—an important NTFP and medicinal plant in the study region—that is used as an illustrative example to gain an in-depth understanding of the possible causal links between globalization, liberalization and livelihood changes. We will show how growing global demand for *safed musli* has led to the overexploitation of wild stocks. As a consequence, the importance of *safed musli* collection (like other NTFPs) for poor rural men and women has diminished. Section 6 puts these processes in the context of other livelihood changes, such as improvements in agriculture and better migrant labour opportunities. These changing livelihood contexts, together with the processes within the NTFP/medicinal plant sector, have resulted in the fragmentation of medicinal plant livelihoods along class, gender and age lines.

In the concluding section 7, we argue that the analyzed paradoxical situation where increased global demand and more integrated markets for medicinal-plant substances did not lead to the improvement of livelihoods of those who traditionally produced or collected these products (*i.e.* poor rural men and women mostly from Adivasi communities) must in part be explained with a lack of appropriate local institutions among the rural poor that could have mediated, and even taken advantage of, the effects of globalization and policy change (including the new subsidy programmes). In the absence of such institutions, globalization and market-oriented reform are likely to create uneven effects, deepen inequalities and render livelihoods less sustainable and more vulnerable.

2. Globalization and Livelihoods

"Globalization" has become a popular catchphrase entailing various, often not very clearly defined, meanings. In the academic literature, globalization is commonly and generally associated with the increased influence of international institutions, organizations and global markets on the day-to-day activities of individuals and households throughout the world. In a review of the Indian globalization discourses, Backhaus (2003) starts—following Anthony Giddens—with a definition of globalization as "a result of the increasingly (spatially and temporally) distanciated consequences of everyday actions... [that] can be at the same time homogenizing as well as fragmenting" (6). In such a view, globalization is not following a "master plan", yet policies (*e.g.*, the market-oriented reforms in India's forestry sector) take an important part in shaping globalization—whether intentionally or unintentionally.

Backhaus identifies and deconstructs various threads of the Indian discourse on globalization. One train of thought views globalization as a process of economic liberalization that has enabled capital to compete in the global marketplace (Shroff, 1999; Stiglitz, 2002) while another group of scholars sees globalization more as the withdrawal of the state that has left portions of society in an increasingly exposed and vulnerable position (Castells, 1997; Hoogvelt, 1997). In practice, economic liberalization and state withdrawal have probably occurred simultaneously in India, as in other countries, and their effects cannot be easily reduced to either improved global competitiveness or increased social vulnerability. The third identified stream of India's discourse sees globalization simply as a process of homogenization, Westernization and the spread of consumerism (Shepard & Hayduk, 2002; Robins, 1997), and thus stands in contrast to the definition above that allows for fragmenting effects as well.

In any case, most observers would agree that India's economic reform since 1991 has been a slow, incomplete and uneven process that has aimed to integrate one of the world's most heavily regulated economies into the global marketplace (for example, Baldev, 1998). The economy has been liberalized bit by bit and sector by sector, some public enterprises have been privatized while others have not, and the bureaucracy as well as government programmes have been restructured only partially (Dreze & Sen, 1995; Harriss-White, 2003). The impacts of the reforms seem to vary between regions, economic sectors and social strata. Although India did not follow a hardcore adjustment strategy but attempted to mitigate the expected negative impacts on the lower classes with development programmes and initiatives, not everybody benefited from the reform, and many—perhaps even the majority—have even been adversely affected (Breman, 1996; Corbridge & Harriss, 2000; Khilnani, 1997).

Due to this uneven nature of India's globalization and liberalization, region- and sector-specific studies appear necessary. For instance, the forest sector generally, and the NTFP and medicinal-plant sector specifically, has gone through a particular set of reforms (section 4) that is bound to have distinct socio-economic impacts. Indeed, liberalization and globalization in this sector have modified the access to timber and non-timber forest resources and the profitability of different forest uses (also versus income opportunities from non-forest-based activities) (Agrawal, 2001; Ballabh & Balooni, 2002; Corbridge & Jewitt, 2004; Kumar, 2004). As we will see, various aspects of the reform in the forest sector, together with "market forces," have globalized the context of individuals, households and firms that depend or once depended on forest resources.

However, such a sectoral approach would fail to capture the implications of reform as they are experienced, and coped with, by individuals and households. In order to get closer to the everyday realities of the rural poor, we use a livelihoods approach. Livelihoods describe the whole set of (forest-based and non-forest-based) activities an individual or household engages in. Thereby, various capabilities based on tangible assets (resources and stores) and intangible assets (claims and access) are combined into a livelihood strategy to produce a living (Chambers & Conway, 1991). Forest-based activities may (and usually are) only one component of a livelihood strategy. Changes in forest-based activities therefore need to be understood in the context of whole livelihood strategies, including the opportunities to pursue other livelihood activities, including farm and non-farm wage labour in the region or nearby urban centres.

Livelihood strategies are not a simple function of a household's capabilities, assets or capitals, but they are also influenced by changing contexts and conditions. The livelihood approach thus goes beyond paying attention to individual or household decision-making to analyse the role of institutions and organizations in influencing access to assets such as land, water or NTFPs. The decisions that determine livelihood strategies are shaped by external forces such as governments, organizations and markets and how they constrain or enhance access to assets (Scoones, 1998). Of particular interest for this study, therefore, is how forest laws and policies, the workings of the forest bureaucracy or the effectiveness of community-based forest user organizations have influenced access to forest resources, including NTFPs and medicinal plants, and how global or domestic markets have shaped the profitability of NTFP livelihood activities (in relation to alternative livelihood opportunities).

3. Methodology and Study Area

A first step in this study has been to assess the market and policy changes in the forest sector, in general, and the NTFP/medicinal-plant sector, in particular. Apart from the study of secondary material (government reports, websites and journal articles), the authors conducted 20 semi-structured interviews with policy-makers, mostly forest officials at the State level.

As the core of the study, first co-author conducted in-depth research in two villages of Chicholi Block, Betul district, during the last four months of 2004. The village-level research looked both at general livelihood dynamics in the liberalization era since the early 1990s as well as at particular changes in the local role of NTFPs and medicinal plants. The qualitative study relied on structured and semi-structured interviews, focus group discussions, social and environmental mapping exercises, as well as participant observation. Betul district, as well as Chicholi Block, were selected by the "Globalization and the Poor" project as to represent the more forested, tribal parts of Madhya Pradesh, and the two study villages have been selected for the purpose of this study to capture different levels of dependence on forest resources.

Finally, we conducted research at the meso level to gain an understanding of the relations between the changing policy and market context, on the one hand, and the changes in livelihood activities at the local level. For this purpose, we have used *safed musli* as an example of an NTFP and medicinal plant that is (or was) significant for local livelihoods and that has attracted increasing domestic and global market demand. While every NTFP has distinct biophysical properties, roles for livelihoods as well as market trends, *safed musli* may show fairly general impact mechanisms of reform and market forces on livelihoods in a pronounced, and therefore well-noticeable, form. The first co-author followed the marketing or commodity chain of *safed musli* and a few other NTFPs to some point, and conducted semi-structured interviews with 13 local NTFP traders as well as with six representatives of pharmaceutical companies in Nagpur and Indore. Furthermore, five forest officials at the divisional and range levels, as well as three representatives of community-based forest user organizations were interviewed to provide insights in the actual implementation and translation of the policy changes on the ground.

Obviously, the study of two villages cannot be representative of the changes in NTFP-based livelihood activities in Madhya Pradesh, or even India, since liberalization and globalization processes have gained momentum in early 1990s. Rather, the aim of this paper is to unveil a set of possible causal links between reform and livelihoods in an explorative way. Also, the results of the village-level studies have been triangulated with the experiences of State-level officials and NGO representatives who generally confirmed our findings.

As mentioned above, Betul district was selected to represent the more forested, tribal parts of Madhya Pradesh. Indeed, betul means without cotton indicating that the poor shallow soil in this hilly forested area is not well suited for intensive cultivation (Department of Agriculture, 2004). Forests, predominantly teak forests, cover 40 per cent of the area in Betul district, and they are divided into 13 timber production units as well as "co-managed" by 638 Joint Forest Management Committees (Department of Forests, 2004; District of Betul, 2003). However, agriculture has become the primary source of livelihoods in the district, and 41 per cent of the land is now classified as cropping area, primarily for wheat, paddy, maize and soybean production (District of Betul, 2003).

In the study of villages too, livelihoods have become predominantly agricultural. In accordance with our selection criteria, village Jangalbari has remained more reliant on forest resources than village Khetpuram, and there are significant livelihood activities in construction and government sectors in both villages. Since Khetpuram is located only 6 km from the town of Chicholi, daily construction work is much easier to access from Khetpuram than for the residents of Jangalbari, which is situated 23 km further west.

Khetpuram consists of 80 households: 49 Gond Scheduled Tribes (ST), 17 Scheduled Castes (SC), primarily Mehra and 14 Other Backward Castes (OBC), split somewhat evenly between the Yadavs and Pawars. The OBC households are more likely to be large landholders and to hold skilled rural non-farm employment (RNFE) than SC and ST households, and OBC households are less likely to be landless or essentially landless with less than enough land to sustain a family as shown in Table 1. Additionally, Yadav (OBC) and Pawar (OBC) men hold all of the official positions of power such as panchayat member, panchayat treasurer, head of Forest Protection Committee and Forest Protection Committee tendu agent. The only exception is

TABLE 1

Distribution of Landholding and Ruralholdings and Non-Farm Employment According to Caste

Village Khetpuram

Households	% of Village	% of Caste Owning > 10 Acres	% of Caste Owning <2.5 Acres	% of Caste in RNF Employment
14 OBC	17.5	26.6	42.48	64.3
17 SC	21.2	11.8	64.7	47.1
49 ST	61.3	8.2	61.2	22.4

Village Jangalbari

Households	% of Village	% of Caste Owning > 10 Acres	% of Caste Owning <2.5 Acres	% of Caste in RNF Employment
15 OBC	28.8	6.7	86.7	2.7
0 SC	0.0	NA	NA	NA
37 ST	71.2	10.8	21.6	0.0

Source: Own field research.

the reserved ST seat on the panchayat council. Khetpuram has been connected to nearby Chicholi town by pacca road for more than 25 years and to the electrical grid for 15 years. Approximately 40 years ago, there were only 15 houses in the village and the dense forests pressed closely to the village's homes and fields but presently women must travel more than two kilometres to the edge of the degraded forest to find fuel wood.

Jangalbari is slightly smaller with 52 households of which 37 are Korku (ST), and 15 Yadav (OBC). Interestingly, the caste-wise pattern of landholdings and RNFE are reversed from those in Khetpuram (and those from Madhya Pradesh more generally). Here, Korku (ST) households control all political and administrative positions and are four times less likely to be essentially landless than OBC households. This reversal of common caste dominance can be directly attributed to the order in which the families came to live here. Until about 50 years ago, when some cattle-herding Yadav (OBC) families migrated from the degraded forests near Chicholi town, the village was a homogeneous Korku (ST) community. The Yadav (OBC) cattle herders were not interested in farming at that time as they felt that the forests would support their cattle that provided the bulk of their income. Even when the government redistributed land in the 1950s, they did not apply to receive their own parcels.

Jangalbari was long isolated from infrastructure improvements such as electricity, all-weather roads and irrigation development schemes. Although a national highway travels near the village, the single lane has only recently been paved. The 2 km link road to the village was improved only in 2002 so that 4-wheel drive vehicles can enter the village. The village was connected to the electrical grid 12 years ago so that the few dug-wells that did exist prior to this had to rely on hand watering. Although the village has grown from only a few houses 50 years ago, the dense forest remains close to the homes and fields, which are squeezed in between the steep forested hillsides.

4. Overview of Market and Policy Changes

Indigenous communities have probably depended on plants to meet their basic medical and other needs for many centuries. According to the World Health Organization (WHO), still over 80 per cent of the world population relies on medicine made from traditional plants for their primary health care needs. Conversely, the pharmaceutical industry views plant wealth as natural capital to be tapped. Forest plants not only embody potentially very valuable genetic resources, but the international market of herbal products has grown to an estimated US $62 billion in 2003, and it is expected to grow even further to US $5 trillion by the year 2050 (WHO, 2004).

In India, the domestic market for alternatives to the Western (allopathic) medicine is growing as well: the market of the so-called Indian systems of medicine and homoeopathy was of the order of US $950 million in 2000, and is expanding day by day (NMPB, 2004). Furthermore, India's exports in medicinal and herbal plants in 2000 were US $100 million and are expected to reach US $700 million annually by 2005 (*Ibid.*). Besides this, there is also a growing demand for natural products including

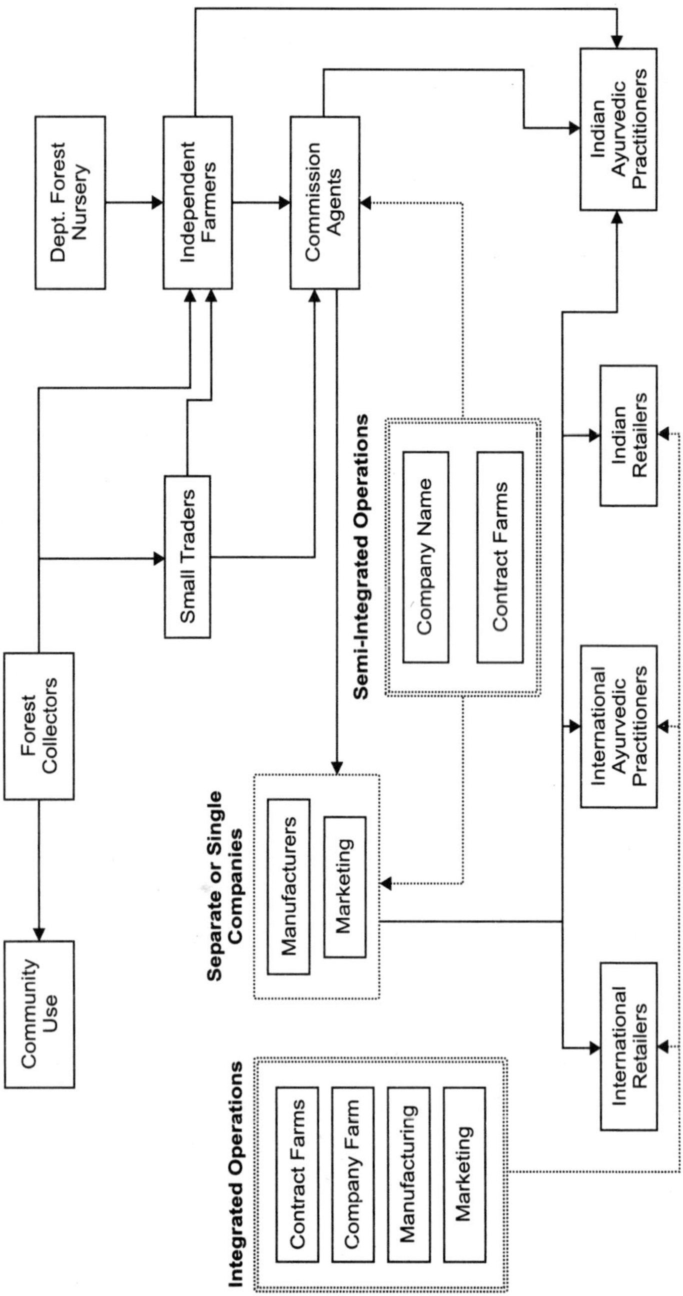

Fig. 1: Commodity chain of India's medicinal plant sector.

food supplements and cosmetics in both domestic and international markets.

Prior to the 1990s, the commodity chain of India's medicinal plant sector looked much like Figure 1 at page 292, without the dashed-line boxes of Semi-Integrated and Integrated Operations and dashed connector lines. Forest communities primarily collected what they needed for subsistence from the forests and sold small surpluses to traders who, in turn, sold the unprocessed medicinal products to commission agents, ayurvedic practitioners and manufacturers of medicines.

More recently, there have been trends toward large-scale cultivation of medicinal plants and toward more integrated operations. Several company farms have started growing medicinal plants. In semi-integrated operations, some of them have also begun to teach "scientific" cultivation methods to contract farmers and to sell planting material to them. A few of these company farms even provide guaranteed buy-back schemes with contract farmers, but the majority leave it to the farmers to find buyers for the medicinal product. This strategy is becoming more common throughout India and primarily in Madhya Pradesh, Gujarat and Maharashtra. In more fully integrated operations, pharmaceutical and chemical manufacturers do everything from cultivating and processing medicinal plants to packaging and marketing their products. Many private companies that existed before liberalization have recognised the growing potential in the herbal and natural medicine sector. Some are looking to increase their exports and others have recently entered the sector as new players.

Parallel to these market changes in the medicinal-plant sector, there have been some significant reforms in the regulation of access to forest resources, including NTFPs and medicinal plants. Forestry has traditionally been one of India's most state-controlled sectors, and since colonial times until the late 1980s and early 1990s, the clear focus had been on extracting timber to create state revenue. The Forest Department has remained in actual control of the lands classified as "protected forest" and "reserved forests", but many recent government orders, programmes and practices generally imply increased market orientation and, at least in theory, increased participation of communities in the management of forest resources.

The National Forest Policy (1988) has provided a new framework that—influenced by an increasingly strong environmentalism in India—adopted more ecological, conservationist goals. Most importantly for the NTFP and medicinal plant sector, the National Forest Policy also outlined a strategy to involve local people in the management of forests in order to limit forest degradation, particularly as a growing population had put increased pressure on timber, fuel wood and fodder. This policy goal became operationalised in the 1990 Government of India Resolution for Joint Forest Management (JFM) obligating the States to institute legislations that provide for the joint management of forest resources by the Forest Department and local people. Madhya Pradesh was quick to come up with its JFM legislation in 1991. The new regulation guaranteed usufructory rights to people living near forests over their locally harvested produce such as fuel wood, fodder, fruits and medicines in exchange for their participation in the management, protection and rehabilitation of local (degraded) forests (Department of Forests, 2003). Crucial to the JFM programme was the constitution of local-level forest user organizations (Forest Protection Committees and Village Forest Committees) that were to become the counterpart of the Forest Department. Till today, more than 14,000 JFM committees have officially been formed in the State. Interviewees among forest officials and NGO representatives suggested that the experience of JFM committees in terms of the programme's conservationist goals is mixed but generally positive, but the programme would generally have failed in terms of enabling true community participation. Indeed, most JFM committees are joint in name only, as they are dominated by local elites and/or the Forest Guard (lowest-level forest official) who is ex-officio secretary of the local committee.

In 1996, Madhya Pradesh went beyond providing usufructory rights to transfer the ownership of NTFPs to local people. However, this was not done through the Forest Department's institutional infrastructure of JFM committees but through the gram sabhas, the local-level panchayat institutions. Furthermore, the net income from the trade of NTFP were redistributed through the Primary Forest Produce Societies, the local-level co-operative societies of the Madhya Pradesh Minor Forest Produce Federation (MPMFPF), which organizes the collection of some nationalised NTFPs such as *tendu patta*, sal seeds and tree gums.

Furthermore, a set of policy changes announced by the State's Forest Department in the Bhopal Declaration in 2003 constituted a shift of the NTFP/medicinal plant sector from direct State control and regulation towards privatization and increased market orientation. For instance, the mandatory transit passes for trade in NTFPs were eliminated, royalties on the sale of non-nationalised NTFPs were abolished, and some NTFPs (*e.g.*, harra) on which the State had had monopoly marketing rights were denationalised. Although the market-oriented reform is far from complete and remains partial and uneven, the measures constitute a paradigm shift within the state towards a market philosophy. This shift—though diverging opinions exist within the state—is also reflected in interview statements from some government officials who opined that "the private sector would be a more efficient manager of resources" or that "[the state] should facilitate the efficiency of private interests."

The paradigmatic shift also has transformed, at least partially, state agencies towards greater market orientation and decreased direct state control. For Madhya Pradesh's NTFP/medicinal-plant sector, the changes in the State's MPMFPF are particularly noteworthy. The Federation was formed in 1984 as part of the Department of Forests with the aim to eliminate middlemen in the collection, storage and trade of NTFPs and to channel more benefits directly to the forest collectors through their primary co-operative societies (MPMFPF, 2004). After the Bhopal Declaration, MPMFPF has limited its responsibility to the collection of only three remaining nationalised NTFPs (*tendu patta*, sal seed and some gums) (Department of Tribal Welfare, 2003). At the same time, the Federation has adopted new and more market-oriented roles. For example, with the objective to facilitate trade in medicinal and herbal products, it started organizing national herbal fairs in 2001 where private traders, manufacturers, NGOs and practitioners of Indian systems of medicine are brought together. Furthermore, MPMFPF has recently built a testing facility for NTFPs as a step towards quality control and market standardisation. The Federation also plans to provide training to their primary co-operatives in collection practices and to support the co-operatives start medicinal plant nurseries, build simple processing units for sal seeds, *tendu patta*, *amla*, honey, etc. as well as create local medical centres where traditional medical practitioners can be trained. The stated goal of this bundle of initiatives is to continue protecting NTFP resources and "traditional" livelihoods of tribals but with a new, more market-oriented approach as opposed to the earlier direct state involvement in the collection and procurement of NTFPs.

Initiatives of the central government, however, have gone beyond providing market support for medicinal plants and targeting only tribal collectors and their primary co-operatives. In 2000, for instance, the Ministry of Health and Family Welfare established the National Medicinal Plants Board (NMPB) and gave it the task to co-ordinate the diverse programmes and schemes in the medicinal-plant sector that operated throughout the country. Most importantly, the NMPB has introduced schemes to promote the commercial cultivation of 32 potentially profitable medicinal plants, mostly on agricultural lands outside the forests (Out of these 32 plants, *safed musli* and *amla* is currently important in Betul district.) The aim of the schemes is to capture a greater share of the growing global medicinal plant market recognizing that India has more than 15,000 medicinal plants but holds only 0.5 per cent of the global export trade in this sector. Another rationale was to release the pressure on the forests and their continually decreasing biodiversity (NMPB, 2004).

In the so-called Contractual Farming Scheme (which in reality is a subsidy more than contract-farming scheme), NMPB reimburses farmers 30 per cent of their investment cost necessary to shift to the (organic) cultivation of the supported medicinal plants. The investment in converting to the cultivation of medicinal plants can cost hundreds of thousands of Rupees per acre (as in the case of *safed musli*) while other products, such as *amla*, can be harvested only three years after planting. As the government subsidies are paid in arrears, only wealthy persons were able to access the programme. Yet their interest in the programme has been substantial because the cultivation of medicinal plants was seen to have potential to produce considerable economic returns regardless of the NMPB's generous subsidy. However, the resulting increased commercial cultivation of selected medicinal plants has also led to a short but huge increase in the demand for planting material that in many cases was still provided from the forests. This created increased ecological pressure on forest resources, at least in the short-term.

5. Case Study on *Safed Musli*

As mentioned above, *safed musli* is one of the medicinal plants that has been supported by NMPB and that has been fairly important for poor people's livelihoods in Betul district. *Safed musli* is a white tuber with green leaves. Globally, its demand is estimated at 35,000 tonnes per annum whereas the annual quantity available in India is only 5,000 tonnes. Prior to the implementation of the NMPB Contractual Farming Scheme, 98 per cent of the 5,000 tonnes available was wild harvested (NMPB, 2004). Furthermore, some companies have begun marketing *safed musli* as a "natural Viagra" throughout the world and demand is expected to increase. We use this NTFP and medicinal plant to illustrate possible changes in livelihoods and forest environments during a time where policy reforms have exposed them increasingly to domestic and global market forces.

Adivasis in Chicholi Block have traditionally collected *safed musli* for consumption as a salad green and in dried form as an energizing tonic. Our research in Jangalbari suggests that 30-40 years ago only a few men and women collected *safed musli* and that it was found in plenty very close to the village. However, in 1992 traders started coming to Jangalbari to buy the dried tubers for Rs. 350-400 per kg. Only seven years later, everyone in the village went to collect *safed musli* from the forest. Prices peaked at Rs. 1,000 per kg (see Table 2), and traders would park their trucks on the highway in the dense forest waiting for collectors to come out and sell the tubers. Some villagers would pack food and work in the forest for up to a month. They would come out only to sell what they had found and then return back to the woods. However, the resource started dwindling because of over-harvesting and also because some "stupid people from the village"—as one Adivasi informant put it—did not harvest the tubers properly but just dug up everything they could find. By 2000, people started selling wet *safed musli*, which reaped only Rs. 50 per kg from traders coming to the village. During the fieldwork in 2004, there was not any *safed musli* left in the forests near Jangalbari. It has become so rare that most village residents stated that they had not seen any wild *safed musli* plant in two or three years. Women have stopped collecting the plant altogether, and only a very few men now take the time to search for it deeper in the woods. They go as far as 50 km into the forest but find very little, and the prices have come down as well (see Table 2).

The availability of other important NTFPs in Chicholi Block, such as the *chironji*, *amla* and *baharra* trees, has decreased too. Villagers explained this resource depletion not only with the increased market orientation but also with population pressure that has encouraged people to cut down everything but teak trees, which are protected by law. Valuable NTFP trees thus have been used as fuel wood for cooking and even as firewood for brick kilns. Furthermore, respondents stated that some collectors among themselves would be too "lazy" to climb the trees for picking the valuable fruits. Instead, they would break whole branches or cut down entire trees in order to harvest the fruit.

TABLE 2

Safed Musli Prices Rs. per Kg

Year	Indore Trader			Village Jangalbari	
	Dry Cultivated	Dry Forest	Wet Cultivated	Wet Forest	Dry Forest
1992					350-40
1996	1200		65		
2000-01	1800-240	700-1200		50-10	1000
2001-02	1800-220	600-900		50-10	
2002-03	900-150	500-700	20	50	
2003-04	700-100	500-600		40-5	100-15

Source: Own field research.

The number of farmers cultivating *safed musli* in Chicholi Block grew to more 20 in 2004 from only two in 1998. Most of these farmers have no more than 2-5 acres planted with *safed musli* but at least two farmers grow *safed musli* on more than 10 acres. Many cultivators watched the prices for *safed musli* climb through the 1990s and, unhappy with the declining margins in the production of soybean, they decided to experiment with this medicinal plant. Indeed, the prices for *safed musli* rose rapidly throughout the 1990s, peaked around 1999-2001 but have declined sharply since. Furthermore, the price for wet *safed musli* (propagules used for planting) declined to very low rates after the peak in 2000-2001 in response to the declining market prices for the medicinal product and because increased numbers of propagules have become available from the fields as opposed to the forest.

Safed musli probably shows the socio-economic and environmental implications of market forces and changed policies in a pronounced way. The possibility of a "market bubble" created by local demand for propagules, the potential for rapid resource depletion due to unsustainable collection practices and the significant government subsidies do not exist for every NTFP to the same degree as for *safed musli*. In any case, apart from pointing to the potential volatility of markets, the case study also reveals some shortcomings in government policy and the absence of institutions that could mitigate negative implications of market forces for livelihoods and local environments.

The deregulation of Madhya Pradesh's NTFP sector did lead to some of the desired impacts. It freed up the flow of *safed musli* (and other medicinal plants)—even from remote forests—as witnessed by the proliferation of small traders who since recently are continuously scouring remote villages. However, this has created a steady pressure on particular forest resources, as collectors do not stop harvesting products until it is no longer economically worthwhile due to increasing scarcity. Furthermore, by denationalising most NTFPs, ceasing the collection of royalties and eliminating transit passes, the Forest Department has not only withdrawn from the regulation of these forest resources but also weakened its monitoring capacity, which would be crucial for the development of sustainable *in situ* production of medicinal plants.

Furthermore, the NMPB's subsidy schemes had in many cases the opposite of its intended effect to conserve wild stocks through their substitution with cultivated plants. The scheme did not foresee the rapid increase in demand for planting material that encouraged a 'gold rush mentality' in Betul and elsewhere and that resulted in unsustainable extraction of the resource from the forests. Apart from its environmental consequences, the NMPB scheme resulted in the transference of a livelihood opportunity of Adivasi men and women to non-Adivasi asset-rich men—farmers and urban professionals. Because of the expected (and overestimated) profits, many richer farmers in Chicholi Block took up *safed musli* cultivation. Even town-based doctors and lawyers bought or rented land just to take part in the NMPB scheme. Since the cultivation costs of *safed musli* (and most other medicinal plants) are very high, only people with wealth were able to take advantage of the opportunity provided by freer markets and the subsidies. Consequently, the original group of collectors increasingly found themselves as casual labourers on *safed musli* fields working for a comparatively low rate, Rs. 25-40 per day.

In sum, traditional collecting activities have been transformed into large-scale cultivation enterprises where the wealthy have been able to capture the largest share of the benefits from the most valuable products. By contrast, the poorest forest collectors have been left with a highly degraded resource base that may no longer support them when they most need it. In the case of *safed musli*, the combination of globally integrated pharmaceutical companies and *laissez faire* government policies contributed to unsustainable resource use and to a widening of the gap between wealthy and poor classes.

The above-mentioned negative environmental and socio-economic implications could neither be mitigated by local-level organizations, such as the JFM committees or the primary co-operative societies of the MPMFPF. Forest Protection Committees in the studied villages failed to become institutions of effective community participation that could have had any potential to regulate the local extraction of *safed musli* (and other NTFPs) necessary for sustainable forest management. The villagers associate the JFM committees with the Forest Department rather than with themselves. Also, the primary co-operatives are regarded as the Forest Department's body to organize the collection of *tendu patta*, which is viewed as wage labour rather than the application of the granted ownership rights to local NTFPs. The MPMFPF's increasingly market-oriented perspective may even have reinforced a worldview that endorses the commercial development of nature. Indeed, Adivasi people in Jangalbari and Khetpuram seem to view NTFPs primarily as economic opportunity.

6. Wider Livelihood Changes and Contexts

The movement away from the collection of *safed musli* and other NTFPs in Chicholi Block needs to be seen in wider contexts that are not all related to the forest sector. Important changes have particularly taken place in the agricultural sector over the past 15 years. Much later than in most regions of India and partly because of ecological constraints, Green Revolution technologies have become important in Chicholi Block only since the 1990s, thus during an era of liberalization and globalization rather than state-led modernisation as elsewhere. In the mid-1990s, irrigation capacity was greatly enhanced in this region through several small-scale government irrigation schemes. This was supported by the electrification of Jangalbari in 1992 that made the use of electrical pumps for well irrigation possible. Furthermore, farmers gained access to improved hybrid seed varieties, fertilisers and pesticides. Also, the cultivation of soybean started much later here than in the more fertile Malwa region. Between 1992 and 2003, for example, the area of irrigated land in Jangalbari grew by 300 per cent, the net acreage of productive land increased by 21 per cent, the number of cultivated crops doubled (especially vegetables were added) and the production of wheat and soybean tripled (District of Betul, 2004). Irrigation has enabled farmers to produce wheat in the rabi season for subsistence. This has allowed them to grow soybean for cash in kharif resulting in reduced cultivation of coarse grains such as *kordu* and *kutki*. Generally, the subsistence nature of agriculture has diminished in the shadow of marketisation—the more so as farmers now take on loans to produce cash crops. Furthermore, wage labour is increasingly paid in cash as opposed to in kind of foodgrains.

These agricultural changes in Chicholi Block did not only arrive comparatively late but they have also not been as dramatic as in other districts, such as nearby Harda. The enormous increase in soybean and wheat production in other districts, therefore, has increased the demand for migrant labour. Although migration from Chicholi Block existed prior to market-oriented reform, it recently has become much more widespread and more frequent. Migration provides people a new significant livelihood opportunity, and contributes to larger cash components in household incomes. People in the studied villages now migrate for soybean weeding and harvesting (for which they are paid in cash) in kharif and for the wheat harvest in rabi (for which they are paid in kind). Parallel to the increase in migration, bus service between Betul and Harda districts have tripled over the past 10 years, generally strengthening the communication links to the outside world.

The agricultural intensification, commercialization and monetisation since the 1990s contributed to the modification of forest-based components of rural livelihoods in the study villages, apart from the degradation of forest resources and the volatility of the medicinal plant market as discussed in section 5. Until the early 1990s, nearly all villagers, regardless of class or caste used to collect *mahua*, *tendu patta*, *harra*, *baharra*, *amla*, *chironji*, *guggul*, *safed musli* and other NTFPs as an important part of their subsistence strategy. Families used to eat *mahua* seed and *safed musli* leaves just before the beginning of the rainy season in June as a last resort to keep from starving or to avoid having to take consumption loans. Only the surplus product that was not consumed locally was sold to visiting private traders (an exception is *tendu patta* which has to be sold to government commission agents). After the marketisation of many, and the depletion of most, NTFPs in Chicholi Block, now only the very poorest continue collecting NTFPs. However, only able-bodied men now can use this livelihood activity of the last resort, and women and older people risk becoming further marginalised as they are not able to go the long distances now necessary to find the scarce valuable species.

On the other hand, a majority of villagers no longer seem to have to take seasonal recourse on the consumption of NTFPs, as the *mahua* seeds in June. Indeed, most families have been able to substitute more profitable activities such as agriculture, migration or forest work provided by the government for the collection of NTFPs. Villagers that possess land or other assets that allow them to diversify their livelihood options look upon the forest no longer as a source of subsistence but as a stock portfolio that they draw upon when the market value of particular plants increases. The subsistence function of NTFPs has also declined because villagers have become less likely to rely on natural medicines and traditional cures. They now prefer to go to doctors and buy allopathic medicines.

When we asked men from the study village to rank different livelihood activities according to their own preference, they gave the following ranking in descending order: cultivation on own land, Forest Department labour contracts, wage labour on local agricultural fields, migration and, lastly, NTFP collection. Similarly, women in the study villages prefer to work the family's land rather than migrate for agricultural or construction labour, and NTFP collection remains the option of last resort since the only wild NTFPs located close to the village tend to yield very low cash values. Moreover, the presently most commonly collected NTFPs, such as *mahua*, *amla* and *chironji*, are now coming mostly from trees planted on private land.

7. Conclusion

The study has shown that the original collectors of forest-based medicinal plants in the tribal belt of Madhya Pradesh have not been able to take advantage of new opportunities created by market access and integration, liberalization of the NTFP sector and increased global demand for natural remedies. Paradoxically, the importance of medicinal-plant collection for their livelihoods has even decreased. This is because the "freed" markets themselves undermined the forest resource base, commercial cultivation on agricultural land has in many cases substituted for the forest-based collection of medicinal plants, and the comparatively late agricultural modernisation brought about new alternative livelihood activities. The implications of globalization, liberalization and modernisation have been uneven and led to the fragmentation of the previously forest-dependent livelihoods along class, gender and age lines. Now, NTFP collection remains only a livelihood activity of last resort, and only for able-bodied men who are physically and socially able to go the long distance and spend the long time in forests that have become necessary to search for the valuable medicinal produce.

Of course, it would be naïve to think that growing global demand in a fairly liberalized sector would directly lead to the sustainable improvement of livelihoods of the rural poor. Rather, a multitude of institutions are filtering the effects of increased demand. Indeed, the government subsidy schemes for the commercial cultivation of medicinal plants—which have been successful in terms of take-up and production increase—have pronounced the fragmenting implications of globalization. By contrast, community-based institutions, which would have the potential to act on new challenges and opportunities created by market-oriented reform, have largely been absent in the study area. The JFM committees, the primary co-operatives of MPMFPF and the panchayat gram sabhas all have rights and responsibilities in the NTFP sector, but they constitute formal local-level organizations that have been created from above. In most cases, they do not involve a sense of community ownership or effective community participation. It also seems that only in the case of the primary co-operatives, the policy-makers have directly attempted to bring local-level institutions in line with the market-oriented reform and to facilitate access to the growing NTFP and medicinal plant market. In practice, however, the villagers (all of them official co-operative members) are either not aware of their primary co-operative or regard it simply as the institution designated by the Forest Department to organize the collection of *tendu patta*.

Seeing the continued livelihood importance of the highly regulated and nationalised *tendu patta* collection and procurement, one may be tempted to demand the re-regularisation and nationalisation of NTFPs. *Tendu patta* is not allowed to be harvested outside a prescribed season, which has protected the resource base, and the collectors generally earn more than double the wage they receive for working in *safed musli* fields, for example. However, the costs of monitoring and enforcing government regulations would be very high given the large number of marketed NTFPs, of which many are traded in small quantities only. Collusion between traders and government officials would also be likely to negate the intended environmental impact as well as the socio-economic benefit to Adivasi populations. Strengthening local participatory institutions and linking them to higher-level organizations and markets may remain the best option, although this is a very tall order.

More fundamentally, however, one may challenge the whole market-based approach to "development" and (global) integration. Adivasi communities too increasingly view the forest as a monetary income source as opposed to a renewable storehouse of household supplies, food and medicines. Their forest-related activities and practices are increasingly based on the (fluctuating) market value of particular forest products. This way of using and seeing the forest may contribute to, and be part of, an overall socio-cultural change that has been accompanied by a gradual shift in lifestyle from relatively localised experience and subsistence to increased integration to the global marketplace. Local institutions will be necessary again, not only to reduce the dependence on, and vulnerability to, the ebb and flow of the global market place, but also to attach new local meanings to globalization and to reaching out into the world.

References

Agrawal, A. (2001), The Regulatory Community: Decentralization and the Environment in the Van Panchayats (Forest Councils) of Kumaon, India. *Mountain Research and Development*, 21(3), 208-211.

Backhaus, N. (2003), The Globalization Discourse. IP 6 Institutional Change and Livelihood Strategies Working Paper No. 2. The Swiss National Centre of Competence in Research North-South.

Baldev, R. (1998), Political Structure and India's Economic Reforms of the 1990s. *Public Affairs*, 71(3), 335-58.

Ballabh, V. and Balooni, K. (2002), Why Local Resource Management Institutions Decline: A Comparative Analysis of Van (forest) Panchayats and Forest Protection Committees in India. *World Development*, 30(12), 2153-67.

Breman, J. (1996), *Footloose Labour: Working in India's Informal Economy*. Cambridge: Cambridge University Press.

Castells, M. (1997). *The Power of Identity*. Oxford: Blackwell Publishing.

Chambers, R. and Conway, G. (1991), Sustainable Rural Livelihoods: Practical Concepts for the 21st Century. IDS Discussion Paper, No. 296.

Corbridge, S. and Harriss, J. (2000), *Reinventing India: Liberalization, Hindu Nationalism and Popular Democracy*. Malden, Mass.: Blackwell Publishers Inc.

Corbridge, S. and Jewitt, S. (2004), From Forest Struggles to Forest Citizens? Joint Forest Management in the Unquiet Woods of India's Jharkland. Corbridge *et al.* (eds.), *Jharkhand: Environment, Development, Ethnicity*, 232-63. New Delhi: Oxford University Press.

Department of Agriculture (2004), Government of Madhya Pradesh. Accessed at www.mp.nic.in/agriculture.

Department of Forests (2004), Government of Madhya Pradesh. Accessed 21 July 2004. Available at www.mp.nic.in/forest.

Department of Forests (2003), Government of Madhya Pradesh. Accessed 27 February 2004. Available at www.mp.nic.in/forests.

Department of Tribal Welfare (2003), Implementation of the Bhopal Declaration. Government of Madhya Pradesh. Accessed 2 November 2004. Available at www.mp.nic.in/tribal/bhopalghoshana/english/turnover.htm.

District of Betul (2004), Department of the District Magistrate, Village Land Records.

District of Betul (2003), Government of India, Accessed 2 February 2004. Available at www.betul.nic.in.

Dreze, J. & Sen, A. (1995), *India: Economic Development and Social Opportunity*. Toronto: Oxford University Press.

Harriss-White, B. (2003), *India Working: Essays on Society and Economy*. Cambridge: Cambridge University Press.

Hoogvelt, A. (1997), *Globalization and the Postcolonial World: The New Political Economy of Development*. London: Macmillan.

Khilnani, S. (1997), *The Idea of India*. Toronto: Penguin Books Canada Ltd.

Kumar, S. (2004), Does "participation" in Common Pool Resource Management Help the Poor? Corbridge, S. *et al.* (eds.), *Jharkhand: Environment, Development, Ethnicity*, 203-31. New Delhi: Oxford University Press.

MPMFPF (2004), M.P. State Minor Forest Produce (Trading and Development) Co-operative Federation. Accessed 21 October 2004. Available at www.mfpfederation.com.

NMPB (2004), National Medicinal Plants Board, Ministry of Health & Family Welfare, Government of India, Accessed 21 October 2004. Available at www.nmpb.nic.in.

Robins, K. (1997), Encountering Globalization. Held D., & McGrew A. (eds.), *The Global Transformations Reader: An Introduction to the Globalization Debate*, 239-45. Cambridge: Polity Press.

Scoones, I. (1998), *Sustainable Rural Livelihoods: A Framework for Analysis*. IDS Working Paper, 72, 1-22.

Shepard, B. & Hayduk, R. (2002), From ACT UP to the WTO: Urban Protest and Community Building in the Era of Globalization. London: Verso.

Shroff, M. (1999), Globalization: A Stock-taking. *Economic and Political Weekly*, 2, October.

Stiglitz, J. (2002), *Globalization and Its Discontents*. New York: Penguin Books.

WHO (2004), *World Health Organization*, Accessed 14 May 2004, Available at www.who.int/en.

PART III

SOCIETY, INFORMATION TECHNOLOGY AND GENDER

Information Technology and Marginalization: A Sociological Understanding of India

13

Nagaraju Gundemeda

I

Introduction

Technology is one of the greatest engines of economic growth and change in society, and its role has been increasing day by day. Technology is the mediating among the social groups of diverse nature. Like all the major transformations in history, the impact of Information Technology is multidimensional: technological, economic, social and mutation for social development, for people's lives and well-being (Castells, 1999). The invention of computer is seen as one of the pivotal events in the history of human civilization. In the early 1960s, computer technology began to have enormous influence on science, mathematics, engineering, business and commerce. But today's computer technology reaches far beyond the limited scope of early years. Presently, it touches virtually every field of the human activity, and it has transformed many of them beyond recognition (Douglas, 1998).

Castells (1999) cautions that Information Technology may not be the only cause for the changes in our lives but without the new information and communication technologies none of what is changing our lives would be possible. Since the 1990s the entire planet has begun to get organized around telecommunication networks with computers at the heart of information systems and communication processes.

The recent great strides in technology present tremendous opportunities for human development, but achieving the potential depends on what kinds of technologies are to be developed and how technologies are used. The rat race for knowledge, with the advent of knowledge economy at the forefront of the global interaction, a great deal of attention has been focused on information and communication technologies (Human Development Report, 1999).

The blend of computers and communications unleashed an unprecedented exploration of the ways to communicate at the beginning of the 1990s. This period marked a tremendous productive gain, ever-falling losses and rapidly growing networks of computers, which have transformed the computing and communications sector. The first half of the 1990s experienced a shift of Internet from a specialized tool of scientific community to a friendlier network transforming social interaction (*Ibid.*).

The wider application of Information Technology fundamentally shifted the production of services and led to the development of Information Society in most of the developed nations. Some of the symptoms of Information Society are evident even in developing countries like India.

Rise of the Information Society

During the last two decades, success to any field has become practically impossible without Information Technology. In manufacturing, policing, medicine, entertainment, banking and education, or for that matter in any other field, information technology is set to change drastically everything that human beings do in advanced societies (Lyon, 1988).

If we trace the history of information society, it has roots in the literature of 'post-industrialism', a popular social science concept of the 1960s and 1970s, which heralded the end of the industrial capitalist era and the beginning (or start) of a 'service' or 'leisure' society. Particularly Daniel Bell's (1973) work on post-industrial society has become popular in the information society literature. According to him, just as agrarian society was replaced by industrial society as the dominant one, economic emphasis shifted from land to manufacturing. Basically the post-industrial society emerged as a result of the economic tilt towards the service-based society in the later half of the 20th century. To put it succinctly, the hand-mill gives you a society with the feudal lord and the steam mill, that of the industrial capitalist.

Douglas (1998) emphasized that in order to understand the significance of information revolution there is a need to look for historical parallels. The information age has to be understood in the context of the already existing technological advancements particularly in the field of language, writing, and printing. Douglas (1998) argues that Information Technology has begun to radically change the social institutions, workplace, business organizations, culture, family relations and education system. Technology tends to create technocracy, a rule by technocrats or technological experts.

Analytical discussions of James Martin (1978) emphasized the role of information in an era of information age. Alvin Toffler's popular 'Third Wave' concept highlights the significant changes that have occurred historically in social structure. According to Toffler, the first wave is agriculture, the second wave is industry and the third wave is Information Technology.

In this context Lyon (1988) argues that what steam engine (or more properly the clock) was to industrial society the computer is to information society. The roots of the information society idea are not limited to Sociology alone. According to James Beniger (1986), the roots of the so-called Information Society are more properly sought in what he calls the 'control revolution,' analysed at the turn of the century by theorists of bureaucracy, such as Max Weber. Sociological theories have not yet crystallized around the concept of 'information society'.

Like Toffler, Daniel Bell (1980) and Marc Porat (1977) promptly captured the changes occurred in erstwhile society and named the emerging society as post-industrial society. An attempt has been made to provide explanation by highlighting the unique features of the information society such as growth of number of workforce in the service sector, shift in the nature of production, *i.e.* manual to mental/knowledge. While analysing the experience of living in the information society Mark Porat highlights that the consumption of information has become an increasingly necessary and conspicuous aspect of everyday life. However, the question of proper social distribution of information needs to be theorized (Porat, 1977).

New Society and Demand for New Skills

Key to information society discourse is the contention that 'information workers' are rising to a majority within the labour forces of the advanced societies. According to Marc Porat (1977), as early as in 1967, 50 per cent of the American workers were engaged in the 'information sector,' and they received 50 per cent of the total employee remuneration. The number of workforce engaged in the service sector is growing at multifold level cutting across the continents with varying degrees of proportion.

The major outcome of Information Technology is the fundamental shift in the mode of production and organization of work. As the foregoing account implies, the new technology, which shaped the new society significantly, changes the nature of work that is primarily different from the agricultural and industrial societies. The new society sustained by the human resources is of high skilled professionals. Information Technology skill profile tends to change from the concentration on middle-range craft and supervisory skill to increasingly high-range qualification and from narrow specialization to broader, multipurpose skills for information handling. Diversity and flexibility at all levels work as substitute for homogeneity and dedicated systems. In the long run industry of software creation, adoption and application will become a major employer. As microcomputers with large-scale integration have become available, they are being used for an even greater number of applications, range of equipment and systems. According to Douglas (1998), the new computerized servant class would be radically different from those of the past, and it would completely avoid the moral difficulties involved with slave holding and other inequalities through the ages, but it may not avoid all the practical difficulties involved with the existence of social class.

With the foregoing account on the nature and scope of IT, in the following pages we critically analyse the nature of Information society and the social groups who are included and excluded in the newly emerging society. Most of the social scientists and policy-makers notice that there is a new society, which is fundamentally different from the Industrial society that emerged in Europe in general and America in particular during the post World War II. Here, we have presented a brief overview of the scholars who have interpreted the 'new' society from different views and perspectives.

Stonier (1983) forcefully argues that, we live in a post-industrialist society and for better or worse we have moved into an information age. Information society promotes democratic state and strengthens its services. At this juncture, Manual Castells (1999) has raised several questions as, is there a shared meaning for every one? Or must we differentiate people in terms of their specific relationship to the process of social change? If so, what are the criteria for such a differentiation?

In this paper, an attempt has been made to understand the nature and organization of Information Technology industry in India, and to explore what are the social groups who are making use of the opportunities generated by the IT industry and highlights how far the marginal social groups are in position to make of these opportunities leveraged by IT.

Here, a brief analysis has been made to show the spread of Information Technology across the world.

TABLE 1

Internet Use Worldwide (as of August 2001)

Name of the country	Million of users	Percentage of users
World Total	513	8.5
Canada & U.S.	181	57.3
Europe	155	21.3
Latin America	25	4.8
Asia/Pacific/Middle East	149	4.0
Africa	4	0.5

Source: www.nua.ie & www.prb.org.

It is evident from Table 1 that the proportion of the users of computers across the world has been changing significantly from continent to continent, the most contrasting observation could be the proportion of the users of computers in US and Canada is comparable to the rest of the world. The European nations also far ahead of the rest of the continents such as Latin America, Asia/Pacific/Middle East Africa in use of computers in day-to-day life. One can draw a significant conclusion that the spread of IT is only limited to the most developed countries in the world, whereas the rest of the world is not experienced the diffusion of technology in more effective form.

As a part of the software development, regions and firms that concentrate on the most advanced production and management systems are increasingly attracting talent from around the world, while leaving aside a significant fraction of their own populations whose educational level and cultural/technical skills do not fit the requirements of the new production system. For example, the Silicon Valley, the world centre for production of Information Technology is attracting every year thousands of engineers and scientists from China, Taiwan, Singapore, Korea, Israel, Russia and Western Europe in general and India in particular (Castells, 1999).

Kloet (2002) notices that within Asia, one easily identifies a clear division between the developed countries such as South Korea, Taiwan, Hong Kong, Singapore and Japan compared to the developing countries like China and Indonesia. Table 2 presents the level of connectivity in a selected number of Asian countries.

According to Jeroen de Kloet (2002), there are significant differences in the spread of Internet between the north and south (East and West). Within the continents like Asia, one can notice tremendous variations between the developed and developing countries and he also observes that within the country like China, the Western region is lagging behind in the use of Internet compared to proportion of users in coastal region of the same country. Most of the scholars in academic discourse and media name the new emerging social reality as under the term "The Digital Divide." As Kloet claims that the USAID report, "more and more concern is being shown about the impact of those left on the other side of the digital divide—the division between the information 'haves' and 'have nots.'"

TABLE 2

Connectivity in Asia

Sl. No.	Name of the country	Millions of users	Percentage of users
1.	Bangladesh	0.07	0.02
2.	China	33.7	2.70
3.	Hong Kong	3.93	54.5
4.	India	5.0	0.49
5.	Indonesia	2.0	0.88
6.	Japan	47.08	37.2
7.	Malaysia	3.7	17.0
8.	Nepal	0.05	0.2
9.	Pakistan	1.2	0.85
10.	Philippines	2.0	2.46
11.	Singapore	1.12	49.3
12.	South Korea	22.2	46.4
13.	Sri Lanka	0.121	0.63
14.	Taiwan	11.6	51.8
15.	Thailand	1.2	1.96
16.	Vietnam	0.1	0.13

Although the Government of India has evolved policies to spread the growth of India by giving slogans like "Internet for All", when we look at the statistics of users, it is much less compared to even the proportion of educated population. The current Internet subscriber base in India is 3.3 million and the user base is 16.5 million. The planned projection is 230 million by the end of the year 2007. The rural areas are far-behind in getting Information Technology and Internet connections.

II

Information Technology Opportunities in the Indian Context

According to The Nasscoms' (National Association of Software and Service Companies), annual survey based on the performance of the Indian IT-ITeS industry (excluding hardware) claims that the overall Indian IT-ITeS industry (including domestic market) grew by 32 per cent during 2004-2005, registering revenues of $22 billion, up from $16.7 billion in 2003-2004. The report also reveals that the Indian software and services exports industry expects a strong growth of around 30 to 32 per cent in 2005-2006, touching revenues of $22.5 billion, Indian software and services exports clocked the revenues of $17.2 billion, registering a growth of 34.5 per cent during 2004-2005.

Annual Nasscom Survey also claims the most important factor that the employee base in the IT sector has grown at a significant rate of 23.6 per cent, from 242,000 in FY 2001-02 to 697,000 in FY 2004-05 and the industry employee base crossed the 1 million mark in the FY ended 05. Without any doubt one can draw a conclusion that Information Technology industry is the only sector, which has the potential to generate employment opportunities at a large scale.

Salary Package of the IT Professionals

If we look at the salaries of the workforce involved in IT sector, one will automatically come to the conclusion that IT workforce is the highest paid group in India. Most of the employees who (in majority) fall under below 30 years of age group tend to draw more than any university professor and IAS officer.

Here, we have presented Table 3, which shows the salaries of IT professionals with number of years of experience on the field.

The Table 3 shows the changing pattern in employee salaries with number of years of experience. It is observed that the fresh employees draw a minimum of Rs. 16,000 per month where the students with non-professional degree background, for example, Ph.D. may hardly get Rs. 15,000 as a starting salary. Within the span of 10 years of service the software professional comfortably draws more than Rs. 10 lakhs, in other words Rs. 83,333 per month, for the university professor in India drawing even half of that salary is definitely a daydream.

TABLE 3

Salaries of IT Professional in India

Salaries:	IT workforce							
Experience	Less than 2 Years		2-5 Years		5-10 Years		Over 10 Years	
Salary per annum	% of employees		% of employees		% of employees		% of employees	
	2004	2003	2004	2003	2004	2003	2004	2003
Less than Rs. 2 lakh	36.5	15.3	9.8	7.5	6	2.9	–	2.3
Rs. 2 to 3 lakh	34	48.6	20.7	24.3	10.5	12.3	3.5	3.3
Rs. 3.1 to 4.5 lakh	24.5	28	34.1	45.9	15	22.9	9.7	11
Rs. 4.6 to 6 lakh	2.5	5.6	22.3	17.6	21.6	30	12.4	20.4
Rs. 6.1 to 8 lakh	1.3	0.8	8.4	4.2	20.7	19	7.1	6.7
Rs. 8.1 to 10 lakh	1.3	0.5	2.7	0.1	12	9.1	13.3	14.6
Rs. 10.1 to 15 lakh	–	1.2	2	0.2	11.7	3.3	28.3	27.4
Rs. 15.1 to 25 lakh	–	–	–	0.1	2.1	0.4	17.7	12.5
Rs. 25.1 to 35 lakh	–	–	–	–	–	–	6.2	1.5
Over Rs. 35 lakh	–	–	–	0.2	0.6	–	1.8	0.3
Average salary (Rs. lakh)	2.6	3	4.2	3.8	6.7	5.4	12.4	9.9
% Change in average salary	–12%		11%		24%		26%	

Source: Data Quest (2004).

The immediate employment opportunities and comparatively higher salaries tend to drive most of the student even cutting across their disciplinary background to the IT related streams in order to get employment opportunities in IT industry. However, the question, which is important to be addressed, is the non-engineering background students are absorbed by IT industry? The answer is defiantly no, if we look at the following graph we could easily understand the disciplinary background of the IT employees.

Engineers are most preferred by the employers of IT industry. Students with technical disciplinary backgrounds such as Engineering and Computer related degrees such MCA and BCA are the most sought after degrees in IT industry. *Data Quest* (DQ) survey found that nearly three-fourths of the respondents (who participated in their survey) had a technical qualification

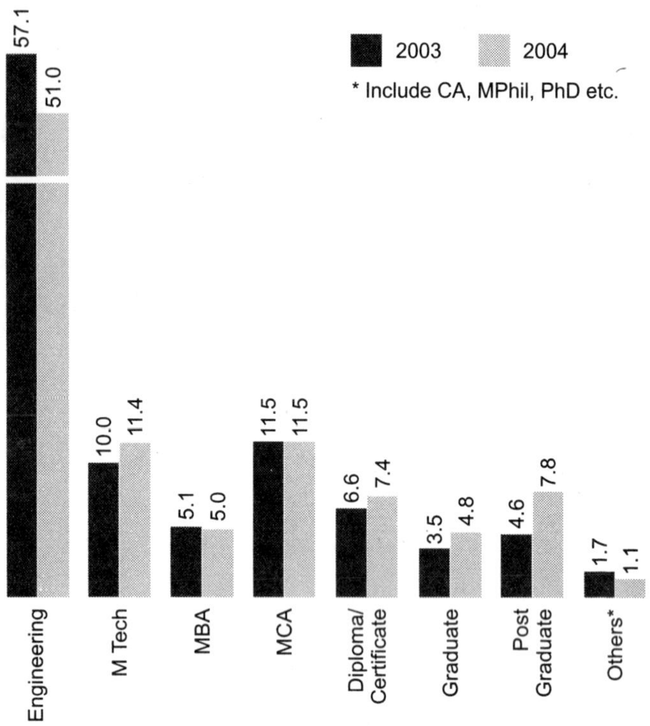

that is either an engineering degree or an MCA. An interesting trend, though, was the paucity of graduates with a business/ management degree.

http://www.dqindia.com/content/top_stories/2004/204100601.asp

A Trend towards Homogenization of Higher Education in India

It is also very clear from job advertisements particularly from early 1980s that one's chances of getting employment are enhanced by the possession of qualifications in micro-electronics, computing, systems analysis, telecommunications, fiber optics, expert systems and so on. The buzzword in Indian higher education today is Information Technology. This can be seen in the proliferation of IT-related courses in colleges and mushroom growth of computer engineering in engineering colleges (Pillai, 2000).

IT education and training is imparted by two sectors in India; formal sector consists of academic institutions such as universities, colleges and special institutions. The private colleges and private institutes such as NIIT, Aptech, CMC and SSI, to name a few which have acquired national stature, and thousands of local institutions spread across the country. This privately instates accounts for training of more than 5 lakh students per year. This sector is popularly known as non-formal sector.

Almost all universities started/expanded degree level programmes in IT. Government has been liberal in giving affiliations to privately run institutes that focus only on IT degree programmes (Maheswari, 2000). More than 700 engineering colleges in the country offer technical degree at graduate and postgraduate level. The formal sector, at degree level (B.Tech./B.E./M.C.A.), is in a position to produce 75,000 graduates every year.

In India, one can witness a shift from traditional disciplines in basic sciences to technologically oriented disciplines, in general and IT education, in particular because of the wide range of opportunities associated with it. According to *The Hindu* (2001), a newspaper, most of the people are spending more money on education than on any other item/activity. Since Independence this is the first time that a good number of Indians have been thrilled at the prospect that a degree in an IT course can offer them good employment in foreign countries as well as in India. The country is witnessing a mushrooming of engineering colleges in large numbers and computer training institutions (*The Hindu* 27-2-2001). What happens to the non-technical background graduates, if only the organized sector like IT has the potential to generate the large-scale employment opportunities?

Here, one can see the serious implications of this kind of trend towards homogenization of higher education. First outcome is if most of the students opt for IT related courses, what happens to the other fundamental disciplines such as Physics, Chemistry, Mathematics and Biological Sciences. It is important to highlight that due to the overemphasis on computer education, the social and economic advantages associated with it led to no seekers for admission into the prestigious science labs like TIFR (Tata Institute of Fundamental Research), Bombay, and most of the universities are suffering from a lack of potential candidates for research in the fundamental sciences which is the base for research and development in science and technology. The second question I would like to highlight is what would happen to the humanities and social sciences streams, if the same trend continues? It has been observed that it is these streams which are hardly hit by the IT craze.

To quote Ambrose Pinto (2000), due to commercialization of education in India, over the last one decade the number of students opting for basic science streams has dropped to less than 19 per cent from the 32 per cent and created fear among the scientific community about the future of research and development in fundamental science.

Over a period of time the accumulated utilitarian value attitude attached to the utility of the subject within popular perception of government functionaries in the State led to evolve a step towards withdrawing of social sciences from under graduate colleges during times of then Chief Minister of Andhra Pradesh, Nara Chandrababu Naidu (*Deccan Chronicle*, 13 December 1999). The IT education and training that began in the 1970s and by the late 1980s received a consistent and considerable attention, as values attached to different streams of education significantly changed in the context of globalization. The Indian higher education is being shaped by technological factors as in the Western context, particularly the computer education virtually transforming the educational ethos and priorities. MNCs and Indian business houses have been entering the educational market in a big way.

According to Chitnis (2000), the caste disparities become evident in significant ways in the process of enrolment of students of disadvantaged castes. Most of these sections were predominantly taking admission into liberal arts and commerce courses at undergraduation and continue into PG and further courses. A very limited number of students were enrolled for science and technology courses. One of the reasons for preferences towards social sciences and humanities among the lower class students is that these streams are considered to be less expensive; secondly, access to these courses is much easier compared to the professional courses. It has been clear that most of the students who opt for social sciences and humanities are students from Dalit, Backwards Castes and Women. However, on the other hand, the proportion of employees in the IT industry with Arts background is almost insignificant. This leads to an assumption/ conclusion that the majority of the marginal sections have been systematically marginalized from the best employment in IT industry.

Fluctuation in the IT industry

One can get an idea of the impact of the slowdown by looking at the observations made by the IT education and training industry reports. It is observed that the computer education industry seems to be facing challenges with changes in student's attitudes due to the slowdown in IT industry.

Owing to the ever-changing scenario in software industry, IT educational institutions both in formal and non-formal sectors, have been challenged to anticipate market shifts and at the same time continue with the basic structure of the academia. Most of the people continue to believe that IT can offer better career options than most of the other disciplines, in spite of the tentative slowdown (*Data Quest*, July 2002). *Data Quest* (2002) highlights that out of 15 lakh students who did some sort of computer course or other during 2001 only 30,000 got jobs. It further confirms the above fact. According to it, out of 5 lakh students who did NIIT courses only 16,000 got jobs. It claims that an overwhelming majority of undergraduates who are responsible for 70 per cent of the industry's revenue realized that quickie courses in non-formal sector would take them nowhere.

The CEO of Aptech admitted that the number of students opting for short-term courses has fallen by 30-40 per cent. This is due to the slowdown in the American economy on which the Indian IT industry mainly depends. According to the survey, out of 4,30,000 students in Aptech 2,00,000 opted for short-term courses, this registered a drop rate of 30-40 per cent (*Data Quest Survey*, 2002).

The recruitment pattern of employment in the IT companies showed that only 20 per cent students with diploma background recruited were able to get employment. It is observed that although IT training market has been expanding in quantity, the quality of faculty to train those knowledge workers is not growing proportionately. This is the basic limitation both in formal and non-formal sector IT institutes (*Data Quest Survey*, 2002).

The changes in IT industry determine the fate of demand for IT education and training or negative growth rate in India reflects the relation between the centre and periphery. According to this perspective, the periphery adjusts itself in correspondence with the needs or requirements of the centre, *i.e.* capitalist developed world.

Rural-Urban Divide in Software Industry

Data Quest (2001) on the basis of survey claims that among the software professionals 65 per cent of those with 2–5 years experience, considered to be the backbone of IT industry hails from the urban cities and towns.

With the foregoing account it is important to overview how far Indian state is successful in popularising technology particularly the information and communication technology across the regions of India.

Level of Awareness and Exclusion

The preliminary analysis on the spread of IT and the users of IT in India may easily lead the scholar to conclude that it is the upper castes and middle classes of the Indian society, who have some basic understanding about the hierarchical caste system.

According to Pradeep Kumar (2004), Information Technology is not spreading to rural areas of India and its scope is very limited. A majority of the people of India is outside the pale of the communication and technology networks. Access to hardware to the majority of the people who are primarily located in rural areas, is relatively impossible, given the economic, literacy and educational levels. IT is confined to a cluster of major urban centres catering to the upper sections and the educated English knowing middle classes. IT is essentially elitist and if it has to deliver a variety of social services, it has to break this barrier.

While the gender composition in the IT sector is male dominated, it is the call centres that employ women in large scale. Since these women have to work at nights, otherwise prohibited by law, the specific issue of security also assumes significance. Wages of the workers in the call centres are very low compared with the wages of those in the software segment. Abuse of women in call centres is a growing phenomenon, to quote Simon Caulkin, "The abuse of Asian call centre staff by customers is symptomatic of corporate mess-up on grand scale" (*The Hindu*, When 'best' is bad, 5-6-05: 13).

Caste Discrimination

Although there is no authentic study about the caste discrimination in the IT industry, it is easy to brush aside the age-old institution of caste system, which has strong roots in India. Backward castes, tribes and Dalits have a tendency to hide their caste in order to escape from the caste discrimination in the IT sector. To quote V. Venkatesan (2002):

> Manoharlal's son completed his B.Tech. in Computer Science from the Regional Engineering College in Kurukshetra, Haryana, and was looking forward to attending the campus interviews. He had secured the sixth position in the college despite his modest background, and there were a number of good positions available in the Information Technology sector. Several big companies held campus interviews and Manoharlal's son attended them. However, to his dismay, his name figured in none of the lists of the selected candidates. Moreover, he saw his classmates who had won lower grades getting selected. Manoharlal, an assistant in the Chandigarh Secretariat of Haryana, was depressed. Some people advised him not to mention in his son's biodata the fact that he belonged to a Scheduled Caste. He acted accordingly, and companies that subsequently interviewed Manoharlal's son decided to recruit him.

This is just one of the incidents coming to notice of the media, there may be lakh of instances where most of the Dalits are discriminated due to their caste background and victims of the discrimination in many walks of life even today for their survival. Although the Indian economy changing from industrial to information based economy, the social modernity is yet to be achieved among social groups whose mindset is ridden with caste prejudices.

The social background of the workforce in the software and ITES/BPO segment is very much important for any study, according to Pradeep Kumar (2004) if one takes caste background of employees in the IT sector, one could easily find that most of the employees predominantly belong to the upper castes. He further argues that perhaps this is one of the sectors where one would not find the presence of Dalits and tribal groups in addition to the backward castes. From top to bottom it is the upper caste people who are engaged in this sector. Thus, it may not be wrong to demand reservation in private sector. The above adds to the elitist nature of the IT sector.

Marika Vicziany (2000) in her paper titled "The prospects for dalit students: A study on the untouchables in India" argues that, in spite of the emergence of neo-economic culture in the Indian urban centres, however, the college going Dalit youth is struggling to find space in the neo-economic order.

According to Vicziany, due to the lower level of skills and education, which is the result of poor grades, the difficulties of sustained study at home and the lack of facilities in the colleges, which they attend, also seriously put them in disadvantageous position. It is a well-known fact that the IT and IT-enabled service industries tend to expect excellent communication skills particularly in English language and familiarity with the technological and professional qualifications in IT streams that hardly include Dalits in the IT fold. According to her, it is the students from the best colleges in Mumbai who get these jobs. The Dalit students are lagging behind due to their lack of competitiveness in the new labour market. In her studies she did not find any Dalit student who was employable in the IT industry as well as IT-enabled services at different levels. Further, she continues, because of their lack of competitiveness, which is reinforced by domestic conditions, restrict access to computers and Internet.

Omvedt (2004) in her article, 'Untouchables in the World of Information Technology' highlights that like any other social castes many Dalits (ex-Untouchables) in India are trying to break into the new world of Information Technology, but they fear to reveal their origins to their colleagues. With caste attitudes continuing to shape marriages, life chances and career opportunities, the fear is understandable. Here, brief analysis has been made based on the empirical work conducted in Andhra Pradesh to understand the relation between the social background and access to IT education and training which is a major agency to get into the world of Information Technology. Data was collected from 225 students who were doing courses on IT in different IT education centres.

TABLE 4

The Level of Awareness and Castes and Gender

Caste	Male	Female	Total
OC	84 (58)	47 (58)	131 (58.2)
BC	48 (33)	24 (30)	72 (32)
SC	12 (09)	09 (11)	21 (9.3)
ST	—	01 (1)	01 (.5)
Total	144 *64* (100)	81 *36* (100)	225 (100)

Note: Figures in the parenthesis are percentage. The italicized numbers indicate the percentage of the total.

The Table 4 gives an impression that the level of awareness is determined by the position/rank of a particular castes group and gender in social hierarchy. The proportion of women in the upper caste category is nearly half that of the men. This trend gives an impression that women's participation in IT education is growing day by day across all caste groups, especially those living in cities. The less representation of both men and women of the downtrodden castes compared to upper castes could be attributed to their socio-economic backwardness. Due to continuous dependence on traditional occupations which are manual and unskilled and their concentration in the rural areas and lack of cultural and social capital, *i.e.* lack of awareness about educational system, lack of education on the part of parents and economic dependence seem to perpetuate the existing inequalities.

Of the 131 students from 225 belonging to upper caste, 104 reported that their fathers' educational level is bachelors degree and above. In the case of backward caste students the majority reported that their fathers' education is bachelors degree. In the case of SC students, the majority reported that their fathers' educational level was bachelors and above. It shows that the SC students had taken advantage of protective discrimination to achieve higher levels of education. In the case of the single ST student his father had bachelor degree level education. It indicates that irrespective of caste background, the students hail from highly educated households (Nagaraju, 2004).

To understand the pertinent role of parental educational impact, here we quote the statement of two women students whose parents' qualifications vary significantly. The contrast becomes evident, one woman student whose father is a B.Tech. graduate and happened to be CEO of one private firm felt that "IT education is essential for the development of women to lead independent life. My father right from the beginning used to discuss about the IT industry development, IT jobs and the potential of it." This has motivated her to go for IT education.

On the other hand, another student from rural background whose father had primary education felt that "I have joined the IT education by the advice of a counselor of the IT education centre. I am doing a basic course in this IT centre, it is very difficult to understand the jargon and operation of this programmes."

The above two cases show the contrast in the awareness of students about IT education. Lareau (1997) claims that the impact of family background on children's education is most effective and explains that social class is a major predictor of educational and occupational achievement. Educational institutions play a crucial role in the process of social reproduction, and sort out students into social categories that award credentials and opportunities for mobility (Collins, 1979).

TABLE 5

Social Networks in IT Industry and Education (Number of respondents who have relatives working in Industry)

Response	Frequency	Percentage
Yes	91	40
No	134	60
Total	225	100

Source: Nagaraju, G. (2004).

Social networks tend play an important role in gaining access to information pertaining to the job opportunities as well as getting into IT industry. Most of the students who have relatives working as software professionals did indicate that their relatives motivated them to pursue IT courses. Relatives play a crucial role in providing information about the appropriate IT courses, job prospects and other related information.

Here, it is important to mention the Bourdieu (1997) concept of social capital. The basic argument is that wealth in the form of knowledge or ideas plays a key role in shaping the society. It is extension of Marxist idea of economic capital, which highlights that possessors of this capital wield considerable power over others in gaining preferred occupational positions. Even in educational system the success and failure is predominantly dictated by the extent to which individuals possess social capital.

According to the Australian scholar Vicziany (2001), Dalit students do not belong to the community networks, which generate information about job prospects. These networks provide up-to-date information about which jobs are available where. Moreover, given the competitiveness of the Indian job market for graduates, community and family connections and recommendations remain an important consideration in making appointments. In the case of small, backyard operators employing perhaps no more than a dozen people, information about job opportunities travels by word of mouth along well-defined community networks which reflect the social standing of the entrepreneur. If the entrepreneur is a Parsi, Muslim, Brahmin or Christian, they are likely to employ people from the same community not necessarily because they deliberately exclude others but because these communities reflect the routes along which information flows in urban India. Professional networks are also an important aspect of labour recruitment. According to Vicziany (2001), the recruitment of labour in the IT industry reflects a more generalized pattern of recruitment in Mumbai. Preliminary inquiries with the managers of twelve McDonald's restaurants in Mumbai showed that in all cases except one, no Dalits were employed. In the outlet, which did employ Dalits, there were about five; this represented some 10 per cent of the workforce at that particular restaurant. It seems that they simply do not present themselves for employment. They do not do so, because they are excluded from the social networks, which generate information about where those jobs exist. These trends imply that Dalits are not aware of the opportunities opened up by the IT industry.

Highlighting the importance of IT in the information society, Mike Chege (2002) rightly points out that bridging the Digital Divide is not something that emerges after addressing the core issues of development; in fact, IT is the most critical component in addressing the challenges of development in the 21st century. There is no dichotomy between the Digital Divide and the broader social and economic divides, which the development process should address. Failure to address the Digital Divide will only exacerbate the existing social and economic inequalities between countries and diverse social groups.

Conclusion

Emphasis on the use and application of Information Technology in diverse spheres in everyday life has been growing day by day across the world, even the developing countries like India are not exception to this trend. India defiantly ceased the opportunities generated by the IT industry. However, to aspire for the position one should acquire skills in IT. Here education, IT literacy and skills play a vital role in creating awareness as well shaping the students to aspire for the employment opportunities generated by the IT industry. When we look at the educational level of India even after five and half decades of Independence only 65-70 per cent of its population is literate and remaining one-third continue to be illiterate. The general analysis indicates that most of this one-third hail from the marginal sections such as Dalits, Tribes, Backward Castes and Women.

The same trend is also found in the case of Information Technology, most of the IT literacy and IT industries are predominantly concentrated in the urban centres and towns and strengthening the gap between the rural and urban areas in India. The empirical study also reveals that social, economic and educational background of the parents plays an important role in determining and conditioning the social groups to access IT opportunities.

The analysis of the socio-economic background of the students and profile of employees in IT industry reveals that most of the social groups who directly or indirectly benefit from the IT opportunities hail from the upper castes and middle classes, whereas the Dalits, tribal groups and backward sections of the Indian society have been simultaneously marginalized from the digital world. Even the agriculture revolution bypassed the Dalits and other marginal categories, the industrial revolution also fails to accommodate this underprivileged section and lastly the Information Technology revolution emerged in the dawn of new millennium set to exclude the traditionally excluded categories such as the Dalits and tribal groups.

References

Bourdieu, P. (1997), Forms of Social Capital. H. Halsey, *et al.* (ed.), *Education, Culture, Economy and Society*. Oxford: Oxford University Press.

Castells, M. (1999), Information Technology, Globalization and Social Development. *UNRISD Discussion Paper, Vol. 114. Geneva: United Nations Research Institute for Social Development.* www.uoguelph.ca/~res/pacts/COIN/references.htm.

Chege, Mike (2002), Bridging the Digital Divide: ICT is not the Panacea. http://www.apnic.net/mailing-lists/s-asia-it/archive/2002/11/msg00047.html.

Chhabra, Mohit (2004), The DQ-IDC India Salary Survey '04, http://www.dqindia.com/content/top_stories/2004/204100601.asp.

Chitins, Suma (1975), Higher Education and the Scheduled Castes. *Journal of Higher Education*, 112 (Autumn): 167-78.

Chitnis, Suma (2000), The Challenge of Access in Indian Higher Education. *Liberal Education,* 86 (4) (Fall): 10-17.

Chowdary, T.H. (2000), Information Technology in the Services of Government and People of Andhra Pradesh. *Pravasandhrula Pratyeka Sanchika*, 29(4): 305-09. Telugu Academy: Hyderabad.

Collins, R. (1979), *The Credential Society*. New York: Academic Press.

Douglas, Robertson (1998), *New Renaissance: Computer and the Next Level of Civilisation*. New York: Oxford University Press.

Jeroen de, Kloet (2002), *Digitisation and Its Asian Discontents: The Internet, Politics and Hacking in China and Indonesia,* First Monday, Vol. 7, No. 9. URL: http://firstmonday.org/issues/issue7_9/kloet/index.html.

Kumar, Pradeep (2004), Offsourcing of Services: The Case of India. Paper presented in workshop on geographical outsourcing of services, hcic-gemdev seminar trade and development, Paris, 3rd & 4th June, 2004, hussonet.free.fr/mondiali.htm-39k.

Lareau, A. (1997), Social-Class Differentials in Family-School Relationships: The Importance of Cultural Capital. A.H. Halsey, *et al.* (eds.), *Education, Culture, Economy and Society*. Oxford: Oxford University Publications.

Lyon, D. (1988), *The Information Society Issues and Illusions*. Cambridge: Polity Press.

Maheswari, S.N. (2000), IT Education in India: Incorporation of Quality. *The Journal of Public Administration*, July-Sep., xlvi (3): 364-74.

Martin, J. (1978), *The Wired Society*. Harmondsworth: Penguin.

Nagaraju, Gundemeda (2004), Social Differentials and Access: A Study of Private Information Technology Education and Training in Andhra Pradesh, Unpublished Ph.D. thesis submitted to University of Hyderabad, Hyderabad.

Omvedt, Gail (2004), Untouchables in the World of Information Technology, http://www.findarticles.com/p/articles/mi_m2242/is_1660_284/ai_n6141995/pg_2.

Pillai, G. (2000), Higher Education in the 21st Century. *Social Action*, 50 (4): 390-403.

Pinto, A. (2000), Globalization and the Changing Ideology of Indian Higher Education. *Social Action*, 50 (4): 333-347.

Rani, S. and Varma, Y. (2001), Reality? Not Anymore! *Data Quest*, Vol. XIX, No. 9: 60-68.

Stonier, T. (1983), *The Wealth of Information: A Profile of the Post-Industrial Economy*. New Jersey: Ablex.

Team, D.Q. (2001), IT Training Institutions in India. *Data Quest*, 20(11).

Team, D.Q. (2002), The Year of Survival. *Data Quest*, 20(13).

Toffler, A. (1980), *The Third Wave*. London: Pan.

Varma, Yograj and Sarita, R. (2001), Reality? Not Anymore! *Data Quest*, May, First Issue.

Venkatesan, V. (2002), *The Dalit Cause*, Vol. 19, Issue 3, http://www.frontlineonnet.com/fl1903/19030920.htm.

Vicziany, Marika (2000), The Prospects for Dalit Students. Paper presented in European South Asian Studies Association Conference, Edinburgh University 5 to 9 September 2000, Globalisation, economic liberalization and employment, http://www.arts.monash.edu.au/mai/mas/globalisation_dalit.rtf.

Contesting or Reinforcing Hegemony? Social and Cultural Habitus of Young Female Employees in ITES

14

Martina Mettgenberg

"Nationalising Crisis" is primarily concerned with the increasing antagonisms between social classes enforced by the divide between the public and the private as well as the connected social divide. One such antagonistic employment is connected to the growth of IT Enabled Services (ITES). This sector has created numerous chances of new employment for, what could be argued to be a certain class. The research is concerned with the class of people working in this sector and problematises this approach as will be outlined below. This contribution aims to detail the implications for social development of the ITES sector by examining how young women have utilised and have been utilised and hopes to delineate the consequences for their lives.

I. THEORETICAL FRAME

The International Division of Labour and Studying-Up

Societies' development can be seen as progressing dialectically, yet this has been contested by examples of the development of developing nations and the international division of labour. It has been widely recognised that the division of labour has been extended globally to maximise profits. The global production line is split globally with many locations involved in the end-product, creating new classes within and between regions of production. As nations like India have been conceptualised as developing countries, the focus of studies on India has been on agricultural and the poor. Whilst this form of income is the predominant form for a certainly big percentage of the population, as Harriss-White (2002) only recently highlighted, the focus on who is working in urban centres and so-called white-collar jobs reveals the mechanism of power and hegemony. Who are the people working in this sector, what are their backgrounds and future aspirations, what life-choices do they make to achieve these? Do they make choices or are the choices made for them? This paper presumes that there's a local elite that administrates and possibly facilitates the International Division of Labour. Yet, who are these in 2005? What is their role and what exactly does this elite do? Studying-up is a method adopted as a consequence of this conceptualisation and hopes to reveal more about the fine tuning of current events in the "International Division of Labour."

Modernisation and Modernity

India's recent development is due to technological advances and enabled the expansion of the division of labour to an international scale. Next to cultural hegemonies and inherited drive for competition, modernisation is a quantifiable, socio-economic process and undoubtedly and observably ongoing. In particular, Information and Communication Technology (ICT), combined with the age-old capitalist quest for an ever cheaper location for the production of goods and services, accelerated the performance of back-office operations by employees in different time zones. In 1991 India embarked on a series of economic reforms, which enabled more private sector foreign investment into India and created numerous free-trade zones (FTZ).

One such zone is Gurgaon, a district in Haryana close to Delhi, which hosts a variety of MNCs and SMEs. In November 2003 the district development agency announced plans to establish a new FTZ around Garhi Harsanu in Gurgaon district hosting primarily Information Technology Enabled Services (ITES).[1] ITES incorporate data centre management, software development, call centre operations, and desktop and network support. Gurgaon, moreover, is a place for experiments in e-government and as such incorporates software development for the public sector. Within these obviously work people, yet who and what their motivations will be explored below.

The research conceptualises modernity to be integral to modernization, as concepts of modernity facilitate hegemony and thus the acceptance of modernization. Modernity differs from meanings and imaginings of modernization in specific localities. As a concept, modernity is not so much taken for granted and adopted, but contradictorily, locally forged and developed (Osella and Osella, 2000: 260), whilst also sometimes including orthodox traditions (Thangararajah in Osella and Gardner, 2003), hence it is more precise, yet simultaneously more imprecise (Van der Veer, 1999), to talk of modernities. For the purpose of this research it can simply be highlighted that narratives diverge and awareness towards the multiplicity of voices has to be upheld. As Osella and Osella remark: "Whilst modernity such as found in classical theory might never exist anywhere, ideas (concepts and ideals) of something called modernity certainly do exist and are continually appealed to in people's economic endeavours, political projects and identity" (2000: 247). In more practical terms this means that the acting out of modernity is also class specific and crystallises at the intersection of gender and class, as will become apparent in the themes of consumption, marriages and dowry. For now, it should also be emphasised that assumed qualities of modernity are not necessarily universal and "new" (257-59; Prakash 1996 and 1999; Chatterjee 1993 and Chakrabarty 1989), but are related to traditional ideas and concepts. They might depart from tradition and pluralize the narratives available to actors. Or they might dilute tradition, thus being heterogenised by tradition. Both cases are obviously based on tradition and only come into being through tradition (*Ibid.*, 259). As a result Indian modernities create additional narratives to the existing European uni-linear master-narrative derived from modernization theory (Osella and Gardner, 2003). The place of these isn't either one or the other, but is heterogeneous and constantly contested and perpetuated. In both cases though, these are manifest in discourses and practices of individuals and are, depending on *etic* or *emic* perspectives (De Neve in Gardner and Osella, 2003), imbued with power to become master-narratives, thus becoming hegemony/ies.

Modernity and Habitus

If, as Osella and Osella remark: "Whilst modernity such as found in classical theory might never exist anywhere, ideas (concepts and ideals) of something called modernity certainly do exist and are continually appealed to in people's economic endeavours, political projects and identity" (2000: 247) and the narratives of modernity vary and are multiple identities and their fragmentations are more actual than ever before. In the case of India, "the agents of this reflexive engagement with both are those ambivalent 'strangers' (Bauman, 1991) or hybrids (Latour, 1993), the products of western modernity—the western-educated elites—who rework and 'traditionalise' modernity for a home audience" according to Osella and Osella (2000: 259).

What are the processes that make these strangers/hybrids? How could this work in detail? Reproduction and transformation are such processes as Harvey (1989) points out by drawing on Haegerstrand, Bourdieu and Foucault. Reproduction can be conceptualised in terms of time trajectories (Haegerstrand, 1975, in Harvey, 1989), since one day has to be structured into different activities and roles have to be fitted into that, hence it obviously dictates job and family and every other activity. Harvey (1989: 213) furthermore draws on Foucault to illuminate how the physical body exists in time and space. Space then becomes a container of power, which usually constrains but sometimes liberates processes of becoming. De Certeau affirms that social practices get ordered along time and space. Time and space influence people through social practices that can be seen to have been converted into social control.

Yet, it has been demonstrated that social practices and discourses are not only perpetuated and that individuals are not determined and governed by them, but also change them as Bourdieu's theory of habitus express. Since a group such as the middle-class in India exists in all diversity, the symbolism of space might be hard to maintain. Bourdieu (1977) points out the ambiguity of assigning divisions of a group into the spatio-temporal organization: "It is here where the fuzzy logic of practice works wonders in enabling the group to achieve as much social and logical integration as is compatible with the diversity imposed by the division of labour between the sexes, the ages, the occupations (smith, butcher)" (in Harvey, 1989: 215). This then makes transformation possible.

Myth and symbolism play a significant role in the perpetuation of values, however, capitalism seems to have difficulties finding stable myths. Conceptions of space and time change, as do practices and discourses, which are external signs of these changes. Spatial practices though become imbued with class meaning under specific constellations of class, gender, community, ethnicity, race and thus Harvey puts these "practices into historical materialist conceptions of capitalist modernization," *i.e.* emphasizes the dialectic explosive relationship.

Vatuk's ethnography of a white middle-class neighbourhood in Meerut, in which differentiations are made along the lines of modern and traditional (1972: 166-67), the content of each is not corresponding to Western ideas of modern and traditional. Furthermore, beyond the local ideas and conceptions of modernity are other perceptions of modernity on an individual level, which again influence/relate to modernity: gender, generational differences, regional differences, religious differences and caste (de Haan, 2003: 198, in Gardner and Osella, F., *Migration Modernity and Social Transformation in South Asia*). Even more detailed, De Neve (2003: *Ibid.*, 251-80) identifies differences between discourses and practices and introduces emic and etic levels of judgements regarding modern/traditional attributes of people, *i.e.* rural labour migrants from Tirupur in Tamil Nadu in this case. Identifying the locations of modernities will allow me to specify flows and interactions in a more precise, less antagonistic framework thus acknowledging hybridity, contradictions and "traditions" as integral.

My focus is firstly on the household and the workplace as arenas where meanings are generated, and secondly, on spaces of consumption such as cafes, restaurants or malls. Such spheres are observable spaces in which modernities are practiced and narrated and as such they are spheres in which the questions I raise can be studied.

Middle Class(es)

In what ways are modernity, habitus and hegemony connected with/to the urban Delhite middle-class? How might studying consumption in connection with the female middle-class give valuable insights into social reproduction and transformation? The theme of social transformation and reproduction is intrinsically linked to the question of hegemony, thus this research explores the relation of the middle class to hegemony.

Theoretically, the middle class is located between the upper class and working class. Depending on the social system, the upper class consists of aristocrats, owners of the means of production, whilst the working class is supposed to be the producers of goods and services. There does not seem to be place for the middle class in this dialectic, dichotomous theory. Crudely, the middle class might be seen as the administrators of the means of production who oversee the production, but do not hold the means of production themselves. This view however is more complicated than laid out here and largely depends on the stage of the society and its economic stage as well as its administrative structure. Share options on the stock market, as a stake in the control over the means of production, furthermore complicate the situation if possession of the means of production is supposed to be the marker for the class. From a Marxist point of view the economic position of a class influences the social, cultural and political attitudes, and thus fashions class's actions. Deshpande (2004) firstly discusses the term "middle class" and its usage in India from a Marxist perspective, concludes the middle class does not have a place in the dichotomous model consisting of capitalists and workers (Deshpande, 2004: 127). Thus the classic Marxist dichotomy is only of limited applicability for an empirical study of economic and socio-cultural identity deriving from employment in India as is proposed here.

Instead, Deshpande identifies the class system as remainders of the caste system and argues that these are still present in what he calls "the rough and tumble politics of identity" (2004) in contemporary India. His view is that the caste system is still prevalent although class is now the discourse to identify people.

Deshpande points out that higher classes still have an overwhelming percentage of members from higher castes, which makes caste still a vital factor to arrive at a higher class. His point strengthens the argument that it is vital for my research to look at caste and caste/class mobility. The Indian context has been largely influenced by viewing class as a new concept superseding caste and being more fluid than the existing caste system due to its organization along meritocratic rather than hereditary criteria (Berreman).

However, caste as well as class are nonetheless systems of stratification and merely represent a shift in criteria for social stratification, rather than a novelty. More importantly then, it is vital to understand the means and symbols of transcending boundaries of class and caste. Next to economic criteria, the project attempts to analyse terms and definitions of the middle class and look beyond their economic preferences into their political and social history, cultural and social preferences and aspirations. From her experience in Hyderabad, Säävälä (2003) defines the term's usage as "in everyday interactions" classed in the middle between the elite and the poor by her lower-caste research participants (234-35). However, she also gathered, that as to be seen to be middle-class, the members have to have a secure economic standing, education and high caste would not be enough to make a family middle-class. Furthermore, it is necessary to live in a middle-class area to be seen as middle-class (*Ibid.*, 235). Education, caste, economics and residency then seem to be the vital factors to determine class in the Indian middle-class context. Säävälä (2003) furthermore problematises the situation of the new middle-class as between their old poorer lower caste and the new place in the middle class, where they often do not find acceptance. Strategies to nonetheless establish oneself successfully are then highlighted through religiosity/sanskritization for example (see Säävälä above). Classes are then socially and politically important, yet socially a class's inclinations are not homogenous and do not directly derive from their economic position. However, they are of social importance and contrary to their importance very little has been published on the middle class, according to Deshpande (2004: 128). Rather than essentialising however, researching processes of hegemony aims to detect links, networks and flows between these factors.

Economically, India has until recently been seen as a rural backward society, yet Sen (1999) points out that the rural/urban transformation is far from complete and India's modernity is a myth. However, since 1991's reforms by Manmohan Singh the production and employment areas increased in the service sector and thus gave India the image of a fast developing nation, so much so that the recent presidential election campaign of the BJP proudly declared "India" to be "shining." Dampening the hype are reports about the lack of infrastructure and basic amenities such as water, electricity and a functioning sewage system (*Down to Earth*, January 31, 2004: 27-37). Apart from this India's employment possibilities have rapidly improved for a few chosen ones as prestigious IITs and foreign investment document. Caste has been linked to occupation and the fulfilment of a certain occupation and vocation through *dharma* which was handed down with one's genes. The choice of occupation was then limited through the *dharmic* caste rules for the individual. That also implied that prestigious occupations were inaccessible for aspiring socially/upwardly mobile people/individuals. Yet, through industrialisation and new employment possibilities, plus increased mobility prestige has become accessible. Requirements are, for example, education, which is followed by a suitably high income [Bailey (...), Säävälä (2003)] earned in a not necessarily steady, hereditary life-long occupation. Outsourcing can be seen as a big part of this development especially for newly graduated young men and women.

Varma (1998) describes phases of the middle class in political and economic history as well as the middle class's relationship to global changes and differentiates inside developments. Macaulay's minute on Indian education in 1835 aimed to educate Indians as a "class of persons, Indian in blood and colour, but English in taste, opinions, morals and intellect," who would serve as interpreters and stakeholders between the colonial powers and the Indian masses. Varma argues that despite India's millenia-old own civilization, this policy succeeded within a century, as has been markedly demonstrated by Nehru and the Anglo-Indian elite, which led the first decades of independent India and somewhat overruled Gandhian grass-roots politics. Politically, the middle class was loyal to the Congress Party thus being involved in nation-building and its administration. This history seems to justify the middle class's role in maintaining and building hegemony and seems to advance the argument that the middle class is on the forefront of implementing social transformation in the project of development after the model of Western modernity.

However, a shift in loyalty after the death of Nehru in 1964 and the assassination of Indira Gandhi in 1984, fractured middle class's loyalties and rung in a change. Until economic betterment of India in 1964 Varma (1998) sees the middle class engulfed/focuses more on the global realm for its social and economic development. Caste associations, revival of primordial ties and alliances and a bizarre invention of tradition as in the increase of national parties are only a few phenomena documenting a new era which paradoxically focuses on "the home" and Hindu-values (RSS, VHP, BJP) on one level, whilst on another level celebrates "the world" in forms of global modernist ambitions, consumption preferences and new forms of employment (Osella and Osella, 2000).

This dichotomy and ambiguity justifies a closer look at the middle class as a group in particular in terms of transformation and reproduction. Whilst caste status is often associated with ritual purity through marriage, occupation and a closed kinship network, class is significantly determined by production/occupation and has in the Indian context often been associated with the display of consumer goods, which can be argued to turn acquired capital into cultural and symbolic capital (Bourdieu, 1990). To summarise, the political history reveals the relationship between politics and middle class and the loyalties to India as a nation and wider influences throughout the 20th Century, in due course fractures and splits as well as alignments and aspirations are highlighted.

The middle class is then far from homogeneous and is not maintaining one hegemony after all, but, if at all, many small hegemonies. Regardless or perhaps especially because of its diversity in shape or form, the middle class is a social location many adhere to. Aspirants to the middle class see this as membership in the significant middle, comforted from decline into the lower classes with their stigma and insecurities and one step closer to the upper classes (Säävälä, 2003; Nisbett, 2005). Thus, it is a desirable class to belong to as well as to study, since precisely because it is such a wide term it does allow for many meanings and simultaneous transformation as well as reproduction, thus making it flexible and interesting enough to belong to and study. To summarise, the middle class is highly differentiated and markers of class are next to economics, education, lifestyle, aesthetic preferences (Bourdieu, 1986) and social network. Thus the term "class" and especially "middle-class" has to be subcategorised and it has to be taken into account that the middle class identifies itself in cultural, economic, aspirational terms and that there are differences between the lower and upper middle class, new and old middle class along the lines of production, income, culture, consumption and aspirations. This also makes the middle class a site for inter-class diversity and a heterogeneous field for reproduction as well as transformation, which in turn is expressed as habitus in discourses and practices revealing aspirations to modernity. Altogether these constitute hegemony.

Primarily then the research seeks to address the questions: Who actually works in call centres? What are their self-ascribed caste and class identities, what is the purpose of their employment, what aspirations does this fulfil and where does the money go that is earned? What does this represent/mean to the actors, *i.e.* young middle-class women and how do they make sense of their lives in discourse and practice?

Women and Work

Women have often been conceptualised as victims of patriarchy (*e.g.* Moore 1999; Ortner 1974), yet as a result of highlighting the subordination of women it has been revealed that they are more than just "victims." The debate of women in development (Searle-Chatterjee, 1976; Sharma, 1979) might have been perpetuating liberal ideas (Kabeer, 1997), yet the focus contributed to seeing women in a different light and led the way to contemporary studies of women emphasising agency (Gold and Raheja, Lamb). These studies utilised the emphasis on suppressed voices of women to discover resistance and an alternative narrative to the master narrative, thus merging with, if not pre-empting 1990's ideas of positionality.

What impact however does employment have on the families, their shape and, more importantly, for female experience of families and households? Kapadia (1995) describes in her ethnography on South Indian non-Brahmin yet upwardly mobile Muthurajah and Pallar women the effects of hypergamous marriage and salaried jobs on female untouchables' lives in Aruloor, Tamil Nadu:

> Whereas both wives and husbands had relatively equal occupations as agricultural workers, this relatively equal relationship has now given way to an extremely unequal one, in which the husband is—and is expected to be—the earner, the wife is transformed from a fellow earner into a financial dependant. (*Ibid.*, 57-58)

She thus concludes that:

> the crowning irony remains, it is in those progressive sections of castes that are economically bettering themselves that women's status is steadily falling. (Kapadia, 1995: 253)

Kapadia's work emphasizes counter-hegemonical views of lower castes as well as redefines what social transformation can mean; rather than buying into the available discourses or going against them she highlights what alternative discourses female South Indians invent and live by and with. She rejects Gramsci's notion of hegemony through the concept of agency and resistance and exemplifies this by looking at discourses and practices of kinship and gender and in particular discusses changes in marital practices through employment patterns education and salaried jobs. Her work greatly supplements Gold and Raheja's work (1994) and is advanced by Leela Fernandes (1997) theoretical framework as discussed below. The impact of dowry on women is also one issue of change in this context. If, as Kapadia stresses, modernization/urbanization/"progress" does de-value women and subordinates them, through firstly, a dichotomous division of labour between wage labour as a male domain and domestic, unpaid labour as its female counterpart, and secondly, through higher dowries demanded despite their own education and high status (1995: 58-60), in how far does a woman's position change through her own wage labour?

Mary Searle-Chatterjee (1981) concludes in her ethnography on sweepers in Benares that gender roles have been transformed through women's responsibility's as wage earner. Women did not only earn at least as much as men and worked in the same jobs, but often earned more through extra work in private houses and also managed the household income (*Ibid.*, 34, 36, 42-43). However, her observation is that discourses differ from practices and so men claim that "housework is done by women who are subordinate to men" (*Ibid.*, 99), whilst Searle-Chatterjee's interviews and observations revealed an equal division of labour (*Ibid.*, 45, 99). Yet, Searle-Chatterjee's example concerns low-caste sweepers, which can be argued to be physically and occupationally separate, as well as caste and aspirationally removed from wider Benares society. Therefore they do not need or wish to conform to another higher class or caste's prescriptions and not even conform to outside norms and hegemonies.

By highlighting women's varied aspects of identity feminist studies have significantly advanced the study of identity and not only illustrated but also advanced the application of ideas of identity. Foucault's and Bourdieu's theories of practice and power relations have been complemented by ideas of Abu-Lughod and Fernandes (1997) and often been illuminated by ethnographies highlighting the multiplicity of identity aspects in women's lives. More importantly, these have illuminated Gramsci's idea of hegemony and resistance and challenges towards this. Feminism and the emphasis on female standpoints has then significantly and originally challenged the idea of hegemony and added agency to the vocabulary of hegemony. As such women and especially middle class women are integral to social practices and discourses, despite their continued marginalisation in the studies surrounding them.

On the basis of Kapadia's findings, it can be argued that class and accompanying status presumptions play a major part in the life choices of women. In what ways, however, do women accept, resist and negotiate these, is what scholars looked at in different time and spatial settings and in what ways female wage labour has influenced these, is furthermore an area to which the proposed research will contribute.

Women, Middle-class Status and Work

Ethnographies of middle-class, urban women as in Sharma (1980) and Vatuk (1982), have highlighted the role of status which might derive from a middle-class standing. These ethnographies expand on the themes from above and lead me to Ursula Sharma's work on women's role within urban migrant communities to Shimla (1986). The most burning questions concern identity formation and transformation through female roles and the influence of female onto the roles they play and change of the roles.

Ursula Sharma (1986), who focused on women's roles in middle-class families in Shimla, Northern India, sees women to be re-producing the conditions for production through essential, domestic work, thus performing vital groundwork for their families and communities. She outlines "networking, gift exchange and arranging marriages" as issues of the household, which are performed by women. It can be argued that it is part of the process of labour force reproduction that social relations of productions are established. Women establish the relations necessary for production not only through biological reproduction, but mainly social reproduction (Edholm, Young, and Harris ,1977). Although women are the persons that establish relations vital for production and housewives are seen as a sign of respectability, their role is not recognized as valuable. A similar picture arises from Sylvia Vatuk (1972), who looked at household structures of white-collar, highly educated middle class families in Meerut and examined whether household structures did change with increasing "urbanisation" and industrialisation. She concludes that households nuclear or joint forms are shifting gradually and are influenced by property ownership of this household, which does not exclude the option of living separately. She also highlights that women's employment was 40 pro mille in her part of Meerut, because it is "low prestige, poorly paid, exhausting and unpleasant," thus pointing out that it is women who keep up the household and that their assigned tasks lay within it, rather than in employment. Teaching however, is an acceptable occupation, but women are only forced into employment through real financial needs. Looking at girls' education, she concludes that it merely serves to secure a good match and has to be slightly inferior to the future husband (80). Urbanisation and increased employment chances then do not seem to be relevant for middle-class women, since they are supposed to be active in the household regardless of its rural or urban location. Standing confirms this by outlining what constitutes respectable jobs outside the household: teaching and nursing are acceptable, whilst clerical work is very prevalent and acceptable, if segregated (1991: 50-52). Moreover, she highlights that, in the case of Calcutta, labour market developments of high male unemployment has "forced" female participation in the labour market (*Ibid.*, 50).

Middle-class women's voluntary welfare work in Madras highlights the relationship between class and women by challenging the boundaries between areas of production and reproduction (Caplan, 1985). The "class" of women is difficult to determine since women's labour force participation is reclining and in any case, their wages are below those of men. A focus on production as significant class marker neglects women's reproduction of culture and actual offspring (*Ibid.*, 12-13), which, as Caplan highlights, is highly significant for class identity. Indeed, the three ethnographies together perpetuate the image of the lower classes resistance to the upper classes through their redefinition of gender roles (Searle-Chatterjee, 1981) upwardly mobile caste succumbing to conformity due to requirements of hegemony (Kapadia, 1995), whilst the upper-castes aim to reproduce these values through welfare organizations and activities (Caplan, 1985). In both cases, women are strongly attached to values of their respective community (Fernandes, 1997), as transporter and/or spearheads of either tradition or novelty. Whilst I would not dispute that women are not "carriers of tradition" (Unnithan-Kumar, 1994), I propose an examination of the processes of reproduction and production of hegemonies by women. As Gold and Raheja pointed out, women's submissiveness is only at the most half-true and often a mere strategy (1994). And if so, how does women's own wage labour contribute to reproduction and/or transformation of these hegemonies?

Fernandes contributed to the awareness that "universalistic categories such as 'women' and 'worker' are contingent on multiple social locations, whether of ethnicity, class, race or gender," and asked how we can "conceptualise the intersections between such categories and identities?" (1997: XIII). Fernandes examines the ways in which boundaries between class, community and gender are produced politically "through institutional, discursive and everyday social and cultural practices" (*Ibid.*, XVIII). In doing so she looks at the dialectics of hegemony and resistance to the labour market, family and community organizations. Drawing on Bourdieu (1985), De Certeau (1988) and Giddens (1981) she lays out how class is constructed dynamically through the process of resistance and hegemony which is dependent on spatial practices and drawing on social, cultural and economic forms. Gender represents a structural force by producing and negotiating patterns within social and cultural life (Fernandes, 1997: 12). Hierarchies between classes and identities are constructed along gendered meanings. Her theoretical position redefines class as a gendered category and conceptualises the category "female worker," through the intersections of community, caste and class and wage labour. In the case of the proposed research there are a few more layers of identity to be added.

II. THE CASE

Women, Middle Class and ITES

Until recently, companies like IBM had policies not to employ women, whilst since 2003 some started staging training camps exclusively for college girls (IBM India: 20 Nov. 2003) and thus establishing a women-preferred recruitment strategy, as women are apparently "more responsible" and "able to work under pressure," as Nisbett was told (2005: 206). A study in Mumbai revealed, based on a small sample of 78 full-time employees, that 96.2 per cent are under 30 years old, with 50 per cent being between 21-25 years old. Furthermore, 59 per cent were female and 87.29 per cent unmarried (Datta, 2004). Educational backgrounds varied with 60.30 per cent being graduates, 32.10 per cent being undergraduates, 29.50 per cent having extra-educational qualifications and only 7.70 per cent being postgraduates. While 61.50 per cent earned between US $220-265, a peak of 38.50 per cent earned US $270-340 (Datta, 2004: 5). This indicates that call centres do indeed employ more women of the 21-25 age bracket, who are unmarried; hence I focus my research on this age and gender group. Furthermore, the recruitment for call centres draws on a young English-speaking, well-educated group of women and men and has been shown to be highly competitive (Remesh, 2004; Nisbett, 2005). Despite seemingly easy access to jobs through walk-in or telephone interviews, the successful completion of call centre training in a college or a company's courses might be a prerequisite, as are markers of a middle-class background such as education and social skills (Mehmood, 30-03-2004). In Mumbai, for instance, the employees are mostly between 19-27 years and graduates with "excellent communication and language skills but not good academic skills" (*Guardian*, Jobs and Money, 06-12-2003: 2-3). Also, the choices and lifestyles of young women are key to building communities, as I will argue in the section on households. It is this intersection of class, age and gender that makes the research unique and useful for understanding India's current adults' lifestyles and preferences. Part of the proposed research is to establish how many people are recruited in Delhi, how and on what skill and task basis they are recruited on, what percentage of these are female and what their social background is, which raises the questions: What skills does an applicant need to be recruited and work in a call centre? How and where does an employee acquire these? And how does employment in ITES contribute to their life plans?

Yet, presuming that many of the employees are female and between 21-25 years old, the questions that arise lie in the areas of marriage choices, dowry, household relations, and consumption. These are moreover observable spaces within which to answer the research questions and observe spatialised language and practices (Fernandes, 1999). How and to what end do individuals use ITES? What do the wages earned in ITES enable them to do?

The Setting

Therefore, the research will be conducted amongst young female employees in ITES in Gurgaon and is based on the presumption that economic transformation in the form of new employment opportunities is followed by social and cultural change, expressed in transformations as well as reproductions (see anthropological literature such as Osella and Osella, 2000; Parry, 1979; Fuller, 1976; Kapadia, 2003; Freeman, 2000; Mills, 1999; Nisbett, 2005; Arun, Heeks and Morgan, 2005; Duncombe, 2004). Key ethnographies of social development in the context of ICT and ITES have focused on shifts in gender relations in the Caribbean and Bangalore respectively, Freeman, 2000 and Nisbett, 2005. Taking its lead from them and recent IDPM publications the proposed research offers a gendered analysis by examining in what ways call centres, as one section of the large ITES segment, are indeed new modes of employment in the context of Gurgaon and Delhi, and what effects this has on household relations, marriage choices and dowry, and consumption in the lives of young women.

Household Relations

Households are maintained through economic and material input, actual maintenance and reproduction, as well as through networking and status maintenance. From a feminist perspective, households have been seen as the smallest unit of society, thus being reproductive relevance and have been highly politicised (Wolf ,1994; Standing, 1991; Moore, 1999).

Existing analyses have in these ways been useful starting points for understanding household management and organization, yet have been based on assumptions about men as the breadwinner of the household (Parry, 1979; Fuller, 1976). In the case of male members of a household, it has been widely acknowledged that urbanization and industrialization, with its implications of changing employment, inheritance and post-marital residence choices, transformed household structures and power relations within the Indian household (*e.g.* Dumont, 1980; Parry, 1979; Fuller, 1976; Berreman, 1979; Fortes ,1949 in Parry, 1979; Sen, 1999; Vatuk, 1972; Ballard, 2001). This view neglects that tasks in the household are divided along gender lines, seniority and length of belonging to the household (Donner, 1999). Women's employment, income and its division can be influenced by these factors (Donner, 1999). Yet apart from their contribution in the household's upkeep, individuals may strive to further their bargaining power in opposition to other members. The questions in this context and for young middle-class women in Delhi are: What kind of household do they live in? And if women are employed who does what with their salary? And what effects does that have on how they perceive their role within the household?

The role of female employment has received attention mainly in the context of poor, either urban, low-caste women (*e.g.* Searle-Chatterjee, 1981) or rural women (*e.g.* De Neve, 2004). Such studies raised questions about who sustains the household and what does economic and social maintenance of the household entail in different castes and classes and contexts of rural and urban environments. They also often highlighted that household income covered through female employment increases women's status in the household and thus changes gender roles (Searle-Chatterjee, 1981; Standing, 1991; Caplan, 1985). If power relations within the household are governed by access to resources (Whitehead, 1981), women's employment and their access to wages can be seen as a substantial contribution to their power.

Furthermore, women's influence in the household and their tasks within the household are also closely linked with their life-stages and the household setting. Donner (1999) has shown that women's influence and standing in the household is greatly influenced by life-stages and fulfilment of expectations of roles within these life-stages. Often motherhood is seen as a substantial and expected mean to raise one's status within the family, thus highlighting the primordial role of women as opposed to a chosen role. In the case of Delhi, I presume to be looking at single, childless women, who possibly have finished their university studies and are working before their marriages.

Within households women are daughters, sisters, possibly daughters-in-law, wives and mothers, and bargain with other household members over household resources. This is particularly interesting in urban contexts and in types of employments, such as call centres, that not allow young women to earn substantial wages, whose social acceptance is contested. Daughters may pay, for example, for a sibling's education or save for their dowry (Sharma, 1986; Vatuk, 1972). Yet, Seeley concludes from the Bangladeshi context: "The status of a woman comes from her family and while her role includes the maintenance of her family as a social institution and as an economic entity, the decision-making powers and economic control are almost always in the hands of men" (*et al.* forthcoming 6). Moreover, such power constellations blur the impact female wages have on the economic maintenance of the household, whilst also maintaining its prestigious façade towards neighbours and future in-laws without mentioning the daughter's help. Yet, wages increase her bargaining power within the household? To what extent is a daughter's income openly acknowledged within the household and the wider family? Keeping Kabeer's (1994) and Wolf's (1994) critique of household economics in mind, what are female wages used for, in what ways do a daughter's wages benefit the household and how does it influence her bargaining power? This research aims to re-examine the debate about Women in Development (WID), "empowerment" and agency *versus* hegemony, yet instead of approaching the subject from a theorised position, the research seeks to work inductive, thus using empirical knowledge to advance these debates and enable understanding ITES' implications for policy development and analysis.

Donner's study of middle-class women in Calcutta highlights that the majority of women do work only before they marry and that their employment activities after marriage are determined by the permission of their in-laws. For an adolescent girl in

Calcutta, expectations are to live relatively secluded and only go out escorted and modestly dressed, whilst expectations of a freshly married daughter-in-law and those of a new mother vary once more and yield different kinds of lifestyles (1999). Status varies through class and it has been argued that female employment is linked closely to presentations of status outside and thus also inside the household (Vatuk, Standing, Donner). This point rings true for middle-class families, in which households and employment depend on each other. In her ethnography about women's class, work and household in Shimla, Sharma records an increased interest in sending unmarried daughters to work and she observes a shift in responsibility from sons to daughters regarding their monetary contribution to the household (1986: 125). This begs the question, how far is a daughter's income used to maintain the middle-class household? Furthermore, Banerjee states that despite women's economic contribution, employment "often burdens the women with the shame to have exposed the family's poverty" (1991: 28). Shame also is further increased through inadequate occupations such as sales or office work (Donner, 1999). Thus, women's contribution to the status of a household through their employment is debatable.

To arrive at an understanding of the interplay of household and women's employment, requires considering the structure of the household: what are the parents' opinions? What are the mother-in-law's attitudes? Are there any unmarried sister-in-laws living in the household or are there brother-in-laws? How do they relate to their agnate sister-in-law? And what are the father-in-law's attitudes? The members of the household and the women's life-stage influence a woman's status within the household and in turn influence if and where women work and what happens with their wages and what status this has.

Furthermore, views on the household and women's role within the household have always been influenced by a concern for women's well-being often phrased in terms of European feminist thought (Standing, 1991). Within this, the family has been seen to perpetuate the sexual division of labour and gender dichotomies (Moore, 1999). Yet, Standing highlighted, who points out that familial support is vital for most women and thus autonomy does not mean individualism (1991: 170). Her findings emphasise that despite familial conflicts, the unit household is of paramount importance to women in India. One would presume that thus employed women contribute all their wages to the family. Yet, Wolf's analysis does differentiate the importance of the household by looking at the assumed strategy of "pooling" of income. She concludes that scholar's perspective on pooling perpetuates the picture of the household as a closed unit with a benevolent head as a decision-maker (1992: 15-19). Instead, she encountered in the context of families of female factory employees in rural Indonesia's daughters making decisions without parental approval and moreover drawing on their poor families' resources for money for themselves. In awareness of presumptions about the household's organization, a standpoint methodology is needed and the research asks: Who makes decisions for whom and how are such decisions implemented and who accepts or resists them? How do females in the household see their role within it and which factors influence their position? How do they experience household economics and what do they think and how do they feel about decision-making?

Tracing strategies of negotiating acceptable practices instigated by local modernities as well as the conception of the modernities involved in the context of young women's employment in the ITES sector is the aim of my research and will. This is particularly interesting in urban contexts and in types of employments, such as call centres, that not only allow young women to earn substantial wages but which are also socially acceptable. Daughters may pay, for example, for a sibling's education or save for their dowry (Sharma, 1986; Vatuk, 1972). Seeley (*et al.* forthcoming 6) concludes from the Bangladeshi context: "The status of a woman comes from her family and while her role includes the maintenance of her family as a social institution and as an economic entity, the decision-making powers and economic control are almost always in the hands of men." Such status considerations blur the impact female wages have on the economic maintenance of the household, whilst also maintaining its prestigious façade towards neighbours and future in-laws without mentioning the daughter's help. Yet, in what ways do her wages benefit the daughter and increase her bargaining power within the household? To what extent is a daughter's income openly acknowledged within the household and the wider family be paramount to addressing questions of transformation and reproduction as experienced by individuals in neo-liberal India?

Marriage Choices and Dowry

Households are not only economically maintained, but also rely on the successful making and upkeep of networks (Vatuk, 1972; Sharma, 1986). As has been pointed out above, women's position does not always improve with marriage and Kapadia as well as Fuller and Parry have indicated that marriage arrangements are dominated by kinship and caste regulations and plays a vital role for status maximization. Marrying female members into a higher caste or class families means not just maintaining but sometimes enhancing the wife-giving family's status and widening their networks. One's daughter's appeal to a higher class/caste family is furthered through her education, which guarantees the bride's ability to speak English and Hindi, mix in educated circles of her future husband and educate future children appropriately (Sharma, 1986). Recent research has further explored what constitutes love marriages and how they are experienced in the context of the Bengali-Hindu middle-class (Donner, 2002), urban Delhites (Mody, 2002) and upwardly mobile, low-caste Izhavas (Osella and Osella, 2000). However, love marriages are often posthumously constructed as arranged marriages. This strategy highlights firstly, degrees of acceptability and a family's attempts to maintain control about future members and secondly, links these two marriage forms to strategies of status maximization. How does their economic position influence their or their families' choice of a husband? How will love matches made in the ITES be accepted and conceptualised? What aspirations do parents and daughters hold towards the "perfect match?" In what contexts may love marriages present an acceptable alternative?

Dowry might be another prerequisite for securing an acceptable match and practices of dowry-giving have been well-documented (Vatuk, 1972; Tambiah, 1973; Sharma, 1986 and 1984; Bhachu in Buijs, 1993; Menski, 1998). Officially, dowry in its many facets is given by the bride's parents, yet Sharma affirms that "wage-earning daughters may buy some items from their wages" (1984: 64) and Seeley (*et al.* forthcoming) reports from Bangladesh that demands for their future dowry forces some rural girls to migrate and work as domestic worker. So how does employment affect young middle-class women's dowries in India? Who is paying and what form do contemporary dowries take? Furthermore, the contents of dowries of Sikhs in the UK create identities, through their different styles and degrees of exclusivity, affiliations with and aspirations to Sloane-Square-SW1 or Oxford-Street-M&S (Bhachu in Buijs, 1993), thus alluding to class and displaying cultural capital (Bourdieu, 1986). What do the contents of the dowry in India symbolize in terms of aspirations to and affiliations with, for example, a modern lifestyle?

However, despite dowry's prohibition by Indian law since 1961[2] cases of dowry demands are ongoing and often life-threatening for the bride/newly-wed wife. Dowry deaths after marriage thus remain widespread and paint a bleak picture of assumed marital bliss.[3] Indicative of the prevalence of cases is the overflowing special women's wing in Tihar jail in Delhi, which was founded at the beginning of 1999 and is the only wing of this kind in the whole of India. The reports in the Indian media and abroad furthermore paint the picture of Indian middle-classes being at the forefront of demanding dowry in the form of "40 sovereigns of gold, Rs. 30,000 in cash, wooden furniture and a Hero Honda motorcycle"[4] or "Rs. 25 lakh, a flat and a car."[5] The Delhi-based lawyer Malavika Rajkotia points out that the number of inmates in Tihar jail's special wing also indicates "how serious dowry demands have become in consumer hungry middle-class Indian families."[6] Dowry here is seen as the fast way to satisfying consumer needs of the groom and his extended family.

If dowry is accepted and given, it seems to be linked to socio-economic independence, as the divergent reports from rural and urban areas show. Twenty-three-year-old Paramjit Kaur from Jalandhar, Punjab married a British Asian man three years ago and he promised to arrange a visa for her and then take her to Britain. Her father gave him £6000 worth of jewellery after the wedding, after which her new husband stopped being in contact. Kaur is apparently still waiting and in the meantime has reported the case to the police and British High Commission.[7] Nisha Sharma's case however reads differently: the twenty-one-year old software engineer from Delhi reported her husband-to-be to the police, when he demanded more dowry in the form of $25,000 in cash and insulted her father, who refused, shortly before the wedding ceremony. Her family supported her fully in her decision and she said she would now focus on her graduation.[8] Six months later Sharma married a computer engineer without exchanging dowry.[9] The example of Nisha Sharma is now in textbooks for secondary schools and inspired debates about the change in social attitudes.[10] The difference in behaviour between the two events/cases above stems from socio-economic circumstances, regional differences and class and caste differences. Kaur's family presumably attempted to achieve a better status for their daughter through marriage to an NRI (Non-Resident Indian), whilst Sharma's family did not need to since their daughter had an independent income and career prospects in India. Quite obviously this enabled Nisha Sharma to turn down dowry demands. However, it has also been pointed out that many women working in ITES do save for their dowries and hope to marry upwardly mobile. Thus the main question in the context of the proposed research is: When do women working in ITES decide to save for their dowry, thus fulfilling their parents and their own wish to marry upwardly mobile/hypergamously and when do they decide to use the monetary power their occupations have given them to not give dowry, but use the status of their jobs to support themselves outside/beyond marriage? BPO can then lead to an increased self-esteem that enables women to make choices and change social habitus (Bourdieu, 1986) or manifest these further through higher spiralling dowries (Gupta, 2000; Remesh, 2004; Datta, 2004).

The (supposed) boom in outsourced ITES can then lead to an increased self-esteem that enables women to make choices and changes within the social habitus (Bourdieu, 1990) or manifest these further through higher spiralling dowries (Gupta, 2000; Remesh, 2004; Datta, 2004). Exploring the strategies of asking for, denying, giving and accepting dowry is one of the aims of the proposed research and will yield valuable insights into the impact of widely available, new employment possibilities on socio-cultural life. This also illuminates the relationship between employment, income, marriage and upward mobility in the light of gender and class subsections. When do women working in ITES decide to save for their dowry, thus fulfilling their parents and their own wish to marry upwardly mobile/hypergamously and when do they decide to use the monetary power of their occupations to not give dowry, but use the status of their jobs to support themselves outside/beyond marriage?

New Modes of Production and New Modes of Consumption?

The above outlined how class can be seen as linked to production and occupation. However, one of the issues to explore is the issue of how status is established, maintained and increased in the "new" middle class. For women, acquisition of status is linked to the occupation of their husbands and, if they work themselves, their own occupations. Next to production and especially if production is not a source of status as in less-prestigious occupations (Osella, 2000; Freeman, 2001; Mills, 1999), scholars have identified consumption as a significant strategy for status enhancement.[11] Where female earnings of wives, daughters or daughters-in-law are not seen as vital for the household's survival (Kabeer, 1991 and 1996; Searle-Chatterjee, 1972; Seeley, 2001 and 2003; Donner, 1999) or used for savings on dowry, they have often been classified as pin-money (*e.g.* Vatuk, 1972) and used for individual seemingly conspicuous consumption.

For my proposed research it then is crucial to understand the "logic of practice" and in particular Bourdieu's theory of "distinction," which explains how economic and social class does not only influence consumption, but how consumption influences social class and enables social mobility as well as erects borders and signifiers of the class system. Which items are purchased, what significance they have has to be addressed as part of my fieldwork. These practices and their discourses also highlight the complexity of individuals and ambigious relation as actors of and against the system as well as expands on how cultural capital can be transformed into social capital and raises questions about the significance of non-economical markers (Bourdieu, 1986). Consumption is an excellent way of converting money/wages/salaries, which are theoretically economic capital, into consumer goods of varying durability, which symbolise cultural capital, thus making "money work twice" (Osella and Osella, 2000: 125). Another example is Nisbett's research, which has highlighted not only purchasing of goods but moreover experiences such as boozing trips (2005), which facilitate belonging to classed and gendered practices making an identity. How goods are acquired, what goods are acquired, what is done with them and what they mean to the acquirer, are the questions this research proposes to address. Preliminary it can be gathered from numerous studies of a similar scope (*e.g.* Freeman, 2000; Nisbett, 2005) that items have class and status connotations are acquired in particular life-stages and are often gendered.

The codes of consumed items are, for example unpicked by Osella and Osella in Kerala, who compare the fashions of the slums with that in the inner city and conclude that fast-living consumer items are rather consumed by the lower middle-class. Freeman (2000) also wrote about clothing and its significance for the workers, in so far as they assist to display alleged upward mobility and wealth. However, Caribbean call centre agents do not earn the salary to afford their fashion and so this display betrays rather than indicates their social status. The Indian example then is equally complex and can only be understood in the context of social position, aspirations and life circumstances (*e.g.* Lakha, 1999: 251-74, in Pinches, ed. 1999). As for the Indian context, consumption and non-consumption is marked by recent economic development. Whilst many public voices announce near-boundless growth of the middle class and their fast-living consumption preferences (Lakha, 1999; Das, 2002), Gupta points out that a distinction needs to be drawn between consumerism and consumption in India since former is often underdeveloped and households purchase one item that then lasts for a long time rather than is replaced as soon as it is unfashionable. His point is that consumption is a myth. Looking at consumption patterns indeed ignores the part of the middle class that does not consume conspicuously, but earns just enough to subsist. What consumption means and what other forms there are to accumulate economic capital (*i.e.* savings, expenditure on *e.g.* education or travels) and display status is thus an important question in understanding the distinction between necessary and conspicuous consumption. What then does "pin-money" (Vatuk, 1972) buy and what does this say about priorities and aspirations?

In much the same way the practices Nisbett highlights demonstrate exclusion from aspired practices and identities and show alternative ways of creating identities. These are for example, exchanging of sunglasses and mobile phones (2005) or the dress sense of tucked-in T-Shirt, pleaded trousers and fake Nike trainers as alternative to middle-class Americanised shirt and khakis with trainers (*Ibid.*, 138). When Nisbett took photographs of his friends and research participants, they exchanged sunglasses and mobile phones and used one of the friends' motorbike as a background prop. The exchange of these goods reveals just how much status having these goods, for however short, induces and what is actually desired. As Freeman's telecommunications workers (2000), these young men endorse fashion as an affordable display of the wealth they aspire to get are excluded from consuming on a larger scale (see also Osella and Osella, 2000: 119-22). This also reveals how their seemingly wealthy façade betrays their net income and if discovered, this disjuncture can be the source of just the opposite effect of establishing an upwardly mobile position. Freeman highlighted that in her account of a female data entry operator being publicly shamed by her former boyfriend with the words: "Don't mind she dress so. When Friday come, she only carryin' home ninety-eight dollars," thus implying that she is "a village girl with a factory wage" despite her exterior as middle-class women with an office-job (2000: 21-22). Outer consumer façade can be at odds with aspirations and economic status, rather than reflecting it proportionally. This then can be called conspicuous consumption. By implication, the research has then to be aware of disjunctures and unravel their meaning to uncover meanings and the debatably "new" hegemony that accompanies employment in ITES.

In connection with new forms of employment other authors have highlighted the significance of sharing and being a generous, big spender and/or exact reciprocity between actors. In the case of urban migrants to Bangkok, Mills describes their free spending on relative on trips home, whilst paying their own ways when going out together in the city. In his ethnography, Nisbett on the other hand describes how spending and sharing increases prestige of individuals within the group and allows spending to be acceptable. Over time, his research participants started to be less close and some started spending their wages earned on themselves, behaviour being taken as an offence by their peers and openly frowned upon.

Yet, frowning upon excessive spending and proud display can express frugality and displays status through near-saintly constraint (Osella and Osella for Kerala, 2000; Mills for Thailand, 1999; Freeman for the Caribbean, 2000). Furthermore, the goods purchased-longevity or short-lived fashion, the way they are purchased, shared or used individually and displayed can be argued to be influenced by lifestages. Especially Osella and Osella highlight the products ranged and then point out that, for example, the importance in land increases when one attempts to settle and thus becomes important to buy. The same applies to a marble floor or the latest motorcycle. It can be argued that goods then also hold connotations about transcience and immanence (Osella and Osella, 2000) and the longer they last, display longevity, maturity and class. They allege that higher classes merely purchase things with a longer lifespan and also invest in education, travel, health care and land are such items for people with higher amounts of money to spend. It is questionable if this is really a sign of sudden unbounded wealth, if we keep Gupta's distinction of consumerism and consumption in mind.

Recent research at the University of Sussex (Nisbett, 2005) has highlighted consumption patterns of young men employed in call centres in Bangalore, which incorporate "boozing trips" with their mates, taking girls out or buying the latest motorcycle and thus symbolize aspirations towards a modernity they forged in interaction with the experiences in their work environments. Yet, one female call centre worker describes her experiences of recruitment and work and sums up a party with her co-remote agents as follows: "there's a lot of peer pressure to be 'cool', to have an 'image'...I just didn't like it and came back in an hour or so.... I don't drink, I don't fag, I don't dance and hate loud music...agle din [my translation: next day]...people teased me, but it's O.K. People get used to you and if you are strong they accept you."[12] In which way then are such activities identified as modern or traditional? To what extent do such "modern" activities allow for social transformation and reproduction? In different geographical contexts gendered practices of consumption have been highlighted by Mills (1999) and Freeman (2000), in which contexts girls and women are often investing in clothes and make-up, rather than boozing trips and cigarettes. My research will focus in particular on the gendered nature of inclusion and participation in such new consumption activities and modes of behaviour by asking the questions: What makes remote agents feel 'cool' and meet their aspirations? How does their working environment in MNC inspire these aspirations and how do women experience the call centre environment and subsequent activities? What activities do call centre employees' earnings allow them to participate in? And how is that in the Indian context? What does purchasing a particular product or experience (*e.g.* facials, nights out, smoking a particular brand of cigarette) mean to young middle-class men and women in India?

Examining meanings of consumption and behavioural patterns along gender lines will assist in understanding transformative and reproductive aspects in the lives of young women through their employment in the New Technology sector and is directly relevant to my key questions. As has been outlined above, call centres recruit a wide range of employees thus enabling studying lower and upper as well as middle-class. However, call centres seem to be the sector where the whole of middle class come together and thus provide a wealth of insight against the backdrop of a site of presumed novelty. This site then is a valuable location for intra-class mobility and will highlight the signifiers of the old and new middle-class through discourses and practices, *e.g.* clothing. BPO, as a new form of employment through its casualisation of labour and preference for female employees, can be seen as the catalyst for the symbolic of consumption. Not because it imposes or enables a "western" or even "modern" mindset, but through the more immediate renumeration that enables satisfying consumer wishes, thus converting economic into cultural capital and enabling display of new status acquired through an otherwise not high-status occupation. These will then reveal how social mobility is practiced and what it is aimed at by whom.

III. AREAS OF ANALYSIS AND CHANGE

This piece is research in progress, yet it can be assumed that ITES has a profound influence on social and cultural aspirations and lifestyles of men and women. The new sectors of employment in ITES are empowering for women in the practical sense that they provide them with an income.

The research could be read in the way of estimating this impact and evaluating its effects. The income then could be seen as not empowering through the way it is used. Wages are used to please others through consumption or "acquiring" a suitable marriage through dowry reveals the exact opposite of empowerment but seems to reproduce and reinforce hegemony. Through giving into the forced hegemony of affording dowry and consume to fit in, the relief from outside pressure is achieved, yet a merely temporary measure. Yet I have also shown that there has been some progression in terms of reinvention in the case of rejection of dowry and the increased self-esteem of some women. In sum however, it is too early for an evaluation and in-depth research into these areas is required.

In any case, to allow for comparison with other countries and societies as well as a deeper understanding of the case, an awareness of the setting should be maintained. Next to the class differences which have been highlighted to be of profound impact on practices and discourses, the environment of Delhi is an appropriate place to understand 20-somethings expression of their lifestyles in societies. On one hand it sets the trend and develops as well as follows hegemonies. On the other it also breaks hegemonies through its size and the possibility to escape the parental gaze. Delhi is furthermore unique through its accumulation for different caste, class, regional and ethnic identities and the possibility of reinvention. Therefore this study also contributes to the literature of urban India. With its close look at the makers and unmakers of hegemonies, the research attempts to deconstruct discourses and practices of the next generation of householders and society-makers.

The focus on women highlights discourses and practices from a gendered standpoint and as has to be emphasised has to stress both subordination and empowerment, reproduction and transformation to whatever proportions found. The focus on the household represents the area of reproductive work, status work as well as bargaining power struggles. Through the conversion of wages into cultural capital and degrees of acknowledgement this is extraordinary site for understanding discourses and practices surrounding young women's lifestyles. Women employed in IT have their own status as we have seen above and therefore reveal degrees of acceptability. In the field of marriage, it is the female's family who give dowry, if they give dowry. Choosing a partner influences young women's lifestyles and future family structures more than anything. Practices surrounding this are fluid as highlighted above and have the potential for reproduction or transformation.

The area of consumption has potential to be an oppressive and forced hegemony. Yet, it has been shown that this has not been recognised by the lower classes and castes and that they deconstruct the idea of conspicuousness. Also, excessive consumption does not equal monetary wealth, as Freeman (2000) has shown and often austerity and buying goods with longevity emphasise higher standing. The practice and discourses of spending are also highly gendered, as Mills (1997), Freeman (2000) and Nisbett (2005) have shown.

Studying modernity, habitus and hegemony in the lives of female young ITES employees assists understanding identity formation and transformation of female roles as well as female agency in the habitus described above. By doing so, we can return to understanding the "state of the nation" and after reaching a thorough understanding of the issues at hand evaluate processes of crisis.

Notes on the Web Informations

1. *See* http://gurgaon.nic.in/f_industry.htm accessed on 15 Nov. 2003.
2. *See* for example Menski, 1998; http://www.indianchild.com/dowry_in_india.htm, accessed on 30-09-2004. Also see Bumiller 1982; Goonesekere 2004; media reports on *e.g.* http://bbc.co.uk/, http://www.indianexpress.com/full_story.php?content_id=36919, 10-12-2003 accessed on 01-10-2004.
3. Bedi (2000), accessed 29-09-2004 on http://news.bbc.co.uk/1/hi/word/south-asia/772896.stm.
4. http://www.indianexpress.com/full_story.php?content_id=40952, 14 February 2004, accessed on 01-10-2004.
5. http://www.indianexpress.com/full_story.php?content_id=36919, 10 December 2003 accessed on 01-10-2004.
6. Bedi (2000), http://news.bbc.co.uk/1/hi/word/south-asia/772896.stm. Accessed on 29-09-2004.
7. *See* Adam Mynott on http://news.bbc.co.uk/1/hi/world/south_asia/2276560.stm. On 23rd September 2002 accessed on 29-09-2004.
8. Rao on http://news.bbc.co.uk/hi/south_asia/3027783.stm. Accessed on 29-09-2004.
9. Chadna on http://bbc.co.uk/go/pr/fr/-/1/hi/world/south_asia/3283989.stm. Accessed on 29-09-2004.
10. *See* Pandey on http://news.bbc.co.uk/go/pr/fr/-/1/hi/world/south_asia/3696562.stm. Accessed on 29-09-2004.
11. Mehmood on http://mail.sarai.net/pipermail/reader-list/2004-March/003576.html. Accessed on 30-03-2004.
12. *Ibid.*

References

AAA Code of Ethics. http://www.aaanet.org/committees/ethics/ethcode.htm accessed on 18-01-2004.

Appadurai, A. and Breckenridge, C. (eds.) (1995), *Consuming Modernity: Public Culture in a South Asian World*. USA: University of Minnesota Press.

Arun, Heeks and Morgan (2005), ICT Initiatives, *Women and Work in Developing Countries: Reinforcing or Changing Gender Inequalities in India*? WP 20, accessed on http://www.sed.manchester.ac.uk/idpm/publications/wp/di/index.htm.

ASA*Ethical Guidelines* http://www.theasa.org/ethics.htm accessed on 18-01-2004.

Balakrishnan, Palan (2004), *Calling from Seattle* on http://www.rediff.com/money/2004/jan/31bpo.htm accessed on 21-03-2003.

Ballard, Roger (2001), The Impact of Kinship on the Economic Dynamics of Transnational Networks. Unpublished paper accessed on 14-02-2003. http://www.transcomm.ox.ac.uk/working%20papers/Ballard.pdf.

Ballard, Roger *et al.* (1994), *Desh Pradesh*: *The South Asian Presence in Britain.* London: C. Hurst and Co. Ltd.

Banerjee, Nirmala (1991), *Indian Women in a Changing Industrial Scenario*. Delhi: Sage.

Bauman, Zygmunt (1991), *Modernity and Ambivalence*. Cambridge: Polity Press.

Bedi, Rahul (01-06-2000), *Jail Crisis for Dowry Crimes* Unknown title http://news.bbc.co.uk/1/hi/world/south_asia/772896.stm accessed 29-09-2004.

Berreman, G.D. (1979), *Caste and Other Inequities*. Meerut; New Delhi: Folklore Institute.

Bhachu, P. (1993), Identities Constructed and Reconstructed: Representations of Asian Women in Britain in Buijs: *Migrant Workers: Crossing Boundaries and Changing Identities*, Oxford: Berg Publications.

Bourdieu, Pierre (1986), *Distinction*: *Critique of the Judgement of Taste*. London: Routledge, Kegan and Paul.

Bourdieu, Pierre (1990), *The Logic of Practice*. Cambridge: Polity Press.

Bourdieu, Pierre (1977), *Outline of a Theory of Practice*. Cambridge: Cambridge University Press.

Bumiller, E. (1990), *May You be the Mother of a Hundred Sons: A Journey Among the Women of India*. New York: Random House.

Cacanas, Z. and Collinson, P. (2003), The Indian Takeaway Based on Big Mac Salaries. *The Guardian*, 06-12-2003.

Chadha, Monica (19-03-2003), Three Weddings and No Dowry on http://news.bbc.co.uk/1/hi/world/south_asia/3283989.stm, accessed on 29-09-2004.

Collinson and Cacanas, The Indian Takeaway Based on Big Mac Salaries. *The Guardian*, 06-12-2003.

Das, G. (2002), *India Unbound*. London: Profile.

Datta, R. (2004), *Worker and Work: A Case Study of an International Call Centre in India*. Unpublished paper presented at the International Labour Process Conference in 5–7-04-2004 at the Amsterdam Inst. for Adv. Labour.

De Neve, Geert (2003), Expectation and Rewards of Modernity: Commitment and Mobility among Rural Migrants in Tirupur, Tamil Nadu. Gardner and Osella (2003), *Migration, Modernity and Social Transformation in South Asia*. Delhi: Sage, 251-81.

De Neve, Geert (forthcoming), *Weaving for IKEA in South India: Subcontracting, Labour Markets and Gender Relations in the Global Value Chain*.

Deshpande, Satish (2004), *Contemporary India: A Sociological View*. Delhi: Penguin.

Doraisamy, Vani (14 February 2004), *TN Bride Spurns Groom and Marries a Guest* http://www.indianexpress.com_full_story.php?content_id=40952 accessed on 01-10-2004.

Dowry Prohibition Act India (1961), amended in 1984 and 1986 on http://wcd.nic.in/dowryprohibitionact.htm accessed on 01-10-2004.

Duncombe, R. (2005), *Growth and Formalisation of Information Systems in Developing Country SMEs*, WP 19 on http://www.ibm.com/news/in/2003/10/2003102702.html accessed on 15 April 2005.

Eriksen, T.H. (1995), *Small Places, Large Issues*. London: Pluto Press.

Fernandes, L. (1999), *Producing Workers: Politics of Gender, Class and Culture in Calcutta Jute Mills*. Philadelphia: UPP.

Freeman, C. (2000), *High Tech and High Heels in the Global Economy*. Durham and London: Duke University Press.

Fuller, C. (1976), *The Nayars Today*. Cambridge: C.U.P.

Gardner, K. and Osella F. (2003), *Migration, Modernity and Social Transformation in South Asia*. Delhi: Sage.

Gilbert, Alorie (October 01, 2003), *Report: Big Blue Still Biggest in Outsourcing* on http://news.com.com/Report+Big+Blue+still+biggest+in+IT+ outsourcing/2100-1011_3-5085055.html accessed on 02-10- 2003.

Goonesekere, Savitri (ed.) (2004), *Violence, Law and Women's Rights in India*. Delhi: Sage Publication.

Gough, Kathleen (1959), The Nayars and the Definition of Marriage. *Journal of the Royal Anthropological Institute*, No. 89, 23-34.

Guha, R. (1983), *Subaltern Studies*. Delhi: Oxford Univeristy Press.

Gupta, Dipankar (1991), *Social Stratification*. Oxford: Oxford University Press.

Gupta, Dipankar (2000), *Mistaken Modernity*. Delhi: Harper Collins Publishers.

Gupta, Dipankar, Gurgaon District Development Agency on http://gurgaon.nic.in/f_industry.htm access on 15 Nov. 2003.

Harriss-White, Barbara (2002), *India Working, Essays on Society and Economy*. Cambridge: CUP.

Harvey, David (1990), *The Condition of Postmodernity*. Malden, Mass., USA: Blackwell.

Heeks, R.B.; Krishna, S.; Nicholson, B. and Sahay, S. (2001), Synching or Sinking: Global Software Outsourcing Relationships, IEEE Software, 18(2): 54-61.

Heeks, R.B.; Krishna, S.; Nicholson, B. and Sahay, S., IBM India *IBM hosts EXITE technology camp to promote IT amongst girls* on http://www.ibm.com/news/in/2003/10/2003102702.html, accessed on 20-11-2003.

Kabeer, N. (1994), *Reversed Realities: Gender Hierarchies in Development Thought*. London: Verso.

Kabeer, N. (1996), Agency, Well-Being and Inequality: Reflections on Gender Dimensions of Poverty. *Poverty, Policy and Aid*, Vol. 27, No. 1, January 1996: 11-21.

Kabeer, N. (1991), *Gender, Production and Well-Being: Rethinking the Household Economy*. Sussex: IDS.

Kapadia, K. (1998), *Siva and Her Sisters: Gender, Caste and Class in Rural South India*. Oxford: Westview.

Lacity and Willcocks (2001), *Global Information Technology Outsourcing: In Search of Business Advantage*. Chichester: Wiley.

Lamb, Sarah (2000), *White Saris and Sweet Mangoes*. Berkeley: University of California.

Latour, B. (1993), *We have Never been Modern*. Hemel Hempstead: Harvester Wheatsheaf.

Mandelbaum, D.G. (1970), *Society in India: Change and Continuity*, Vol. 2. Berkeley: California University Press. McKinsey, *Research Agenda and Publications* on http://www.mckinsey.com/knowledge/

mgi/reports/globaleintegration/newhorizons/newhorizons.asp accessed on 15-09-2004.

Mehmood, Taha, *Call Centres as an Urban Workplace* on http://mail.sarai.net/pipermail/reader-list/2004-March/003576.html accessed on 30-03-2004.

Menski, W. (ed.) (1998), *South Asians and the Dowry Problem*. Stoke-on-Trent: Trentham Books.

Mills, M.B. (1997), Contesting the Margins of Modernity: Women, Migration and Consumption in Thailand, *American Anthropologist,* 24(1): 37-61.

Mitter, S. (1986), Industrial Reconstructuring and Manufacturing Housework: Immigrant Women in the Clothing Industry. *Capital and Class*, Vol. 27, 37-38.

Mitter, S. (1986), *Common Fate, Common Bond: Women in the Global Economy*. London: Pluto Press.

Mitter, S. (2000), *Telework and Teletrade in India: Combining Diverse Perspectives and Visions* accessed on 15-04-2004 http://www. intech. unu.edu/ search/ index.htm.

Mitter, S. and Rowbotham, S. (eds.) (1995), *Women Encounter Technology: Changing Patterns of Employment in the Third World*. London: Routledge.

Mitter, S. and Rowbotham, S. (eds.) (1995), *Women Encounter Technology*. London: Routledge.

Mody, P. (2002), Love and the Law: Love-Marriage in Delhi. *Modern Asian Studies,* 36, 1, 223-56.

Moore, Henrietta (1999), *Anthropological Theory Today*. Cambridge: Polity Press.

Mynott, Adam (23-09-2003), *British Husbands Desert Indian Brides* on http://news.bbc.co.uk/1/hi/world/south_asia/2276560.stm accessed on 29-09-2004.

Nader, Laura (1972), *Up the Anthropologist*.

NASSCOM (ongoing), *Background Sources* on http://www.nasscom.org accessed on 01-10-2003.

Nicholson, Lai, Heeks (2003), *Uncertainty and Coordination in Global Software Projects: A UK/India-Centred Case Study*. Development Informatics WP No. 17, on http://www.sed.manchester.ac.uk/idpm/publications/wp/di/index.htm accessed on 30 May 2005.

Nicholson, B. and Sahay, S. (2005), *Human Resource Development Policy in the Context of Software Exports: Case Evidence from Costa Rica*. Development Informatics WP 23, on http://

www.sed.manchester.ac.uk/idpm/publications/wp/di/index.htm access on 30 May 2005.

Nisbett, N. (2005), *Knowledge, Identity, Place and (Cyber) Space: Growing Up Male and Middle Class in Bangalore*. Sussex University: Unpubl. D.Phil thesis.

Ong, A. (1987), *Spirits of Resistance and Capitalist Discipline: Factory Women in Malaysia*. New York: State University of New York Press.

Ortner, Sherry (1974), Is Female to Male as Nature is to Culture? M.Z. Rosaldo and L. Lamphere (eds.) *Woman, Culture and Society.*

Osella, F. and Osella, C. (2000), *Social Mobility in Kerala: Modernity and Identity in Conflict*. London: Pluto Press.

Osella, F. and Osella, C. (1999), From Transience to Immanence: Consumption, Life-cycle and Social Mobility in Kerala, South India. *Modern Asian Studies,* Vol. 33, No. 44.

Pandey, Geeta (29-09-2004), *Dowry Woman Becomes Textbook Star* on http://news.bbc.co.uk/go/pr/fr/-/1/hi/world/south_asia_3696562.stm accessed on 29-09-2004.

Parry, J. (1979), *Caste and Kinship in Kangra*. London: Routledge.

Parry, J., *et al.* (eds.) (1997), *The Worlds of Indian Industrial Labour*. Delhi: Sage.

Pinches, Michael (ed.) (1999), *Culture and Privilege in Capitalist Asia*. London: Routledge, 1999.

Rao, Rajyasri (14-05-2003), *Dowry Demand Lands Groom in Jail* on http://news.bbc.co.uk/1/hi/world/south_asia/3027683.stm accessed on 29-09-2004.

Remesh, B.P. (2004), Cyber Coolies in BPO. *EPW*, Vol. 39, No. 5, 31. 01-06-02.

Säävälä, Minna (2003), *Auspicious Hindu Houses: The New Middle Classes in India Social Anthropology,* Vol. II, No. 2, 231-47.

Scheper-Hughes, N. (1995), The Primacy of the Ethcial: Propositions for a Militant Anthropology. *Current Anthropology*, Vol. 36, No. 3.

Searle-Chatterjee, M. (1981), *Reversible Sex Roles: The Special Case of Benares Sweepers*. London: Pergamon.

Seeley, Janet (2003), *Livelihood Labelling: Some Conceptual Issues*. Unpublished paper accessed on 23-03-2004 on http://www.livelihoods.org/static/jseeley_NN178.htm

Seeley, Ryan and Khan, Hossain (forthcoming), The Internal Migration of Poor Women in Bangladesh. Paper presented in the Migration Research Seminar at the University of Sussex on 18-02-2004.

Sen, Samita (1999), Beyond the "Working Class": Women's Role in India's Industrialization. *South Asia,* Vol. XII, 2, 95-117.

Sharma, U. (1984), Dowry in North India. Hirschon, R. *Women and/as Property*. London: Croom Helm.

Sharma, U. (1986), *Women's Work, Class and Urban Household in Shimla*. London: N. India Tavistock Publications.

Sharma, U. (1998), *Caste*. Buckingham: Open University Press.

Standing, Hilary (1991), *Independence and Autonomy*. London: Routledge.

Tambiah, S.J. and Goody, J. (1973), *Dowry and Bridewealth*. Cambridge: C.U.P.

Thangarajah, C.Y. (2003), Veiled Constructions: Conflict, Migration and Modernity in Eastern Sri Lanka. Gardner and Osella (2003), *Migration, Modernity and Social Transformation in South Asia*. 141-63, Delhi: Sage.

Unknown author, Dhamal Growth, *Down to Earth*. January 31, 2004, 27-37.

Unknown author, *Dowry in India* on http://www.indianchild.com/dowry_in_india.htm accessed on 30-09-2004.

Unknown author (10-12-2003), *Dowry Torture Taint on Former Cong MP* on http://www.indianexpress.com/full_story.php?content_id=36919 accessed on 01-10-2004.

Van Der Veer, Peter (1995), The Global History of "Modernity." *Journal of the Economic and Social History of the Orient*.

Varma, Pavan K. (1998), *The Great Indian Middle Class*. India: Penguin.

Vatuk, S. (1972), *Kinship and Urbanization: White Collars Migrants in North India*. Berkeley: University of California.

Whitehead, A. (1981), I'm Hungry, Mum: The Politics of Domestic Budgeting. K. Young, C. Wilkowitz and R. McCullagh (eds.), *Of Marriage and the Market*. London: CSE Books.

Wolf, D. (1994), *Factory Daughters: Gender, Household Dynamics and Rural Industrialization in Java*. Berk: University of California Press.

WSIS (2004), *Report of the Geneva Phase of the World Summit on the Information Society*, on http://www.itu.int/dms-pub/itu-s/md/03/wsis/doc/S03-WSIS-DOC-0009!R1!PDF-E.pdf on 15 April 2005.

Yelvington, Kevin A. (1995), *Producing Power: Ethnicity, Gender and Class in a Caribbean Workplace*. USA: Temple U.P.

Legislation as an Agent of Social Change: Widow's Access to Property Rights in Bhima, Maharashtra

15

Karine Bates

INTRODUCTION[1]

In India, the *Hindu Succession Act* (*HSA*) of 1956 allows to claim an equal share to the wife and daughters, along with the sons of the deceased senior male,[2] out of familial property.[3] By giving inheritance rights to daughters and widows, and not only to sons, this Act encourages a radically different organization to the ideal household, commonly referred to as "the Indian joint family."[4] The Act initiates a transformation of Hindu women's status through their rights to property, which entails the transformation of women's rights and duties in India. It also affects men's access to natal property and modifies brother-sister relationships. The long debate over personal laws that took place in the 1950s led Indian legislators to envision laws as potential agents of social change.

Property rights are so crucial to one's place in society that *HSA* has the potential to empower women. The Indian Constitution allows each state to modify personal laws.[5] In 1994, the Government of Maharashtra took further steps to enhance women's access to property, including agricultural land. Maharashtra, like other southern states,[6] has amended the *HSA* to allow women to obtain a share in both the acquired and the ancestral property[7] of the father or husband.[8] Furthermore, the *Maharashtra Agricultural Lands Act* clearly recognizes that wives have a right to the land.

The limited success of the *HSA* can be explained by a complex interplay of factors. A first set of factors is related to the judicial environment. Inspired by the ideology of 'equality', as framed in Western philosophy and by a desire to respect some Hindu legal schools (mainly the Mitakshara), the *HSA* resulted from the combination of two legal philosophies partially at odds with one another. Furthermore, this Act was a legislative initiative implemented in a rapidly changing, young nation whose long history was characterized by various phases of cultural and religious invasions and colonization. In addition, legislative initiatives such as the *HSA* are not alone able to ensure social change because their success depends on the tribunals' and judicial bureaucracy's capacity and/or desire to communicate the outcomes of potential new jurisprudence.

Another set of factors influencing the impact of the *HSA* is that related to the particular social and economic environment that a specific legislation aims to change. The impact of this legislation also depends on the presence or absence, within a specific local context, of the socio-economic factors that allow people to become aware of the legislative changes and give them the appropriate means with which to claim their rights. In addition, the population must perceive the advantages of claiming their rights and have the economic and social tools to face the potential changes instigated by a legislation.

Local and regional practices have often modified the impact that written laws have had on different Hindu legal schools of thoughts. It is in this context of legal pluralism that the policy-makers of independent India elaborated laws for the new state; hence, establishing a new social order concerning access to property. Drawing on the analysis of data compiled during an extensive fieldwork period in the village of Bhima, and complemented by ethno-legal research in Pune tribunals, this paper will provide an analysis of how the current Indian cultural context affects widows' inheritance rights, and access to property and justice in Maharashtra. I will begin this paper with a brief presentation of methodological approach, followed by an overview of my theoretical perspective. I will then discuss the main issues that arose during my ethnographic research, first by underlining the main characteristics of widowhood in Bhima, second by analysing the level of women's legal awareness in this village, and third by describing their relationship with the judicial bureaucracy and court system. Finally, I will provide some insights into various means that could improve women's access to property.

Methodology

In order to understand how Indian women interact with various perceptions of the social order and modes of conflict resolution, it is important to investigate key elements of their lives such as household dynamics, kinship systems, marriage rules, economic resources, inheritance patterns, gender socialization, caste organization and concepts of rights and duties. In addition, to explain access to property rights and the legal system, it is necessary to examine how the social and legal statuses of women in Maharashtra are changing.

There is little recent anthropological research on property in Maharashtra. This lack of information is why I decided to conduct my research in Bhima, a village of Pune district, Western India. Bhima lies on the banks of the Bhima River. Situated approximately 30 kilometres from Pune city, it is located in Shirur Taluka.

BHIMA VILLAGE

In this village, I undertook a survey covering 150 out of the 853 households of the village. My numbers clearly show that most people in Bhima fall under the jurisdiction of the *HSA*. Bhima is predominantly Hindu with 87.4 per cent of its population belonging to this religion.[9] In addition, 8.7 per cent of the population belong to the Buddhist religion.[10] In Maharashtra, 40 per cent to 50 per cent of the rural population belong to the Maratha caste. In Bhima, as well as in the region, Maratha caste is dominant not only in terms of numbers, but also in terms of economic and political influence.

In Bhima there are a primary school, a middle school and a high school. According to the Census of India 2001, in this village, 59 per cent of the male population is literate compared to 41 per cent of the female population. These numbers indicate that Bhima's literacy rate is lower than the Maharashtra and India literacy rates. For India as a whole, 54 per cent of female of the age of 7 and more are literate, for 76 per cent for male. In Maharashtra, female literacy rate is of 68 per cent for female compared to a male rate of 86 per cent.[11]

The main economic activity in Bhima is linked to agriculture with approximately 85 per cent of the population involved in agriculture. In Bhima, during my survey of the village, 48.7 per cent of the households claimed to have a land while 6.6 per cent refused to answer. In 2001, according to the written records of preliminary census results of the *gram panchayat*, 12 women were the owners of these 24.94 hectares of irrigated land. Those numbers mean that 12.28 per cent of the 203 hectares of irrigated land belonged to women, jointly or as sole owner.[12]

The largest plot of land owned by a woman was of 4.6 hectares. The next largest was 4 hectares, followed by 2.8 and 2.4 hectares. The 8 other owners possessed land of 2 hectares or less. If irrigated, 2 hectares is quite a lot by village standards—certainly enough to support a widow and young children. However, in Bhima, many women and men possessing one or two hectares of land and living in the village (and not on their land in the hamlets) were generally not using that land for cultivation because of various problems. One was that if the land is 2 or 3 kilometres from the house, it is too far to go every day to cultivate. Most importantly, it was not possible to check the crops and prevent acts of vandalism.[13]

Shirur Taluka is poor and is renown as being an arid zone, thus one not favourable for agriculture. Indeed, in Bhima, access to irrigation is harder for small landowners because it costs too much to install. In Maharashtra, most of the land is irrigated by well, not by source. Only large lands close to Bhima River are properly irrigated.[14] The other ones would be irrigated by well. According to the 1991 Census, 72 per cent of Bhima's land remained unirrigated compared to 9.5 per cent of irrigated land.[15] *Bajri* and *jowar*, two types of millet, are the principal crops cultivated in Bhima, and this mostly by large landowners. Tractors are the exception, with only three for the whole village. The ploughing is still mostly done with bullocks. Sugar cane, peanuts and different types of vegetables (such as onions, potatoes, beans) are also cultivated.[16] There are three small brick companies as well as another company where car motors are fabricated. Still, such businesses rarely hired people from Bhima because they may not have received the expertise or the training necessary to work in such fields. Moreover, the above-mentioned companies provide mainly part-time and temporary employment. There are some industries at 100 kilometres from Bhima, but most people originating from rural communities cannot benefit from jobs in these industries due to lack of appropriate qualifications. However, such industries may create indirect economic activities.

It is possible for men who own only a small plot of land, or no land at all to find economic security if they are educated. In such cases, an educated male might find government employment or else a permanent job in either a company in Pune or elsewhere in Shirur Taluka. Most school teachers, both men and women, come from outside of Bhima. Yet, because of the schools and the presence of a dispensary, around twenty people (men and women) in Bhima are employed in work related to building maintenance.

Ten women have started some tailoring business. They are able to work from home and their job provides the household with an appreciable extra income. Most of these women received special training in tailoring. This form of education creates valuable long-term economic alternatives and allows women to meet with their household work obligations as they do not have to leave the house during the day to work outside. Less fortunate women work on other's farm as agricultural labourers. Overall, apart from work in the fields, there are few employment opportunities in Bhima itself.

Research Techniques

In Bhima, accompanied by my research assistant Mira, I followed the lives of 35 women (of whom 14 were widows) during a period of 14 months.[17] Ten men also participated in my study which enabled me to explore further nuances of gender issues, married life and inheritance practices. As well as conducting interviews, I collected life and family histories and some marriage and inheritance genealogies through informal discussions with the respondents.[18] To facilitate comparison of the data collected through fieldwork in Bhima, I conducted additional interviews with 30 women (including 12 widows) from several other villages in Pune district.

I combined this research in the village with participant observation techniques in both a lawyer's office and courts in the city of Pune. My legal research included analyses of statutes, jurisprudence, legislative records, court procedures and cases.

This fieldwork in courts enabled me to grasp the subtleties of dispute resolutions and conflict avoidance strategies used by the villagers in Bhima.

Overall, this methodology allowed me to explore the broader social context of widowhood, the reasons why widows do not claim their inheritance rights under the *HSA*, and the elements that could improve widow's access to property.

Theoretical Approach

Ursula Sharma (1980), Bina Agarwal (1994), and Srimati Basu (1999) clearly demonstrate that understanding women's access and rights to land, and other forms of property, is a key element in the study of gender inequality. Various studies confirm Indian women's marginal land and property ownership, despite legal reforms (Agarwal, 1994; Chen and Drèze, 1995; Chen, 2000; Gulati & Gulati, 1993). Sharma (1980), Gulati & Gulati (1993), Agarwal (1994), and Chen & Drèze (1995), also discuss the ways in which notions of 'family' and 'tradition' are used to deprive women of their property rights.

In the same vein, my approach allowed me to contextualize women's relationship to property rights. The central aspect of this context is found in what women perceive to be their 'real security network,' which is found in the organization of household. I am inspired here by the approaches of Kitchlu (1993) and Achutan (2003) on social security, a concept that goes beyond the idea of welfare, "An all-encompassing definition, as adopted in this study, is one where social security is 'regarded as a social means to prevent deprivation and vulnerability to deprivation'" (Kitchlu, 1993: 194; Achutan, 2003: 384).

As will be explained in the next section, widowhood is in a vulnerable position for a Hindu woman in India, which often brings great social and economic insecurity for both her and her children. Barbara Miller (1981) initiated the comparative regional study of women's experience in rural India. She found that women tend to be socially and economically vulnerable in certain phases of their life cycle, specifically in early childhood, the early stages of marriage and widowhood. This finding is supported by Bina Agarwal's (1994) comparative analysis of women and property rights in South Asia. Moreover, anthropologists Ursala Sharma and Martha Chen, as well as the Indian economist Bina Agarwal, have demonstrated that widows are placed in a precarious situation if they do not obtain property through their inheritance rights.

How is it possible then, to explain why widows do not claim their property rights in order to reduce their level of vulnerability within society? This paper shows that women know that they have rights to their father's and husband's property. However, for various reasons, they do not see any advantage to claiming those rights. This does not mean that women are necessarily against the general idea that women should have access to property. Rather, the immediate and practical effects of claiming property are perceived by women to have the potential to create more problems than they are seen to be a source of economics and social improvement.

Also, women often find it difficult to reconcile claiming rights with their duties as daughters (or daughters-in-law) and with the social restrictions associated with widowhood. In this context, before 'shopping forums of justice,' most women (and men) will first 'shop for a space of conflict avoidance.'

Widowhood

According to the National Family Health Survey of 1998-1999, widows form 9 per cent of the Indian female adult population (9 per cent in rural India and 9.2 per cent in urban India) and 10.6 per cent of the adult female population of Maharashtra. However, only 2.5 per cent of the Indian and 1.8 per cent of the Maharasthrian male population are widower.

Those numbers indicate that widowhood is much more common for women than men. The lower rate of widowers can be explained by the fact that women almost always marry husbands who are older than them and those Indian males, throughout time, had the possibility of easy remarriage after the death of their wives, whereas the general practice is that widows won't remarry.[19]

Among Hindus, the ideology of widowhood includes references to some forms of asceticism, sexual control and *sati* (the immolation of the widow upon her husband's funeral pyre). In Bhima, while widows' lives have to be simple and discreet (and must be seen as such), they do not fit the image of strict social exclusion and widows in Maharashtra seem to be, overall, better off than widows in other northern states.[20] Widows now wear colourful bangles but other jewelry is rare. The *mangalsutra*[21] is removed and burned with the husband's body, after which the widow will wear a simpler necklace, which is not made of gold. The *kumkum*[22] is replaced by a black dot. However, in spite of the improvement in widows' status in this region, various social and economic factors still prevent widows from claiming their property rights.

Widows in their *Sasar*

The house is empty. Three weeks ago, it was still a Mang family where a husband and wife were harmoniously raising two daughters, and encouraging them to study so they would not be financially dependant on their future husband and *sasar*[23] members. Overnight, everything changed. Suhas, the father, was hit by a car while getting down from the bus in Bhima after a day of work. After the accident, he was hospitalized in Bhima's dispensary. The next morning, the severity of his condition led to his transfer to a hospital in Pune, where forty-eight hours later he died from complications.

At 41, Anita is now a widow, in charge of Sunita, who is 14 years old, and Manjira, 17 years old. Over the past seven years, Suhas had been a worker in a car company located at approximately 20 kilometres from Bhima. With a monthly salary of 3,500 rupees, he could barely support his family.

Hence, he and his unemployed wife did not have any savings. As is the case with most of the men in Bhima who worked for companies, Suhas had no access to social benefits such as a pension plan, health insurance, or welfare. Adding to this financial stress was the fact that workers rarely had a permanent job and the companies regularly lay them off for a couple of weeks, if not months, every year.

The last time I saw Anita, two weeks after she became a widow, she was a defeated woman, mourning the terrible loss of her husband and anguished over the financial crisis that she, her husband's brothers and his nephews all faced because of the hospital and funeral ceremonies expenses. She did not know what she would do. "I do not know what will happen to me and my daughters. We lost everything. Everything."

Later, when I saw her empty house, with a large, metal padlock on the door, I was shocked. Arobai—a friend of Anita's—told me, "Anita had to go to live with her sister. She left by bus with her daughters. They only had one bag each, nothing else. They are not coming back." That was the end of 18 years of marriage, 18 years of life in her *sasar*. I asked Arobai, "What will happen to the house? She owned it with her husband." Arobai answered, "No one wants to care for her in Bhima now. That's why she left for her sister's place. Her brothers-in-law will rent out her one-room house here to get some money for themselves."

The house was rented a few weeks later, and Anita never came back to her *sasar*. Anita's story illustrates the precarious position of a widow and her unmarried daughters in her *sasar*, the importance of the siblings, and the difficulty she had in gaining access to her property in spite the fact that she held an official title in her house, jointly with her husband. Due to the pressure Anita experienced in her *sasar* after widowhood, she could not have control over her property, which legally represents half of the value of the house. In addition, according to the *HSA*, the other half of the property, which belonged to her husband, should have been divided in the following way: one third for Anita, and one third for each of her daughters.[24]

On the Importance of Siblings

In the previous section, Anita's experience of the loss of her *sasar's* support after the sudden death of her husband illustrates some of the problems widows face as they seek to keep their relationships with their in-laws intact. Regardless of the amount of property which is part of the succession, the condition of a widow in her *sasar* remains difficult, thereby justifying her need to avoid conflict.

Yet this does not mean that a widow automatically leaves her *sasar* after the death of her husband, as it is also not considered proper to come back to stay in *maher*[25] after widowhood. Approximately eight months before she lost her husband, we had a general discussion concerning the state of women after widowhood and the help a widow could receive from her brothers. At that time, Anita told us that if she became a widow she would not want leave Bhima to live with her brother. Part of our dialogue went as follows:

Anita: My brother would be good to me, but it would create tensions with his wife.

Karine: What type of tensions or problems?

Anita: See, if I go to live there with my two daughters, he will wish to help them for education. Then his wife would say that there is no more money for the education of her own children. If he wants to go to see a movie with his wife, my brother will feel bad not to bring me. But if I go, his wife will be angry with me. It is not good for them as a couple.

The discussion I had with Anita revealed the extent to which competition among women is a crucial element in a widow's access to property, which is a symbol of both material and social security. As researchers, we have to go beyond a simple view of male-female competition. Anita's story shows that competition among women is also important.

On the other hand, cooperation among sisters may help a widow survive the crisis caused by the loss of her husband. Rejected by her *sasar*, and not wanting to cause trouble for her brother because of tension with his wife, Anita went to live with her married sister. This is an exceptional case of cooperation between sisters. It is exceptional not because sisters do not want to help one other, but because they are generally constrained by the fact that each depends on her *sasar* for access to resources.

For Vidhya, who has no sisters, it was her brothers who helped her. When we arrived in Bhima, Vidhya had just seen to the marriage of her youngest daughter. It was an important relief for her. Her main preoccupation at that time was that her elder daughter, who had been married for two years, had not yet been able to give birth to a first child. The elder daughter's in-laws were pressing Vidhya to pay for her daughter to have a medical examination to ensure that she could bear children. Vidhya said, "How can I pay for it? I do not have enough money for myself and all my savings were used to marry my younger daughter!" I asked her, "What about your in-laws? They cannot help you?" Vidhya smiled sadly, "What about them? They were even not helping my husband when he was alive!"

Her prosperous brothers-in-law do not help her at all financially, although she is still in contact with them. Yet she does not go visit her *sasar*. Situated 30 kilometres from Bhima, she cannot afford the bus ticket which costs 46 rupees, the equivalent of three or four days work for her. Her mother-in-law comes three or four times a year to visit her. Vidhya says of this situation, "My *sasu* is nice, but her sons are not." Yet she hopes that one day they will decide to support her, and that is why she does not wish to claim her share of her husband's property and maintains a polite relationship with them.

In spite of her low income, Vidhya's life conditions are better than those of other widows due to the support she receives from her brothers—help that was present even before the death of her husband. Although her husband came from a prosperous family of tailors, after fights among his brothers concerning the family business, Vidhya's husband left his household and went to stay in his wife's natal village. Vidhya's parental house was available: her parents were dead and her two brothers were doing business in Pune. They agreed that she, her husband, and their two young unmarried daughters could move into the family house. It was at this time that Vidhya's husband began a tailoring business, which Vidhya kept up after her husband's death. The support Vidhya still receives from her brothers has been crucial, especially since widowhood. Not only have they let her live in the parental house, they also paid the dowries and marriage expenses for her two daughters. Without their help, Vidhya told me that she probably would not have been able to arrange her daughters' marriages.

Knowing the kind of relationship Vidhya had with her brother-in-laws,[26] I introduced the topic of widowhood into our conversation by asking her if widows have a right of their husband's property. Vidhya, like the majority of the women in the village, knew that she had a right to her husband's property after his death. However, she felt that to go to the police or to court in order to gain access to the property would not be well perceived by either the women or the men of Bhima: it is seen to bring shame on the widow and her family. Anyhow, on a practical level, how could she claim her share in *sasar's* property, when even her husband was excluded from it. Had her husband had access to it, or had the partition of the joint family-owned business taken place before his death, the idea of claiming something would have been a more plausible one for Vidhya. "What would I claim exactly? I do not want to work in their business. Anyway, they would not accept me."

In the absence of acceptance of the widow in her *sasar*, siblings are of crucial importance. Yet, the older the widow, the more complicated is the situation. Brothers and sisters may not be alive anymore. Also, after many years of life in their *sasar*, many widows have lost contact with their brothers and sisters. Since Bhima has only been accessible by bus for the last ten years, travel between villages to visit family members has been limited. Indeed, before the bus service, it was even more difficult than it is nowadays for widows to travel to their *maher*. This is what happened to Aji. Her three brothers had not visited her in Bhima for many years. Her *maher*, where her brothers live, is situated 60 kilometres from Bhima. A few years before the death of her husband, she had stopped visiting that place. She said that this was because of the distance and a lack of time due to her own familial obligations. She could not remember exactly, but over the past eight years, (that is, since her widowhood), she had visited them only three or four times.

Women in Bhima do not see the advantages of claiming their inheritance rights. If they claim their inheritance, they risk disrupting their security network along with jeopardizing the reputation of their family. For example, if a young married girl loses her husband and takes the initiative to consult a lawyer to obtain her share in his property, her actions will be very negatively perceived by her own natal family. First of all, she will be perceived as rebellious and undisciplined because she did not ask her natal kin if she should take legal action. However, had she done so, they probably would have refused to go to court anyway. Instead, her brothers (if she had any) would have tried to negotiate with her in-laws to ensure that she continues to be treated well, despite having lost her husband. Secondly, her independent initiative could give the entire family a bad reputation and diminish the possibility of her unmarried brothers and sisters would have in findings suitable partners to marry.

Claiming inheritance rights to her deceased husband's property also shames the widow and her natal family. Rather than going to the court, the brothers of a widow might try to solve the matter directly with the other family. Men also mentioned that it is their duty to help their sisters when they become widows. However, many widows, especially the elder ones, have lost contact with their brothers or receive little help from them in practice. Hence, many widows live with both economic and emotional insecurities. The status of a woman in community greatly decreases, when she loses her husband, unless she has adult sons to protect her.

Avoiding conflict with in-laws is one reason why women would not proceed with claiming inheritance. But there are also other reasons why women would not proceed with administrative actions—reasons which include both a lack of money and education.

The State Legal System

The *Hindu Succession Act* is seldom used by widows. Since 2000, the Supreme Court of India has heard only seven cases related to this Act. Because it is a very complex law, covering various aspects of intestate succession,[27] only three of those cases dealt directly with the issue of widows' inheritance rights. The Bombay High Court has heard five cases related to the *HSA*. The number of Supreme Court and High Court cases is only an indicator of claims under this Act, as most cases would be found at the lower court level. For example, if a widow from Bhima wishes to obtain a share of her husband's property, she will first go to the District Court. Then, in the case of an appeal, the Bombay High Court will hear her case.

When I conducted my research in the Pune District Court, the two judges who specialized in hearing cases on succession told me that over the past years, they had heard only two or three cases concerning widows' inheritance rights. Those cases had been in court for the last five to ten years. The matters were pending due to procedural delays, such as those I describe in the following sections (for example, lack of identity papers or absence of marriage certificate). Because so few widows go to court to claim their inheritance rights and the *HSA* is seldom used, I found it useful to observe non-widowed women and men in Pune's District Court and Family Court.[28] Furthermore, since access to justice is highly procedural, it was extremely instructive to investigate case preparation between lawyers and clients. This procedural facet of the judiciary is very important and too often forgotten by social scientists, anthropologists and legal reformers.

Although the widows participating in my research were mainly of poor and middle-class economic backgrounds, all of their husbands possessed some property: either land, a house, a shop or a business, savings, furniture, etc. Section 14 of the *Hindu Succession Act* states that any property, movable or immovable, possessed by a female Hindu is held by her as 'full' owner and not as 'limited' owner, as it used to be until 1956. Until then, under traditional Hindu law, a woman did not have a full interest in the property, which meant that she could not dispose of and control the property as she desired. The *HSA* provided women with a full right to ownership, not only a limited control over or right of usufruct of the property. To what extent do women in rural Maharashtra benefit from their ownership rights?

Legal Awareness in Bhima

In the case of intestate succession, the *HSA* confers to the widow a succession right in her husband's property. For example, if a Hindu man dies leaving his son, daughter and widow, the property will be divided into three equal shares. When I started my fieldwork in Bhima, I was not expecting that women and men would know the specific rules under the *HSA*. In any society, citizens rarely know the specifics of a law unless they are confronted with the legal system.[29]

Legal awareness is the first step to ensure that people will claim their rights. The following examples show that women in Bhima are aware that they have some rights to property, such as inheritance rights, but they may not know exactly what their rights consist of. Also, as Sangena's case will illustrate, women may know that they have rights in property, but without knowing the procedures for claiming these rights, they lack the means to do so.

One day we visited with Sangena, a woman of the Kumbar caste. She was excited to speak with us, explaining, "My husband and I just bought a piece of land. We will build a house there." After nine years of marriage, they were realizing a dream. When I asked Sangena if she had an official title to the land, we had the following exchange:

Sangena: My husband bought the land and signed the paper. I do not need to sign them because I am married to him.

Karine: So you also own the land?

Sangena: Yes.

Karine: Because you are married, you are automatically entitled to the land and to your future house?

Sangena: Yes. It is like that, it is the law.

Karine: Well, I hope it will not happen, but what if your husband dies?

Sangena: Same thing, I go to court and will give me the title of the property.

Karine: Do you have a proof that you are married?

Sangena: (laughing) Everyone in Bhima knows I am married! Why would I need to prove it?

Sangena is aware that if she were to become a widow, she would have rights to her husband's property. Yet her knowledge of her rights ends there. A widow does not have to go to court to obtain her inheritance. The *HSA* can be implemented through administrative paper work, as long as the widow has control over the necessary documents, such as the marriage certificate and the death certificate of her husband.

However, such administrative procedures may take a long time, might cost money, and may also involve a certain level of education due to the complexity of their requirements. For example, Sangena has the impression that you can prove your marriage by hearsay, that is by the mere fact that people in Bhima know that she is married. In fact, she would need more than that to prove to the pertinent administrative authorities that she was her husband's official wife. Sangena possesses wedding photos, ration cards and photos of her children, which she keeps locked in a cupboard. These photos and the ration cards (indicating her name, the name of her husband and the names of their three children) may sufficiently prove their marriage. But what would really facilitate her claim to her husband's property would be to have an official marriage certificate, which like most women in Bhima, she does not have.

When I asked unmarried or married women, as well as widows, the general question of whether widows have a right to the property of their husbands, the majority of them answered that it was possible after his death. Only two widows, who belong to the age group of 60 and more, told me that they did not know about their rights. One of the widows, named Aji, said, "Why would I have a right to my husband's land? I am a widow now. No one cares about me. I do not know about law." Aji is now approximately 70 years old and her husband died around 10 years ago.

Throughout the discussions, it was never mentioned that the law divided the property between various heirs, such as the widow and the adult children (sons and daughters). The possibility of making a will was never raised. No one said that a will could change the legal situation and, therefore, deprive a widow of her right to property. Another interesting finding is that Buddhist women of Bhima were unaware that they fell under the Hindu laws.

In Bhima, of the 14 widows from whom I collected stories, four claimed to have received their share of the property of their husband (house or land) after his death. However, according to the official records I could consult, only two Maratha widows (aged over 60) were the official owners of the houses in which they live and none of these four women owned land.

One Mang widow believed that her name as the sole owner of the property of her deceased husband was automatically registered at the *Gram Panchayat* office.[30] After her husband committed suicide 10 years ago, Shilpa was left in a position of extreme poverty with the full responsibility for her son and daughter who were respectively 16 and 13 at that time. Here is part of our dialogue.

Karine: Are you the official owner of your house?

Shilpa: Yes, it belongs to me. When my husband died, I became the owner.

Karine: Did you have to do paperwork to have an official title in the house?

Shilpa: No, when my husband died, the *Gram Panchayat* knew about it. I told them. Then they put my name as the only owner.

Karine: Did they give you a paper, a proof of your ownership?

Shilpa: Why would they give me that? I do not read. I have no education. I know they did it. And I pay all taxes.

There are two interesting comments worth underlining here. The mere fact that this village institution knows about someone's death does not ensure the registration of the widow as the owner. An interesting point lies in the trust Shilpa places in the *Gram Panchayat*. Other women also showed similar confidence in what the *Gram Panchayat* would do in terms of administrative paperwork. Their reactions are mainly explained by their lack of education regarding the limited powers of this institution. The widow herself must initiate the paperwork. In general, men are the ones taking care of such administrative matters. Thus, when a woman loses her husband, she relies on the male members of her *sasar* to take care of administrative work and she does not wish to interfere in order to avoid conflicts with them.

Overall, women know the main principle of 'the law' that provides them with inheritance rights. However, their very limited knowledge of the necessary parameters of the law and surrounding bureaucracy is one of the factors explaining why they do not claim their inheritance rights.

Relationships with the Bureaucracy

Arobai: The *Gram Panchayat* told me that I can get a small pension as a widow. But I have to go to Shirur to get a death certificate and fill out paper work. I went last week to Shirur. It cost me 30 rupees to take the bus. They gave me forms to fill out. How can I do that? I am illiterate! I have to go with someone who can understand the questions and fill out the papers. After that, I have to go to another office, I do not remember why, then get another paper. It will take the whole day. Who can come with me? My son works every day. We are poor. He cannot lose one day of work.

Karine: No one else can go with you?

Arobai: Who can come? We are all Mang, all uneducated. And have no money.

Karine: The other day you told me why you did not go to put the house under your name and

Eknath's [her son]. Would you need to pay also for that paper work?

Arobai: Everything costs money. It is like that nowadays. It will cost money for each procedure. There are fees at every step. Small fees, but I am so poor. And I do not understand what to do? It is very complicated.

The dense bureaucracy of the legal system and the governmental apparatus partly explains why access to justice is limited for widows. During my observation of court proceedings in Pune, I realized that gaining access to property is often a highly technical procedure. As mentioned earlier, in order to obtain this right, a widow has to produce her husband's death certificate. The ease with which the widow is able to obtain the desired certificate seems to vary. Firstly, it is not always easy for a widow to go to the *Gram Panchayat, Talathi's* office[31] or governmental offices by herself. For most women, the paperwork that follows the death of their husbands will be the first administrative work that they have ever had to tackle on their own. Even women who are breadwinners are not necessarily familiar with administrative work or comfortable with negotiating with government agencies. The intricacies of governmental administration also transform the task of finding a simple piece of information into a real challenge, which can be very discouraging for someone who is unfamiliar with such procedures and bureaucratic work in general.

Widows in Bhima, in other villages of Shirur Tahsil, as well as in Pune, often told me about their concern and despair regarding administrative procedures. Indeed, their frustration is such that it is not uncommon to find widows who have given up pursuing access to their husband's pension or to other types of property to which they have a right.

At the beginning of the previous section, I presented the case of Sangena, a married Kumbar woman who was very happy because she and her husband had just acquired a house. She thought that the mere fact of being married guaranteed her title in the house. However, the matter is much more complicated than what she believed:

Karine: Let's say that you fight with your husband—I hope it will not happen—but let's say something happens between you and your husband, and you have to leave your husband, what will happen to your house? Will you get something?

Sangena: If I leave my husband, then I get nothing. But if he threw me out of the house, then he would have to give me a share of the property.

Karine: In that last case, is it automatic?

Sangena: Yes, I will go to court and ask for it. They will give me my share.

Karine: In which court would you go to?

Sangena: Pune.

In such a case, however, the wife would not really have any legal claim on the house unless the deed was registered jointly in her name. Moreover, her legal standing might be dubious if she lacks a marriage certificate (as most wives do). When someone deals with a modern legal system, such as the Indian one, and its surrounding bureaucracy, the officers are less likely not to know the identity of the person. Hence, the bureaucrats will first make sure that the person is officially an Indian citizen and that the person's request is put in the proper jurisdiction or local governmental office. Identity cards indicating, among other things, the name, address and marital status of a person can facilitate the paperwork necessary to access some economic resources (such as widow's access to a part of the husband's pension). Yet, individual identity papers are not common.

Contrary to the requirements of the state law, marriages are almost never registered, and so it is very hard to prove officially that one is married. In Sangena's case, we have seen various ways that can be used to prove marriage in the absence of a registered marriage certificate. Individual identity cards are rarely held by villagers—these are more in the hands of economically affluent classes and highly educated urban citizens. In villages such as Bhima, administrative proof of one's existence would generally be merged within the household. For most villagers, it is their ration cards that indicate the names of every household member. Most often, these cards are in the possession of the male head of household. The situation is similar for other identity documents such as caste certificates and birth certificates. On the one hand, this means that identity documents are almost never kept in the hands of a woman, but rather held by her father or, after marriage, by her husband.

On the other hand, male members of the household do not necessarily even have such identity papers in their control. Married or not, it is not uncommon for men to have to ask their father for access to the ration card in order to obtain a bank loan, apply for a job, etc.

In the absence of such papers, it is not impossible to deal with the bureaucracy, banks, etc. but it creates delays. It may also create unexpected expenses. For example, to 'replace' the ration card, a person can obtain a notice from a lawyer that proves their identity. This involves additional fees. Of course, the effects are even more detrimental for the poorest. Another facet of the problem resides in the fact that the less education someone has, the harder it is for them to deal with all these procedures.

Once the husband dies, the widow must prove that her ration card truly belonged to her husband. When it is difficult to prove that someone was your husband, it will be even harder to claim rights to his property. Wedding photos and invitations often constitute evidence that the wedding occurred, but only if the widow can lay her hands on them. Most often, the widow will have to go to court to obtain official recognition that those constitute accurate evidence of her marriage.

And to go to court, one needs a lawyer. How easy is it for a women in Bhima to have access to a lawyer?

Do You Know a Lawyer?

There are no lawyers in Bhima. None of the respondents personally knew one. Male and female respondents told me that, in order to find a lawyer, one would have to go to Pune and Shirur, cities that are situated 30 kilometres from Bhima.

Therefore, if a woman is still in her *sasar* after widowhood, how can she hide such a long trip from her in-laws, so as not to alert them about her intention to claim her rights? As a widow is not normally free to go out of Bhima unaccompanied, even to the market three kilometres away from the village, how can she secretly go to Pune to find a lawyer? At this point, it is pertinent to explore the alternatives to filing a lawsuit.

Nowadays, caste *Panchayats* (caste councils, led by the elders of the caste) are not very active in areas surrounding, and including Bhima (except in some tribal communities). However, even before the creation of a national court system, caste *Panchayats* did not really deal with 'women's issues,' except in cases where a property claim created a dispute between two families.

Women may go to a women's organization to obtain advice or conflict mediation. In Pune district, such organizations are concentrated in the city of Pune and its immediate surrounding areas. But Bhima is too far from such organizations, which are non-existent in the village itself and nearby towns.

Overall, there are few institutions and organizations that offer alternatives for conflict resolution. We have seen why and how women tend to avoid conflicts. To a certain extent, the process of claiming rights itself requires women to defy or deviate from the behavioural norms that define womanhood. Once in the realm of the legal system, and on the margins of its bureaucracy, women—and men—have to modify the way they present and interpret their life experiences to fit within the parameters of the legal culture of a particular court. An individual's level of education and capacity for communication with a lawyer plays a vital role in the extent to which the claimant can shape his or her persona in order to achieve the status and identity recognized—and heard—by the legal system.

To go to court is a shame for a widow and her family. Some men told me that before going to court, the brothers of a widow will try to resolve matters with her husband's family. Some men also said that it is their duty to help their sister when she becomes a widow. In practice, most widows, especially the elder ones have lost contact with their brothers or receive little help from them. If a widow finally brings her case to court, it is not often an individual decision: it will be a familial decision. Both financial and psychological support from her brothers and extended family are often necessary (but not always available) in order to confront the legal system.

Fighting for Property Rights in Court: "All That Money for Nothing!"

As we have seen, legal awareness does not necessarily ensure that women will claim their property rights. In Bhima, I met only one widow who went to court to claim her succession rights. Manisha, 35 years old, came back to stay with her Maratha family in Bhima five years ago, after her husband died. She now lives in her elder brother's house, with his wife and their three children. Her mother, who is also a widow, resides with them as well. Her mother is a very articulate woman of around 60 years. She is the head of the household, takes part in all decisions, and is well respected by her children. She is the one who told me her daughter's story.

Manisha's mother (Mm): We spent Rs. 25,000 for nothing! All that money for nothing! The judge gave her [my daughter] nothing!

Karine: How did the judge justify his decision?

Mm: The judge said that because Manisha did not have children from her husband, she did not have a right in her husband's property.

Karine: Really! How come?

Mm: This is what he said. I understand nothing in these things. We are uneducated, we do not know. See, these are the papers.

Manisha's court case lasted for ten years and the widow as well as her family had to spend more than Rs. 25,000. The judge finally decided that she could not obtain a share in the husband's property because she had no children. In the written judgement, it is not clear why the judge came to that decision. The *HSA* does not stipulate that a widow can inherit only if she has children.[32] Normally, claimants do not receive a copy of the judgement and just hear what is going on in court.[33]

The costs associated with heavy bureaucracy are important factors in influencing people's access to justice.[34] Since the mid-1990s, women litigants in Maharashtra are exempt from paying court fees in cases relating to maintenance, property, violence, and divorce. Nevertheless, the cost for lawyers' services remain high. In one case, a widow claimed compensation for her husband's fatal accident but had no money leftover afterwards to claim her share in his property. Women in Bhima are not aware that they may have access to a government lawyer through Legal Aid. However, obtaining a lawyer through Legal Aid requires not only patience but also the capacity to deal with bureaucratic matters.

The Impact of a Decision in Favour of a Widow

What if the decision of the court had been in favour of Manisha? If a court decides in favour of a widow, is it the end of the matter? The answer is no, as the judgement still needs to be executed. In this section, we will briefly explore the difficulties that winning claimants face in seeing a court decision carried out.

The ability to enforce a court decision depends on a variety of factors, among them both the financial and personal capacities of a claimant to communicate and/or 'deal' with the judicial bureaucracy as well as the willingness of the guilty party to abide by the court order. To illustrate these two aspects the enforcement process, I will briefly outline the story of Nanda, a Maratha widow of Pune, who now lives 20 kilometres from her *sasar*.

Nanda is a widow of 45 years old from the Chambar caste. She was granted her inheritance rights by the Bombay High Court after 15 years of judicial procedures and more than Rs. 50,000 in legal expenses. Her father and two brothers encouraged her to claim her rights and financially supported her throughout the whole court procedure. However, although the judgement was delivered three years ago, Nanda has yet to receive her share of the land (10 acres) and business of her husband's brothers (in the form of monetary compensation).

The main reason for this delay is that her brothers-in-law bribed the local police to stop the execution of the court decision. The police took the money, and in return they agreed to help to prevent Nanda from accessing her piece of land in her *sasar* by harassing her and by refusing to recognize the court order.

The brothers-in-law also produced a woman in the police office, who claimed that she was Nanda. This woman told the police that she no longer wanted her share in the property and she claimed to forfeit her inheritance rights by signing a document to this effect. The village authorities turned a blind eye to fraudulent manoeuvre, although they knew that the woman was not Nanda. Moreover, Nanda saw the falsified document and denied that it held her signature. But the village authorities would not listen to her. As she and her four children (two sons and two daughters) had to leave her *sasar*, has not been easy for her to influence and control what is going on there. Like many other widows, she does not belong in her *sasar* since her husband died. In addition, this widow and her children have been subject to various acts of intimidation from the in-laws with the aim to discourage her from claiming her rights. For example, they threatened her younger son (who was 12 at the time), to break his legs if his mother continue to claim her rights.

Nanda, her father, and two brothers are already in debt. Fees continue to accumulate because the lawyer's services are still required in order to ensure that the legal decision is enforced and upheld. But there is no guarantee that the judgement will be enforced. In addition to the lack of money, Nanda's children, who are almost all adults, now demand their mother to drop the case. They are discouraged by the length and costs of the legal procedures, but, most of all, by the lack of tangible results. In addition, her children are also concerned about their future weddings. This implies expenditures, especially for the daughters because of the dowry practice. Although the four children have jobs, their meager income does not allow them to save any money.

Complex procedures, along with intimidation from the in-laws, greatly reduce the possibility that the court decisions will be implemented, and further increase the costs of the judicial process. Where can women find such money? Once they become widows, especially when they are young, they have to go back to their *maher*. There, they have to find a job, most likely as agricultural labourers in rural areas. Such casual employment does not provide much money to save. Therefore, unless the members of her *maher* can afford to assist her financially, going to court is not feasible for most women.

It is usually after his death that a wife becomes aware of husband's financial situation. This sometimes brings unpleasant surprises, as in cases where the husband had acquired heavy debts. In such cases, the widow has to repay these debts in addition to providing for the family's basic needs.[35]

Negotiating Access to Justice, Economic Resources and Education

In a transitional context of legal pluralism and rapid socio-economic change, before "shopping for forums of justice" (Benda-Beckmann, 1984), women will first—and not necessarily consciously—shop for "avoidance of conflict forums." If the Indian State wishes to implement state legal reforms, then education and access to various types of economic resources must be more available in rural areas. As demonstrated by Nobel Prize (in Economic Sciences) recipient, Amartya Sen, education, economic participation and property rights are all interrelated (Drèze and Sen, 2002). All these factors give more agency to men and women and increase their capacity to participate in various areas of social life. They become less vulnerable when they have access to a broader range of resources that can be used to help cope with and recover adversity and tragedy when one becomes a widow.

As demonstrated by the economists Jean Drèze and Amartya Sen, the role of education (along with health care) is crucial in promoting social change—and often even more so than legislative reforms (Drèze and Sen, 2002). Over the last decades, the persistent increase in literacy rate for men and women, women's increased access to education in the formal and informal sectors, and the better community acceptance of women going out of Bhima for education and jobs indicate a deep movement towards social changes leading to greater gender equality.[36] Those factors may, in the long-term, reduce the negative impacts of social indicators associated with the North (such as the prevalence of patrilocality and patrilineal inheritance patterns). In Maharashtra, and Bhima, positive effects of education are already found in the reduction of mortality rates and decreasing fertility rates. With regards to the topic at hand, it is also relevant to note that widowhood is less difficult now than it was 30 to 40 years ago. Education has also played an important role in eliminating some of the discrimination based on caste or widowhood. There is also a slight but persistent increase in job opportunities now available to women and widows.

In fact, women and men in Bhima were proud to talk about the improved position of women in the community, especially with regards to women's access to higher levels of education:

Lakshmi: Nowadays, everyone goes to school, women and men. It is good for Mang people like us. We can get as much education as other. I could not go to school, but see, my son go to the university. People do not regard us as being as backward as before.

Karine: Do you think that it changes some things for women?

Lakshmi: Someone who went to school is always more respected. The woman can find a more educated husband, with a better job.

Karine: But is an educated woman better treated by her husband?

Lakshmi: Not always. But if she has a good job, then the husband is happier with her.

Lakshmi is herself illiterate, as is her daughter, Alka, who is ashamed of this situation.

Karine: Does the fact that you have a job and bring back a small income to the house improve your relationship with your husband?

Alka: We are poor. My parents, who do very well, do not help us. I am ashamed when my husband asks them for money. I have to work.

Karine: Does your husband appreciate your financial contribution?

Alka: Yes. It is good. But if I was educated, it would be better. I could have found a better job. And I could read. I would have liked to read. Now, I can only sell brooms at the market place. It is very little money and it is hard.

Alka stayed in her *maher* after her marriage and lived in a one-room house with her husband and three children. Her parents exemplify economic mobility within the caste system. They have three different businesses (a general store, a small enterprise making and selling brooms, and a rickshaw). Alka's brothers benefit from this, but Alka is excluded from the joint family's financial expansion. She has a fifth grade education, but it was with great sadness that she spoke of her illiteracy. Her elder brother has married a woman who is 28 years old, like Alka. Alka's sister-in-law has a M.A. degree in literature. She reads the *Bhagavad-Gita* in its original Sanskrit every night to her in-laws during the family prayer time. Her husband is less educated, having completed the eleventh grade. They made a love marriage, and she is respected in her *sasar*.

What is the role of education in terms of legal awareness in Bhima? When I asked women how they learned about the existence of property rights, two answers arose consistently: from television and through hearsay from other villagers. In that regard, education (schooling) was never mentioned as a factor of legal awareness. Yet the villagers believe that young girls and boys should go to school as it increases their chances of finding better jobs. Moreover, education has an obvious effect on the ability to fill out official forms and to navigate through the bureaucracy.

As I observed in the Pune District Court and Pune Family Court, education provides the claimants with many tools necessary to understand and negotiate within the processes taking place within these tribunals and with the overall bureaucracy. Ethnographic research conducted in the United States by Conley and O'Barr (1998) underlines that the power of law is embedded in judicial language. "Law is a language, and it is through this language that the macro-dynamics of law's power play themselves out" (O'Barr, 1998: 112; Mertz, 1994).[37] For example, people who speak assertively are more likely to be believed by the courts than people who speak deferentially (O'Barr, 1982).[38] The *rule-oriented* claimants, compared to *relational-oriented* claimants, are favoured by judges of small claims in the courts in the United States because the forms of language they use are better understood by the courts (Conley & O'Barr, 1990: 58-59).[39]

For various reasons, it is not easy for Indian women to be 'rule-oriented' When they speak in front of a judge, at the Family Court or District Court, or when they deal with bureaucracy, these women are often speaking in public for the first time.[40] Not only is speaking in public an intimidating experience, but the fact that women and men have to speak about their personal lives and their relationships with other household members, makes the entire process somewhat humiliating or demeaning. Another aspect of the judicial bureaucracy renders access to the national legal system even more complex. In Family and District Courts, the court hearings are in Marathi but the paperwork is in English. Therefore, most claimants have to sign documents that they cannot understand.[41] Within that context, claimants rely completely on their lawyers, not only to make sense of legal system jargon, but also to have someone translate from English into Marathi.[42]

In Pune district, education is not the only social factor influencing women's relationship with the legal system. Yet, it is certainly an important element in the process of re-shaping an identity that will fit the requirements of the state legal system and that will facilitate access and control over resources. With education, the social mobility of women will increase and they will have more varied opportunities of employment. Hence, women may become less vulnerable and dependent on their *maher* and *sasar* for economic resources and as security network.

Conclusion

Since Indian Independence, the social changes that have occurred in Bhima for both men and women, including widows, suggest that in the long run, legal reforms concerning property rights may be utilized by the population. Ultimately, however, it will be social changes—particularly education—that will promote legal reforms, and not the reverse.

Contemporary Indian governments have proposed legal reforms introducing concepts of individual rights, along with an administrative and judicial bureaucracy relying on a mechanism of evidence that rests upon the provable existence of individual citizens. The goal of the research was to evaluate, through various ethnographic research techniques, why *HSA* is not used. Social aspects of the difficulty to claim rights can change in the long-term especially through education and the development of new forms of employment. Yet, the bureaucracy of Maharashtra (and of the Indian state as a whole) is, in itself, not providing citizens with the adequate means with which to implement those rights advocated by the national legal system.

Because social security includes state interventions as well as economic and social support provided by the family and community (Achutan, 2003), it is important for the government to ensure institutional changes, such as facilitating access to governmental offices, taking serious means to communicate the content of legislation and the procedures to be followed by the claimants, creating legal aid services—such as legal aid clinics, and reducing the costs of legal procedures. Without such national and local initiatives, widows will remain without real access to property. In addition, the overall education of the population with regards to their rights is important in order to ensure long term changes. Moreover, the State must encourage local initiatives that aim to, on the one hand, support communities as they face changes brought about by the reallocation of land and other forms of property, and on the other hand, educate the population of the benefits of the changes in property rights.

Notes

1. This paper is based on my Ph.D. thesis, submitted to the Department of Anthropology, McGill University, January 2005. My sincere thanks to the Apte family who made me feel at home in Pune and who were so generous helping me with my research. I would like to thank the people of the village of Bhima who, with great generosity, welcomed me into their community during my fieldwork in India. Similarly, I am indebted to all the people in Pune who invited me into their homes, thereby allowing me to witness most aspects of Maharashtrian society. I would also like to thank my Research Assistant, Mira, for her generous collaboration on my Doctorate project and for her friendship.

   Such research would not have been possible on either an intellectual or a personal level without the continued support of McGill University's Department of Anthropology. Many professors of the Department showed support to my research project. More specifically, I would like to thank my thesis supervisor Professor Donald W. Attwood for his inspiring guidance throughout my Master's and Ph.D. research as well as for his generous presence while reading drafts of my thesis. Also, I would like to thank Professor Laurel Bossen for always being there for me. Special thanks to Professor Jane Glenn of the McGill Faculty of Law for her continuous support.

   The research on which this paper is based was funded by the *Social Sciences and Humanities Research Council of Canada*, the Alma Mater Fund of McGill University, the *Centre for Society, Technology and Development* (Department of Anthropology, McGill University) and the *McGill Centre for Research and Teaching on Women*. Another part of the funding for my research comes from the Government of India (GoI) through the India Studies Programme of the *Shastri Indo-Canadian Institute* (SICI). Neither the GoI nor the SICI nor other granting agencies necessarily endorse the views expressed herein.

   Finally, my thanks to Martha Radice for helping me revise earlier portions of this manuscript, to thanks also to Melissa Bull who helped, through her many revisions, shape my paper, and to Gillian Chilibeck whose suggestions and commentaries have been very enlightening.
2. The *HSA* applies to all Hindus, Buddhists, Sikhs and Jains (but not to Scheduled Tribes—unless otherwise indicated by the Central Government).
3. According to the *HSA*, the preferential heirs of a Hindu male are his children (daughters and sons), his widow and his mother. They are

part of what the Act refers to as Class 1 heirs. The father of an Hindu male is not a "preferential heir."

4. This joint family is both patrilineal and patrilocal. The traditional ideal is that every Hindu couple aspires to have a household composed of themselves, several sons, and their wives and children (Shah 1988: 35). Like property rights and legal interpretations of succession rights, the joint family has always been subject to regional variations. However, very few households achieve this goal for various reasons (Shah 1988: 36). The deviations from the norm are often caused by demographic accident and lack of opportunity (Attwood 1995: 4).
5. The Constitution divides legislative powers between the Union and the States. It is a quasi-federal Constitution in that it is applicable to all States. The Union Government has exclusive powers to legislate on matters enumerated in List I of the Seventh Schedule of the Constitution. The State Governments have exclusive jurisdiction over matters enumerated in List II of the Seventh Schedule. The Union and the states have concurrent powers over matters in List III of the Seventh Schedule. Personal or customary laws in List III govern matters such as marriage, divorce, intestacy, succession, joint family and partition and adoption. Consequently, personal laws applicable to Hindus in one State need not necessarily apply to Hindus in other States.
6. Kerala, Karnataka, Andhra Pradesh and Tamil Nadu.
7. Ancestral property is formed in the following way. In Maharashtra, prior to Independence, the inheritance pattern before the *HSA* was patrilineal and the Mitakshara was the predominant school of law. Under Mitakshara, the property was divided among male heirs *per stirpes* (between branches) and not *per capita* (Attwood 1995). This *per stirpes* division led to the creation of a coparcenary. This coparcenary was a community of interests and rights under the possession of the joint family. When a Hindu male died, the property he had inherited by birth from his father, paternal grandfather or paternal great-grandfather, would through his agnatic descent, which is his sons, agnatic grandsons, and agnatic great-grandsons.
8. Ancestral property cannot be willed away by the father.
9. On a national level, Hindus form 80.5 per cent of the population and in Maharashtra they form 80.4 per cent.
10. Only 2.6 per cent are Muslims and 1.3 per cent are Christians.
11. In terms of literacy rate, Maharashtra is above the national average for both male and female categories. Yet, Maharashtra is falling between Kerala rates (88 per cent for female and 94 per cent for male) and Uttar Pradesh (44 per cent for female and 71 per cent for male) (Drèze and Sen 2002).

12. I briefly had access to these records under the surveillance of the *gram panchayat's* clerk. Although the *Gram Sevak* gave me his 'permission' (I only needed an informal permission because tax and land records are public documents), Mira (my research assistant) and I only had one hour to consult pages of documents because that was the time the clerk had for us. He never had time on other days. Data on unirrigated land were not yet available because the compilation of the 2001 census was not yet completed.
13. The police quarters are in Shirur, 30 kilometres from Bhima. It is in the hands of the population of Bhima to prevent acts of vandalism and theft.
14. Most population of Bhima does not live close to the river. Water supply is available through village hand pumps for two or three hours in the morning. Some women directly go to the river to wash clothes, which represents a walk of half kilometre from the center of the village.
15. Forests make up 4.5 per cent of the land, cultivatable waste represents 7.1 per cent and 6.9 per cent of the area is not available for cultivation, as it is used for housing, etc.
16. Bhima is not a market town. Once a week, villagers go to the market at around two kilometres from Bhima.
17. The first, starting in March 2001, consisted of intensive ethnographic research, while during the second, from September 2001 until May 2002, I undertook legal analysis in addition to ethnographic research. Accompanied by a research assistant, I visited these people regularly during my four months in Bhima and the following nine months when I was based in Pune.
18. The participants in the study belonged to different castes, classes and age groups and had different levels of education. The widows had lost their husbands to various causes, such as accidents, old age and disease.
19. According to the *Hindu Widow's Remarriage Act* (1983), the widows can remarry.
20. None of the respondents I interviewed could remember hearing about cases of *sati*, not even during their grandmothers' or great-grandmothers' time, although they knew that this practice used to be common in North India. Some women mentioned instances of widows having their heads shaved, but these cases occurred over 40 years ago and mostly among Marathas. The practice does not take place nowadays.
21. A woman's bridal necklace made of black pearls with two ornaments and five gold beads.

22. The red dot on the forehead worn by a married woman.
23. In-laws' house.
24. Because both daughters were minors, Anita would have had the responsibility to take care of their share until they are adults.
25. A woman's maternal (and paternal) home.
26. Her husband had no sister.
27. Section 3(g) of the *HSA*: "intestate"—a person is deemed to die intestate in respect of property of which he or she has not made a testamentary disposition capable of taking effect.

    It is important to note that testamentary disposition are seldom in a village like Bhima, even in materially affluent families.
28. These court disputes were directly related to property issues in cases of alimony, land partition, pension claims and marriage registration certificates, and indirectly in cases of separation and divorce.
29. At such a time, there are normally bureaucrats and officers are there to explain the content of an act and how an individual's rights can be claimed.
30. The *Gram Panchayat* elected Village Council.
31. The *Talathi* is the salaried village accountant and revenue collector.
32. In spite of this lack of clarity, Manisha and her mother were wise to ask for a copy from the lawyer. Even though they were not successful in their claim, the claimants benefit from what consists in a confirmation of the procedures that took place in court.
33. The lawyer does not automatically receive a copy of the written judgement. A lawyer needs to formally request a copy of the judgement, a written version of the judge's decision that may become available months after the court decision has been rendered. In the same vein, a lawyer does not automatically give a copy of the judgement to his or her client. He/she may do so out of courtesy, but generally, the client needs to request it from the lawyer (or directly from the court). It is most likely that the client will pay for the photocopying, as well as for shipping and handling fees.
34. For examples, a death certificate costs ten rupees per copy while it will cost 25 to 50 rupees to officially register the new owner of a land or a house at the Talathi's office. Although these fees can be considered as being nominal, it may not be so for women who are agricultural labours and/or who have limited control over her income (if any).
35. Married women are often unfamiliar with banking procedures, as bank accounts are generally managed by the husband. Women seldom have savings in their name. Joint accounts may be under the name of

both husband and wife, but the wife is often unaware of how much is in the joint account. Also, some women believe that both signatures are necessary to withdraw the money, which is not always the case, as it depends on the instructions given to the bank at the time the account is opened.

36. In Maharashtra, social reformers such as Dhondo Keshav Karve, Justice Mahadeo Govind Ranade, Shahu Maharaj, Jotirao Govindrao Phule, Bhaurao Paigonda Patil and Dr. B.R. Ambedkar worked for the spread for education in rural and urban Maharashtra. In addition, each of these activists also took specific measures to render education accessible to women, including widows. Moreover, their actions were often shaped by a desire to modify castes relationships towards greater equality. Their actions still influence contemporary India.
37. A similar dynamic between law and language has been observed in non-western settings.
38. This study was an interdisciplinary work: it combined anthropology, linguistics, social psychology and law.
39. Small claims courts were chosen as a site of study because these courts offer a legal environment in which judges invited the litigants to tell their story open-endedly, unlike in formal courtrooms.
40. This is also the case for many men.
41. In addition to which the judge 'repeats' in English the 'statements' of the parties to the case and of the witnesses, statements that were made in Marathi. This is necessary so that the clerk can transcribe the 'facts' in English for the court records. Such a translation is not precise and involves a great deal of interpretation of the facts by the judge, in addition to the transformations of meanings due to the normal process of translation. The construction of narratives by disputants, the community and the court is an integral part of the disputing process (Just 1991), and these elements should be taken into account while studying access to justice.
42. Preferably, all the paperwork has to be completed by a legal professional, a lawyer, since the language is very difficult for a layperson to understand. It is also important that the lawyer prepares the client for her court appearance. The claimant has to feel confident enough to listen carefully to what the judge or other lawyers are asking and to answer in a coherent manner. One requirement of the court discourse is that the witness should provide a chronological account of her story. To increase the chance of being listened to and understood by the judge, a good lawyer will help the client in organizing the facts.

References

Achutan, Nisha Sahai (2003), Elderly Rural Widows in India: A Study of their Social Security Issues and Concerns: An Analytical Review of Existing Literature. *Indian Social Science Review*, 5(2): 383-408.

Agarwal, Bina (1994), *A Field of One's Own: Gender and Land Rights in South Asia*. Cambridge: Cambridge University Press.

Attwood, Donald W. (1995), Inequality among Brothers and Sisters. Working Papers, Centre for Society, Technology and Development, McGill University.

Basu, Srimati (1999), *She Comes to Take Her Rights*. New York: SUNY.

Benda-Beckmann, Keebet von (1984), *The Broken Staircase to Consensus: Village Justice and State Courts in Manangkabau*. Dordrecht, The Netherlands: Foris.

Chen, Martha (2000), *Perpetual Mourning: Widowhood in Rural India*. New Delhi: Oxford University.

Chen, M. and Drèze, J. (1995), Recent Research on Widows in India. *Economic and Political Weekly*, Sept. 30.

Conley, J.M. and O'Barr, W.M. (1990), *Rules versus Relationships: The Ethnography of Legal Discourse*. Chicago: University of Chicago Press.

Conley, J.M. and O'Barr, W.M. (1998), *Just Words: Law, Language, and Power* (*Language and Legal Discourse*). Chicago: Chicago University Press.

Drèze, J. and Sen, A. (2002), *India: Development and Participation*. New Delhi: Oxford University Press.

Gulati, M. and Gulati, Leela (1993), Remnants of Matriliny: Widows of Two Kerala Villages. *Manushi*, 76: 32-34.

Just, Peter (1991), Conflict Resolution and Moral Community among the Dou Donggo. *Conflict Resolution: Cross-cultural Perspective*, K. Arruch, P.W. Black and J.A. Scimecca (eds.), *Contributions in Ethnic Studies*, 28. New York: Greenwood University Press.

Kitchlu, T.N. (1993), *Widows in India*. New-Delhi: Ashish Publishing House.

Mertz, Elizabeth (1994), Legal Language: Pragmatics, Poetics, and Social Power. *Annual Review of Anthropology*, 23: 435-55.

Miller, B.D. (1981), *The Endangered Sex*. New York: Cornell University Press.

National Family Health Survey (2000), *NFHS: India*. Mumbai: International Institute for Population Sciences.

O'Barr, W.M. (1982), *Linguistic Evidence: Language, Power and Strategy in the Courtroom*. New York: Academic Press.

Shah, A.M. (1988), The Phase of Dispersal in the Indian Family Process. *Sociological Bulletin*, 37(1): 33-47.

Sharma, Ursula (1980), *Women, Work, and Property in North West India.* London: Tavistock.

Contributors

Brij Mohan, Professor of Social Work, Louisiana State University, Baton Rouge, LA 70808, USA. He is founding Editor-in-Chief of New Global Development (www.newglobaldevelopment.com) now published as *Journal of Comparative Social Welfare* by Routledge (Taylor and Francis).

Pritam Singh, Senior Lecturer in Economics, Department of Economics, Oxford Brookings University, UK.

B. Mishra, Faculty, Department of Economics, North-Eastern Hill University, Shillong, Meghalaya, India.

P.S. Suresh, Faculty, Department of Economics, North-Eastern Hill University, Shillong, Meghalaya, India.

K.Z. Ovung, Lecturer, Department of Economics, Mt. Tiyi College, Wokha, Nagaland, India.

Bhabani Shankar Nayak, Doctoral Research Fellow and Tutor in Development Studies (CDE), University of Sussex, Brighton, UK.

Eswarappa Kasi, ICSSR Doctoral Fellow, Department of Anthropology, University of Hyderabad, Central University (P.O.), Hyderabad, Andhra Pradesh, India.

R. Siva Prasad, Associate Professor, Department of Anthropology, University of Hyderabad, Central University (P.O.), Hyderabad, Andhra Pradesh, India.

Mamata Swain, Professor and Head, Department of Economics, North Orissa University, Baripada, Orissa, India.

Deepak Kumar Das, Reader, Engineering Faculty, Water and Land Management Institute, Cuttack, Orissa, India.

S.S. Rath, Reader in Economics, Sambalpur University, Orissa, India.

Sadananda Sahoo, Research Fellow, Institute of Applied Manpower Research, Narela, Delhi, India.

Samantha Syiem, Doctoral Candidate in Development Studies (CDE), University of Sussex, UK.

Felix Padel is a freelance anthropologist who obtained his doctorate in social anthropology/sociology from Oxford University and the Delhi School of Economics.

Samarendra Das is a journalist and film-maker from Orissa, India.

Judy Whitehead, Department of Anthropology, University of Lethbridge, Lethbridge, Canada.

Garry Fehr, Department of Geography, University of Guelph, Guelph, Ontario, Canada.

René Véron, Department of Geography, University of Guelph, Guelph, Ontario, Canada.

Nagaraju Gundemeda, Lecturer, Department of Sociology, University of Hyderabad, Central University (P.O.), Hyderabad, Andhra Pradesh, India.

Martina Mettgenberg, Department of Anthropology, University of Sussex, Brighton, UK.

Karine Bates, Post Doctoral Fellow, Department of Anthropology, Université de Montréal, Montréal, Canada.